CRISWELL'S

CURRENCY SERIES

VOL. 1

4th Edition

CONFEDERATE AND SOUTHERN STATES CURRENCY

A Descriptive Listing, Including Rarity and Values

by

Grover C. Criswell, Jr.

THE CONFEDERATE STATES OF AMERICA

and all of the

SOUTHERN STATES

including

"The Florida Republic"
and
"The Republic and Government of Texas"
and
"The Indian Territories"

A listing of all known contemporary counterfeits is included for the first time.

also by the same author

Confederate Bonds (second edition in preparation)
North American Currency

other paper money books from the publisher

Comprehensive Catalog of U.S. Paper Money fifth edition by Gene Hessler
United States Essay, Proof and Specimen Notes by Gene Hessler
An Illustrated History of U.S. Loans 1776-1892 by Gene Hessler
Military Payment Certificates by Fred Schwan
Prisoner of War and Concentration Camp Money by Lance Campbell

Library of Congress Card Catalog Number
92-17386

International Standard Book Number
0-931960-20-7

BNR Press
132 East Second Street
Port Clinton, Ohio 43452-1115

(419) 732-6683 FAX (419) 732-6683

contact the author at

Criswell's
15001 NE 248th Ave
Salt Springs, FL 32134

Foreword

In 1978 when I was preparing *World War II Military Currency,* I asked Grover Criswell to write a foreword which he gladly did. Now nearly 15 years later, I get to sneak a few words into this marvelous new edition of *Confederate and Southern States Currency.* This foreword and a few other things will be surprises to Grover as the first time that he will see them is in print.

In many ways Grover gave me my start in numismatic writing and therefore publishing when he accepted my earliest attempts for the *Bank Note Reporter* which he founded in 1973. Since that time I have enjoyed greatly the opportunity to write for that and other periodicals.

It has been an extreme pleasure for me to be associated with the production of this edition of a classic reference. I have certainly learned a lot about Confederate and southern states paper money!

Many people have been waiting for this edition for at least five years. I am not sure exactly when Grover first announced its imminent release, but it has been a long time. I am sure that there are some who are skeptical that he had more than good intentions.

Take it from me, Grover was very close to publishing the book at least five times. When the materials were turned over to us for publication, I saw the results of multiple preparations.

Each edition of this classic has been noteworthy and this is no exception. The sections on counterfeit notes and Indian nations is special. The discovery of a major new type note is also of great significance. Grover calls it one of the greatest discoveries in the past 100 years of Confederate note collecting.

In many ways the book is the result of the microprocessor. We have set all new type which allowed for some new features, but we also have maintained the familiar style with which collectors have become comfortable for the last 30 years. For many years Grover has been famous for his late night phone calls. Now he has perfected the technique with the fax machine. The fax machine was an absolute miracle as we were preparing the manuscript. Once we got started in earnest, we may have set several records in numismatic publishing. The last set of price changes were made only three weeks before the first book was in a collector's hands!

Of course the project was also a trial of patience and the other virtues as you can probably imagine, but I think that the results were worth the test.

A start has been made of illustrating the backs of the notes listed here. This is a trend which we certainly plan to continue. We also very much would like to replace the photographs of the most obscure notes which have not been available for photography in recent years. If you have access to material of this kind, please let us hear from you!

There are more improvements to be made. We will count on your helping us!

Fred

Author's Preface

Writing acknowledgements is always a hard thing to do. One always feels like a special note of thanks could be written to each one who has written a letter to remind you of each new discovery. Then there are those who send you a photocopy of every note they have run across. Then, too, there are the ones who loaned you their entire collections to photograph, etc. Some are collectors, some are dealers, some are relatives, and all are friends.

Special words are now necessary for a very special few: The four girls, without whom I just couldn't have kept things straight since the last editions are: my wife, Dolly; Janice Doub; Martha Griffee; and Beverly Halbert. I love you all.

To Hugh Shull, who has been like a son to me for many years, and without whose continued pushing and badgering I probably wouldn't have gotten this book as correct as it is in information and pricing. He has done yeoman work in both these areas, besides helping to gather details and illustrations together over many years. You're now a Colonel, too!

To Brent Hughes, Confederate financial scholar, historian and artist par extraordinaire, I tip my hat. He has always shared information, and readily loaned it, as well as made special drawings and information for me. His work is prominent throughout the book, as it is throughout the paper money fraternity.

To Dr. Douglas Ball, who has never hesitated to give me new information as he found it, and who has always volunteered his opinion on types and varieties of notes and their rarities, I say thanks much. Dinner's on me.

To my adopted (almost) kids Randy and Linda Ockerman who have lived and worked with me over the years: I love you both and appreciate your help and encouragement. Come on back home.

Last but not least, to my son Grover Criswell III, I say thanks for being the head of Criswell's Publications. I'm glad you turned this big headache over to Fred...

Fred? - Oh, yes...Fred! Fred Schwan, owner of BNR Press. Thanks much for your help and understanding, coupled with your everlasting love for "fax machines" and "overnight delivery services!" It's been lengthy, but fun! (Did we really have the world's longest fax?)

Grover C.

IN MEMORIAM

Too many good friends and contributors have passed on. Their contributions in kind to earlier editions were no greater than their contributions in spirit to this editon.

Walt Alcott
Ben O. Anderson
Tom Bain
D. O. Barrett
Aubrey Bebee
Dr. Julian Blanchard
Dr. Warren F. Brown
C. A. Brownell
Maurice Burgett
Joh Paul Butler
Amon Carter, Jr.
Affleck Charlie
Phil Chase
L. A. Cook
David Cox
Tom Crigler
B. J. Dantone
August F. Dietz
Ben Douglas
Ben Dubose
Dr. Harold Faggart
Aaron Feldman
Harley L. Freeman
Jack Friedberg
Claude Fuller
Ralph Goldstone
Stanley F. Horn
Raynor Hubbell
Herb Jenne
Dr. Walter B. Jones
Sidney Jones
Sol Kaplan

Art Kelly
W. H. Kelly
S. C. Kerksis
Michael Kolman, Jr.
Abe Kosoff
Major H. A. Lamberton
Harry J. Lemley
Louis Lenz
George Malpass
Fred R. Markhoff
Bob Medlar
B. Max Mehl
Herb Melnick
D. C. Montgomery
Dr. John A. Muscalus
Alfred E. Newman
George Nicholson
Chuck O'Donnell
C. E. Osmun
Roy T. Payne
William Philpot
Claude Rankin
C. R. Ross
Matt Rothert
Lucius S. Ruder
Bolling Stanely
Jake B. Sureck
Tom Warefield
James White
D. C. Wismer

ACKNOWLEDGEMENTS

Many collectors, dealers, and friends have helped in countless ways with this and earlier editions. Specifically, the following have loaned notes, information, photographs, and given selflessly of their time for which I am greatfully indebted.

Marvin Ashmore
Charles Avery
Henry Bach
Douglas Ball
Autence & Baxter Bason
Adeline Bebee
Dr. J. R. Betson, Jr.
Hank Biencink
Tom Biley
Gordon Bleuler
Christian Blom
M. J. Bly
William A. Bond
John Bostwick
Dave Bowers
Bill Brady
Walter Breen
Jerry Briggs
Colin Bruce, II
Charles Bryan
Wiliam J. Bryan
Debbie & Jack Buchert
David Bushnell
Bob Cardiff
Daniel Cassidy
M. L. Chew
Neil Chiappa
Guy Cifre'
Owen B. Cook
Ryron Cook
Everett K. Cooper
H. G. Corbin
Arnold M. Cowan
Mike Crabb
James Curto
Tom Denly
Em M. Enderby
Steve Feller
Don Fisher
David M. Foley
John J. Ford, Jr.
Dennis Forgue
Leonard & Paul Garland
Dorthy Gerschenson
Steve Goldsmith
Brian Green
Nancy Green
Carling Gresham
Frank Hannah
Harold Hauser
Randy Haynie
John Heleva
Warren Henderson
Diane & John Herzog
John Hickman
Don Higgins
Dick Hobber, Jr.
Ron Horstman
Brent Hughes
Bill Hurt
James Johnson
Richard Jones
Art Kagin
H. Kaslove
William H. Kelly
Grace L. Kent
Richard Kirk
Turner Kirkland
Michael L. Kolman
Chester Krause
Kurt Krueger
R. J. Lindesmith
Jack Lindner
Morris Lowenstern
Gene Mack
Hardie Maloney
Larry Marsh
David Martin
Michelle Masse'
Henry McCarl
Donald C. McClanahan
M. Clinton McGee
C. A. McGlamery
Gordon McHenry
Elvin Miller
Larry Miller
Gene Mintz
Purnie Moore
Judith & Claude Murphy
Dwight Musser
R. E. Neville, Jr.
Eric P. Newman
Robert C. Nichols
J. V. Nielson, Jr.
Linda & Randy Ockerman
Jasper Payne
Roy Pennell
Ralph Plumb
H. Leroy Pope
Dr. Sam Proctor
Clarence Rareshide
Bill Reed
Edward C. Rochette
John N. Rowe, III
John L. Satenstein
David Saulman
Jim Sazama
Herman Schindler
Herb & Martha Schingoethe
Fred Schwan
Austin M. Sheheen, Jr.
Hugh Shull
Arlie Slabuagh
H. B. Solmson
Howard E. Spain
Harvey Stack
Duane Staggers
Leonard W. Stark
Mel Stark
Howard Stebbins, Jr.
Garland Stephens
Keith Strawn
David Strebe
Ted Sturm
JJames Thompson
John E. Tidwell
Dr. Joseph Vacca
C. V. Valance
Bill Vaughan
Bill Waken
R. E. Wallace
Flannan Walsh
David Walsworth
Fritz Weber
Dr. B. H. Webster
Raymond & Roger Weil
Tom Werner
Charles Wormser
N. A. Wright

CONTENTS

BASIC INFORMATION ABOUT CONFEDERATE MONEY . . .

The paper money illustrated and described herein is that currency which was issued by the central Confederate Government and the states which made up the Confederacy. The first Confederate issues were printed in New York City, which had close ties to the South through trade and commerce. It is a little known or publicized fact that the city of New York would have liked to secede from the "Union" and the "State" and join the South. They stayed in sympathy with the South through most of 1861.

Starting in early April 1861 the first Confederate notes went into circulation. There were interest bearing notes paying "One cent per day" per $100.00. It stated on each note "Twelve months after date The Confederate States of America will pay to bearer"...The fourth and final redemption date which appeared on the 1863 notes, and until the end, read "Two years after a Ratification of a treaty of peace..." etc.

Because some notes had early redemption dates, some were interest bearing, and others needed to be withdrawn for various reasons. "Cancellations" were used.

FUNDAMENTALS

Type notes

Confederate notes have "T" or type numbers assigned for the major types only. This is to insurestandard simplicity for type note collectos. There are no "T" numbers on Southern state notes but all notes have an individual catalog number to assist in identification and communications.

Rarity

Each note is given a rarity (R) number between 1 and 11, with number 11 used only for items which exist in a quantity of only one to five pieces. The higher the rarity number, the rarerthe currency. The rarity number is basued upon the number of notes now existing, rather than the quantity printed. Rarity is shown in parenthesis following the denomination of each notes.

Values

The figures shown for the notes lited herein are retail market value as determined from price lists and by recent auction reports. IN many cases "rare," "very rare," or "extremely rare" are used in lieu of value for the entire note, or just for the "unciruclatred" figure. This is because thre are no recent recorded sales of such pieces. Values for these items are usually determined on the merits of the individual piece at the time it is offered. The authro will be glad to give his opinionin such cases. A general "rule of thumb" is that major tyhpe notes bring more than minor varieties. The popularity of certain tyepps and designs of ntoes also is a factor in their current market prices; and "availability" is always a factor.

Contemporary Counterfeits

Notes that were issued during the period that the genuine notes were in circulation are called contemporary counterfeits. The collecting of "Confederate counterfeits" in particular has become very popular over the last twenty years. For the first time a listing is include of all of the Confederate, and most of the Southern states countefeits. There will undoubtedly be many additions to this section and persons with such notes or information about them are urged to correspond with the authro so that all suhc invaluable information can be included in the next edition.

Printers

There were many firms which printed notes for the Confederate government, and others who engraved plates, or did both for the Confederacy and the states. Various combinations of names make for numerous minor varieties, and only the major ones are covered herein.

Bogus Notes

"Contemporary" notes which circulated and/or were thought to be genuine although not resembling legitimate notes are called bogus notes. Such pieces are extremely interesting and are included in the catalog. It is likely that additional discoveries will surface in this area and reports are requested.

Serial or Plate Letters

Serial or plate letters are those letters usually next to the serial numbers. For example, if a note was printed in a sheet of four, there would be four serial numbers the same, each with the four different plate letters. "Series" and other added information were usually printed so that the issuer could differentiate printings and quantities, etc.

In the listings plate letters are given for each note. This allows the use of the book as a check list even for the most detailed collector.

Flourishes

Only major flourish changes are listed, where these were obvious "intentional" design changes, rather than minor variations caused by worn or re-engraved plates and plate repairs.

Reprints

Reprints are generally notes that were made from the 1880s to the present day. Usually they were made by an offset or photogravure process and they *always show up with signature in black ink* the same as the rest of the design of the note (see signatures). This is the easiest way to tell genuine notes from reproductions.

The paper used for printing most of the Confederate notes was white, although pink paper was used in 1862 for $1 through $20 notes, in 1863 for 50 cents through $2 notes and on the 50 cents notes of 1864. Most of the Southern state and other entities used white paper ninety-nine percent of the time except in a few cases where blue paper was used. No brown or parchment-like paper was **ever** used, *and the paper did not turn brown over the years.*

Signatures on Notes

Signatures and signature combinations on hand-signed notes are only listed in separate categories, where they are of great importance.

The first six Confederate notes issued, the four from Montgomery as well as type 5 and 6 from Richmond, were hand signed by the "register" and "treasurer" themselves. Thereafter, because the treasury secretary felt hand signatures helped prevent counterfeiting, and because of the quantities of notes spewing forth, clerks were hired to sign "for Register" and "for Treasurer." There were about 200 different people who signed for each treasury official, making for thousands of signature combinations. Mostly the clerks were women, many the wives or daughters of soldiers who had been killed in action. Since the notes were signed in Richmond through April of 1864 (when all operations were removed to Columbia, S.C.), most of the signers were from there, some moved to Columbia, and others were hired in Columbia.

In the case of Confederate notes, there were only four notes with printed rather than hand-signed signatures: T-47 (XX2), T-48 (XX3), T-63, and T-72. All others were hand-signed in brown ink.

Ninety-eight percent of notes other than Confederate were also signed mostly in brown ink but some few in red or blue. Virtually none were signed in black ink (see reprints).

It is most interesting to many people to find that they had relatives who signed Confederate money, and many people search for such notes. From the classic *Register of the Confederate Debt*, by Raphael P. Thian, we have copied the listing of the clerks who signed for the register and treasurer. See if you have an ancestor listed!

Names of Signers of Treasury Notes//For Treasurer

* Transferred ^ Ladies

Adams, Miss S. J.
Gill, Miss Isabel L.
Morris, Miss C. S.
Allen, Miss Maria
Gilliam, Robert
Morris, Miss M. J.*
Allen, William G.
Gills, E. W.
Mumford, Miss C. C.
Ambler, Mrs. Jennie
Gist, Mrs. M. S.
Neill, Miss Sophia
Angel, Mrs. J. H.
Goddin, Edward C.
Nelson, Miss Kate
Archer, Miss Lizzie*
Godwin, Miss Missouri
Nethers, J.
Armstrong, Miss L.
Goodloe, Harrel H.
Newton, Miss M.
Ashby, F. Westwood
Goodwin, Miss Nannie
Nicholas, Miss Mary S.
Ashford, Craven
Gott, Miss Julia F.
Ott, John
Bagby, P.C.*^
Graham, Miss H.
Overton, Mrs. Rebecca
Bain, R.
Grattan, Miss Sallie G.
Palmer, Miss Nellie*
Baker, Miss E. A.
Gray, Albert W.
Patton, Anthony
Balaguer, Mrs. H. M.
Gray, Mrs. A. E.
Payne, R. M.
Baldwin, C. A.
Green, Mrs. E. C.
Pellet, Miss A. P.*
Ball, Miss R. F.
Gwynn, Mrs. M.
Points, Miss Adele
Banks, Miss M.
Hamilton, Miss M. E.*
Porter, Miss E. P.*
Bartlett, Miss H.
Harrison, Miss A.
Quarles, Mrs. Mary L.
Bass, N. A.
Harvey, William L.*
Read, Miss Emma S.*
Beall, Miss E. O.
Hatch, Thomas J.
Reeves, Miss M. C.
Bell, Miss E. M.
Haynes, Miss Riche
Rind, Miss Virginia M.
Bell, Thomas W.
Henderson, John E.*
Ringgold, Mrs. Mary
Bell, Thomas W.
Heth, Miss Kitty
Sanxay, Miss Sophia G.
Benton, Miss Ida
Hix, A. P.
Savage, Miss M. L.
Berry, B. H.
Hix, Mrs C.
Scott, Miss S.
Boyd, Miss M.
Hoge, W. T.
Selden, Miss Maria
Breeden, Miss Louis
Holmes, Mrs. L. L.
Semple, Miss Nannie
Bridges, Clifford C.
Hooe, Philip B.
Shaver, Miss Sally F.
Bridges, Miss V.
Irvine, Mrs. M. C.
Shook, H. C.
Briggs, Mrs. Virginia B.
Jacobs, Mrs. J. A.
Simmons, Miss S. R.
Brown, T. W.*
Jacobs, S. B.
Sims, Miss L.
Bunting, J.
Jones, E. W.
Skinner, Miss C.
Caldwell, Mrs. A.
Jones, John A.
Sleker, Miss Emma
Capron, Miss Annie B.
Jones, John W.
Smallye, Mrs W. L.
Carr, John H.
Jones, Mrs. Mary*
Sommers, Mrs. M.
Carrington, Miss M. J.
Joplin, James C.
Sparnick, Henry
Carter, Mrs. L.
Keesee, Thomas O.
Stalnaker, Miss C.
Christian, Mrs. M. B.
Kelly, Miss E.*
Stanard, Miss Virginia M
Clark, Miss S.*
Kepler, H.
Starke, Miss H.
Clarke, Miss Bettie J.*
Kingman, Miss Mary M.
Stocker, Miss F.
Cone, Mrs. Hattie Berrien
Knox, Mrs. Mary S.
Stuart, Miss A. S.
Cooper, Miss Mary E.
Korff, Miss Kate
Tennent, John C.
Darby, Miss Mary
Lambert, Miss Sally
Tighe, R. H. L.
Dargan, Miss M. A.
Layne, Mrs. E. D.
Todd, William R.
Davies, Miss Virginia K.*
Leigh, C.
Tompkins, James H.
Dennison, Miss E. A.
Levin, L. J.
Trescot, Miss E. C.
Dewees, Miss M. A.
Lewis, John S.
Tyler, Miss V. M.
Dickins, Miss Fannie M.
Link, Frank H.
Wade, Mrs. M. F.*
Dimity, J. B. S.
Logan, Miss J.
Walford, T. D.
Dinkins, T. Waties
Loughborough, Mrs M.
Waller, Mrs. M. C.
Dix, John S
Loyd, Miss Georgia
Waties, Mrs. Fannie
Douglas, Miss Joan*
Lyon, D.
Watkins, Mrs. Hortense
Douglass, Miss H. M.*
Macmurdo, Miss Rosa
Watts, A. S.
Doyle, Walter J.
Marshall, Miss M. L.
Weisiger, F. C.
Dudley, Mrs. Harry E.
Marshall, O. M.
Wells, Mrs. S. K.*
Ellery, Mrs. Julia
Mason, Miss Eva*
West, A.
Fauntleroy, Miss E. H.
Maurice, C. S.
White, Miss C. P.
Faxon, J. W.
Mayo, Miss Martha T.
White, William H.
Fort, Miss H.
McCants, Miss S.
Williams, Hampton C.
Fuller, Miss Sallie G.
McCully, Mrs. Elilza M.
Wills, Miss Elvira
Gale, Thomas G.
McGowan, Miss O. R.
Wilson, Mrs. Josephine
Garnett, Miss Mary W.
Miller, Miss Allice M.
Wise, Miss S.
Garrett, Miss W. A.
Minor, Mrs. Lucy C.
Wray, Mrs. Fannie
Giles, Miss N.
Moise, Mrs. H. L.
Young, M. M.
Giles, Miss F. G.*
Moore, Miss H.

Names of Signers of Treasury Notes//For Register

* Transferred ^ Ladies

Abbott, Mrs. B. M.
Hamilton, Miss M. E.*
Palmer, Miss Nellie*
Acosta, Mrs. Julia A.
Hancock, William
Parry, Mrs. A. S.
Adams, Mrs. E. A.
Harper, Mrs. M. E.
Payne, Miss Betty M.
Alexander, Miss H. E.
Harris, J. H.
Pellet, Miss A. P.*
Allen, William H.
Harvey, William L.*
Pelot, Mrs. S. L.
Apperson, Miss M. S.
Hayes, S. C.
Pendleton, Miss Emma W.
Archer, Miss Lizzie*
Henderson, John E.
Penrifoy, Mrs. V. M.
Arthur, Mill L.
Henry, Miss L.
Percival, Miss C. E.
Bagby, P. C.*^
Herbert, Mrs. H.
Pleasants, Miss P.
Bailey, Miss M. W.
Heriot, Miss H. P.
Pleasants, Mrs. M.
Barnwell, Mill H.
Hill, Jr. R.
Porter, Miss E. P.*
Bernard, Miss Fannie E.
Holt, John T.
Proctor, Mrs. E. S.
Black, Miss M. J.
Howell, Miss K. P.
Randolph, Miss S. A.
Boykin, Miss Nannie
Huard, Miss S. L.
Read, Miss Emma S.*
Boykin, Robert V.
Huger, Mrs. Caroline P.
Rhett, Mrs. F. M.
Brady, Miss M. E.
Hughes, Mrs. S. E.
Richardson, Miss Nannie
Brisbane, Miss N.
Hunt, J. H.

Riggs, Myron C.
Brown, T. W.*
Hunter, Miss L. M.
Robinson, W. R.
Bryan, Mrs. H. E.
Jackson, J. T.
Rogers, Louis P.
Caldwwell, W. P.
Jarvis, Miss M. F.
Rothrock, William
Cary, Mrs M. F.
Johnson, C. H.
Royster, Mrs. L. C.
Clark, Miss S.*
Johnson, Miss S.
Sale, John O.
Clarke, Miss Bettie J.*
Johnson, Mrs. M. S.
Sands, Johnson
Cocke, William Archer
Johnston, Gabriel
Saunders, Miss Margaret
Coffin, Miss Eliza M.
Johnston, Mrs. J. L.
Savage, Miss Parkie
Connor, Miss Julia M.
Jones, Miss Fannie C.
Sessions, Mrs. O.
Cooke, James H.
Jones, R. S.
Sinton, Samuel
Cooke, Miss Hattie L.
Jones, Mrs. Mary*
Slade, W. O.
Cooke, Mrs. Isabella A.
Keim, C. W.
Smith, E. H.
Courtney, Mrs. L.
Kelly, Miss E.*
Smith, Herbert
Crouch, T. L.
Kennedy, Miss A.
Snead, W. T.
Cullen, Miss M. E.
King, Miss R. B.
Snyder, John O.
Dabney, Miss Bettie
Kinney, J. M.
Southall, Miss Sallie
Davies, Miss Virginia*

Kirby, Mrs. Mary B.
Spottswood, Miss Lucy
Davis, Miss Ella
Kirk, Mrs Martha A.
Stanard, Miss E.
DeLeon, Miss Isabel
Lathrope, Miss M. C.
Stevens, Mrs. M. F.
Delony, Robert J.
Laurens, Mrs. Eliza B.
Swords, Joseph P.
Devine, Miss Lizzie
Laval, Miss S. E.
Talley, Miss Susan A.
DeWitt, Bennet M.
Lyon, Miss Bella T.
Taylor, Charles S.
Dickson, J. T.
Macon, Miss Lydia
Taylor, Mrs. Miriam
Dixon, Mrs. M.
Marks, Mrs. F. H.
Thayer, C. C.
Doar, Miss S. A.
Mason, Miss Eva*
Thomas, Miss H. C.
Dorsey, R. J.
Massic, E. L.
Tiffey, Miss Julia B.
Douglas, Miss Joan
Matthews, J. J.
Tinsley, S. G.
Douglass, Miss H. M.
Matthews, Miss Emily
Treadwell, Mrs. J. D.
Downman, W. Y.
McCarthy, Miss Jane
Tyler, Miss Betty W.
Dunbar, W. G.
McGarr, Miss Jennie
Upshur, Mrs Mary E.
Dutcher, S.
McRae, Miss B.
Veal, Miss C. C.
Eggleston, J. W.
McRae, Richard
Via, Miss Josephine
Ellett, Miss S. C.
Meade, Miss Charlote R.
Wade, William A.

Ellett, Temple
Michel, Miss L. G.
Wade, Mrs. M. F.*
Elliott, Miss L. W.
Miller, Thomas J.
Walker, Miss Kate
Foran, Mrs. A. M.
Miller, W.
Waller, William
Forde, L.
Mills, R. A.
Walston, William B.
French, W. T.
Mobley, Miss M. A.
Walthall, C.
Gaither, Mrs. M. S.
Morris, Miss M. J.*
Warren, G. N.
Garlick, Miss Elilzabeth
Morrison, Miss Mary W.
Watkins, A. S.
Garrett, G. W.
Morton, Miss M. C.
Watson, Miss Virginia C.
Gay, Miss M.
Nelson, J.
Wells, S. K.*^
Gibb, Miss M. A.
Newman, Miss Ada
Windle, C. F.
Gibson, J.
Norris, Mrs. L. A.
Wingate, Mrs. N. E.
Gifford, Mrs. M. A.
Norton, Mrs. Mary E.
Winston, Meriwether
Giles, F. G.
Nott, William
Winston, Miss E. C.
Gilliam, Miss M. E.
Nulty, E.
Woodward, Miss M.
Gilman, William S.
Orr, Henry E.
Yates, Mrs. M. A.
Grayson, T. Fitzbugh
Pace, Miss M. E.
Zealy, Miss Anna W.

CONFEDERATE "T" NUMBER
CHECK LIST
(For keeping notations on a type collection or cross cataloging).

1861

T1	$1000
T2	$500
T3	$100
T4	$50
T5	$100
T6	$50
T7	$100
T8	$50
XX1	$20
T9	$20
T10	$10
T11	$5
T12	$5
T13	$100
T14	$50
T15	$50
T16	$50
T17	$20
T18	$20
T19	$20
T20	$20
T21	$20
T22	$10
T23	$10
T24	$10
T25	$10
T26	$10
T27	$10
T28	$10
T29	$10
T30	$10
T31	$5
T32	$5
T32 1/2	$5
T33	$5
T34	$5
T35	$5
T36	$5
T37	$5
T38	$2

1862

T39	$100	
T40	$100	
T41	$100	
T42	$2	
T43	$2	
T44	$1	
T44	$1	
T45	$1	
T46	$10	
T47	$20	(XX2)
T48	$10	(XX3)
T49	$100	
T50	$50	
T51	$20	
T52	$10	
T53	$5	
T54	$2	
T55	$1	

1863

T56	$100
T57	$50
T58	$20
T59	$10
T60	$5
T61	$2
T62	$1
T63	50c

1864

T64	$500
T65	$100
T66	$50
T67	$20
T68	$10
T69	$5
T70	$2
T71	$1
T72	50c

THE CONFEDERATE STATES OF AMERICA
1861
MONTGOMERY ALABAMA ISSUE

$1,000,000 Authorized by Act of "March 9th."

Written Dates "1861."

All of the Montgomery issues of Confederate notes were signed by hand by "Alex B. Clitherall" and "E. C. Elmore," "Register" and "Treasurer" respectively with the following exception. At the very end of the $500 denomination issue, about a dozen or so notes were signed by "C. T. Jones, Acting Register."

"National Bank Note Co., New York."

T1

Black with green overprint. Bears Interest "Ten Cents Per Day." 607 issued.
(John C. Calhoun at left. Andrew Jackson at right.)

1 $1000 (9) Serial letter A $5,000.00 $16,000.00

T2

Black with green overprint.. Bears interest, "Five Cents Per Day." 607 issued.
(Vignette *Cattle Crossing a Brook.*)

2 $500 (9) Serial letter A $4,500.00 $15,000.00

Signed by "C. T. Jones, Acting Register."

2A $500 (11) Serial letter A $8,500.00 $22,000.00

T3

Black with green overprint. Bears interest "One Cent Per Day." 1,606 issued.
(Railway Train. Minerva at left.)

3 $100 (8) Serial letter A $1750.00 $5500.00

T4

Black with green overprint.. Bears interest, "Half a cent per day." 1606 issued.
(Slaves hoeing cotton.)

4 $50 (8) Serial Letter A $1600.00 $4500.00

RICHMOND, VA. ISSUE

By the American Bank Note Co., New York;
Although ostensibly by the "Southern Bank Note Company."

5,798 issued of each

T5

Black. with green overprint. Red fiber paper. Bears interest "One cent per day."
(Railway train. Justice left and Minerva right.)

5 $100 (6) Serial Letter B $295.00 $750.00

T6

Black. with green overprint. Red fiber paper. Bears interest "Half a Cent Per Day."
(Pallas & Ceres Seated on Bale of Cotton. Washington at right.)

6 $50 (6) Serial Letter B $250.00 $650.00

$20,000,000 Authorized by Act of "May 16th, 1861."

All "HOYER & LUDWIG, RICHMOND, VIRGINIA."
All lithographed date "July 25th, 1861."

T7

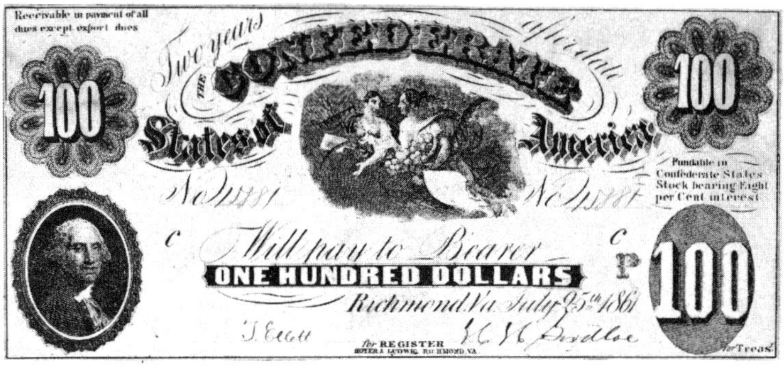

(Ceres and Proserpina Flying. Washington at left.)
"For" before "Treas'r" is printed.

7	$100 (8)	Serial Letter B	$200.00	$500.00
		"For" before "Treas'r" is written.		
8	$100 (8)	Serial Letter B	$200.00	$500.00
		"For" before "Treas'r" missing.		
9	$100 (10)	Serial Letter B	$300.00	$800.00
		"For" before "Treas'r" printed. Bond paper.		
10	$100 (7)	Serial Letter C	$200.00	$500.00
		Same on thin paper.		
11	$100 (7)	Serial Letter C	$200.00	$500.00
		"For" before "Treas'r" written, bond paper.		
12	$100 (10)	Serial Letter C	$250.00	$600.00
		Same on thin paper.		
13	$100 (7)	Serial Letter C	$200.00	$600.00

Remarks: numbers 8 and 9 changed from the previous edition.

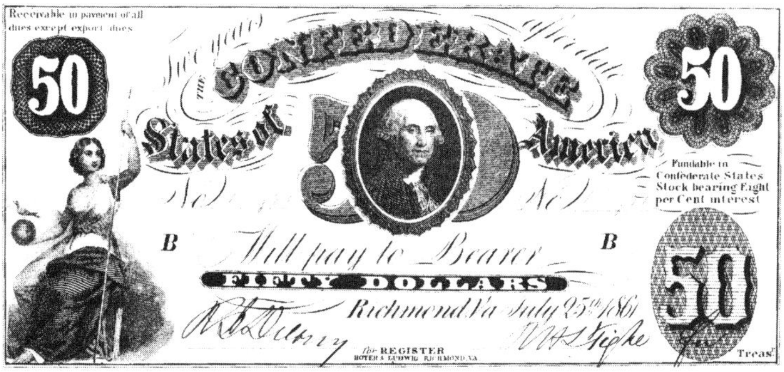

T8

(Washington, Tellus at left.)

"For" before "Treas'r" is printed.

14 $50 (8) Serial Letter B $60.00 $100.00

"For" before "Treas'r" is written.

15 $50 (6) Serial Letter B $45.00 $80.00

No "For" before "Treas'r."

16 $50 (8) Serial Letter B $60.00 $140.00

"For" written over "Treas'r."

17 $50 (8) Serial Letter B $60.00 $140.00

"For" before "Treas'r" is printed.

18 $50 (5) Serial Letter Bb $45.00 $80.00

"For" before "Treas'r" is printed, on bond paper.

19 $50 (6) Serial Letter C $45.00 $85.00

Same on thin paper.

20 $50 (5) Serial Letter C $45.00 $85.00

"For" before "Treas'r" is written, on bond paper.

21 $50 (9) Serial Letter C $80.00 $120.00

Same on thin paper.

22 $50 (5) Serial Letter C $45.00 $10.00

Remarks: numbers 16 through 18 have been revised. The $50 notes with serial letter Bb ("For" before "Treas'r" written) does not exist. The former number 18 was a duplication of number 16.

Special Section

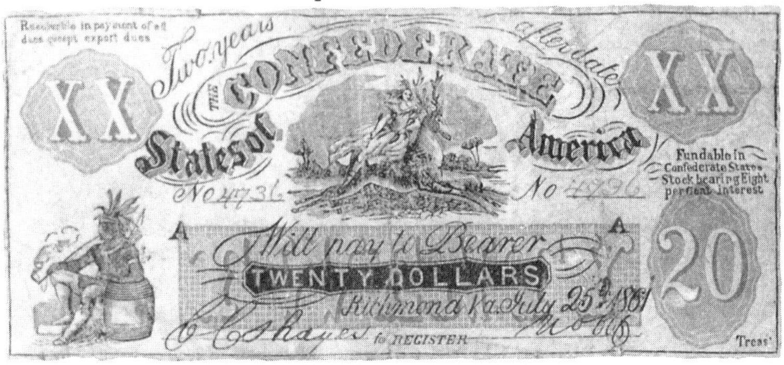

Female Riding Deer Bogus Notes

Numismatic scholar Brent Hughes has done an in-depth study on the well known Female Riding Deer (FRD) bogus notes. His article on the subject has been used with his permission to constitute this new special feature.

In discussing the FRD notes we should be careful about the use of the words "producer" and "originator." Sam Upham was undoubtedly the producer of the notes bearing his logo, but he was not the originator. Sam was just a shop owner who was smart enough to jump on an opportunity. He was not an artist himself and had no good reason to employ one. You and I both know that when Sam offered to pay three times face value in gold for any rebel note that he could copy, the whole city beat a path to his door. And even if he had not advertised this offer, the federal government would have supplied all the notes, paper, ink and equipment he needed. The more I look at Sam's operation the more I am convinced that it looks very much like a Civil War era CIA operation. Sam produced a ton of the copies and stayed with it until the Feds felt that this usefulness was over, at which time he suddenly went out of business. Same way today.

This note is bogus, a printer's fantasy. The design was never issued by the Confederacy. Its origis in unknown but evidence points to a printer in Virginia.

It is found today in three face design varieties the third of which sometimes has postwar letterpress back designs in various colors of ink and paper.

XXI	as described	$75.00	$200.00

Female riding deer vignette, back blank.

BOGUS XXI-A

Small black rectangle after "E" of "CONFEDERATE" at top of note. Red "TWENTY" overprint is wide, overlapping the plate letters "A" slightly. The serial number if printed is 6430. The serial number may also be written or the space may be blank. The "R" in "Richmond" has normal serifs.

XXI-A1: Printed signatures and serial numbers, with Upham logo.
XXI-A2: Same without Upham logo.
XXI-A3: Printed signature, written serial numbers, with Upham logo.
XXI-A4: Same without Upham logo.

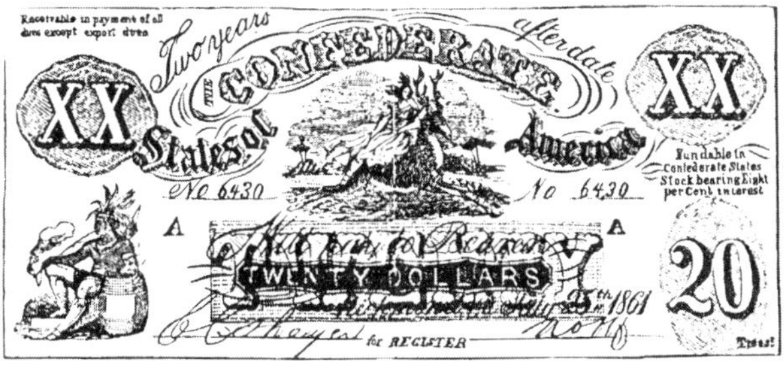

BOGUS XXI-B

Shorter small black rectangle after "E" of "CONFEDERATE" at top of note. Red "TWENTY" overprint is narrow with plate letters "A" not covered. No cross bar on the "f" in "States of." Block-separation gap is visible as white vertical line through center vignette. Serial number is printed 6430. The "R" in "Richmond" has normal serifs.

XXI-B1: Printed signatures and serial numbers.

BOGUS XXI-C

No small black rectangle after "E" of "CONFEDERATE"at top of note. The red "TWENTY" overprint is wide, overlapping plate letters "A" slightly. The serial number is written. The left stroke of the "R" in "Richmond" has a definite hook on the bottom. White area of barrel at left is almost a pure square with not short shading lines. "XX" and "20" counters have very fine cross-hatching. Some backs are blank; other may be red, orange green or yellow on face or back. Paper varies in tint and may be watermarked.

XXI-C1: Printed signatures, written seral numbers, plain paper.
XXI-C2: Printed signatures, written serial numbers, paper is watermarked "KASHMIR BOND."

Back design A

Back design B

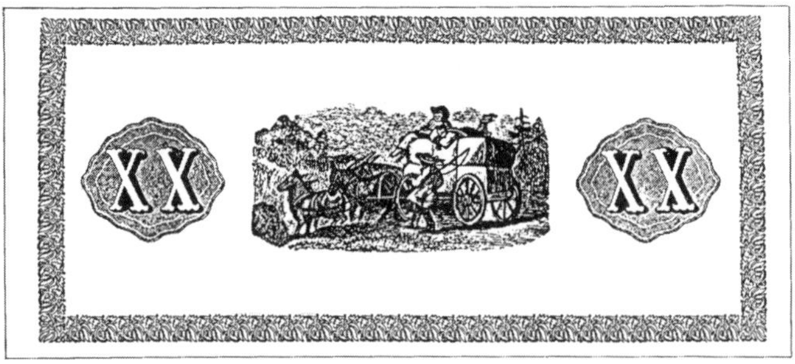

Back Design C

Back Design D

Back Design E

Back Design F

Back Design G

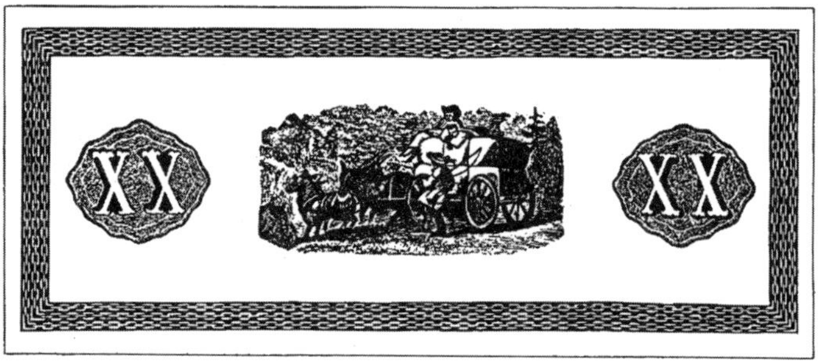

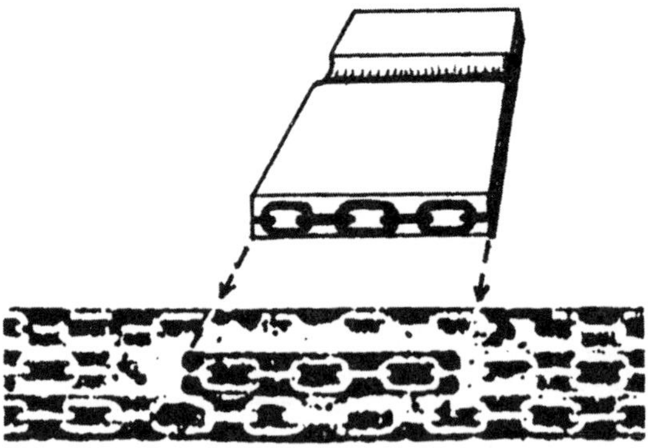

Enlarged portion of unretouched chain-lings border frame and piece of type probably used to construct the border design. Note three-link piece of type inside border was too high, leaving white area around it during the printing process.

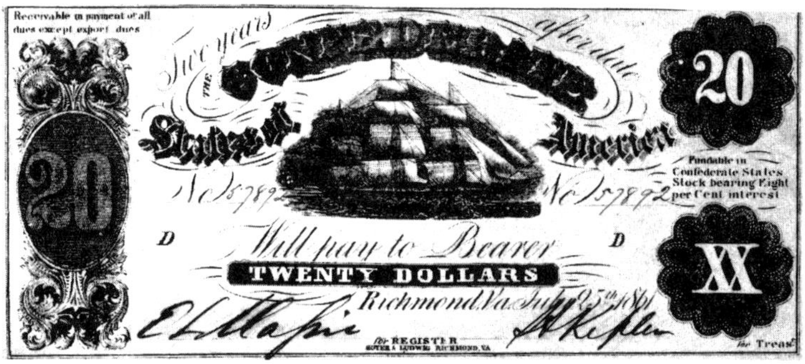

T9

(Large Sailing Vessel. "20" at left.)

No.	Denomination	Description		
		"For Treas'r" is printed.		
23	$20 (6)	Serial Letter B	$45.00	$100.00
		"For Treas'r" is printed twice.		
24	$20 (10)	Serial letter B	$90.00	$225.00
		"For Treas'r" is printed once.		
25	$20 (6)	Serial letter C	$45.00	$100.00
		"For Treas'r" printed once at lower right corner.		
26	$20 (5)	Serial letter Cc	$45.00	$100.00
		"For Treas'r" printed once under "1861."		
27	$20 (5)	Serial Letter Cc	$45.00	$100.00
		"For Treas'r" is printed twice.		
28	$20 (7)	Serial letter Cc	$45.00	$100.00
		Small "XX," "For Treas'r" is printed, bond paper.		
29	$20 (6)	Serial letter Cc	$80.00	$200.00
		Same, thin paper.		
29A	$20 (10)	Serial letter Ccc	$45.00	$150.00
		Large "XX," "For Treas'r" is printed.		
29B	$20 (4)	Serial letter Ccc	$45.00	$100.00
		Large "XX," "For Register" and "For Treas'r" written.		
30	$20 (9)	Serial letter Ccc	$85.00	$225.00
		Small "XX," "For Treas'r" is printed, bond paper.		
31	$20 (5)	Serial letter D	$45.00	$100.00
		Small "XX," "For Treas'r" is printed, thin paper.		
32	$20 (4)	Serial letter D	$45.00	$100.00
		Large "XX," "For Treas'r" is printed.		
33	$20 (7)	Serial letter D	$45.00	$100.00
		Same, but "XX" inverted.		
33A	$20 (9)	Serial letter D	$75.00	$200.00

T10

(Liberty seated by eagle, and shield with flag.)

Remarks: there are at least 42 minor varieties of this note, including a supposed 10 or 11 stars on shield. Usually the stars are so indistinct that a note may show from 6 to 15 stars. The other differences are in minute changes in the size of the "10" in the upper corners. Only the major types are listed here.

		Large "10" upper left "For" printed *over* "Treas'r."		
34	$10 (7)	A	$100.00	$650.00
		No "For" over "Treas'r."		
34A	$10 (9)	A	$375.00	Ex Rare
		Large "10" upper left. "For" printed *before* "Treas'r."		
35	$10 (6)	A	$100.00	$650.00
		Large "10," "For" printed *before* and *over* "Treas'r."		
35A	$10 (9)	A	$175.00	$725.00
		Small "10" upper left. "For" written *before* "Treas'r."		
36	$10 (6)	A	$100.00	$650.00
		Small "10" upper left, "For" printed *over* "Treas'r."		
37	$10 (6)	A	$75.00	$475.00
		Large "10" upper left, "For" printed *before* "Treas'r."		
38	$10 (8)	B	$120.00	$550.00
		Large "10" upper left, "For" printed *over* "Treas'r."		
38A	$10 (8)	B	$120.00	$525.00
		Large "10," "For" written over "Treas'r."		
39	$10 (9)	B	$200.00	$650.00
		Large "10" upper left, "For" printed *before* "Treas'r."		
40	$10 (7)	C	$150.00	$800.00
		Large "10" upper left, "For" printed *over* "Treas'r."		
40A	$10 (6)	C	$80.00	$485.00
		Large "10" upper left, "For" written *over* "Treas'r."		
40B	$10 (8)	C	$125.00	$650.00
		No "For" before or over "Treas'r."		
40C	$10 (9)	C	$125.00	$650.00
		"Before" written before "Treas'r."		
41	$10 (10)	C	$250.00	$800.00

T11

(Liberty seated by eagle. Sailor left.)

"For" before "Treas'r" is printed.

42 $5 (8) Serial letter B $750.00 very rare

Error, two "Fs," one 4mm before "For" of "Treasurer."

43 $5 (8) Serial letter B $800.00 very rare

44 $5 (7) Serial letter Bb $600.00 $5000.00

45 $5 (10) "ies" shows in upper left $1200.00 ex rare

Remarks: the former numbers 43 and 45 with "For" before "Treas'r" written do not exist.

"J. Manouvrier, New Orl's."
Written date "July 25th, 1861"

T12

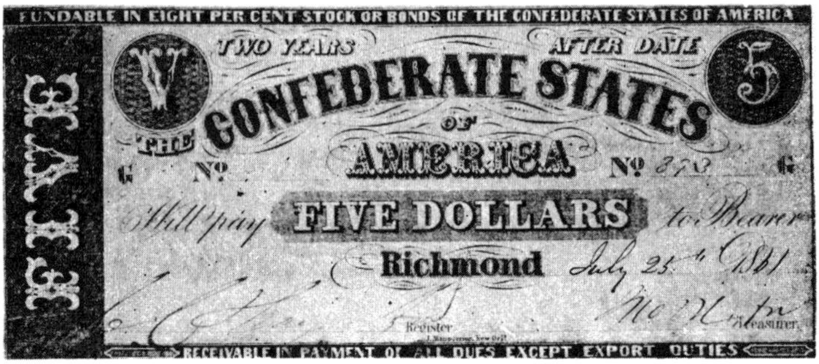

"Confederate States of America" in blue on blue back.

46	\$5 (8)	Serial letter F	\$400.00	\$4250.00
47	\$5 (8)	Serial letter G	\$400.00	\$4250.00
48	\$5 (8)	Serial letter H	\$400.00	\$4250.00
49	\$5 (8)	Serial letter I	\$400.00	\$4250.00

\$100,000,000 Authorized by Act of "Aug. 19th, 1861."
\$50,000,000 Authorized by Act of "Dec. 24th, 1861."

"Hoyer & Ludwig, Richmond, VA."

Lithographic date, "September 2nd, 2d, & 2, 1861."

T13

(Slave loading cotton, sailor left.)

50	\$100 (5)	Serial letter A	\$30.00	\$75.00

51	$100 (6)	Serial letter B	$40.00	$95.00
52	$100 (6)	Serial letter C	$40.00	$95.00
53	$100 (6)	Serial letter D	$40.00	$95.00
54	$100 (6)	Serial letter E	$40.00	$95.00
55	$100 (6)	CA, DA, EA, FA, GA, HA, JA KA, LA, MA, NA, OA	$40.00	$95.00

Same as number 55 but a period after the first letter F A.

55A	$100 (6)	CA, DA, EA, FA, GA, HA, JA KA, LA, MA, NA, OA	$40.00	$110.00
56	$100 (5)	AC, AD, AE, AF, AG, AH, AI AJ, AK	$40.00	$75.00

Same as 56 but no flourishes under America.

56A	$100 (8)	AC, AD, AE, AF, AG, AH, AI, AJ, AK	$45.00	$150.00
57	$100 (5)	A1, A2, A3, A4, A5, A6, A7, A8	$40.00	$75.00

Flourishes between "Confederate" and "States."

58	$100 (6)	A1, A2, A3, A4, A5, A6, A7, A8	$40.00	$95.00

T14

(Moneta seated by treasure chests. Sailor left.)

59	$50 (4)	Serial letter A	$30.00	$50.00
60	$50 (6)	Serial letter B	$30.00	$55.00
61	$50 (6)	Serial letter C	$30.00	$55.00
62	$50 (6)	Serial letter D	$30.00	$55.00
63	$50 (6)	Serial letter E	$30.00	$55.00

Small uppercase "D" above and to the right of "A."

64	$50 (4)	Serial letter AD	$30.00	$50.00

		Large uppercase "D" above and to the right of "A"		
65	$50 (3)	Serial letter AD	$30.00	$50.00
		Block letter "D" above and to right of "A."		
66	$50 (9)	Serial letter AD	$95.00	$195.00
67	$50 (9)	Serial letter AE	$95.00	$195.00
68	$50 (9)	Serial letter AF	$95.00	$195.00
69	$50 (9)	Serial letter AG	$30.00	$195.00
70	$50 (9)	Serial letter AH	$95.00	$195.00
71	$50 (9)	Serial letter AI	$95.00	$195.00
Note, AJ, formerly listed as #72, does not exist				
73	$50 (9)	Serial letter AK	$95.00	$195.00
74	$50 (9)	Serial letter AL	$95.00	$195.00
		Small numeral above and to right of "A."		
75	$50 (4)	A1, A2, A3, A4, A5, A6, A7, A8	$30.00	$75.00
		Large numeral above and to right of "A."		
76	$50 (4)	A1, A2, A3, A4, A5, A6, A7, A8	$30.00	$75.00
		Flourishes between "Confederate" and "States."		
77	$50 (4)	A1, A2, A3, A4, A5, A6, A7, A8	$30.00	$85.00
78	$50 (7)	A9, A10, A11, A12, A13, A14, A15, A16	$35.00	$90.00

* * * * * * * * * * *

"Southern Bank Note Company"

T15

Black with red overprint on red fiber paper.
(Railway train. Justice right. Hope with Anchor left.)

79	$50 (8)	Serial letter A	$875.00	$6000.00

"Keatinge & Ball, Richmond, VA."

T16

Black with green overprint.
(Jefferson Davis)

Engravers names above "Fundable" at left side.

Red fiber paper

80	$50 (4)	WA, XA, YA, ZA	$40.00	$195.00
		Watermarked "CSA" in script letters.		
81	$50 (5)	WA, XA, YA, ZA	$45.00	$210.00
		Watermarked "CSA" in block letters.		
82	$50 (7)	WA XA YA ZA	$50.00	$225.00

Engravers names below "Fundable" at left end.

83	$50 (4)	WA, XA, WA, ZA	$40.00	$195.00
		Watermarked "CSA" in script letters.		
84	$50 (4)	WA, XA, YA, ZA	$40.00	$195.00
		Watermarked "CSA" in block letters.		
85	$50 (4)	WA, XA, YA, ZA	$65.00	$250.00
		Plain, unwatermarked paper.		
86	$50 (4)	WA, XA, YA, ZA	$50.00	$195.00

"2nd Series"

Engravers names above "Fundable" at left end.

87	$50 (5)	WA, XA, YA, ZA	$40.00	$195.00
		Watermarked "CSA" in script letterss.		
88	$50 (6)	WA, XA, YA, ZA	$45.00	$225.00
		Watermarked "CSA" in block letters.		
89	$50 (6)	WA, XA, YA, ZA	$45.00	$225.00
		Watermarked "J. Whatman. 1862."		
90	$50 (7)	WA, ZA	$95.00	$275.00

Engravers names below "Fundable" at left end.

91	$50 (5)	WA, XA, YA, ZA	$40.00	$195.00
		Watermarked "CSA" in script letters.		
92	$50 (6)	WA, XA, YA, ZA	$45.00	$215.00
		Watermarked "CSA" in block letters.		
93	$50 (7)	WA, XA, YA, ZA	$50.00	$225.00
		Watermarked "J. Whatman. 1862."		
94	$50 (7)	WA, ZA	$95.00	$275.00

NO SERIES

Unwatermarked, red fiber paper

95	$50 (11)	Serial letter 1A	extremely rare
96	$50 (11)	Serial letter 2A	extremely rare
97	$50 (11)	Serial letter 3A	extremely rare
98	$50 (11)	Serial letter 4A	extremely rare

* * * * * * *

"Hoyer & Ludwig, Richmond, VA."

T17

Black with green ornamentation overprint.
(Ceres Seated Between Commerce & Navigation, Liberty left.)

"For" before "Treas'r" is printed.
Plain paper

99 $20 (7) Serial letter A $125.00 $295.00

"For" before "Treas'r" is printed.
Paper watermarked "Ten.."

99A $20 (10) Serial letter A $225.00 $450.00

"For" is written over "Treas'r" and "Register."

100 $20 (9) Serial letter A $180.00 $375.00

Hoyer & Ludwig, Richmond, VA."

T18

(Large sailing vessel. Sailor at capstan left.)

101	$20 (4)	Serial Letter A	$20.00	$80.00
102	$20 (4)	B C D E F G H I K L M N O P Q R	$20.00	$80.00
103	$20 (6)	Serial letters S T	$60.00	$100.00

		Large "b" before "A."		
104	$20 (7)	Serial letters bA	$70.00	$110.00
		Small "b" before A.		
105	$20 (4)	bA	$20.00	$80.00
		Small upper case letter before "A."		
106	$20 (3)	BA CA DA EA FA GA HA IA KA LA	$20.00	$80.00
		Large upper case letter before "A."		
107	$20 (3)	BA CA DA EA FA GA HA IA KA LA	$20.00	$80.00
		Large upper case letter with period before "A."		
108	$20 (3)	BA CA DA EA FA GA HA IA KA LA	$20.00	$60.00
		Large upper case letter before "A," inverted "XX."		
109	$20 (8)	DA	$100.00	$250.00
		Small "A" before upper case letter		
110	$20 (5)	aC	$32.00	$90.00
111	$20 (5)	aD	$32.00	$90.00
112	$20 (5)	aE	$32.00	$90.00
113	$20 (5)	aF	$32.00	$90.00

Note: beware of counterfeits of numbers 110 through 113. The counterfeits have no period after the small letter.

		Lower case letter followed by same upper case letter.		
114	$20 (7)	bB cC dD eE fF gG hH iI kK lL mM nN oO pP qQ rR sS tT	$50.00	$150.00
		Large upper case letter above "A."		
115	$20 (9)	AC	$150.00	$250.00
		Large letter above and close to "A."		
116	$20 (4)	AD AE AF AG AH AI AK AL	$20.00	$80.00
		Large letter above and distant from "A."		
117	$20 (5)	AD AE AF AG AH AI AK AL	$24.00	$90.00
		Large upper case letter above "A."		
118	$20 (9)	AM		very rare
119	$20 (9)	AN		very rare
120	$20 (9)	AO		very rare
121	$20 (9)	AP		very rare
122	$20 (9)	AQ		very rare

123	$20 (9)	AR		very rare
124	$20 (9)	AS		very rare
125	$20 (9)	AT		very rare
126	$20 (9)	AU		very rare
		Small upper case letters above and close to "A."		
127	$20 (4)	AD AE AF AG AH AI AK AL	$20.00	$80.00
		Small upper case letters above and distant from "A."		
128	$20 (5)	AD AE AF AG AH AI AK AL	$32.00	$90.00
		Numeral over "A."		
129	$20 (3)	A1 A2 A3 A4 A5 A6 A7 A8 A9 A10 A11 A12 A13 A14 A15 A16 A19 A20 A21 A22 A23 A24 A25 A26	$20.00	$80.00
129A	$20 (6)	A17 A18	$40.00	$150.00
		Numeral before "A."		
130	$20 (3)	19A 20A 21A 22A 23A 24A 25A 26A	$20.00	$80.00

Flourishes between "CONFEDERATE" and "STATES."

131	$20 (6)	A10 A11 A12 A13 A14 A15 A16	$30.00	$100.00
131A	$20 (8)	A17 A18		very rare
		Large numeral over "A."		
132	$20 (4)	A19 A20 A21 A22 A23 A24 A25 A26	$20.00	$40.00
		Small numeral over "A."		
133	$20 (4)	A19 A20 A21 A22 A23 A24 A25 A26	$20.00	$40.00
		"Treas'r" in "For Treas'r" is misspelled "Teas'r."		
133A	$20 (9)	A24		very rare
		Flourishes are heavy, no flag at main mast.		
134	$20 (5)	A19 A20 A21 A22 A23 A24 A25 A26	$25.00	$60.00

"J.T. Patterson, Columbia, S.C."

SECOND SERIES

		Small numeral at right of "A."		
135	$20 (9)	A1 A2 A3 A4 A5 A6 A7 A8	$65.00	$175.00
		Large Numeral at right of "A."		
136	$20 (6)	A1 A2 A3 A4 A5 A6 A7 A8	$40.00	$110.00

* * * * * *

"SOUTHERN BANK NOTE COMPANY"

T19

Black with red overprint on red fiber paper.

(Navigation Seated by Charts, Minerva left, blacksmith right.)

137 $20 (8) Serial Letter A $600.00 $2750.00

Note: the above type printed on plain paper which formerly was listed as number 138 is now believed not to exist.

T20

(Industry seated between cupid and beehive, bust of A. H. Stevens left.)

"B. DUNCAN, COLUMBIA, S.C."

"First Series," unwatermarked.

139 $20 (5) 1 2 3 4 5 6 7 8 $25.00 $110.00

First series, watermarked "CSA" in script letters.

140 $20 (8) 1 2 3 4 5 6 7 8 $75.00 $300.00

"B. DUNCAN, RICHMOND"
First Series

141	$20 (3)	1 2 3 4 5 6 7 8 9 10	$20.00	$95.00

Error: "First Series: numeral "1" at left, "5" at right.

141A	$20 (10)	1/5 3/5	extremely rare	

"2 Series"

142	$20 (3)	1 2 3 4 5 6 7 8 9 10	$18.00	$90.00

Note: beware of counterfeit, "2 Series," numeral "6."

"3 Series"

143	$20 (4)	1 2 3 4 5 6 7 8 9 10	$20.00	$85.00

"Only the word "Series"

143A	$20 (11)	6	extremely rare	

"Keatinge & Ball, Columbia, S.C."

T21

(Alexander H. Stephens)

BLACK, WITH YELLOW GREEN ORNAMENTATION OVERPRINT

Plain Paper

144	$20 (5)	W X Y Z	$100.00	$350.00

Watermarked "N Y"

144A	$20 (10)	W X Y Z		very rare

DARK GREEN ORNAMENTATION OVERPRINT

Plain Paper

145	$20 (5)	W X Y Z	$100.00	$350.00

Watermarked "CSA" in block letters.

146	$20 (6)	W X Y Z	$150.00	$400.00

Watermarked "CSA" in script letters.

147	$20 (6)	W X Y Z	$150.00	$400.00

Watermarked "J. Whatman. 1862."

148	$20 (7)	W Z	$160.00	$475.00

Watermarked "N Y."

149	$20 (10)	W X Y Z	$250.00	$800.00

"Southern Bank Note Company, New Orleans"

T22

Black with red overprint on red fiber paper.

(Group of Indians. Thetis left, Maiden with "X" at right.)

150	$10 (7)	Serial letter A	$150.00	$495.00
151	$10 (7)	Serial letter B	$150.00	$495.00
152	$10 (8)	Serial letter C	$195.00	$575.00

* * * * * * * * * * *

"Leggett, Keatinge & Ball, Richmond, VA."

T23

Black with orange-red overprint.
(Wagonload of Cotton, Harvesting Sugar Care at right, John E. Ward left.)

		Plain paper		
153	$10 (7)	Serial letter A	$150.00	$1800.00
		Red fiber paper		
154	$10 (8)	Serial letter A1	$225.00	$2500.00
		Plain paper		
155	$10 (10)	Serial letter A1		very rare

T24

Black with orange-red overprint.
(R.M.T. Hunter left, vignette of child right.)
"Leggett, Keatinge & Ball, Richmond, VA."

		Plain paper		
156	$10 (4)	H I J K	$45.00	$350.00
		Red fiber paper		
156A	$10 (8)	H I J K	$75.00	$475.00
		Watermarked "CSA" in block letters.		
157	$10 (6)	H I J K	$60.00	$425.00

Watermarked "CSA" in script letters.

158 $10 (6) H I J K $65.00 $425.00

Watermarked "Ten"

159 $10 (7) H I J K $90.00 $450.00

Watermarked "J. Whatman. 1862."

160 $10 (6) H K $80.00 $425.00

"Keatinge & Ball, Richmond VA."

Plain paper

161 $10 (6) H I J K $45.00 $350.00

Red fiber paper

162 $10 (8) H I J K $75.00 $475.00

Watermarked "CSA" in block letters.

163 $10 (5) H I J K $60.00 $425.00

Watermarked "CSA" in script letters.

164 $10 (4) H I J K $55.00 $350.00

Watermarked "Ten."

165 $10 (6) H I J K $85.00 $425.00

Watermarked "J. Whatman. 1862."

166 $10 (7) H K $75.00 $450.00

Watermarked "NY."

167 $10 (9) H I J K $250.00 $1000.00

"Keatinge & Ball, Richmond, VA."

T25

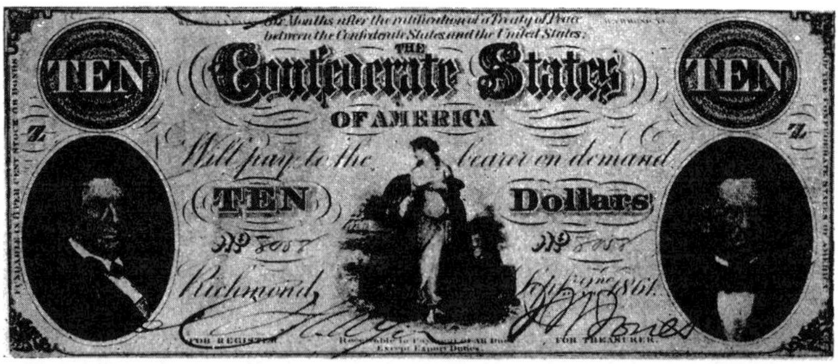

(Hope with Anchor, R.M.T. Hunter left, C. G. Memminger right.)

Plain paper

168 $10 (5) W X Y Z $37.50 $250.00

Same, no dash over "Bearer."

168A $10 (6) Z $45.00 $300.00

Watermarked "CSA" in block letters.

169 $10 (5) W X Y Z $40.00 $250.00

			Same, no dash over "Bearer."		
169A	$10 (6)	Z		$40.00	$250.00
			Watermarked "J. Whatman."		
170	$10 (7)	W Z		$65.00	$325.00
			Same, no dash over "Bearer."		
170A	$10 (5)	Z		$50.00	$315.00
			Watermarked "Hodgkinson & Co. Wookey Hole Mill."		
171	$10 (9)	W Z		$110.00	very rare
			Same, no dash over "Bearer."		
171A	$10 (9)	Z		$120.00	very rare

Note: the author is of the opinion that none of the above types exist in "2nd Series," including that formerly listed as number 172.

"Keatinge & Ball. Richmond, VA."

T26

(Hope with anchor, R.M.T. Hunter left, C.G. Memminger right.)

There are three types of red "X" "X" overprint. That section of the note on which the overprints appear is illustrated at 200%.

Solid red "X" "X" overprint.

NO SERIES

			Plain paper		
173	$10 (5)	W X Y Z		$25.00	$200.00
			Same, no dash over "Bearer."		
174	$10 (6)	Z		$30.00	$225.00
			Watermarked "CSA" in block letters.		
175	$10 (5)	W X Y Z		$25.00	$200.00
			Same, no dash over "Bearer."		
176	$10 (6)	Z		$30.00	$225.00
			Watermarked "CSA" in script letters.		
177	$10 (5)	W X Y Z		$25.00	$200.00
			Same, no dash over "Bearer."		
178	$10 (6)	Z		$30.00	$225.00
			Plain paper, "Of" before "The" is omitted.		
179	$10 (7)	W X		$45.00	$250.00
			Same, no dash over "Bearer."		
180	$10 (7)	Z		$50.00	$275.00
			Watermarked "CSA" in block letters. "Of" before "The" is omitted.		
181	$10 (7)	W X		$50.00	$275.00
			Same, no dash over "Bearer."		
182	$10 (7)	Z		$50.00	$295.00
			Watermarked "CSA" in script letters. "Of" before "The" is omitted.		
183	$10 (8)	W X		$65.00	$295.00
			Same, no dash over "Bearer."		
184	$10 (8)	Z		$75.00	$295.00
			Watermarked "Hodgkinson & Co. Wookey Hole Mill."		
184E	$10 (11)	W Z		extremely rare	

Note: only counterfeits are known of notes which were formerly listed as 185-188.

Coarse lace "X" "X" overprint.

NO SERIES

			Plain paper		
189	$10 (8)	W X Y Z		$65.00	$250.00

Same, no dash over "Bearer."

190 $10 (9) Z $70.00 $275.00

Watermarked "CSA" in block letters.

191 $10 (9) W X Y Z $40.00 $275.00

Same, no dash over "Bearer."

192 $10 (6) Z $60.00 $225.00

Watermarked "CSA" in script letters.

193 $10 (4) W X Y Z $30.00 $200.00

Same, no dash over "Bearer."

194 $10 (7) Z $50.00 $250.00

Watermarked "CSA" in script letters. "Of" before "The" is omitted.

199 $10 (8) W X $65.00 $250.00

Same, no dash over "Bearer."

200 $10 (8) Z $75.00 very rare

2nd SERIES

Plain paper

201 $10 (6) W X Y Z $35.00 $225.00

Same, no dash over "Bearer."

202 $10 (7) Z $50.00 $250.00

Watermarked "CSA" in block letters.

203 $10 (8) W X Y Z $50.00 $250.00

Same, no dash over "Bearer."

204 $10 (9) Z $90.00 very rare

Watermarked "CSA" in script letters.

205 $10 (8) W X Y Z $85.00 very rare

Same, no dash over "Bearer."

206 $10 (9) Z very rare

Watermarked "J. Whatman. 1862."

207 $10 (9) W Z very rare

Same, no dash over "Bearer."

208 $10 (10) Z very rare

Plain paper, "Of" before "The" is omitted.

209 $10 (9) W X very rare

Same, no dash over "Bearer."

210 $10 (10) Z very rare

Fine lace "X" "X" red overprint.

NO SERIES

		Plain paper		
211	$10 (7)	W X Y Z	$45.00	$250.00
		Same, no dash over "Bearer."		
212	$10 (8)	Z	$65.00	$275.00
		"Of" before "The" is omitted.		
212A	$10 (10)	W X Y Z		very rare
		Watermarked "CSA" in block letters.		
213	$10 (4)	W X Y Z	$30.00	$195.00
		"Of" before "The" is omitted.		
213A	$10 (10)	W X		very rare
		Same, no dash over "Bearer."		
214	$10 (6)	Z	$60.00	$225.00
		Watermarked "CSA" in script letters.		
214A	$10 (10)	Z	$75.00	$350.00
		Same, no dash over "Bearer."		
214B	$10 (9)	Z	$95.00	$295.00
		Watermarked "Hodgkinson & Co. Wookey Hole Mill."		
214C	$10 (10)	W Z		very rare

Note: only counterfeits are known of notes formerly listed as 215 - 220A.

"Lith. of Hoyer & Ludwig. Richmond, VA."

T27

(Liberty seated by shield and eagle.)

221	$10 (9)	Serial Letter Ab	$1,200	$35,000

The plates used for printing the numbered varieties vary slightly from those for the "Ab" notes.

222	$10 (11)	Serial letter A9	extremely rare
223	$10 (11)	Serial letter A10	extremely rare
224	$10 (11)	Serial letter A11	extremely rare
225	$10 (11)	Serial letter A12	extremely rare
226	$10 (11)	Serial letter A13	extremely rare
227	$10 (11)	Serial letter A14	extremely rare
228	$10 (11)	Serial letter A15	extremely rare
229	$10 (11)	Serial letter A16	extremely rare

T28

(Ceres and Commerce with an urn.)

"Hoyer & Ludwig. Richmond, VA."

Small numeral below "A."

230 $10 (4) A9 A10 A11 A12 A13 A14 A15 A16 $25.00 $175.00

Large numeral below "A."

231 $10 (4) A9 A10 A11 A12 A13 A14 A15 A16 $25.00 $175.00

Small numeral at right of "A."

232 $10 (4) A9 A10 A11 A12 A13 A14 A15 A16 $25.00 $175.00

Same, period after numeral.

232A $10 (4) A9 A10 A11 A12 A13 A14 A15 A16 $25.00 $175.00

Large numeral at right of "A."

233 $10 (4) A9 A10 A11 A12 A13 A14 A15 A16 $25.00 $175.00

Large numeral over "A."

234 $10 (5) A9 A10 A11 A12 A13 A14 A15 A16 $20.00 $175.00

"J. T. Paterson, Columbia, S.C."

Small numeral below "A."

235 $10 (4) A9 A10 A11 A12 A13 A14 A15 A16 $25.00 $175.00

Same, period after numeral.

235A $10 (5) A9 A10 A11 A12 A13 A14 A15 A16 $20.00 $200.00

Large numeral below "A."

236 $10 (4) A9 A10 A11 A12 A13 A14 A15 A16 $25.00 $200.00

Watermarked "CSA" in block letters.

236A $10 (9) A9 A10 A11 A12 A13 A14 A15 A16 $100.00 $475.00

Same as 235, but period after numeral.

236B $10 (5) A9 A10 A11 A12 A13 A14 A15 A16 $40.00 $200.00

T29

(Slave picking cotton.)

"B. Duncan, Richmond, VA."

237 $10 (6) A B C D E F G H $100.00 $650.00

* * * * * * *

T30

(General Francis Marion's "Sweet Potato Dinner" R.M.T. Hunter left, Minerva right.)

"B. Duncan, Columbia, S.C."

"First Series"

238 $10 (4) 1 2 3 4 5 6 7 8 $30.00 $115.00

WITHOUT ENGRAVER'S NAME

"Second Series"

239 $10 (5) 1 2 3 4 5 6 7 8 $35.00 $125.00

Error: "Second Series," numeral "5" at left, "1" at right.

240 $10 (10) 5/1 $300.00 $1500.00

"Third Series"

241 $10 (7) 1 2 3 4 5 6 7 8 $37.50 $137.50

"B. Duncan, Columbia, S.C."

"Fourth Series"

242	$10 (4)	1 2 3 4 5 6 7 8 9 10	$30.00	$95.00

"Southern Bank Note Company, New Orleans"

T31

Black with red overprint on red fiber paper.
(Minerva left, Agriculture, Commerce, Industry, Justice and Liberty seated at center.
Statue of Washington right.)

243	$5 (6)	Serial letter A	$125.00	$650.00
244	$5 (6)	Serial letter B	$125.00	$650.00
245	$5 (7)	Serial letter C	$195.00	$850.00

* * * * * * * *

"Leggett, Keatinge & Ball, Richmond, VA."

T32

Black with orange red overprint.

(Machinist with hammer, boy in oval left.)

Plain paper

246	$5 (8)	Serial letter A	$150.00	$1000.00

Plain paper

248	$5 (10)	Serial letter AA	$195.00	$1500.00

Red fiber paper

249 $5 (8) Serial letter AA $150.00 $1200.00

"Leggett, Keatinge, & Ball, Richmond, VA."

T32 ½

Black with *black* overprint.
(Machinist with hammer, boy in oval at left.)

The Amazing New "Blacksmith" Note

An important new discovery has just come to light. It is a Confederate States of America (CSA) $5 "Blacksmith Note (Criswell Type-32)," serial number 9387/A with a black rather than the "normal" red-orange color. This is a major discovery. It is the first major type to be discovered in the 127 years since collectors first became interested in listing various types!

Careful examination of the note by experts establishes that the piece is certainly a genuine note in which the "5 FIVE V" overprint is printed in black instead of the specified red-orange color.

One of the experts made the following comments about the note which answers many questions about the note and also sheds interesting light on many other aspects of CSA currency.

> "A careful measurement of the elements shows that this overprint is precisely the same as the same overprint printed in red-orange. The elements are also in the same locations.
>
> "The major factor proving that the note is genuine is that the overprint impression in black ink bleeds through the paper while the other black printing did not. This indicates that the same plate that was used to print the red-orange overprint was also used to print the black. In order to get an easily visible impression of light-colored

> inks on currency, it is necessary for more ink to be applied than would be used if the ink were black. The engraver accomplished this by making the cuts deeper to hold more ink during the printing process. These deeper cuts on the plate would have produced a normal red-orange impression by depositing more red-orange ink on the paper, but when black ink was used instead, it left a heavier-than-normal deposit of black ink which bled through.
>
> "I know of no chemical process whereby someone might have changed red-orange ink to black, nor do I know of any natural oxidation or other process which would have altered the red-orange ink to black. I believe that the overprint was originally printed in black.
>
> "This note was signed, numbered and issued. It circulated extensively and was apparently turned in during one of the Confederate government's redemption campaigns. Note that someone wrote the word "Cancelled" in brown ink, vertically at the middle of the bill, and added an "X" in the same brown ink on each end. This method of cancellation was commonly used when equipment to cut out the signatures or other parts of the note was not available.
>
> "Fold marks on the back indicate that the note was folded three times so that it could be carried in a wallet or money belt."

It is highly likely that the printers ran out of red-orange ink before printing the total 10,000 sheets as needed. They simply re-inked the machine and finished the run with a black on black overprint little realizing that they were creating a new "Type note."

As further evidence of how a situation could have occurred where the pressman might have run out of ink, the expert quotation continues:

> "I can only speculate as to why this note was made or was issued anyway. My guess is that the note was printed during a time when conditions at the Treasury Department were most chaotic. Military supplies contractors were literally standing in line outside Memminger's office waiting to be paid for their goods. Currency printers were getting drunk on the job, fighting among themselves, setting fires and in general making things miserable for Memminger. On August 28, 1861 the secretary ordered Samuel Schmidt, manager of the Southern Bank Note Company of New Orleans, to move his equipment to Richmond. Schmidt would not cooperate so the Confederate

government settled the matter by declaring Schmidt's parent company, the American Bank Note Company of New York, an enemy alien. The equipment in New Orleans was seized and turned over to Leggett, Keatinge & Ball in Richmond.

> "Just as things began to settle down, Memminger told Keatinge and Ball to remove Leggett from the firm or else he would close them down. Leggett's name was soon removed from the plates but not before the "Blacksmith" notes were completed. It was so hot in Richmond during the day that a lot of note printing was done between 6 p.m. and 2 a.m. The men still suffered because ice from the north had been cut off, making printing very difficult.
>
> "Under such conditions it is not surprising that many errors were made. Most were caught however and were never delivered to the Treasury Department. Perhaps this note was part of a single sheet that was printed with black overprint. It may have been set aside to be destroyed but in order to complete the order Keatinge may have decided to send it along to avoid delay in getting paid. Memminger was a stingy person who made life miserable for his currency contractors, so Keatinge may have slipped one through on him.
>
> "Temple Ellett and Harrel Goodlow, the two men who signed all these notes, were being paid to sign notes, not to examine them. Obviously, in the midst of red, black sheets would have stood out. But the two signed the notes anyway and sent them on to be cut apart and issued. Memminger's tellers would have not been inclined to reject them. They paid the notes out in the normal course of business. With so many different designs in circulation, most people would have accepted the notes and passed them on."

Further examination in the future may yield some idea as to how many of these notes, or sheets of notes, may have been printed and issued. If red-orange notes with high serial numbers are located, it is possible, but not necessarily a fact, that red-orange ink might have been acquired the next day (or whatever), and the balance of the run finished in the proper color.

If the black on black was the end of the run there could still be higher numbers as they could have been stacked below the reds as well as within. Maybe just enough were "signed" at the end to make an even 10,000. How many? Who knows?

T33

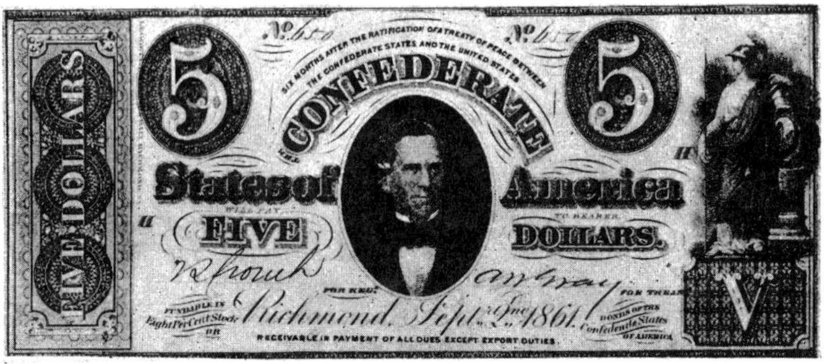

Black with blue and yellow-green ornamentation overprints.
(C. G. Memminger, Minerva right.)

Plain paper.

The listings for type 33 have been revised to account for two distinct color varieties: blue-green and yellow-green. The numbers formerly listed as 258 through 261 are included.

"Leggett, Keatinge & Ball, Richmond, Va," facing in.

250	$5 (5) H I J K			
	a. blue-green	H I J K	$75.00	$450.00
	b. yellow-green	H I J K	$75.00	$450.00

"Va" dropped at end of engravers' names.

250A	$5 (8) H I J K			
	a. blue-green	H I J K	$95.00	$495.00
	b. yellow-green	H I J K	$95.00	$495.00

"Leggett, Keatinge & Ball, Richmond, VA" facing out.

250B	$5 (6) H I J K			
	a. blue-green	H I J K	$75.00	$450.00
	b. yellow-green	H I J K	$75.00	$450.00

"VA" dropped at end of engravers' names.

250C	$5 (8) H I J K			
	a. blue-green	H I J K	$95.00	$450.00
	b. yellow-green	H I J K	$95.00	$450.00

Paper watermarked "CSA" in block letters.

"Leggett, Keatinge & Ball, Richmond, Va." facing in.

252	$5 (6) H I J K			
	a. blue-green	H I J K	$95.00	$450.00
	b. yellow-green	H I J K	$95.00	$450.00

"Va." dropped at end of engravers' names.

252A $5 (8) H I J K

a. blue-green	H I J K	$95.00	$450.00
b. yellow-green	H I J K	$95.00	$450.00

"Leggett, Keatinge & Ball, Richmond, VA." facing out.

252B $5 (6) H I J K

a. blue-green	H I J K	$95.00	$450.00
b. yellow-green	H I J K	$95.00	$450.00

"VA." dropped at end of engravers' names.

252C $5 (8) H I J K

a. blue-green	H I J K	$95.00	$450.00
b. yellow-green	H I J K	$95.00	$450.00

Watermarked "Five"

"Leggett, Keatinge & Ball. Richmond, VA." facing in.

253 $5 (6) H I J K

a. blue-green	H I J K	$95.00	$450.00
b. yellow-green	H I J K	$95.00	$450.00

"Va." dropped at end of engravers' names.

253E $5 (8) H I J K

a. blue-green	H I J K	$95.00	$450.00
b. yellow-green	H I J K	$95.00	$450.00

"Leggett, Keatinge & Ball. Richmond, VA." facing out..

250F $5 (6) H I J K

a. blue-green	H I J K	$95.00	$450.00
b. yellow-green	H I J K	$95.00	$450.00

"Va." dropped at end of engravers' names.

253G $5 (8) H I J K

a. blue-green	H I J K	$95.00	$450.00
b. yellow-green	H I J K	$95.00	$450.00

Watermarked "J. Whatman. 1862"

"Leggett, Keatinge & Ball. Richmond, VA." facing in.

253A $5 (7) H K

a. blue-green	H K	$95.00	$450.00
b. yellow-green	H K	$95.00	$450.00

"Va." dropped at end of engravers' names.

253B $5 (8) H K

a. blue-green	H K	$95.00	$450.00
b. yellow-green	H K	$95.00	$450.00

"Leggett, Keatinge & Ball. Richmond, VA." facing out.

253C $5 (6) H K

a. blue-green	H K	$95.00	$450.00
b. yellow-green	H K	$95.00	$450.00

Watermarked "J. Whatman. 1862."

"Va." dropped at end of engravers' names.

253D	$5 (8) H K			
	a. blue-green	H K	$95.00	$450.00
	b. yellow-green	H K	$95.00	$450.00

Plain Paper.

"Keatinge & Ball. Richmond, VA." facing in.

254	$5 (6) H I J K L M N O			
	a. blue-green	H I J K L M N O	$95.00	$450.00
	b. yellow-green	H I J K L M N O	$95.00	$450.00

"Va." dropped at end of engravers' names.

254B	$5 (8) H I J K L M N O			
	a. blue-green	H I J K L M N O	$95.00	$450.00
	b. yellow-green	H I J K L M N O	$95.00	$450.00

"Keatinge & Ball. Richmond, VA." facing out.

254A	$5 (6) H I J K L M N O			
	a. blue-green	H I J K L M N O	$95.00	$450.00
	b. yellow-green	H I J K L M N O	$95.00	$450.00

"Va." dropped at end of engravers' names.

254C	$5 (8) H I J K L M N O			
	a. blue-green	H I J K L M N O	$95.00	$450.00
	b. yellow-green	H I J K L M N O	$95.00	$450.00

Watermarked "CSA" in block letters.

"Keatinge & Ball. Richmond, VA." facing in.

255	$5 (5) H I J K L M N O			
	a. blue-green	H I J K L M N O	$95.00	$450.00
	b. yellow-green	H I J K L M N O	$95.00	$450.00

"Va." dropped at end of engravers' names.

255A	$5 (8) H I J K L M N O			
	a. blue-green	H I J K L M N O	$95.00	$450.00
	b. yellow-green	H I J K L M N O	$95.00	$450.00

"Keatinge & Ball. Richmond, VA." facing out.

255B	$5 (6) H I J K L M N O			
	a. blue-green	H I J K L M N O	$95.00	$450.00
	b. yellow-green	H I J K L M N O	$95.00	$450.00

"Va." dropped at end of engravers' names.

255C	$5 (8) H I J K L M N O			
	a. blue-green	H I J K L M N O	$95.00	$450.00
	b. yellow-green	H I J K L M N O	$95.00	$450.00

Watermarked "J. Whatman. 1862"

"Leggett, Keatinge & Ball. Richmond, VA." facing in.

256 $5 (7) H K L O

a. blue-green	H K L O	$125.00	$475.00
b. yellow-green	H K L O	$125.00	$475.00

"Va." dropped at end of engravers' names.

256E $5 (9) H K L O

a. blue-green	H K L O	$125.00	$475.00
b. yellow-green	H K L O	$125.00	$475.00

"Leggett, Keatinge & Ball. Richmond, VA." facing out.

250F $5 (8) H K L O

a. blue-green	H K L O	$125.00	$475.00
b. yellow-green	H K L O	$125.00	$475.00

"Va." dropped at end of engravers' names.

256G $5 (9) H K L O

a. blue-green	H K L O	$125.00	$475.00
b. yellow-green	H K L O	$125.00	$475.00

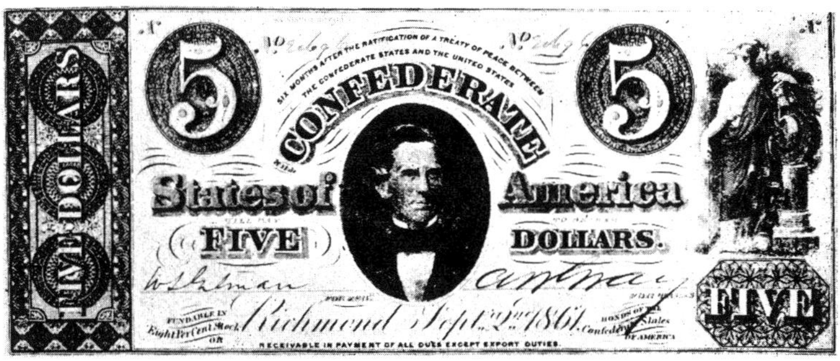

T34

(C. G. Memminger, Minerva at right.)

"Keatinge & Ball, Richmond, VA.," engravers

Plain paper

262	$5 (5)	W X Y Z	$30.00	$200.00

Same as 262 but "o" instead of "c" in "receivable."

262A	$5 (5)	Y	$60.00	$300.00

Watermarked "CSA" in block letters.

263	$5 (4)	W X Y Z	$28.00	$200.00

Same as 263 but "o" instead of "c" in "receivable."

263A	$5 (5)	Y	$60.00	$325.00

Watermarked "CSA" in script letters.

264	$5 (5)	W X Z	$45.00	$260.00

264A	$5 (5)	Y	$60.00	$300.00
		Watermarked "J. Whatman. 1862."		
265	$5 (7)	W Z	$75.00	$235.00
		Watermarked "Hodgkinson & Co. Wookey Hole Mill."		
265A	$5 (9)	W Z	$125.00	$350.00

WITHOUT NAMES OF ENGRAVERS

		Plain paper		
266	$5 (6)	H I J K	$30.00	$210.00
		Watermarked "CSA" in block letters.		
267	$5 (5)	H I J K	$30.00	$200.00
		Watermarked "CSA" in script letters.		
268	$5 (5)	H I J K	$30.00	$210.00
		Watermarked "J. Whatman 1862."		
269	$5 (7)	H K	$85.00	$300.00
		Watermarked "Hodgkinson & Co. Wookey Hole Mill."		
270	$5 (9)	H K	$150.00	$500.00

"Lith. of Hoyer & Ludwig. Richmond, Va."

T35

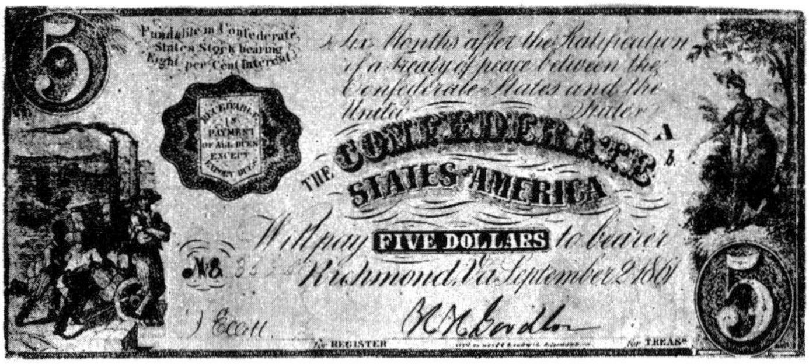

(Loading cotton left, "Indian Princess" right.)

271	$5 (9)	Serial letter Ab	$2,750	$60,000

******

T36

(Ceres seated on bale of cotton, sailor left).

"Hoyer & Ludwig. Richmond."

Numeral before "A."

272 $5 (5) 9A 10A 11A 12A 13A 14A 15A 16A $20.00 $95.00

"J.T. Paterson, Columbia, S.C."

Numeral before "A."

274 $5 (3) 9A 10A 11A 12A 13A 14A 15A 16A $20.00 $85.00

"J.T. Paterson & Co. Columbia, S.C."

Numeral before "A."

276 $5 (3) 9A 10A 11A 12A 13A 14A 15A 16A $20.00 $85.00

278 $5 (3) 9A 10A 11A 12A 13A 14A 15A 16A $20.00 $85.00

Same, watermarked "CSA" in block letters.

280 $5 (6) 9A 10A 11A 12A 13A 14A 15A 16A $60.00 $150.00

Same, watermarked "CSA" in script letters.

281 $5 (6) 9A 10A 11A 12A 13A 14A 15A 16A $60.00 $195.00

THIRD SERIES

Numeral before "A."

282 $5 (10) 9A 10A 11A 12A 13A 14A 15A 16A $200.00 v. rare

T37 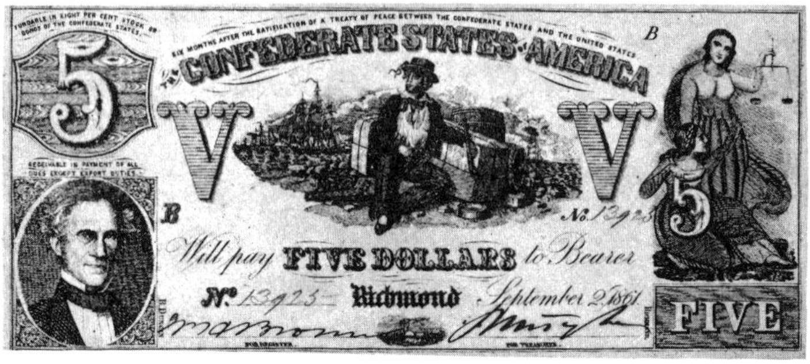

(Sailor seated beside bales of cotton, C.G. Memminger left, Justice and Ceres right.)

"B. Duncan, Richmond."

284 $5 (6) 1 2 3 4 5 6 7 8 $30.00 $275.00

"B. Duncan, Columbia, S.C."

285 $5 (6) 1 2 3 4 5 6 7 8 $35.00 $300.00

"B. Duncan, Columbia, S.C."

Dated "September 2, 1861," through an error. No Confederate note of less than $5 was authorized in 1861.

T38 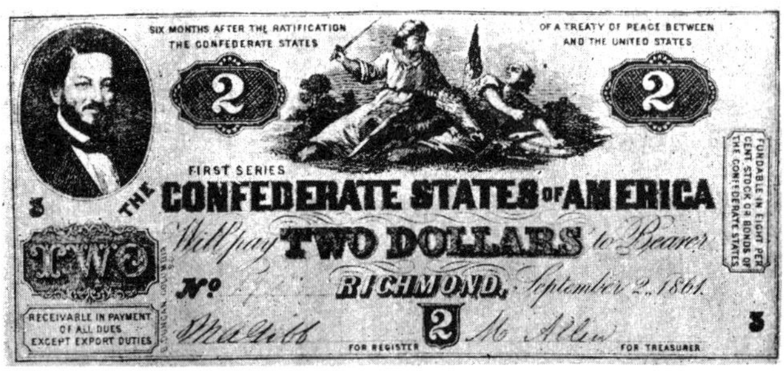

(Personification of South striking down Union, J.P. Benjamin left.)

286 $2 (8) 1 2 3 4 5 6 7 8 9 10 $400.00 $4500.00

Error: numeral "1" at left, numeral "10" at right.

286A $2 (10) 1/10 $950.00 ex rare

1862

$165,000,000 Authorized by Act of April 17th, 1862.

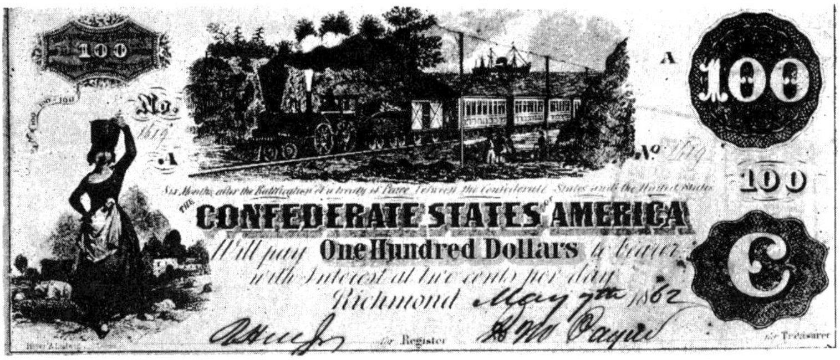

T39

(Railway train--straight steam from locomotive--milkmaid left.)

Bears "Interest at Two Cents Per Day."
DATED MAY 5 TO MAY 9, 1862
"Hoyer & Ludwig. Richmond, Va."

287 $100 (7) A $40.00 $60.00

Serial letter below "A."

289 $100 (7) Ab Ac Ad Ae Af Ag Ah $40.00 $60.00

Error: period after serial letter.

289A $100 (8) Ab Ac Ad Ae Af Ag Ah $50.00 $90.00

VARIOUS WRITTEN DATES, MAY THROUGH OCTOBER, 1862

J. T. Paterson, Columbia, S.C. (at lower left).

Small letter below "A."

290 $100 (4) Aa Ab Ac Ad Ae Af Ag Ah $25.00 $45.00

Large letter below "A."

291 $100 (4) Aa Ab Ac Ad Ae Af Ag Ah $25.00 $45.00

Small letter below "A."

292 $100 (6) Aa Ab Ac Ad Ae Af Ag Ah $25.00 $45.00

Capital letter "A" elongated.

293 $100 (5) Aa Ab Ac Ad Ae Af Ag Ah $25.00 $45.00

"J.T. Paterson & Co., Columbia, S.C." (at lower right)

Small letter below "A."

294 $100 (4) Aa Ab Ac Ad Ae Af Ag Ah $25.00 $45.00

Large letter below "A."

296 $100 (5) Aa Ab Ac Ad Ae Af Ag Ah $25.00 $45.00

Small letter below "A," treasurer printed twice.

296A $100 (10) Ah $150.00 $200.00

Remarks; numbers 290 through 297 come with a period after some combinations, and without on others, but not both.

"J. T. Paterson & Co. Columbia, S.C."

T40

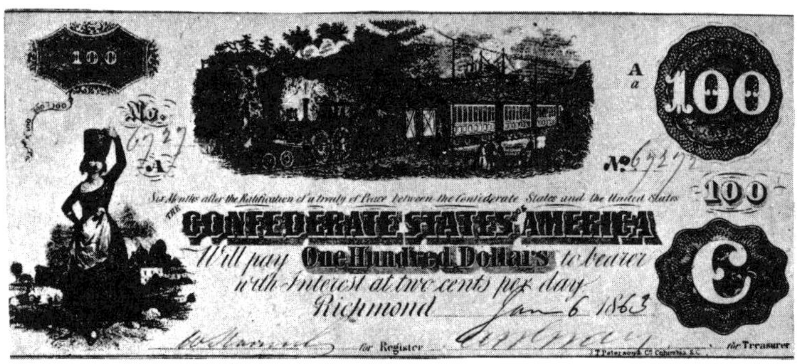

(Railway train--diffused steam from locomotive--milkmaid left.)

Bears "Interest at Two Cents Per Day."

VARIOUS WRITTEN DATES, MAY THROUGH OCTOBER, 1862

Small letter below "A."

298 $100 (4) Aa Ab Ac Ad Ae Af Ag Ah $25.00 $45.00

Large letter below "A."

300 $100 (6) Aa Ab Ac Ad Ae Af Ag Ah $25.00 $50.00

Small letter below "A," watermarked "CSA" in block letters.

302 $100 (6) Aa Ab Ac Ad Ae Af Ag Ah $25.00 $45.00

Large letter below "A," watermarked "CSA" in block letters.

304 $100 (7) Aa Ab Ac Ad Ae Af Ag Ah $35.00 $60.00

Small letter below "A," watermarked "CSA" in script letters.

306 $100 (5) Aa Ab Ac Ad Ae Af Ag Ah $30.00 $50.00

Large letter below "A," watermarked "CSA" in script letters.

307 $100 (6) Aa Ab Ac Ad Ae Af Ag Ah $35.00 $60.00

DATED JANUARY (UP TO THE 8TH), 1863

Small letter below "A."

308 $100 (7) Aa Ab Ac Ad Ae Af Ag Ah $25.00 $50.00

Large letter below "A."

309 $100 (8) Aa Ab Ac Ad Ae Af Ag Ah $35.00 $65.00

"Keatinge & Ball, Columbia, S.C."

Note: on these notes there are two types of ornamental scrolls in the upper right corners. They will be listed as scroll No. 1 and No. 2 as illustrated.

Scroll 1

Scroll 2

T41

(Slaves hoeing cotton. J.C. Calhoun left, Minerva at right).

"Hundred" overprint in orange-red, bears "Interest at Two Cents Per Day."

Dated "August 26th, 1862." (Date all written), scroll No. 1.

Plain Paper

310 $100 (8) W X Y Z $60.00 $100.00

Watermarked "CSA" in block letters.

311 $100 (7) W X Y Z $60.00 $95.00

Watermarked "CSA" in script letters.

312 $100 (6) W X Y Z very rare

Watermarked "J. Whatman. 1862."

313 $100 (10) W Z very rare

Watermarked "Hodgkinson & Co. Wookey Hole Mill."

314 $100 (10) W Z very rare

Written dates, Aug. to Dec. "1862." ("186" of date is engraved).

Bottom frame line goes under word "Except."

Plain paper, scroll no. 1.

315 $100 (4) W X Y Z $30.00 $45.00

Same as above but frame line stops at "Except."

315A $100 (4) W X Y Z $30.00 $45.00

Scroll number 2

316 $100 (5) W X Y Z $30.00 $45.00

Same as above but frame line stops at "Except."

316A $100 (5) W X Y Z $30.00 $45.00

Watermarked "CSA" in block letters, scroll number 1.

317 $100 (5) W X Y Z $30.00 $45.00

Same as above but frame line stops at "Except."

317A $100 (5) W X Y Z $30.00 $45.00

Scroll number 2

318 $100 (4) W X Y Z $30.00 $45.00

Same as above but frame line stops at "Except."

318A $100 (4) W X Y Z $30.00 $45.00

Watermarked "CSA" in script letters, scroll number 1.

319 $100 (4) W X Y Z $30.00 $45.00

Same as above but frame line stops at "Except."

319A $100 (5) W X Y Z $30.00 $45.00

Scroll number 2

320 $100 (4) W X Y Z $30.00 $45.00

Same as above but frame line stops at "Except."

320A $100 (6) W X Y Z $30.00 $45.00

Same as above, but "For Treasurer" at left and right.

320C $100 (9) Z $300.00 v. rare

Watermarked "J. Whatman. 1862," scroll number 1.

321 $100 (7) W Z $40.00 $65.00

Same as above but frame line stops at "Except."

321A $100 (7) W Z $40.00 $65.00

Scroll number 2.

322 $100 (7) W Z $40.00 $65.00

Same as above but frame line stops at "Except."

322A $100 (7) W Z $40.00 $65.00

Watermarked "Hodgkinson & Co. Wookey Hole Mill.," scroll number 1.

323 $100 (9) W Z $90.00 $200.00

Same as above but frame line stops at "Except."

323A	$100 (9)	W Z	$90.00	$200.00

Scroll number 2

324	$100 (9)	W Z	$95.00	$210.00

Same as above but frame line stops at "Except."

324A	$100 (9)	W Z	$95.00	$210.00

Dated January 1st to January 8th, 1863

Plain paper, scroll number 1.

325	$100 (6)	W X Y Z	$30.00	$50.00

Same as above but frame line stops at "Except."

325A	$100 (6)	W X Y Z	$30.00	$50.00

Scroll number 2

326	$100 (7)	W X Y Z	$30.00	$50.00

Same as above but frame line stops at "Except."

326A	$100 (8)	W X Y Z	$30.00	$50.00

Watermarked "CSA" in block letters, scroll number 1.

327	$100 (8)	W X Y Z	$35.00	$70.00

Same as above but frame line stops at "Except."

327A	$100 (8)	W X Y Z	$35.00	$70.00

Scroll number 2

328	$100 (7)	W X Y Z	$35.00	$70.00

Same as above but frame line stops at "Except."

328A	$100 (7)	W X Y Z	$35.00	$70.00

Watermarked "J. Whatman. 1862," scroll number 1.

330	$100 (8)	W Z	$45.00	$85.00

Same as above but frame line stops at "Except."

330A	$100 (8)	W Z	$45.00	$85.00

Scroll number 2

331	$100 (8)	W Z	$45.00	$85.00

Same as above but frame line stops at "Except."

331A	$100 (8)	W Z	$45.00	$85.00

$5,000,000 Authorized by Act of April 18th, 1862.
$5,000,000 Authorized by Act of September 23rd, 1862.

"B. Duncan, Columbia, S.C."

T42

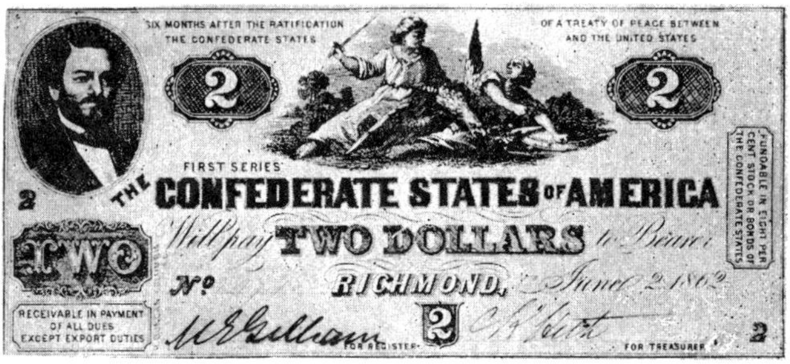

(Personification of South striking down Union, J.P. Benjamin left).

		First series		
334	$2 (4)	1 2 3 4 5 6 7 8 9 10	$35.00	$150.00
		First series, double flourish to "J" in June.		
335	$2 (4)	1 2 3 4 5 6 7 8 9 10	$35.00	$150.00
		Second series		
336	$2 (4)	1 2 3 4 5 6 7 8 9 10	$35.00	$150.00
		Error: numeral "1" at left, numeral "10" at right.		
336A	$2 (10)	1/10	$200.00	$1200.00
		Third series		
337	$2 (4)	1 2 3 4 5 6 7 8 9 10 11 12	$35.00	$150.00

* * * * * *

"B. Duncan, Columbia, S.C."

T43

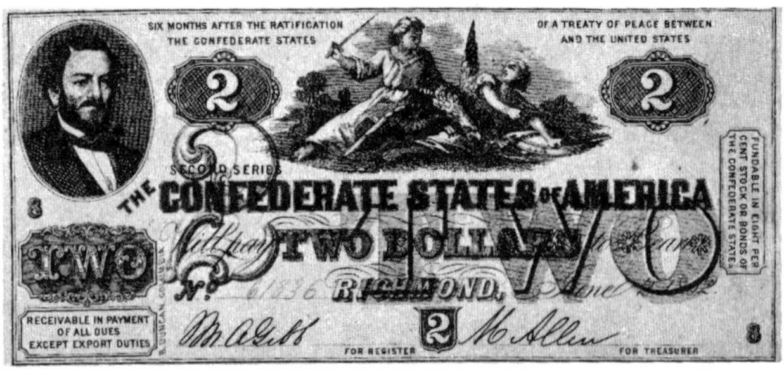

(Personification of South striking down Union, J.P. Benjamin left).
"2" and "TWO" in green overprint.

Second series

338 $2 (6) 1 2 3 4 5 6 7 8 9 10 $75.00 $1000.00

Error: numeral "1" at left, numeral "10" at right.

338A $2 (10) 1/10 very rare

"B. Duncan, Columbia, S.C."

T44

(Steamship at sea, Lucy Holcombe Pickens right, Liberty at left.)

First series

339 $1 (4) 1 2 3 4 5 6 7 8 9 10 $25.00 $95.00

Second series

340 $1 (4) 1 2 3 4 5 6 7 8 9 10 $25.00 $95.00

Third series

341 $1 (4) 1 2 3 4 5 6 7 8 9 10 11 12 $25.00 $90.00

* * * * *

"B. Duncan, Columbia, S.C."

T45

(Steamship at sea, Lucy Holcombe Pickens right, Liberty at left.)

"1" and "One" green overprint

Second series

342 $1 (6) 1 2 3 4 5 6 7 8 9 10 $40.00 $400.00

First series

342A $1 (5) 1 2 3 4 5 6 7 8 9 10 $40.00 $400.00

This is a Sept. 2, 1861 note, dated through error "September 2, 1862."

No engravers names, but a product of Hoyer & Ludwig!

T46

(Ceres reclining on cotton bales, R. M. T. Hunter at right.)

Terms of redemption read "Six *Months* after."

343 $10 (4) I J K L M N O P $22.50 $150.00

Terms of redemption read "Six *Month* After."

344 $10 (4) I J K L M N O P $22.50 $150.00

* * * * *

PRINTED SIGNATURE NOTES

Essay notes...bogus notes...on and on the story has gone for years, over a hundred to be exact. The two notes following have always been collected as types, and were thought to be "essay pieces" which were produced to show the member of the Confederate Congress that printed signatures "could survive" and be economically feasible.

Several different theories exist as to where, when, and how these pieces were made. The fact that only a few dozen are known, and that they have turned up in old collections as well as in"hoards" of genuine currency has promulgated the mystery that surrounds them.

In listing them this time, numbers XX2 and XX3 have been assigned in addition to the type number because of how paradoxically these notes (even though suspect for years) have proven to be among the most sought after, and desirable pieces in Confederate note collecting.

These were formerly listed as numbers 345 and 346.

"KEATINGE & BALL, COLUMBUS, S.C."

T47

(Liberty seated on bale of cotton, R.M.T. Hunter at right.) Printed signatures.

XX2 $20 (10) N $1200.00 ex. rare

T48

(Ceres holding sheaf of wheat, R. M. T. Hunter at right.) Printed signatures.

XX3 $10 (10) N $1200.00 ex rare

$90,000,000 Authorized by Act of Oct. 13th, 1862
"Keatinge & Ball, Columbia, S.C."

T49

(Lucy Holcombe Pickens, George W. Randolph right).
Fancy green back.

NO SERIES

Plain paper

347 $100 (7) A B C D $75.00 $195.00

With inverted back.

347IB $100 (11)A B C D very rare

Watermarked "CSA" in block letters, with wavy borderline.

348 $100 (6) A B C D $60.00 $175.00

Watermarked "J. Whatman. 1862."

348A $100 (9) A D very rare

Watermarked "Hodgkinson & Co. Wookey Hole Mill."

348B $100 (9) A D ex rare

2nd SERIES

Watermarked "CSA" in block letters, with wavy borderline.

349 $100 (9) A B C D $100.00 $250.00

Note: a contemporary counterfeit exists on plain paper. It is believed that no genuine pieces exist on plain paper.

T50

Black with green overprint. Ornate green back.
(Jefferson Davis)

All "3rd SERIES"

"Keatinge & Ball. Richmond, Va."
Engravers' names above "Fundable" at left end.

Plain paper

350	$50 (6)	WA XA YA ZA	$40.00	$125.00

Watermarked "CSA" in block letters with wavy borderline.

351	$50 (4)	WA XA YA ZA	$40.00	$125.00

Watermarked "CSA" in script letters.

352	$50 (6)	WA XA YA ZA	$60.00	$150.00

Watermarked "J. Whatman. 1862."

352A	$50 (8)	WA ZA	$80.00	$195.00

"Keatinge & Ball. Richmond, Va."
Engravers' names below, "Fundable" at left end.

Plain paper

353	$50 (6)	WA XA YA ZA	$40.00	$125.00

Watermarked "CSA" in block letters.

354	$50 (6)	WA XA YA ZA	$40.00	$125.00

Watermarked "CSA" in block letters, with wavy borderline.

355	$50 (4)	WA XA YA ZA	$40.00	$125.00

Watermarked "CSA" in script letters.

356 $50 (4) WA XA YA ZA $40.00 $125.00

Watermarked "J. Whatman. 1862."

356A $50 (8) WA ZA $95.00 $195.00

"Keatinge & Ball. Columbia, S.C."

Engravers' names above "Fundable" at left end.

Two flourishes under "de" of Confederate." Plain paper.

357 $50 (5) WA XA YA ZA $45.00 $125.00

Same, watermarked "CSA" in block letters.

358 $50 (4) WA XA YA ZA $45.00 $125.00

Same, watermarked "J. Whatman. 1862."

359 $50 (8) WA ZA $85.00 $195.00

Same, watermarked "CSA" in block letters with wavy borderline.

360 $50 (5) WA XA YA ZA $40.00 $125.00

Three flourishes under "de" of "Confederate," watermarked "CSA" in block letters.

361 $50 (9) XA YA ZA $45.00 $210.00

Error: "Ratification, etc." in place of "Six Months, etc."

361A $50 (10) WA $200.00 $395.00

Same, watermarked "CSA" in block letters, with wavy borderline.

362 $50 (4) WA XA YA ZA $40.00 $125.00

Same, plain paper

362A $50 (7) WA XA YA ZA $45.00 $150.00

* * * * *

All "Engraved by Keatinge & Ball. Columbia, S.C."

T51

(State capitol at Nashville, Tennessee, A. H. Stephens.)

Fancy blue back

"Printed by J. T. Paterson & Co." (on lower margin). "1st Series."

363 $20 (5) A B C D E F G H $40.00 $150.00

Same, except "Printed By" is omitted.

364 $20 (7) A B C D E F G H $55.00 $175.00

No printer's name, "1st Series," face of tower on capitol *is* shaded.

365 $20 (5) A B C D E F G H $40.00 $150.00

Same, face of tower on capitol *is not* shaded.

366 $20 (4) A B C D E F G H $35.00 $150.00

Same, except "Engraved by Keatinge & Ball. Columbia, S.C." is doubled (in plate transfer).

366A $20 (10) A very rare

Same, face of tower on capitol is shaded, period after first serial letter.

367 $20 (6) A B C D E F G H $40.00 $150.00

"B Duncan" (on lower right margin), "1st Series."

368 $20 (7) A B C D E F G H $50.00 $175.00

"Printed by B. Duncan" (on lower margin), "1st Series."

368A $20 (8) A B C D E F G H $60.00 $195.00

"Engraved by Keatinge & Ball. Columbia, S.C."
Printed on pink paper.

T52

Fancy blue back.
(State Capitol at Columbia, S.C., R. M. T. Hunter.)
"Printed by B. Duncan," no series.

369 $10 (3) A B C D E F G H $22.00 $65.00

		Same as 369 with inverted back.		
369IB	$10 (11)			very rare
		Same, "2 Series"		
371	$10 (3)	A B C D E F G H	$22.00	$65.00
		Same, "3. Series" (far from top of note).		
372	$10 (6)	A B C D E F G H	$25.00	$80.00
		"3 Series" (near top of note).		
373	$10 (4)	A B C D E F G H	$26.00	$70.00
		Same as above with inverted back.		
373IB	$10 (11)			very rare
		Same, "4. Series" (far from top of note).		
374	$10 (5)	A B C D E F G H	$25.00	$75.00
		Same, but serial letters differ at top of note.		
374A	$10 (11)C/G		extremely rare	
		Same, "4. Series" (near top of note).		
375	$10 (4)	A B C D E F G H	$22.00	$65.00
		Same as above with inverted back.		
375IB	$10 (11)			very rare
		"Ptd. by Evans & Cogswell," no series.		
376	$10 (3)	A B C D E F G H	$20.00	$60.00
		Same, "3rd Series" in small letters (on left end).		
377	$10 (6)	A B C D E F G H	$25.00	$80.00
		Same as above with inverted back.		
377IB	$10 (11)			very rare
		Same, "3. Series" in large letters.		
378	$10 (8)	A B C D E F G H	$40.00	$85.00
		Errors, in that two printers' names appear next to each other on the left end. "Ptd. by Evans & Cogswell." "Printed by B. Duncan." "3 Series." (on right end).		
378A	$10 (9)	A B C D E F G H	$75.00	$200.00
		Same, "4. Series"		
378B	$10 (9)	A B C D E F G H	$75.00	$180.00
		Same as above with inverted back.		
378BIB	$10 (11)	A B C D E F G H		very rare
		"Ptd. by Evans & Cogswell." "B. Dunc." showing, "3.Series" (all on left end).		
378C	$10 (9)	E	$80.00	$225.00

All "Engraved by Keatinge & Ball. Columbia, S.C."
Printed on pink paper.

T53

(State capitol at Richmond, Va. C.G. Memminger.)

Fancy blue back

No printers' names, "1st Series" (on left end).

379	$5 (5)	A B C D E F G H	$25.00	$65.00
		Same, "2nd series."		
380	$5 (4)	A B C D E F G H	$23.00	$60.00
		"Printed by J. T. Paterson & Co.," "1st Series."		
381	$5 (7)	A B C D E F G H	$40.00	$80.00
		"Lithog'd by J. T. Paterson & Co." "1st Series."		
382	$5 (5)	A B C D E F G H	$25.00	$65.00
		Same, "2nd Series."		
383	$5 (5)	A B C D E F G H	$25.00	$65.00

		Error: "2nd Series" with mismatched serial letters.		
384	$5 (8)	H/A C/GG/C	$165.00	$425.00
		"J.T. Paterson & Co." "2nd Series."		
385	$5 (6)	A B C D E F G H	$60.00	$175.00
		"Lithog'd by J.T. Paterson & Co." "3rd Series"		
387	$5 (5)	A B C D E F G H	$25.00	$60.00
		"Ptd. by Evans & Cogswell." "2nd Series"		
388	$5 (3)	A B C D E F G H	$25.00	$60.00
		Error: "2nd Series" with mismatched serial letters.		
389	$5 (9)	D/A	$250.00	$450.00
		"Ptd. by Evans & Cogswell," "Lithog'd by J. T. Paterson & Co." "2nd Series"		
390	$5 (7)	A B C D E F G H	$40.00	$95.00
		"Ptd. by Evans & Cogswell," "J.T. Paterson & Co." "2nd Series"		
390B	$5 (8)	A B C D E F G H	$95.00	$300.00

All "Engraved by Keatinge & Ball. Columbia, S.C."
Printed on pink paper.

T54

(Judah P. Benjamin.)

"1ST SERIES"

		No periods		
391	$2 (5)	B C D E F G H I	$30.00	$60.00
		Periods after both serial letters.		
392	$2 (5)	B C D E F G H I	$30.00	$60.00
		Period after right serial letter.		
392A	$2 (7)	D	$40.00	$75.00
		Period after left serial letter.		
392B	$2 (8)	E	$45.00	$80.00

Period before 1st and after last serial letter.

392C	$2 (8)	D	$45.00	$85.00

Flourishes about the serial letters.

393	$2 (6)	B C D E F G H I	$35.00	$75.00

Skeleton serial letters.

394	$2 (5)	B C D E F G H I	$30.00	$60.00

Same, flourishes about the serial letters.

394A	$2 (6)	B C D E F G H I	$40.00	$70.00

Same as 394 but period after serial letters.

394B	$2 (9)	B C D E F G H I	$55.00	$100.00

"2nd Series"

Period after both serial letters.

395	$2 (7)	B C D E F G H I	$40.00	$80.00

"PRINTED BY J. T. PATERSON & CO."

No series

396	$2 (5)	A	$30.00	$60.00

Two specimen backs which were never adopted or used.

396pf

401pf

These proofs of backs for Confederate States of America notes are very rare. Very little information is available on them.

All "Engraved by Keatinge & Ball. Columbia, S.C."
Printed on pink paper.

T55

(Clement C. Clay)

"1st SERIES"

No periods

397	$1 (4)	B C D E F G H I	$50.00	$125.00

Period after right serial letter.

397A	$1 (7)	H I	$50.00	$150.00

Period after both serial letters.

398	$1 (5)	B C D E F G H I	$50.00	$150.00

Skeleton serial letters.

399	$1 (6)	B C D E F G H I	$50.00	$175.00

"2ND SERIES"

Period after both serial letters.

400	$1 (7)	B C D E F G H I	$50.00	$150.00

"PRINTED BY B. DUNCAN"

No series

Script serial letter

401	$1 (6)	A	$50.00	$150.00

1863

$50,000,000 Authorized Monthly, from April, 1863 to January, 1864 by Act of March 23rd, 1863

All of the notes of this year are dated April 6th, 1863, but a red overprinted date appears on all of the $5, $10, $20, $50, and $100 denominations showing the year and month of issue. For the first time, all of the types that can conceivably exist have been listed. Most, but not all of these, have been personally observed by the author. A special numbering system has been established to accommodate these listings, and the rarity is shown, individually, for each issue.

ALL ENGRAVED BY "KEATINGE & BALL. COLUMBIA, S.C."

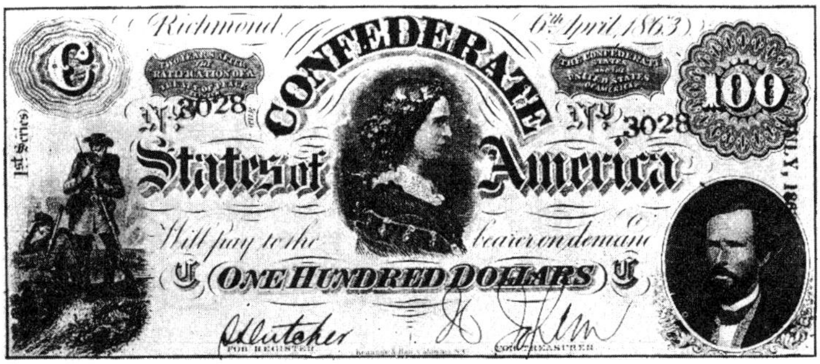

T56

T56

(Lucy H. Pickens, two soldiers left, George W. Randolph right.) Green back..

Watermarked "CSA" in block letters, with wavy borderline, no series.

402 $100 (4) A B C D $45.00 $100.00

November, 1863

402/8 $100 (4) A B C D

December, 1863

402/9 $100 (4) A B C D

January, 1864

402/10 $100 (4) A B C D

Watermarked "CSA" in block letters, with wavy borderline,"1st Series."

403 $100 (4) A B C D $45.00 $100.00

April, 1863

403/1 $100 (6) A B C D

May, 1863

403/2 $100 (6) A B C D

June, 1863

403/3 $100 (5) A B C D

July, 1863

403/4 $100 (6) A B C D

August, 1863

403/5 $100 (5) A B C D

September, 1863

403/6 $100 (6) A B C D

October, 1863

403/7 $100 (5) A B C D

Same, flourishes in front of "1st Series."

404 $100 (4) A B C D $50.00 $110.00

May, 1863

404/2 $100 (4) A B C D

June, 1863

404/3 $100 (5) A B C D

July, 1863

404/4 $100 (5) A B C D

August, 1863

404/5 $100 (5) A B C D

September, 1863

404/6 $100 (5) A B C D

October, 1863

404/7 $100 (5) A B C D

November, 1863

404/8 $100 (5) A B C D

Note: "2nd series" overprints which appear on this issue are believed to be bogus. Unwatermarked contemporary counterfeits of number 403 exist.

T57

Black with green overprint.
Ornate green back.
(Jefferson Davis)

"Keatinge & Ball. Richmond, VA" (above "Fundable" at left end).
Watermarked "CSA" in block letters, with wavy borderline, "1st series."

406 $50 (5) WA XA YA ZA $45.00 $75.00

April, 1863

406/1 $50 (5) WA XA YA ZA

May, 1863

406/2 $50 (5) WA XA YA ZA

June, 1863

406/3 $50 (6) WA XA YA ZA

July, 1863

406/4 $50 (4) WA XA YA ZA

August, 1863

406/5 $50 (4) WA XA YA ZA

September, 1863

406/6 $50 (5) WA XA YA ZA

October, 1863

406/7 $50 (4) WA XA YA ZA

November, 1863

406/8 $50 (5) WA XA YA ZA

December, 1863

406/9 $50 (4) WA XA YA ZA

"Keatinge & Ball. Richmond, VA." (Below "Fundable" at left end.)

Plain paper, "1st Series"

"April, 1863"

407 $50 (10) WA XA YA ZA $150.00 $375.00

"Keatinge & Ball. Richmond, VA." (Below "Fundable" at left end.)

Watermarked "CSA" in block letters, with wavy borderline, "1st Series."

408 $50 (4) WA XA YA ZA $45.00 $75.00

April, 1863

408/1 $50 (6) WA XA YA ZA

May, 1863

408/2 $50 (5) WA XA YA ZA

June, 1863

408/3 $50 (6) WA XA YA ZA

July, 1863

408/4 $50 (4) WA XA YA ZA

August, 1863

408/5 $50 (4) WA XA YA ZA

September, 1863

408/6 $50 (5) WA XA YA ZA

October, 1863

408/7 $50 (4) WA XA YA ZA

November, 1863

408/8 $50 (4) WA XA YA ZA

December, 1863

408/9 $50 (4) WA XA YA ZA

"Keatinge & Ball. Columbia, S.C." (*Above* "Fundable" at left end.)

Plain paper, no "series."

409 $50 (11) WA XA YA ZA extremely rare

April, 1863

409/1 $50 11) WA XA YA ZA

May, 1863

409/2 $50 (11) WA XA YA ZA

"Keatinge & Ball. Columbia, S.C." *(Above* "Fundable" at left end.)

Watermarked "CSA" in block letters, with wavy borderline, no series.

410 $50 (8) WA XA YA ZA $60.00 $110.00

January 1864

410/10 $50 (8) WA XA YA ZA

February 1864

410/11 $50 (8) WA XA YA ZA

"Keatinge & Ball. Columbia, S.C." (*Above* "Fundable" at left end.)
Watermarked "CSA" in block letters, with wavy borderline, no series.
Flourish over "Con" of "Confederate."

411 $50 (9) WA XA YA ZA $75.00 $125.00

December 1863
411/9 $50 (11) WA XA YA ZA
January 1864
411/10 $50 (9) WA XA YA ZA
February 1864
411/11 $50 (9) WA XA YA ZA

"Keatinge & Ball. Columbia, S.C." (*Above* "Fundable" at left end.)
Watermarked "CSA" in block letters, with wavy borderline.
"1st Series" in large letters, no period after "Series."

412 $50 (3) WA XA YA ZA $45.00 $75.00

July, 1863
412/4 $50 (3) WA XA YA ZA
August, 1863
412/5 $50 (3) WA XA YA ZA
September, 1863
412/6 $50 (4) WA XA YA ZA
October, 1863
412/7 $50 (3) WA XA YA ZA
November, 1863
412/8 $50 (4) WA XA YA ZA
December, 1863
412/9 $50 (3) WA XA YA ZA

Same as 412 but with period after "Series."

413 $50 (3) WA XA YA ZA $45.00 $75.00

June, 1863
413/3 $50 (11) WA XA YA ZA
July, 1863
413/4 $50 (3) WA XA YA ZA
August, 1863
413/5 $50 (3) WA XA YA ZA
September, 1863
413/6 $50 (4) WA XA YA ZA
October, 1863
413/7 $50 (3) WA XA YA ZA
November, 1863
413/8 $50 (3) WA XA YA ZA
December, 1863
413/9 $50 (3) WA XA YA ZA

"Keatinge & Ball. Columbia, S.C." (*Above* "Fundable" at left end.)
Watermarked "CSA" in block letters, with wavy borderline.
"1st Series" in small letters, flourish over "Con" of "Confederate.
No period after "Series."

414 $50 (8) WA XA YA ZA $60.00 $95.00

April, 1863
414/1 $50 (5) WA XA YA ZA
May, 1863
414/2 $50 (5) WA XA YA ZA
June, 1863
414/3 $50 (9) WA XA YA ZA
July, 1863
414/4 $50 (4) WA XA YA ZA
August, 1863
414/5 $50 (4) WA XA YA ZA
September, 1863
414/6 $50 (10) WA XA YA ZA
October, 1863
414/7 $50 (10) WA XA YA ZA
November, 1863
414/8 $50 (5) WA XA YA ZA
December, 1863
414/9 $50 (4) WA XA YA ZA

Same as above, but plain paper.
"April. 1863"

414A $50 (10) WA XA YA ZA $150.00 $275.00

"Keatinge & Ball. Richmond, VA." (*Above* "Fundable" at left end.)
Watermarked "CSA" in block letters, with wavy borderline.
"1st Series" in small letters, flourish over "Con" of Confederate,"
period after "series."

415 $50 (3) WA XA YA ZA $45.00 $75.00

August, 1863
415/5 $50 (3) WA XA YA ZA
September, 1863
415/6 $50 (4) WA XA YA ZA
October, 1863
415/7 $50 (3) WA XA YA ZA
November, 1863
415/8 $50 (4) WA XA YA ZA
December, 1863
415/9 $50 (5) WA XA YA ZA
January, 1864
415/10 $50 (5) WA XA YA ZA

"Keatinge & Ball. Richmond, VA." (*Above* "Fundable" at left end.)
Watermarked "CSA" in block letters, with wavy borderline.
"1st Series" in small letters, period after "series."

416 $50 (10) WA XA YA ZA $100.00 $200.00

April, 1863

416/1 $50 (6) WA XA YA ZA

May, 1863

416/2 $50 (5) WA XA YA ZA

June, 1863

416/3 $50 (6) WA XA YA ZA

Same as above, *No* period after series.
only two flourished under "de" of "Confederate."

417 $50 (4) WA XA YA ZA $45.00 $75.00

April, 1863

417/1 $50 (4) WA XA YA ZA

May, 1863

417/2 $50 (4) WA XA YA ZA

June, 1863

417/3 $50 (5) WA XA YA ZA

July, 1863

417/4 $50 (4) WA XA YA ZA

August, 1863

417/5 $50 (4) WA XA YA ZA

September, 1863

417/6 $50 (4) WA XA YA ZA

Same as above but on plain paper.
"April 1863"

417A $50 (10) WA XA YA ZA $80.00 $150.00

All "Engraved by Keatinge & Ball. Columbia, S.C."

T58

(State capitol at Nashville, Tennessee, A.H. Stephens.)

T58

Fancy blue back.

"1st Series." Plain paper.

418 $20 (3) A B C D E F G H $25.00 $60.00

April, 1863

418/1 $20 (3) A B C D E F G H

May, 1863

418/2 $20 (5) A B C D E F G H

All below "Litho. by Evans and Cogswell."

No series, watermarked "CSA" in block letters.

"July, 1863," (October, 1863)

420 $20 (8) A B C D E F G H $30.00 $90.00

No series, watermarked "CSA" in block letters, with wavy borderline.

420A $20 (10) A B C D E F G H $50.00 $110.00

July, 1863

420A/4 $20 (8) A B C D E F G H

October, 1863

420A/7 $20 (9) A B C D E F G H

Same as 420 but watermarked "J. Whatman."

420B $20 (10) A B C D E F G H $300.00 ex rare

July, 1863

420B/4 $20 (10) A B C D E F G H

October, 1863

420B/7 $20 (10) A B C D E F G H

Same as 420 but watermarked "Hodgkinson and Co. Wookey Hole Mill."

420C $20 (11) A B C D E F G H extremely rare

July, 1863

420C/4 $20 (11) A B C D E F G H

October, 1863

420C/7 $20 (11) A B C D E F G H

"1st Series," plain paper.

421 $20 (4) A B C D E F G H $35.00 $70.00

April, 1863

421/1 $20 (4) A B C D E F G H

May, 1863

421/2 $20 (4) A B C D E F G H

July, 1863

421/4 $20 (4) A B C D E F G H

"2nd Series." watermarked"CSA" in block letters, with wavy borderline, serial letters far from top of note.

Error: "1st Series." plain paper, serial letter "A" left, "E" right.

"May, 1863"

422 $20 (10) A E $150.00 $300.00

"2nd Series." plain paper, serial letters far from top of note (see 426).

423 $20 (3) A B C D E F G H $25.00 $65.00

April, 1863

423/1 $20 (9) A B C D E F G H

May, 1863

423/2 $20 (5) A B C D E F G H

June, 1863

423/3 $20 (4) A B C D E F G H

July, 1863

423/4 $20 (3) A B C D E F G H

August, 1863

423/5 $20 (4) A B C D E F G H

"2nd Series," watermarked "CSA" in block letters, with wavy borderline. Serial letters far from top of note.

424 $20 (3) A B C D E F G H $25.00 $60.00

June, 1863

424/3 $20 (4) A B C D E F G H

July, 1863

424/4 $20 (3) A B C D E F G H

August, 1863

424/5 $20 (4) A B C D E F G H

October, 1863

424/7 $20 (7) A B C D E F G H

Same as above but serial letters near top of note.

425 $20 (5) A B C D E F G H $30.00 $75.00

June, 1863

425/3 $20 (6) A B C D E F G H

July, 1863

425/4 $20 (5) A B C D E F G H

August, 1863

425/5 $20 (6) A B C D E F G H

"2nd Series." plain paper, serial letters near top of note.

426 $20 (4) A B C D E F G H $28.00 $65.00

April, 1863

426/1 $20 (9) A B C D E F G H

May, 1863

426/2 $20 (5) A B C D E F G H

June, 1863

426/3 $20 (5) A B C D E F G H

July, 1863

426/4 $20 (5) A B C D E F G H

August, 1863

426/5 $20 (4) A B C D E F G H

"3rd Series," plain paper.

427 $20 (5) A B C D E F G H $30.00 $65.00

July, 1863

427/4 $20 (8) A B C D E F G H

August, 1863

427/5 $20 (9) A B C D E F G H

September, 1863

427/6 $20 (5) A B C D E F G H

October, 1863

427/7 $20 (6) A B C D E F G H

"3rd Series," watermarked "CSA" in block letters, with wavy borderline.

428 $20 (3) A B C D E F G H $25.00 $60.00

June, 1863

428/3 $20 (4) A B C D E F G H

July, 1863

428/4 $20 (3) A B C D E F G H

August, 1863

428/5 $20 (4) A B C D E F G H

September, 1863

428/6 $20 (3) A B C D E F G H

October, 1863

428/7 $20 (5) A B C D E F G H

"Printed by J. T. Patterson & Co."
"1st Series."
"April, 1863."

428A $20 (8) A B C D E F G H $55.00 $120.00

Same as 428 except watermarked "CSA" in block letters

428B $20 (8) A B C D E F G H $55.00 $125.00

June, 1863

428B/3 $20 (8) A B C D E F G H

July, 1863

428B/4 $20 (8) A B C D E F G H

August, 1863

428B/5 $20 (8) A B C D E F G H

September, 1863

428B/6 $20 (8) A B C D E F G H

October, 1863

428B/7 $20 (9) A B C D E F G H

All "Engraved by Keatinge & Ball. Columbia, S.C."

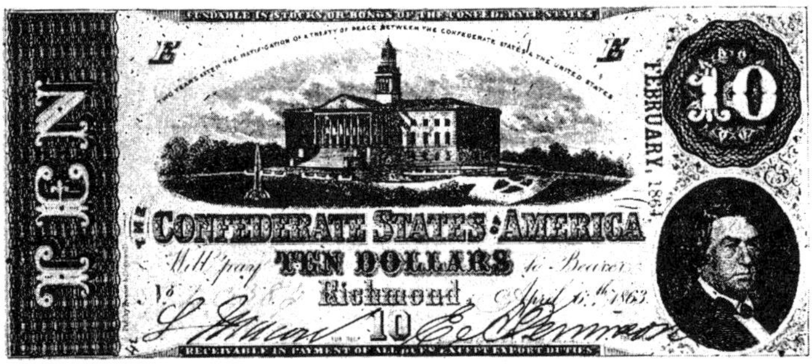

T59

(State capitol at Columbia, S.C., R. M. T. Hunter.)
Blue back.

"Ptd. by Evans & Cogswell."
Plain paper, no series.

429 $10 (4) A B C D E F G H $20.00 $50.00

December 1863

429/9 $10 (10) A B C D E F G H

January 1864

429/10 $10 (4) A B C D E F G H

February 1864

429/11 $10 (4) A B C D E F G H

Same, "1st Series" (in small letters).

430 $10 (3) A B C D E F G H $20.00 $45.00

April, 1863

430/1 $10 (5) A B C D E F G H

May, 1863

430/2 $10 (3) A B C D E F G H

November, 1863

430/8 $10 (4) A B C D E F G H

December, 1863

430/9 $10 (4) A B C D E F G H

January, 1864

430/10 $10 (5) A B C D E F G H

Note: those types formerly listed as 431, 432, 432A; and 433 are counterfeits and have been dropped.

Same as above, plain paper, "5th Series."

434 $10 (5) A B C D E F G H $20.00 $45.00

April, 1863

434/1 $10 (8) A B C D E F G H

September, 1863

434/6 $10 (5) A B C D E F G H

November, 1863

434/8 $10 (6) A B C D E F G H

December, 1863

434/9 $10 (5) A B C D E F G H

Same, plain paper, "5th Series," "Duncan" on left end.
"December, 1863" overprint.

434A $10 (10) A B C D E F G H $60.00 $100.00

"Lithod by Evans & Cogswell."
Plain paper, no series.

435 $10 (3) A B C D E F G H $20.00 $40.00

August, 1863

435/5 $10 (4) A B C D E F G H

September, 1863

435/6 $10 (10) A B C D E F G H

October, 1863

435/7 $10 (4) A B C D E F G H

November, 1863

435/8 $10 (3) A B C D E F G H

December, 1863

435/9 $10 (4) A B C D E F G H

January, 1864

435/10 $10 (4) A B C D E F G H

October, 1863

435IB $10 (10) A B C D E F G H very rare

Plain paper, "1st Series" in large letters, serial letters *far from* top of note.

436 $10 (4) A B C D E F G H $22.00 $45.00

May, 1863

436/2 $10 (4) A B C D E F G H

June, 1863

436/3 $10 (4) A B C D E F G H

July, 1863

436/4 $10 (5) A B C D E F G H

Plain paper, "1st" series in large letters, serial letters *near* top of note.

437 $10 (4) A B C D E F G H $25.00 $50.00

May, 1863

437/2 $10 (4) A B C D E F G H

June, 1863

437/3 $10 (4) A B C D E F G H

July, 1863

437/4 $10 (5) A B C D E F G H

August, 1863

437/5 $10 (9) A B C D E F G H

Watermarked "CSA" in block letters, with wavy borderline.
"1st Series" in large letters, serial letters near *top* of note.

438 $10 (5) A B C D E F G H $25.00 $50.00

June, 1863

438/3 $10 (5) A B C D E F G H

July, 1863

438/4 $10 (5) A B C D E F G H

October, 1863

438/7 $10 (11) A B C D E F G H

Plain paper, "1st Series" in small letters, serial letter *far* from top of note.

439 $10 (4) A B C D E F G H $25.00 $50.00

April, 1863

439/1 $10 (6) A B C D E F G H

May, 1863

439/2 $10 (4) A B C D E F G H

June, 1863

439/3 $10 (4) A B C D E F G H

July, 1863

439/4 $10 (9) A B C D E F G H

August, 1863

439/5 $10 (9) A B C D E F G H

September, 1863

439/6 $10 (10) A B C D E F G H

Plain paper, "1st Series" in small letters, serial letter *near* top of note.

440 $10 (4) A B C D E F G H $25.00 $50.00

April, 1863

440/1 $10 (7) A B C D E F G H

May, 1863

440/2 $10 (4) A B C D E F G H

June, 1863

440/3 $10 (4) A B C D E F G H

July, 1863

440/4 $10 (5) A B C D E F G H

August, 1863

440/5 $10 (4) A B C D E F G H

September, 1863

440/6 $10 (4) A B C D E F G H

October, 1863

440/7 $10 (4) A B C D E F G H

November, 1863

440/8 $10 (5) A B C D E F G H

December, 1863

440/9 $10 (5) A B C D E F G H

January, 1864

440/10 $10 (5) A B C D E F G H

February, 1864

440/11 $10 (4) A B C D E F G H

Plain paper, "1st Series" in small letters.
ERROR: Serial letter "A" left, "C" right.

441 $10 (9) A/C $250.00 $300.00

May, 1863

441/2 $10 (9) A/C

June, 1863

441/3 $10 (9) A/C

August, 1863

441/5 $10 (10) A/C

Plain paper, "2nd Series" in large letters.

442 $10 (3) A B C D E F G H $20.00 $40.00

June, 1863

442/3 $10 (3) A B C D E F G H

July, 1863

442/4 $10 (4) A B C D E F G H

August, 1863

442/5 $10 (4) A B C D E F G H

September, 1863

442/6 $10 (4) A B C D E F G H

October, 1863

442/7 $10 (4) A B C D E F G H

November, 1863

442/8 $10 (4) A B C D E F G H

December, 1863

442/9 $10 (5) A B C D E F G H

January, 1864

442/10 $10 (5) A B C D E F G H

INVERTED BACKS

442IB $10 (10) A B C D E F G H very rare

September, 1863

442IB/6 $10 (10) A B C D E F G H

October, 1863

442IB/7 $10 (10) A B C D E F G H

Watermarked "CSA" in block letters, "2nd Series."

442B $10 (3) A B C D E F G H $20.00 $40.00

July, 1863

442B/4 $10 (4) A B C D E F G H

August, 1863

442B/5 $10 (6) A B C D E F G H

September, 1863

442B/6 $10 (4) A B C D E F G H

Watermarked "J. Green & Son 1862."

442C $10 (11) A B C D E F G H extremely rare

Watermarked "CSA" in block letters, with wavy borderline, "2nd Series."

Serial letters *far from* top of note.

443 $10 (3) A B C D E F G H $20.00 $40.00

June, 1863

443/3 $10 (3) A B C D E F G H

July, 1863

443/4 $10 (4) A B C D E F G H

August, 1863

443/5 $10 (4) A B C D E F G H

September, 1863

443/6 $10 (3) A B C D E F G H

October, 1863

443/7 $10 (4) A B C D E F G H

November, 1863

443/8 $10 (3) A B C D E F G H

December, 1863

443/9 $10 (3) A B C D E F G H

Same as 443 but "Lighog'd. by J.T. Patterson and Co." left end.

443A $10 (8) A B C D E F G H $75.00 $150.00

Watermarked "CSA" in block letters, with wavy borderline.
"2nd Series." "JULY, 1863"

444 $10 (4) A B C D E F G H $15.00 $40.00

Watermarked "J. Whatman. 1862." "2nd Series."

444A $10 (9) A B C D E F G H $75.00 $175.00

July, 1863

444A/4 $10 (10) A B C D E F G H

December, 1863

444A/9 $10 (9) A B C D E F G H

"Printed by B. Duncan" (left end).
"1. Series" (right end), plain paper.
"April, 1863"

445A $10 (8) A B C D E F G H $40.00 $125.00

Watermarked "CSA" in block letters, with wavy borderline, "2nd Series."

446A $10 (4) A B C D E F G H $75.00 $125.00

July, 1863

446A/4 $10 (5) A B C D E F G H

August, 1863

446A/5 $10 (4) A B C D E F G H

September, 1863

446A/6 $10 (5) A B C D E F G H

November, 1863

446A/8 $10 (4) A B C D E F G H

December, 1863

446A/9 $10 (5) A B C D E F G H

Note: on types T-59 and T-60 many varieties had bogus "series," engravers' names, etc. added to make collector varieties in the 1870s.

All "Engraved by Keatinge & Ball. Columbia, S.C." Engravers' names on lower margin.

T60

Fancy blue back
(State capitol at Richmond, Va. C.G. Memminger.)

Plain paper, "2nd Series."

448 $5 (9) A B C D E F G H $45.00 $80.00

June, 1863

448/3 $5 (9) A B C D E F G H

July, 1863

448/4 $5 (9) A B C D E F G H

August, 1863

448/5 $5 (11) A B C D E F G H

INVERTED BACKS

448IB $5 (9) A B C D E F G H very rare

June, 1863

448IB/3 $5 (9) A B C D E F G H

July, 1863

448IB/4 $5 (10) A B C D E F G H

August, 1863

448IB/5 $5 (10) A B C D E F G H

Plain paper, "3rd Series."

449 $5 (9) A B C D E F G H $45.00 $80.00

August, 1863

449/5 $5 (9) A B C D E F G H

October, 1863

449/7 $5 (9) A B C D E F G H

"Lithog'd by J.T. Paterson & Co. Plain Paper, "1st Series."
No issuance overprint

450NO $5 (11) A B C D E F G H extremely rare

450 $5 (3) A B C D E F G H $20.00 $40.00

April, 1863

450/1 $5 (3) A B C D E F G H

May, 1863

450/2 $5 (4) A B C D E F G H

June, 1863

450/3 $5 (4) A B C D E F G H

July, 1863

450/4 $5 (10) A B C D E F G H

August, 1863

450/5 $5 (4) A B C D E F G H

September, 1863

450/6 $5 (10) A B C D E F G H

October, 1863

450/7 $5 (11) A B C D E F G H

November, 1863

450/8 $5 (11) A B C D E F G H

January, 1864

450/10 $5 (5) A B C D E F G H

February, 1864

450/11 $5 (3) A B C D E F G H

Same as 450 but with inverted back.

450IB $5 (8) A B C D E F G H very rare

ERROR: same but reads "St Series" (no "1").

450A $5 (8) B C D E

April, 1863

450A/1 $5 (8) B C D E

May, 1863

450A/2 $5 (9) B C D E

ERRORS: Serial letters at left and right are different. "1st Series."

451 $5 (9) E/A C/A A/D E/ $75.00 $95.00

April, 1863

451/1 $5 (9) E/A C/A A/D E/

May, 1863

451/2 $5 (9) C/A A/D E/A E/

Plain paper, "2nd Series."

453 $5 (3) A B C D E F G H $20.00 $40.00

May, 1863

453/2 $5 (8) A B C D E F G H

June, 1863

453/3 $5 (5) A B C D E F G H

July, 1863

453/4 $5 (3) A B C D E F G H

August, 1863

453/5 $5 (3) A B C D E F G H

September, 1863

453/6 $5 (6) A B C D E F G H

October, 1863

453/7 $5 (6) A B C D E F G H

November, 1863

453/8 $5 (3) A B C D E F G H

January, 1864

453/10 $5 (10) A B C D E F G H

February, 1864

453/11 $5 (10) A B C D E F G H

September, 1863

453IB $5 (10) A B C D E F G H very rare

"2nd Series." Watermarked "CSA" in block letters.

454 $5 (3) A B C D E F G H $20.00 $40.00

June, 1863

454/3 $5 (5) A B C D E F G H

July, 1863

454/4 $5 (3) A B C D E F G H

August, 1863

454/5 $5 (5) A B C D E F G H

October, 1863

454/7 $5 (7) A B C D E F G H

November, 1863

454/8 $5 (7) A B C D E F G H

"2nd Series." Watermarked "CSA" in block letters with wavy borderline.

454A $5 (8) A B C D E F G H $45.00 $75.00

April, 1863

454A/1 $5 (11) A B C D E F G H

May, 1863

454A/2 $5 (8) A B C D E F G H

June, 1863

454A/3 $5 (9) A B C D E F G H

July, 1863

454A/4 $5 (9) A B C D E F G H

August, 1863

454A/5 $5 (10) A B C D E F G H

"2nd Series." Watermarked "J. Whatman, 1862."

455 $5 (7) A B C D E F G H $35.00 $70.00

June, 1863

455/3 $5 (7) A B C D E F G H

July, 1863

455/4 $5 (8) A B C D E F G H

August, 1863

455/5 $5 (9) A B C D E F G H

"2nd Series." Watermarked "Hodgkinson & Co. Wookey Hole Mill."

456 $5 (7) A D E H $125.00 $300.00

June, 1863

456/3 $5 (9) A D E H

July, 1863

456/4 $5 (8) A D E H

August, 1863

456/5 $5 (8) A D E H

"3rd Series" in small letters ("3rd" varies in size).
Watermarked "CSA" in block letters with wavy borderline.

457 $5 (4) A B C D E F G H $20.00 $45.00

July, 1863

457/4 $5 (4) A B C D E F G H

August, 1863

457/5 $5 (5) A B C D E F G H

September, 1863

457/6 $5 (10) A B C D E F G H

October 1863

457/7 $5 (7) A B C D E F G H

November 1863

457/8 $5 (8) A B C D E F G H

Inverted backs

July 1863

457IB/4 $5 (10)A B C D E F G H very rare

"3d Series" in large letters, plain paper.

458 $5 (6) A B C D E F G H $25.00 $50.00

August, 1863

458/5 $5 (7) A B C D E F G H

September, 1863

458/6 $5 (6) A B C D E F G H

October, 1863

458/7 $5 (6) A B C D E F G H

November, 1863

458/8 $5 (11) A B C D E F G H

January, 1864

458/10 $5 (11) A B C D E F G H

"3rd Series" in large letters.
Watermarked "CSA" in block letters with wavy borderline.

459 $5 (5) A B C D E F G H $20.00 $45.00

July, 1863

459/4 $5 (5) A B C D E F G H

August, 1863

459/5 $5 (5) A B C D E F G H

September, 1863

459/6 $5 (9) A B C D E F G H

October 1863

459/7 $5 (5) A B C D E F G H

November 1863

459/8 $5 (5) A B C D E F G H

February, 1864

459/11 $5 (5) A B C D E F G H

"Engraved by Keatinge & Ball, Columbia, S.C." (on lower margin).
"Lithog'd by J. T. Paterson & So." (on left end).
"2nd Series," plain paper. Serial letter *far from* the top of the note.

460 $5 (8) A B C D E F G H $35.00 $60.00

May, 1863

460/2 $5 (10) A B C D E F G H

June, 1863

460/3 $5 (10) A B C D E F G H

July, 1863

460/4 $5 (8) A B C D E F G H

Same as above. Serial letter *near top* of note.

461 $5 (9) A B C D E F G H $45.00 $80.00

June, 1863

461/4 $5 (9) A B C D E F G H

July, 1863

461/5 $5 (10) A B C D E F G H

"3rd Series" plain paper.

462 $5 (5) A B C D E F G H $20.00 $35.00

July, 1863

462/4 $5 (3) A B C D E F G H

August, 1863

462/5 $5 (4) A B C D E F G H

September, 1863

462/6 $5 (4) A B C D E F G H

October, 1863

462/7 $5 (4) A B C D E F G H

December, 1863

462/9 $5 (5) A B C D E F G H

January, 1864

462/10 $5 (5) A B C D E F G H

February, 1864

462/11 $5 (9) A B C D E F G H

"Engraved by Keatinge & Ball, Columbia, S.C." (on lower margin).
"Lithog'd by Evans & Cogswell" (on lower margin).
No series, plain paper.

463 $5 (4) A B C D E F G H $20.00 $35.00

August, 1863

463/5 $5 (8) A B C D E F G H

September, 1863

463/6 $5 (4) A B C D E F G H

October 1863

463/7 $5 (4) A B C D E F G H

November 1863

463/8 $5 (8) A B C D E F G H

December, 1863

463/9 $5 (5) A B C D E F G H

January, 1864

463/10 $5 (5) A B C D E F G H

February, 1864

463/11 $5 (7) A B C D E F G H

Inverted backs

September, 1863

463IB/6 $5 (10) A B C D E F G H very rare

January, 1863

463IB/10 $5 (10) A B C D E F G H very rare

Same as 463 but "Litho. by J.T. Paterson and Co.," instead of Evans and Cogswell.

463A $5 (9) A B C D E F G H $75.00 $180.00

"Engraved by Keatinge & Ball, Columbia, S.C." (on lower margin).
"Lithog'd by Evans & Cogswell" (on left end).
No series, plain paper.
Letters and words in "Lithog'd by Evans & Cogswell" are close together.

464 $5 (3) A B C D E F G H $20.00 $35.00

August, 1863
464/5 $5 (3) A B C D E F G H
September, 1863
464/6 $5 (3) A B C D E F G H
October 1863
464/7 $5 (3) A B C D E F G H
November 1863
464/8 $5 (4) A B C D E F G H
December, 1863
464/9 $5 (4) A B C D E F G H
January, 1864
464/10 $5 (4) A B C D E F G H
February, 1864
464/11 $5 (3) A B C D E F G H

Inverted backs

464IB $5 (10)A B C D E F G H very rare

September, 1863
464IB/6 $5 (10) A B C D E F G H
December, 1863
464IB/9 $5 (10) A B C D E F G H
February, 1863
464IB/11 $5 (10) A B C D E F G H

As above but letters and words are extended across most of the left end.

464A $5 (8) A B C D E F G H $40.00 $80.00

September, 1863
464A/6 $5 (8) A B C D E F G H
October 1863
464A/7 $5 (9) A B C D E F G H
December, 1863
464A/ 9 $5 (10) A B C D E F G H
January, 1864
464A/10 $5 (8) A B C D E F G H
February, 1864
464A/11 $5 (7) A B C D E F G H

"3rd Series," plain paper.

465 $5 (4) A B C D E F G H $22.00 $60.00

September, 1863

465/6 $5 (5) A B C D E F G H

October 1863

465/7 $5 (10) A B C D E F G H

November 1863

465/8 $5 (4) A B C D E F G H

December, 1863

465/9 $5 (5) A B C D E F G H

January, 1864

465/10 $5 (5) A B C D E F G H

February, 1864

465/11 $5 (10) A B C D E F G H

"Engraved by Keatinge & Ball, Columbia, S.C." (on lower margin).
"Evans & Cogswell, Litho" (in very small letters at left end).
"3rd Series," plain paper.

468 $5 (9) A B C D E F G H $75.00 $150.00

August, 1863

468/5 $5 (10) A B C D E F G H

September, 1863

468/6 $5 (11) A B C D E F G H

October 1863

468/7 $5 (9) A B C D E F G H

"Engraved by Keatinge & Ball, Columbia, S.C." (on lower margin).
"Litho'd by J.T. Paterson & Co." (on lower margin).
"Ptd. by Evans & Cogswell" (on left end).

"1st Series," plain paper, "April, 1863."

469 $5 (9) D $65.00 $175.00

Same as 469 but no series instead of "1st Series."

469A $5 (10) D $95.00 $175.00

Pink paper.

T61

(Judah P. Benjamin)

"Engraved by Keatinge & Ball. Columbia, S.C."

"1st Series"

470	$2 (6)	A B C D E F G H	$60.00	$225.00

"2nd Series"

471	$2 (5)	A B C D E F G H	$55.00	$200.00

"Engraved by Keatinge & Ball. Columbia, S.C."
"Lithog'd by Evans & Cogswell" (on left end).

No series

472	$2 (7)	A B C D E F G H	$60.00	$250.00

"2nd series"

473	$2 (6)	A B C D E F G H	$55.00	$210.00

"Engraved by Keatinge & Ball. Columbia, S.C."

Pink paper

T62

(Clement C. Clay)

"1st series"

Period after both serial letters.

474 $1 (5) A B C D E F G H $50.00 $70.00

Period after the first serial letter.

475 $1 (7) A B C D E F G H $50.00 $75.00

Period after the last serial letter.

476 $1 (7) A B C D E F G H $50.00 $75.00

Period each side of the last serial letter.

477 $1 (7) A B C D E F G H $50.00 $75.00

Period each side of the first serial letter.

477A $1 (9) A B C D E F G H $65.00 $120.00

"2nd Series"

Period after both serial letters.

478 $1 (5) A B C D E F G H $50.00 $70.00

Period each side of the last serial letter.

479 $1 (7) A B C D E F G H $60.00 $75.00

Period on each side of the first serial letter.

479A $1 (8) A B C D E F G H $65.00 $100.00

"Lithog'd by Evans & Cogswell" (on left end).
No series

No periods

480 $1 (6) A B C D E F G H $50.00 $70.00

Period before both serial letters.

481 $1 (7) A B C D E F G H $50.00 $80.00

Period before first serial letter.

482 $1 (7) A B C D E F G H $50.00 $80.00

Period before the last serial letter.

483 $1 (7) A B C D E F G H $50.00 $80.00

"2nd Series"

Period before both serial letters.

484 $1 (6) A B C D E F G H $50.00 $80.00

Period before the last serial letter.

484A $1 (8) A B C D E F G H $50.00 $100.00

"Archer & Daly. Richmond, Va."
Pink paper

T63

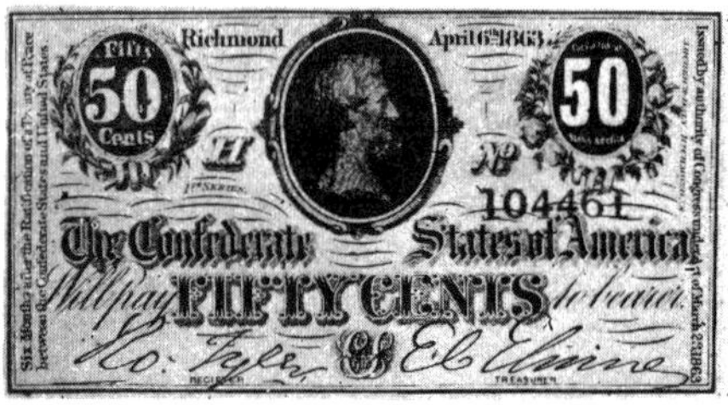

(Bust of Jefferson Davis)

"1st Series"

Flourishes above the serial letter.

485	$.50 (3)	A B C D E F G H	$15.00	$30.00

No flourishes above the serial letter.

486	$.50 (10)	A B C D E F G H	$75.00	$150.00

"2nd Series"

Flourishes above the serial letter.

487	$.50 (4)	A B C D E F G H	$15.00	$30.00

No flourishes above the serial letter.

488	$.50 (6)	A B C D E F G H	$20.00	$30.00

1864

$200,000,000 was authorized by Act of February 17th, 1864, but the actual amount issued was probably much larger and the amount printed even greater. Thus there are many minor varieties of each type. Only the important variety differences (which have been recognized for the last 40 to 60 years), plus a few major types previously unknown are listed. The most common Confederate notes appear in this year.

All notes of this year are dated "Feb. 17th, 1864."

"Keatinge & Ball. Columbia, S.C."

T64

Black with reddish, horizontal line overprint.
(Equestrian statue of Washington Confederate flag at left.
General T. J. "Stonewall" Jackson at right..)

489	$500 (7) A B C D	$200.00	$350.00

Black with dark red, very detailed, horizontal lines in background.

489A	$500 (7) A B C D	$325.00	$650.00

"Keatinge & Ball. Columbia, S.C."

T65

(Lucy Pickens at center, two soldiers left, and Geo. W. Randolph at right.)
Black with reddish overprint. Intricate blue back with "Hundred" in large letters.

No series.

490 $100 (4) A B C D $50.00 $85.00

Same as last, but 1/4 inch shorter.

491 $100 (5) A B C D $50.00 $90.00

"Series I" (full size).

493 $100 (4) A B C D $50.00 $85.00

"Series II" (full size).

494 $100 (4) A B C D $50.00 $85.00

Note: at least 20 different tiny variations in the length of flourishes, dashes, etc., on the above $100 type notes (T65) have been noted.

"Keatinge & Ball. Columbia, S.C."

T66

Black with reddish overprint.
Blue back with "Fifty" in large letters.
(Portrait of Jefferson Davis.)

No flourish over "CON" of "CONFEDERATE."

		No Series.		
495	$50 (3)	WA XA YA ZA	$40.00	$75.00
		"1st Series."		
496	$50 (3)	WA XA YA ZA	$40.00	$75.00
		"2 Series."		
497	$50 (3)	WA XA YA ZA	$40.00	$75.00
		"3 Series."		
498	$50 (3)	WA XA YA ZA	$40.00	$75.00
		"4 Series."		
499	$50 (3)	WA XA YA ZA	$40.00	$75.00

Flourish over "CON" of "CONFEDERATE."
No Series.

500	$50 (4)	WA XA YA ZA	$40.00	$75.00

		"1st Series."		
501	$50 (5)	WA XA YA ZA	$40.00	$75.00
		"2 Series."		
502	$50 (4)	WA XA YA ZA	$40.00	$75.00
		"3 Series."		
503	$50 (6)	WA XA YA ZA	$40.00	$75.00

Note: upward of 25 minor changes in flourish size and shape on the $50.00 notes have been identified.

"Keatinge & Ball. Columbia, S.C."

T67

Reddish network background overprint, intricate blue back with "Twenty" in large letters. (State capitol at Nashville, Tennessee, A. H. Stephens at right).

TWO FLOURISHES OVER "ICA" OF "AMERICA."

		No series		
504	$20 (2)	A B C D	$20.00	$18.00

Error: frame at upper left reads "Six Months After..." Frame at upper right reads "Two years after a ratification..."

504A	$20 (10)	B	$255.00	$450.00
		Series 1		
505	$20 (2)	A B C D	$20.00	$35.00

No.	Denomination	Plates	Series	Price 1	Price 2
506	$20 (2)	A B C D	Series 2	$20.00	$35.00
507	$20 (2)	A B C D	Series 3	$20.00	$35.00
508	$20 (2)	A B C D	Series 4	$20.00	$35.00
509	$20 (2)	A B C D	Series 5	$20.00	$35.00
510	$20 (2)	A B C D	VI Series	$20.00	$35.00
511	$20 (2)	A B C D	VII Series	$20.00	$35.00
512	$20 (2)	A B C D	VIII Series	$20.00	$35.00
513	$20 (2)	A B C D	IX Series	$20.00	$35.00
514	$20 (2)	A B C D	X Series	$20.00	$35.00
515	$20 (2)	A B C D	XI Series	$20.00	$35.00

ONE FLOURISH OVER "ICA" OF "AMERICA."
THREE FLOURISHES OVER "THE" ABOVE "CONFEDERATE."

No.	Denomination	Plates	Series	Price 1	Price 2
516	$20 (4)	A B C D	No series	$25.00	$40.00
517	$20 (4)	A B C D	Series 1	$25.00	$40.00
518	$20 (4)	A B C D	Series 2	$25.00	$40.00
519	$20 (4)	A B C D	Series 3	$25.00	$40.00
520	$20 (4)	A B C D	Series 4	$25.00	$40.00
521	$20 (4)	A B C D	Series 5	$25.00	$40.00
522	$20 (4)	A B C D	VI Series	$25.00	$40.00
523	$20 (4)	A B C D	VII Series	$25.00	$40.00
524	$20 (4)	A B C D	VIII Series	$25.00	$40.00
525	$20 (5)	A B C D	IX Series	$25.00	$40.00
526	$20 (5)	A B C D	X Series	$25.00	$40.00
527	$20 (4)	A B C D	XI Series	$25.00	$40.00

ONE FLOURISH OVER "ICA" OF "AMERICA."
NO FLOURISHES OVER "THE" ABOVE "CONFEDERATE."

		No series		
528	$20 (6) D		$35.00	$50.00
		Series 1		
529	$20 (6) D		$35.00	$50.00
		Series 2		
530	$20 (6) D		$35.00	$50.00
		Series 3		
531	$20 (6) D		$35.00	$50.00
		Series 4		
532	$20 (6) D		$35.00	$50.00
		Series 5		
533	$20 (6) D		$35.00	$50.00
		VI Series		
534	$20 (6) D		$35.00	$50.00
		VII Series		
535	$20 (6) D		$35.00	$50.00
		VIII Series		
536	$20 (6) D		$35.00	$50.00
		IX Series		
537	$20 (5) D		$35.00	$50.00
		X Series		
538	$20 (5) D		$35.00	$50.00
		XI Series		
539	$20 (6) D		$35.00	$50.00

Note: more than 15 minute differences in the size and shape of the flourishes on the $20 notes have been noted. No serial letter other than "D" has been observed for number 528 through 539.

"Keatinge & Ball. Columbia, S.C."
"Ptd by Evans & Cogswell" (on left end).

T68

Black with reddish overprint. (Horses pulling cannon, R.M.T. Hunter at right.)
Intricate blue back with "Ten" in large letters.

		No series.		
540	$10 (2)	A B C D E F G H	$18.00	$30.00
		Same, but only one serial letter at top, left.		
540A	$10 (9)	G/	$90.00	$250.00
		"1st Series" (Roman type).		
541	$10 (2)	A B C D E F G H	$18.00	$30.00
		Same as above.		
541A	$10 (10)	B/A	$150.00	$300.00
		"1st Series" (italics).		
542	$10 (3)	A B C D E F G H	$20.00	$35.00
		"2 Series."		
543	$10 (2)	A B C D E F G H	$18.00	$30.00
		"2nd Series."		
544	$10 (6)	A B C D E F G H	$20.00	$35.00

		"3 Series."		
545	$10 (3)	A B C D E F G H	$20.00	$30.00
		Same, but serial letters are different at each side of note.		
545A	$10 (9)	A/C C/A	$125.00	$275.00
545B	$10 (8)	backward E-3	$50.00	$175.00
		"4 Series."		
546	$10 (1)	A B C D E F G H	$18.00	$30.00
		"5 Series."		
547	$10 (1)	A B C D E F G H	$18.00	$30.00
		Same as 547 but serial letters are different.		
547A	$10 (9)	B/C G/C	$150.00	$325.00
		Error in that some of the letters only show partially.		
547B	$10 (9)		$75.00	$125.00
		"6 Series."		
548	$10 (1)	A B C D E F G H	$18.00	$30.00
		"7 Series."		
549	$10 (1)	A B C D E F G H	$18.00	$30.00
		"7. Series."		
549A	$10 (5)	A B C D E F G H	$20.00	$35.00
		"7.. Series."		
549B	$10 (5)	A B C D E F G H	$20.00	$35.00
		"8 Series."		
550	$10 (1)	A B C D E F G H	$18.00	$30.00
		"9 Series."		
551	$10 (1)	A B C D E F G H	$18.00	$30.00
		"10 Series."		
552	$10 (1)	A B C D E F G H	$18.00	$30.00
		Same but serial letters are different (or lacking) on left and right end.		
553	$10 (9)	/G A/C B/A C/A E/A	$150.00	$300.00

Note: upward of 30 tiny changes in size or style of the series numbers in the $10 notes have been identified.

* * * * *

"Engraved by Keatinge & Ball. Columbia, S.C."

T69

Reddish network overprint background.
(State capitol at Richmond, Va, C. G. Memminger at right.)

T69

Intricate blue back with "Five" in large letters.

		No series		
558	$5 (2)	A B C D E F G H	$20.00	$35.00
		"1 Series" (at extreme right end).		
559	$5 (2)	A B C D E F G H	$20.00	$35.00
		"Series 2"		
560	$5 (1)	A B C D E F G H	$20.00	$35.00
		"Series 3."		
561	$5 (1)	A B C D E F G H	$20.00	$35.00
		"Series 4."		
562	$5 (1)	A B C D E F G H	$20.00	$35.00
		"Series 5."		
563	$5 (1)	A B C D E F G H	$20.00	$35.00
		"Series 6."		
564	$5 (1)	A B C D E F G H	$20.00	$35.00
		"Series 7"		
565	$5 (3)	A B C D E F G H	$20.00	$35.00

T70

Black with reddish, network background overprint.
(Judah P. Benjamin.)

"Engraved by Keatinge & Ball. Columbia, S.C."

566	$2 (7)	A B C D E F G H	$35.00	$90.00

"Engraved and Printed by Keatinge & Ball."

No periods.

567	$2 (4)	A B C D E F G H	$35.00	$55.00

Period before each serial letter.

567A	$2 (5)	A B C D E F G H	$35.00	$55.00

Period before the first serial letter.

568	$2 (5)	A B C D E F G H	$35.00	$55.00

Period before the last serial letter.

568A	$2 (6)	A B C D E F G H	$35.00	$55.00

"Engraved by Keatinge & Ball. Columbia, S.C."
"Lithog'd by Evans & Cogswell."

No periods.

569	$2 (4)	A B C D E F G H	$45.00	$80.00

Period before each serial letter.

570	$2 (5)	A B C D E F G H	$45.00	$80.00

Period before the first serial letter.

571	$2 (7)	A B C D E F G H	$35.00	$60.00

T71

Black red-orange overprint.
(Clement C. Clay.)

"Engraved by Keatinge & Ball."

572	$1 (7)	A B C D E F G H	$55.00	$95.00

"Engraved & Printed by Keatinge & Ball."

No periods.

573	$1 (6)	A B C D E F G H	$50.00	$85.00

Period before 1st serial letter only.

573A	$1 (8)	A B C D E F G H	$55.00	$95.00

Period before each serial letter.

574 $1 (4) A B C D E F G H $55.00 $95.00

Period before each serial letter and after the last.

574A $1 (6) A B C D E F G H $55.00 $95.00

Period after each serial letter.

575 $1 (6) A B C D E F G H $55.00 $95.00

"Engraved by Keatinge & Ball. Columbia, S.C."
"Lithog'd. by Evans & Cogswell."

No periods.

576 $1 (4) A B C D E F G H $55.00 $95.00

Period before the first serial letter.

576A $1 (6) A B C D E F G H $55.00 $95.00

Period before the last serial letter

576B $1 (7) A B C D E F G H $55.00 $95.00

Period before each serial letter.

577 $1 (4) A B C D E F G H $55.00 $95.00

"Engraved by Archer & Halpin. Richmond, VA."

Pink paper

T72

(Bust of Jefferson Davis.)

"1st Series"

578 50c (3) A B C D E F G H I $15.00 $22.00

Same as 578 but slate blue black ink (only a small number made).

578A 50c (9) A B C D E F G H I $50.00 $100.00

"2nd Series"

579 50c (7) A B C D E F G H I $20.00 $35.00

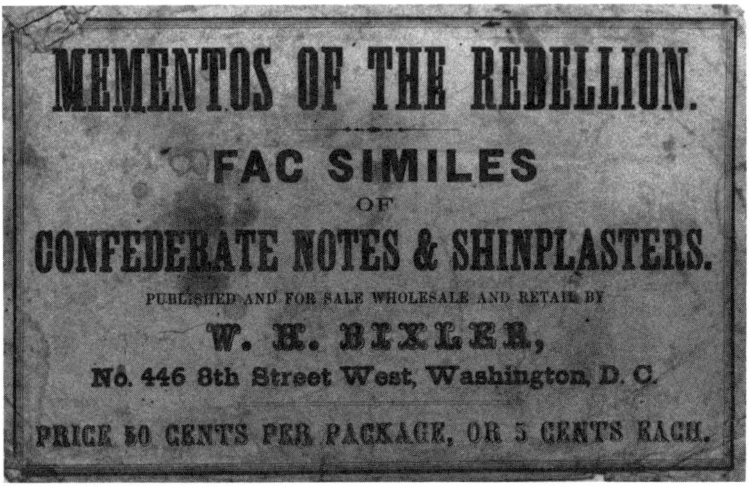

This is an envelope which apparenty contained "facsimile Confederate notes." It is not known if this envelope contained Upham or some other types of counterfeits. The envelope is green and appears to be contemporary.

CONFEDERATE COUNTERFEITS

This section is the most important addition since the introduction of the first edition of this catalog in 1957.

Counterfeiters played a major role in the gradual collapse of the Confederacy's financial structure. In quality their products range from notes based on crude woodcuts created by newspaper and magazine artists to exquisite copies that almost defy detection. Today's collectors are fortunate that many of the counterfeit notes which were produced during the Civil War somehow survived and provide a fascinating field of study in themselves.

These contemporary notes should not be confused with the many reproductions which have been produced in recent years and which were sold in souvenir stands or given away as premiums by breakfast cereal makers. Such notes, although interesting, have no place in serious numismatics.

Two-thirds or more of Confederate counterfeit notes were produced and sold by Samuel Upham, a Philadelphia shopkeeper, or were made by others using plates sold by Upham when he went out of business. Upham always insisted that he produced only facsimiles for the souvenir market. Yet his inscription was always printed on the margin of the note in such a way that it could be easily trimmed off and the note passed into circulation as genuine. Thus Union soldiers were able to send them home as captured "prizes." Thousands of other Upham or Upham-like notes were used by smugglers to buy cotton from unsuspecting plantation owners. So many notes were trimmed that in today's market an Upham note with his inscription intact brings about double the price of a trimmed example.

Long after the Civil War ended, Sam Upham boasted that Jefferson Davis had offered a reward in gold for his "corpus, dead or alive." He proudly admitted that during his career as producer of Confederate "facsimiles" he printed a total of 1,564,050 notes. To this number must be added the thousands of notes which were produced by his competitors and successors. An Upham broadside advertising his products is reproduced on the following page.

The "Havana" counterfeits of 1864 are another most interesting study. In 1958, with the help of personal friends in Havana, I came close to finding the actual plates which were used to make these notes. Unfortunately, the parties having the information about the plates and their use died before I could complete my negotiations.

I have tried to make my list of contemporary counterfeits as complete and accurate as possible. If any collector has notes which are not listed here, I hope that he/she will contact us so that such items may be added in future editions.

The counterfeit notes that follow have the same numbers as the regular Criswell number (types and regular) with the addition of a "CT" prefix.

This envelope apparently contained "facsimile Confederate notes." It is not known whether this envelope contained Upham or some other type of counterfeits. It appears to be contemporary, and is printed in dark green.

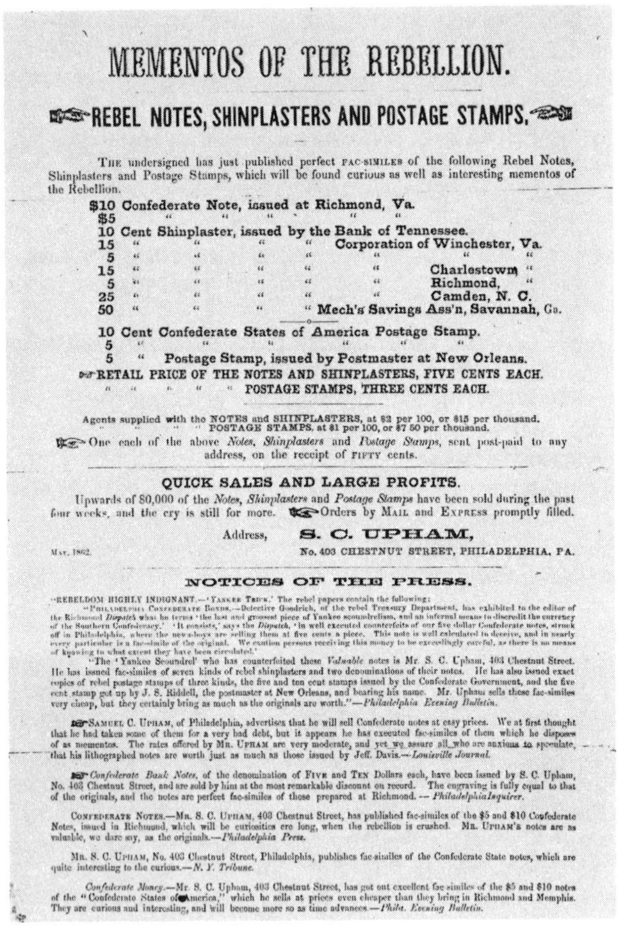

MEMENTOS OF THE REBELLION.

REBEL NOTES, SHINPLASTERS AND POSTAGE STAMPS.

THE undersigned has just published perfect FAC-SIMILES of the following Rebel Notes, Shinplasters and Postage Stamps, which will be found curious as well as interesting mementos of the Rebellion.

$10 Confederate Note, issued at Richmond, Va.
$5 " " " " "
10 Cent Shinplaster, issued by the Bank of Tennessee.
15 " " " " Corporation of Winchester, Va.
5 " " " " " " "
15 " " " " " Charlestown "
5 " " " " " Richmond, "
25 " " " " " Camden, N. C.
50 " " " " Mech's Savings Ass'n, Savannah, Ga.

10 Cent Confederate States of America Postage Stamp.
5 " " " " " "
5 " Postage Stamp, issued by Postmaster at New Orleans.
RETAIL PRICE OF THE NOTES AND SHINPLASTERS, FIVE CENTS EACH.
" " " " " POSTAGE STAMPS, THREE CENTS EACH.

Agents supplied with the NOTES and SHINPLASTERS, at $2 per 100, or $15 per thousand.
" " " " POSTAGE STAMPS, at $1 per 100, or $7 50 per thousand.

One each of the above *Notes, Shinplasters* and *Postage Stamps*, sent post-paid to any address, on the receipt of FIFTY cents.

QUICK SALES AND LARGE PROFITS.

Upwards of 80,000 of the *Notes, Shinplasters* and *Postage Stamps* have been sold during the past four weeks, and the cry is still for more. Orders by MAIL and EXPRESS promptly filled.

Address, S. C. UPHAM,
No. 403 CHESTNUT STREET, PHILADELPHIA, PA.

MAY, 1862.

NOTICES OF THE PRESS.

"REBELDOM HIGHLY INDIGNANT.—'YANKEE TRICK.' The rebel papers contain the following:

"PHILADELPHIA CONFEDERATE BONDS.—Detective Goodrich, of the rebel Treasury Department, has exhibited to the editor of the Richmond *Dispatch* what he terms 'the last and grossest piece of Yankee scoundrelism, and an infernal means to discredit the currency of the Southern Confederacy.' 'It consists,' says the *Dispatch*, 'in well executed counterfeits of our five dollar Confederate notes, struck off in Philadelphia, where the news-boys are selling them at five cents a piece. This note is well calculated to deceive, and in nearly every particular is a fac-simile of the original. We caution persons receiving this money to be exceedingly careful, as there is no means of knowing to what extent they have been circulated.'

"The 'Yankee Scoundrel' who has counterfeited these *Valuable* notes is Mr. S. C. Upham, 403 Chestnut Street. He has issued fac-similes of seven kinds of rebel shinplasters and two denominations of their notes. He has also issued exact copies of rebel postage stamps of three kinds, the five and ten cent stamps issued by the Confederate Government, and the five cent stamp got up by J. S. Riddell, the postmaster at New Orleans, and bearing his name. Mr. Upham sells these fac-similes very cheap, but they certainly bring as much as the originals are worth."—*Philadelphia Evening Bulletin.*

SAMUEL C. UPHAM, of Philadelphia, advertises that he will sell Confederate notes at easy prices. We at first thought that he had taken some of them for a very bad debt, but it appears he has executed fac-similes of them which he disposes of as mementos. The rates offered by MR. UPHAM are very moderate, and yet we assure all who are anxious to speculate, that his lithographed notes are worth just as much as those issued by Jeff. Davis.—*Louisville Journal.*

Confederate Bank Notes, of the denomination of FIVE and TEN Dollars each, have been issued by S. C. Upham, No. 403 Chestnut Street, and are sold by him at the most remarkable discount on record. The engraving is fully equal to that of the originals, and the notes are perfect fac-similes of those prepared at Richmond. — *Philadelphia Inquirer.*

CONFEDERATE NOTES.—MR. S. C. UPHAM, 403 Chestnut Street, has published fac-similes of the $5 and $10 Confederate Notes, issued in Richmond, which will be curiosities ere long, when the rebellion is crushed. MR. UPHAM'S notes are as valuable, we dare say, as the originals.—*Philadelphia Press.*

MR. S. C. UPHAM, No. 403 Chestnut Street, Philadelphia, publishes fac-similes of the Confederate State notes, which are quite interesting to the curious.—*N. Y. Tribune.*

Confederate Money.—Mr. S. C. Upham, 403 Chestnut Street, has got out excellent fac-similes of the $5 and $10 notes of the "Confederate States of America," which he sells at prices even cheaper than they bring in Richmond and Memphis. They are curious and interesting, and will become more so as time advances.—*Phila. Evening Bulletin.*

Rare broadside offering Upham counterfeits.

CT-8

On this lithographed counterfeit of Type 8 Confederate notes, Washington has a "prissy" mouth, and there are two medium size flourishs over "America." The medallion at lower right with "50" is tilted to the left.

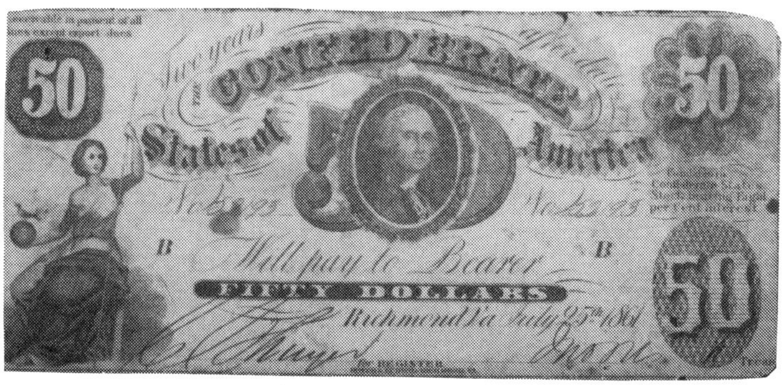

Printed signatures and written serial numbers.

CT8/15 $50 (9) Serial letter B $150.00 $275.00

Washington has a "slit" in his mouth extending down on his right side. The "50" medallion is also tilted to the left.

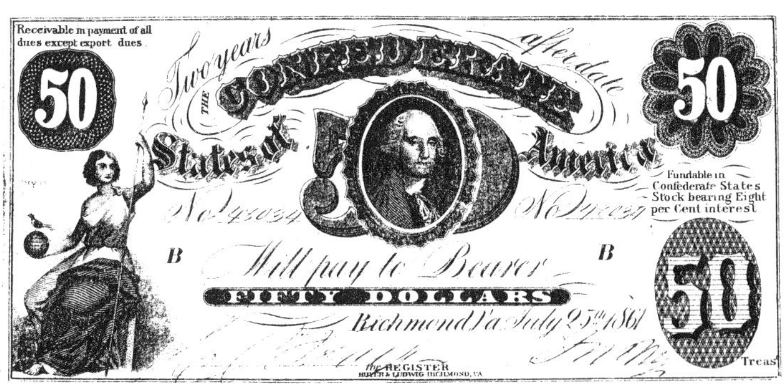

Written signatures and serial numbers.

CT8/15A $50 (7) Serial letter B $75.00 $125.00

CT-10

This is a wood cut facsimile of Type 10 Confederate notes. There is a top on the "R" in "Richmond." There is no cross bar on the "f" in "of" and no comma between "Richmond" and "Va." There is a loose lock of hair on Miss Liberty which is pronounced and points upward toward her eye, and the mouth of Hope with the anchor is but a slanted slash. "Noyer" instead of "Hoyer."

Printed signatures and serial numbers.

CT10/38 $10 (6) Serial letter B $75.00 $135.00

There is no top on the "R" in "Richmond," and there is a comma between "Richmond" and "Va." The line from seated Liberty's hair appears to be more to be her ear and points down. Hope with the anchor has a better mouth but a cleft line in her chin giving her mouth a vertical appearance. "Noyer" instead of "Hoyer."

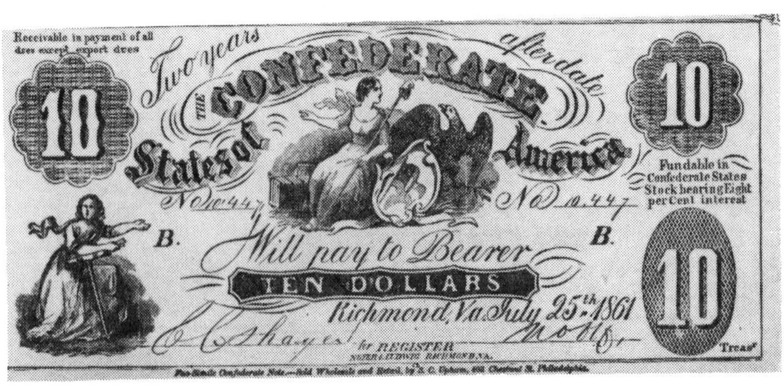

Printed signatures and serial numbers, serial letter B.

CT10/38A $10 (7) serial letter B $70.00 $185.00

Printed signatures and written serial numbers (or blank).

CT10/38B $10 (7) Serial letter B $75.00 $185.00

Written signatures and serial numbers.

CT10/38C $10 (7) Serial letter B $80.00 $140.00

A large green "CSA" has been added to the note.

Printed signatures and serial numbers.

CT10/C $10 (9) Serial letter B $95.00 $200.00

Same as CT10C but written signatures and serial numbers.

CT10/D $10 (9) Serial letter B $100.00 $275.00

Large red "CSA" has been added to the note.

CT10/E $10 (11)Serial letter B $250.00 $500.00

CT-11

Printed signatures, written numbers

CT11/44 $5 (10) Serial letter Bb $300.00 $750.00

CT-13

This is a lithographed counterfeit of the Type 13 Confederate note. The sailor's skin around the immediate facial area is very dark and make him look like he has a beard.

Written signatures and serial numbers

CT13/50 $100 (7) Serial letter A $50.00 $100.00

Written signatures and serial numbers.

CT13/55 $100 (8) Serial letters FA, GA $60.00 $125.00

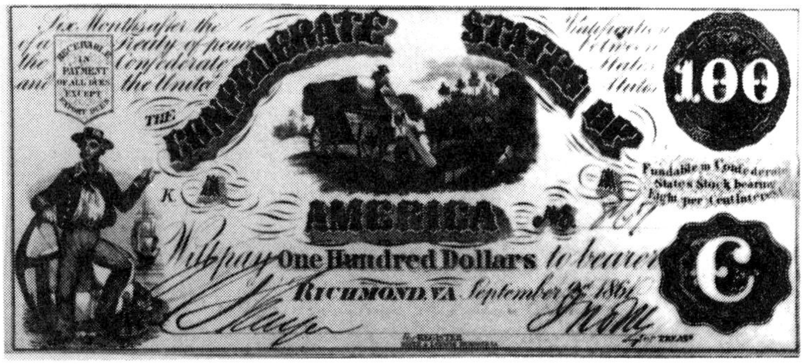

Written signatures and serial numbers.

CT13/55 $100 (8) Serial letters KA $60.00 $125.00

Written signatures and serial numbers

CT13/56 $100 (7) Serial letters A, I $55.00 $100.00

Sailor at left has both eyes, and there are three flourishes under "of."
Printed signatures and numbers.

CT13/56A $100 (4) Serial letters A G $55.00 $100.00

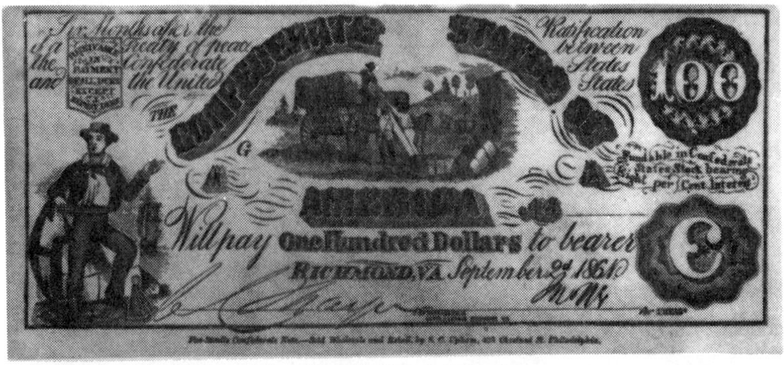

Printed signatures and written number (or blank).

CT13/56B $100 (4)Serial letters A G $45.00 $90.00

Written signatures and written number (or blank)

CT13/57 $100 (8) Serial letters A4 (two plates) $40.00 $75.00

Printed signatures and written serial numbers.

CT13/58 $100 (8) Serial letter A4, A6 $40.00 $100.00

CT-14

This is a lithographed counterfeit of T-14 Confederate note. The exposed left hand of the sailor without a hat appears more like a spindle of yarn.

Written signatures and serial numbers.

CT14/59 $50 (7) Serial letter A $35.00 $100.00

The hair of the sailor without a hat is blowing wildly, unlike the genuine note where the hair is plastered to the head.

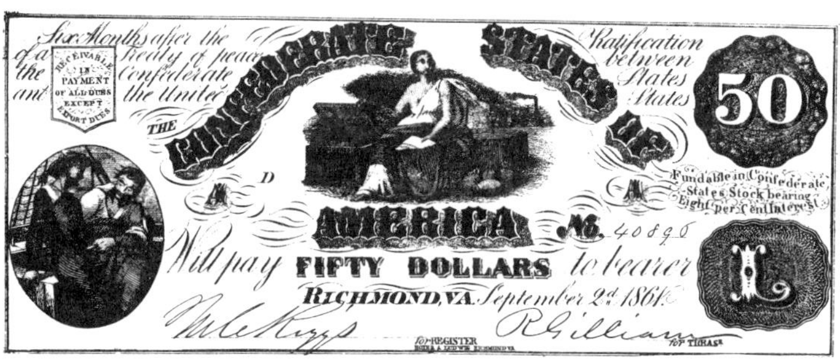

Written signatures and serial numbers.

CT14/64 $50 (7) Serial letters A D $40.00 $80.00

Unlike the genuine pieces the sailor without a hat has three sharply divided strands of hair. Written signatures and serial numbers.

CT14/75 $50 (7) Serial letter A2 $40.00 $80.00

CT14/75A $50 (8) Serial letter A3 $50.00 $90.00

The sailor without a hat has four very even strands of hair.

Written signatures and serial numbers.

CT14/75B $50 (7) Serial letter A3 $40.00 $80.00

The cheeks of the sailor without a hat are undefined
and are not separated from the neck by shading as on the genuine note.

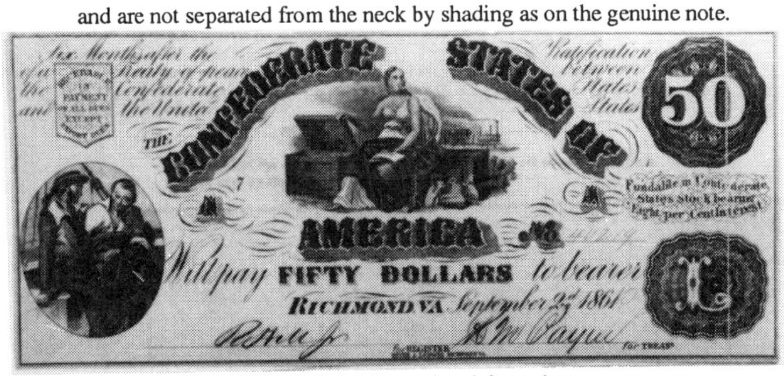

Written signatures and serial numbers.

CT14/75C $50 (7) Serial letter A7, A5 $40.00 $80.00

A woodcut facsimile of a T-14 (probably done by Upham).
Printed signatures and printed serial numbers.

CT14/75D $50 (6) Serial letter A1 $40.00 $60.00

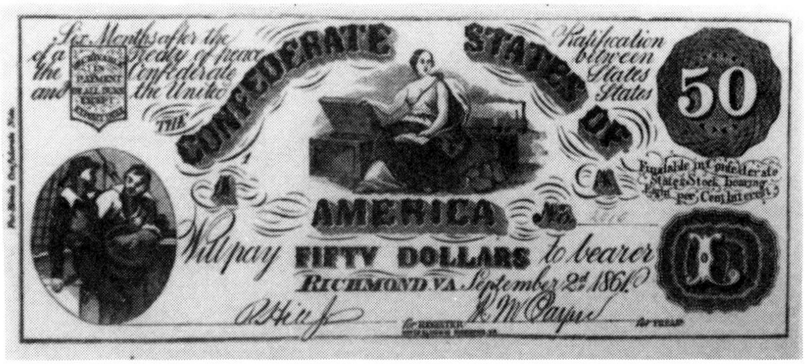

Printed signatures and written serial numbers (or blank).

CT14/75E $50 (8) Serial letter A1 $40.00 $90.00

Printed signatures and written numbers (or blank).

CT14/75F $50 (5) Serial letters A-2, A3, A-12 $35.00 $65.00

Written signatures and serial numbers.

CT14/75G $50 (5) Serial letter A2, A3, A12 $35.00 $65.00

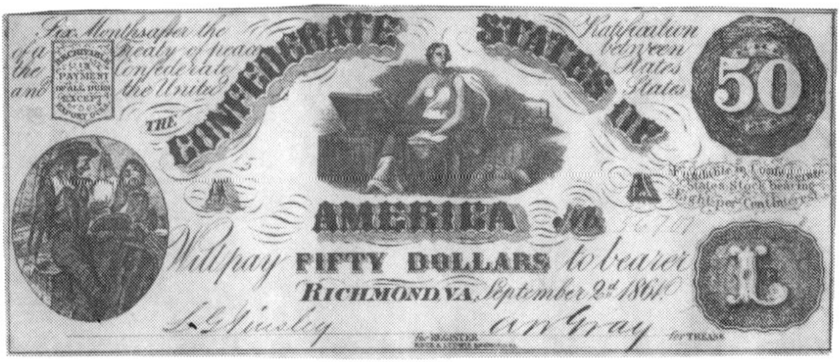

Written signatures and written serial numbers (or blank).

CT14/77 $50 (9) Serial letter A5 $50.00 $100.00

CT-16

On this lithographed counterfeit, the leaf design in the upper left corner of the note has a distinct curl pointing down from the bottom of the design, somewhat like the genuine note but different from other varieties of this counterfeit.

Printed signatures with written serial numbers (or blank).

CT16/86 $50 (8) Serial letter XA $35.00 $85.00

Same as CT16/86 but red fiber paper.

CT16/86A $50 (9) Serial letter XA $75.00 $125.00

Unlike the genuine note the green underprint of this counterfeit has the rays "outlined" around the number fifty at the center bottom.

Printed signatures with written serial numbers (or blank).

CT16/86B $50 (8) Serial letter XA $50.00 $100.00

The curl at the bottom of the leaf design in the upper left corner points up.
Written signatures and serial number (or blank)

CT16/86C $50 (8) Serial letter XA $75.00 $150.00

CT-18

On this lithographed counterfeit of T-18 Confederate note, the sailor has a very dark blotchy face in which the mouth and eyes are almost obscure. Plate letter "A."

Printed signatures and written numbers.

CT18/101 $20 (6)Serial letter A $35.00 $80.00

Printed signatures and serial numbers

CT18/102 $20 (6)Serial letter K $35.00 $80.00

Written signatures and serial numbers

CT18/102A $20 (6)Serial letter K $35.00 $80.00

Written signatures and serial numbers.

The sailor has a large pupil in his eye and a "patchy" beard.

CT18/107 $20 (6) Serial letter F-A $45.00 $90.00

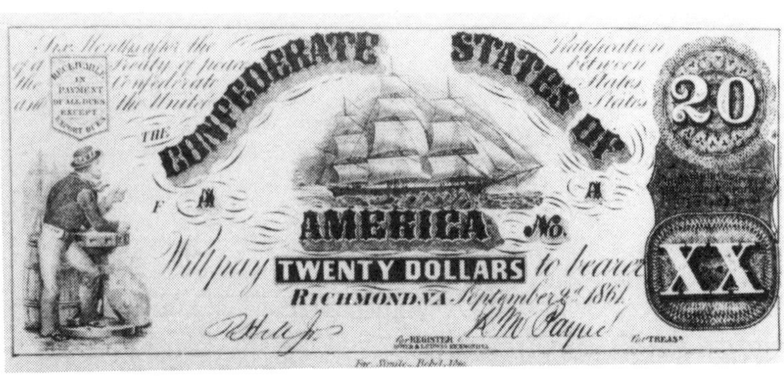

Printed signatures and written serial numbers (or blank).

CT18/107A $20 (8) Serial letter F A $50.00 $100.00

The sailor has no chin but has an exaggerated jutting beard which almost makes the sailor appear to have his mouth wide open.

Written signatures and serial numbers.

CT18/116 $20 (6) Serial letter A E $45.00 $90.00

The eye of the sailor is large, white, and heavily outlined.

Printed signatures and written serial numbers (or blank).

CT18/129 $20 (8) Serial letter A F 26 $75.00 $125.00

Similar to CT18/129

Written signatures and serial numbers (or blank).

CT18/129A $20 (6) Serial letter A-F 26 $75.00 $125.00

Printed signatures and written serial numbers (or blank).

CT18/129B $20 (6) Serial letter A F $75.00 $125.00

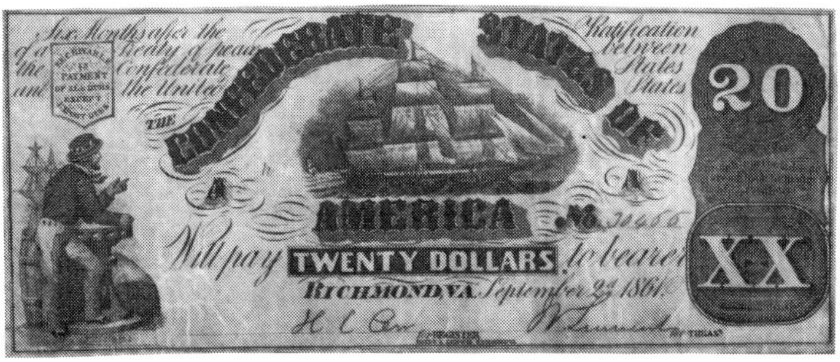

Small case letter above "A." Written signatures and serial numbers (or blank).

CT18/129D $20 (6) Serial letter Ah $40.00 $100.00

Written signatures and serial numbers (or blank).

CT18/130 $20 (6) Serial letter 5A $40.00 $95.00

This is an Upham-style woodcut facsimile.

All notes have flourishes between "Confederate" and "States."

Printed signatures and written number (or blank).

CT18/130B $20 (9) Serial letter 25A $75.00 $150.00

Written signatures and written numbers (or blank).

CT18/130C $20 (9) Serial letter 25A $75.00 $150.00

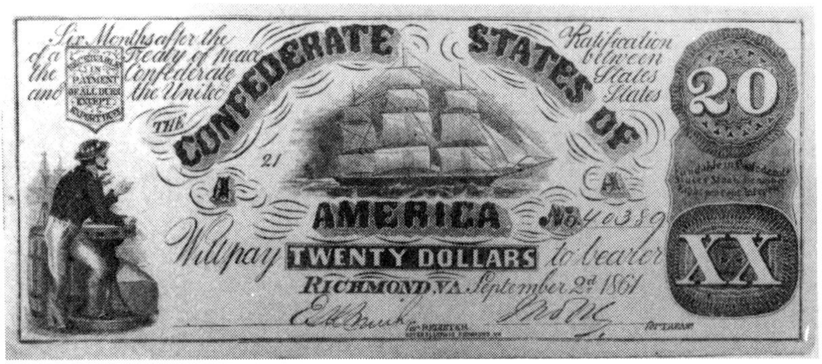

Printed signatures and serial numbers.

CT18/132 $20 (6) Serial letter A21 $35.00 $80.00

Printed signatures and written number (or blank).

CT18/132A $20 (5) Serial letter A21 $35.00 $75.00

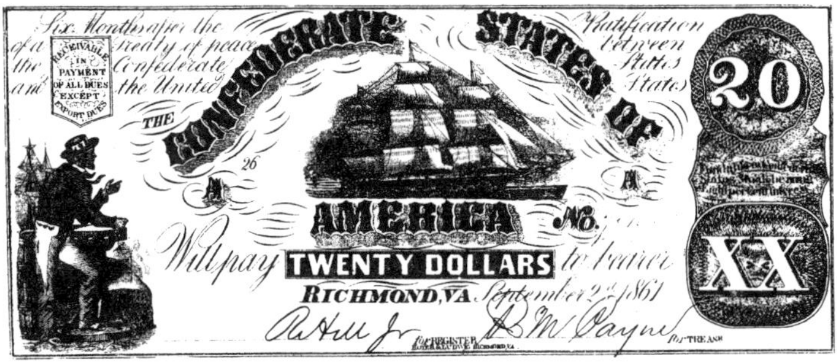

Written signatures and serial numbers (or blank).

CT18/132B $20 (7) Serial letter A26 $50.00 $90.00

CT-19

This is a woodcut facsimile of a T-19 Confederate note. It has three small vertical apostrophe-like marks over the "d" in "Confederate" and the "e" in "America." It also has periods after "New Orleans" and "Treasurer" like the genuine note.

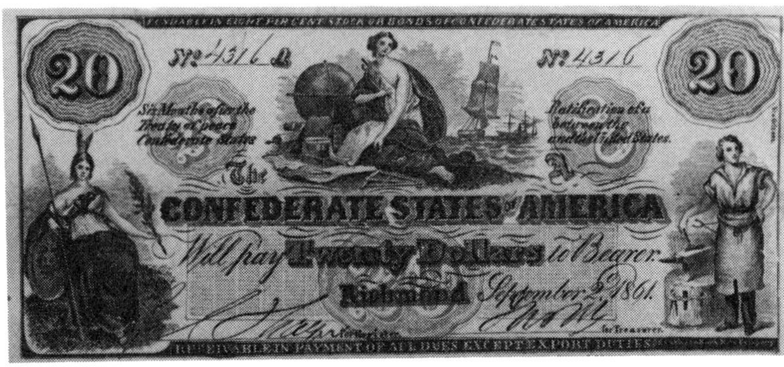

Printed signatures and serial number 4316.

CT19/137 $20 (6) Serial letter A $60.00 $150.00

Printed signatures and written serial numbers (or blank).

CT19/137A $20 (7) Serial letter A $75.00 $150.00

Written signatures and serial numbers.

CT19/137B $20 (6) Serial letter A $75.00 $175.00

No small vertical flourish marks over the "d" in "Confederate" nor over the "e" in "America." No periods after "New Orleans" and "Treasurer."

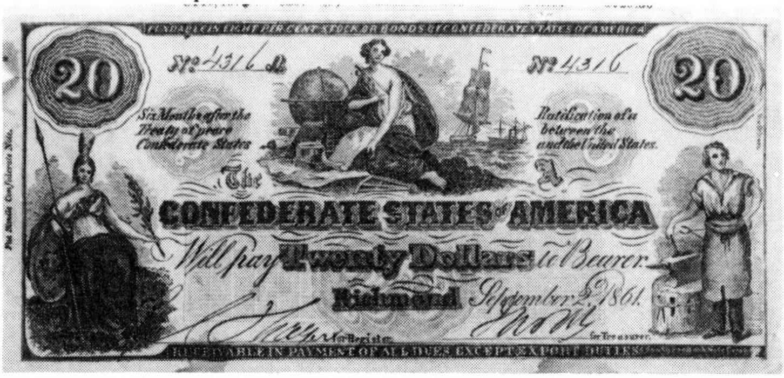

Printed signatures and written serial numbers (or blank).

CT19/137F $20 (5) Serial letter A $75.00 $160.00

Similar to CT19/137B
Written signatures and serial numbers (or blank).

CT19/137G $20 (5) Serial letter A $75.00 $160.00

CT-20

This note has a distinctly different face on Industry. Stephens appears to be looking slightly to his left rather than straight ahead as on genuine pieces. Plate No. 2, First Series. Hope with anchor also has an odd face.

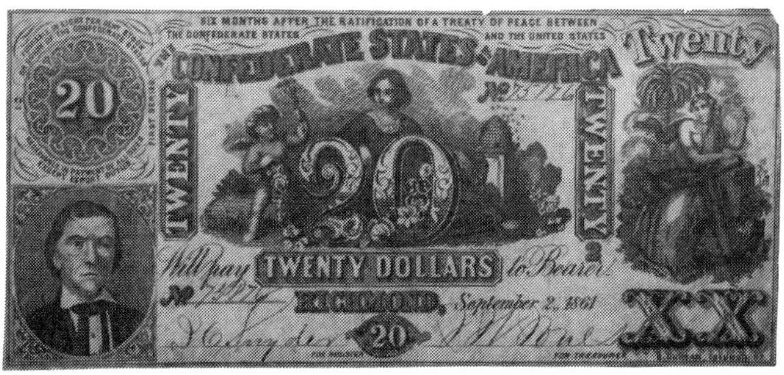

Written signatures and serial numbers.

CT20/139 $20 (7) Serial letter 2 $60.00 $110.00

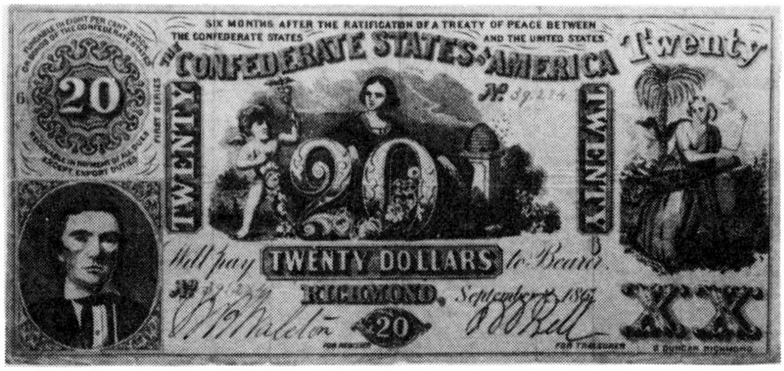

CT20/139A	$20 (8)	Serial letter 2	$85.00	$135.00

On this lithographed counterfeit, Stephens has very dark shadows on both cheeks which make the area below his eyes appear too white. Plate number 6, First Series.

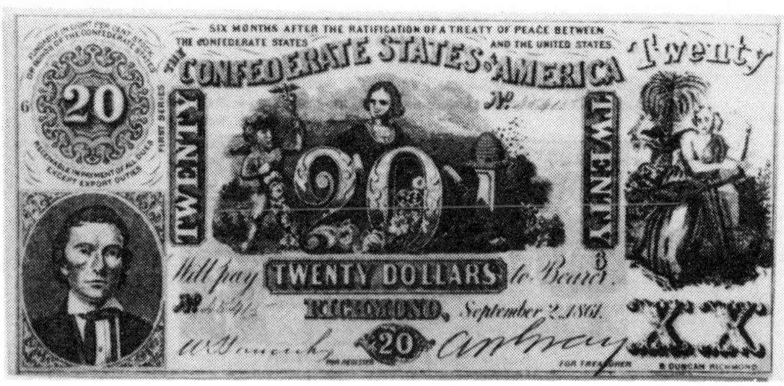

Printed Signatures and written serial numbers.

CT20/141	$20 (5)	Serial letter 6	$35.00	$85.00

Written signatures and serial numbers.

CT20/141A	$20 (5)	Serial letter 6	$35.00	$85.00
CT20/141B	$20 (7)	Serial letter 2	$40.00	$75.00
CT20/141C	$20 (7)	Serial letter 4	$40.00	$75.00

Similar to CT20/141 but watermarked "J. Whatman"

Written signatures and serial numbers.

CT20/141D	$20 (9)	Serial letter 6	$100.00	$150.00

Stephens has heavy creases on the right side of his mouth and where his nose and eyebrows meet.
Plate No. 6. Second Series.

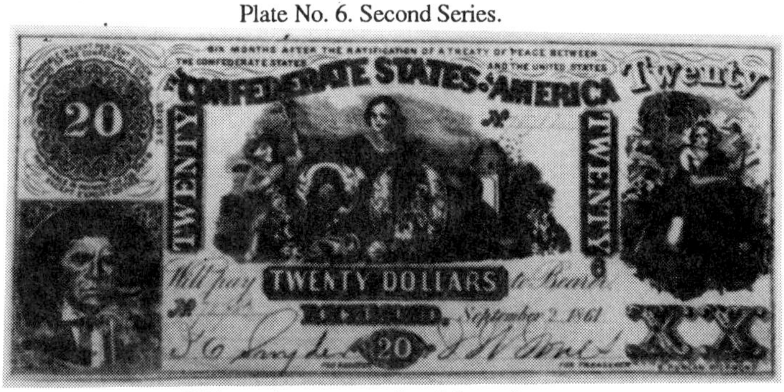

Written signatures and serial numbers.

CT20/142 $20 (5) Serial letter 6 $35.00 $85.00

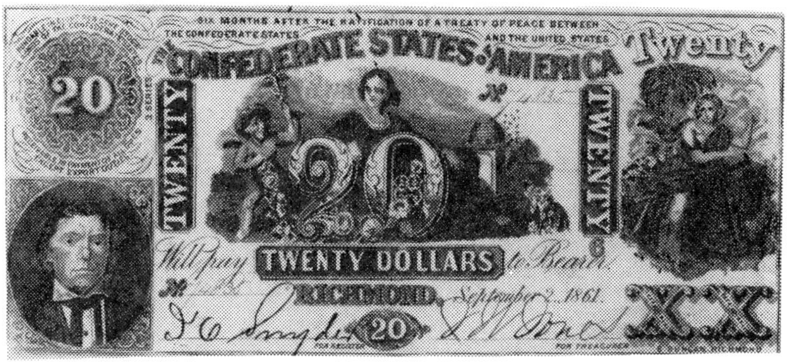

CT20/143 $20 (9) Serial letter 6 $50.00 $100.00

CT-22

This is a woodcut facsimile of a T-22 Confederate note. There is a grove of pines to the right of the Indian family and "New Orleans" vertically at the far left side of the note. This variety is sometimes on red fiber paper.

Printed signatures and serial numbers.

CT22/152 $10 (5) Serial letter C $45.00 $80.00

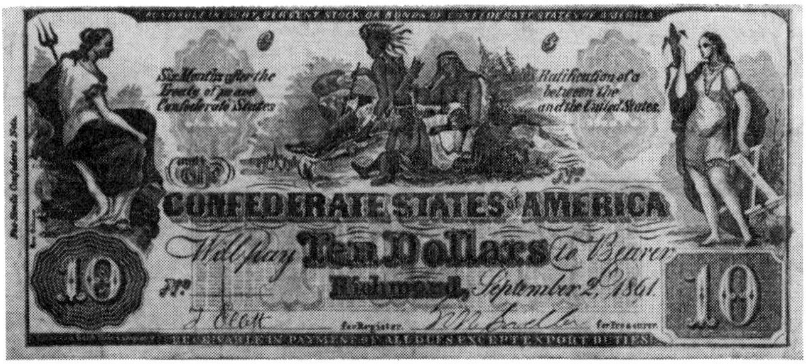

Printed signatures and written serial numbers (or blank)

CT22/152A $10 (5) Serial letter C $45.00 $ 80.00

No red overprint, printed signatures and written serial numbers (or blank).

CT22/152B $10 (9) Serial letter C $100.00 $200.00

"ADRIAN SHARP" imprint on margin at left end.

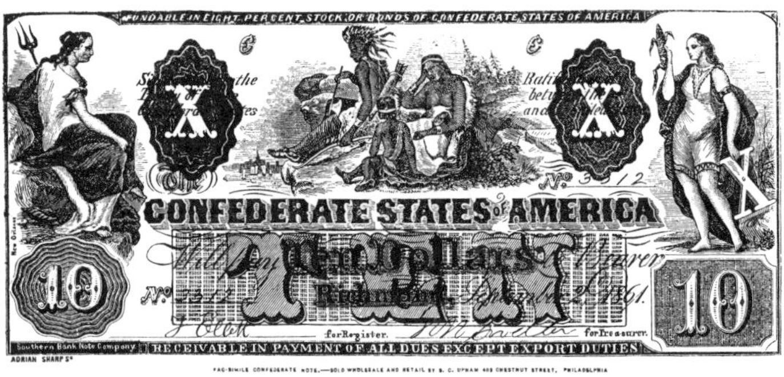

Printed signatures and numbers.

CT22/152C $10 (9) Serial letter C $100.00 $150.00

The grove of pines to the right of the Indian family is omitted. No "New Orleans" vertically on the far left side of the note.

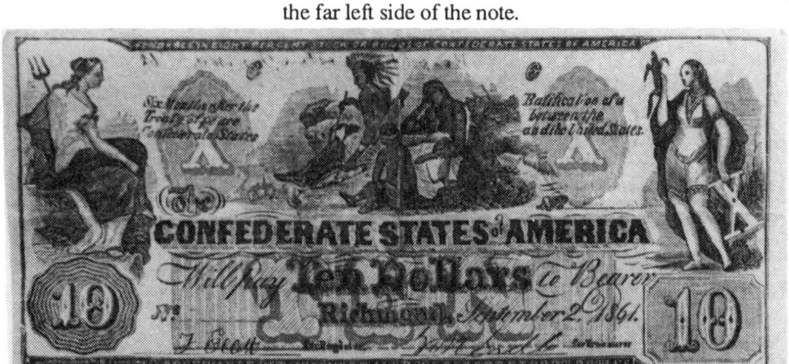

Printed signatures and serial numbers (or blank).

CT22/152D $10 (5) Serial letter C $40.00 $75.00

CT-25

On this lithographed counterfeit, Hunter on the left has a very distinct curl or lock of his hair making a complete loop just above his right ear. This same note was also printed with red "X"s to make it a type 26 note. Moreover, the cut for Memminger on the right was used to make a counterfeit type 33 note.

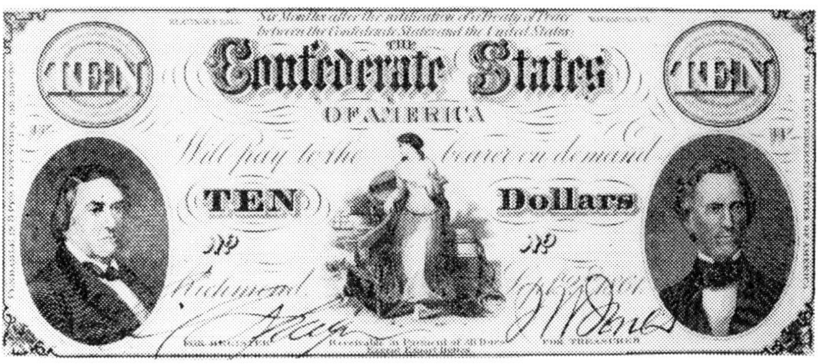

Printed signatures and written serial numbers (or blank).

CT25/168 $10 (7) Serial letter W $35.00 $75.00

Similar to CT25/168. Written signatures and serial numbers (or blank).

CT25/168A $10 (8) Serial letter W $60.00 $90.00

Hunter on the left has a pronounced wrinkle below his right eye, and Memminger at right also has pronounced shading about his right eye and at the bridge of the nose. Plate letter "X."

Written signatures and serial numbers (or blank).

CT25/168B $10 (7) Serial letter X $60.00 $120.00

Printed signatures and written serial numbers (or blank).

CT25/168C $10 (7) Serial letter X $60.00 $120.00

CT-26

This counterfeit is the same as CT25/168 above with the addition of two red "XX" to the face of the note. Hunter at left of the note has a "loop" of hair above his right ear.

Written signatures and serial numbers (or blank).

CT26/173 $10 (7) Serial letter W $100.00 $150.00

CT-28

Woodcut facsimile.

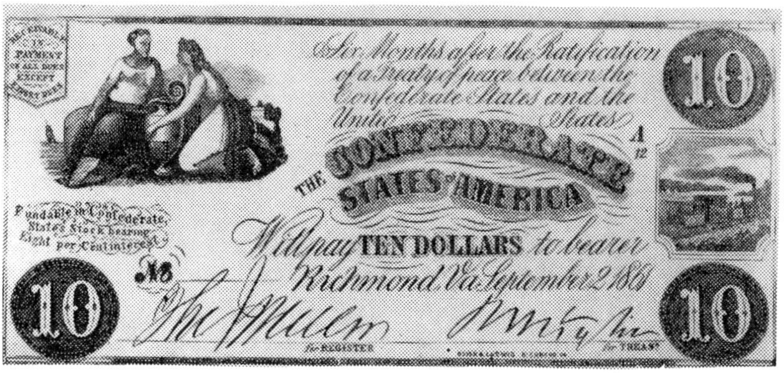

Printed signatures and written serial numbers (or blank).

CT28/230	$10 (6)	Serial letter A-1	$275.00	$125.00

Printed signatures and serial numbers.

CT28/230A	$10 (8)	Serial letter A-10, A-12	$85.00	$140.00

CT-29

This is an excellent lithographed counterfeit. However, it is marked "R. Duncan," in the lower left corner rather than "B. Duncan" as on the genuine. This note was printed in sheets with probably plate letters "A" through "H."

Printed signatures and written serial letters (or blank).

CT29/237	$10 (8)	Serial letters A B C D E F G H	$80.00	$150.00

Similar to CT29/237 with written signatures and serial letters.

CT29/237A	$10 (6)	Serial letter A B C D E F G H	$75.00	$150.00

CT-31

This was Upham's first facsimile. It is a woodcut with printed signatures and often with the printed serial number 364. It was reproduced from the February 24, 1862 issue of the *Philadelphia Inquirer*. It has "New Orleans" near the left bottom of the note and flourishes over the "A" in "States."

Red overprint "5," "Five."

Printed signatures and serial numbers.

CT31/245 $5 (5) Serial letter C $35.00 $90.00

No "New Orleans" on the notes, and the right serial letter "C" is missing, with red overprint "5 FIVE 5."

Printed signatures and serial numbers.

CT31/245A $5 (5) No serial letter $30.00 $100.00

Printed signatures and written serial numbers.

CT31/245B $5 (5) No serial letter $30.00 $100.00

Written signatures and serial numbers.

CT31/245C $5 (5) No serial letter $30.00 $100.00

"New Orleans" near left bottom of the note and no flourishes over the "A" in "States."

Red overprint "5 FIVE 5."

Printed signatures and serial numbers.

CT31/245D $5 (5) Serial letter C $75.00 $150.00

Green "5 FIVE 5" overprint.

CT31/245E $5 (9) Serial letter C $125.00 $250.00

CT-33

This lithographed counterfeit was produced as a high grade, two-color facsimile. The same engraving of Memminger was used as on the type 25, and 26 notes. The green underprint on the counterfeit is distinctly more blue-green than on the genuine note.

Printed signatures and written serial numbers.

CT33/250 $5 (5) Serial letter J $30.00 $90.00

This is a woodcut facsimile. The vertical printer's name is missing from the left side of the note, and the left serial letter "J" is also missing. The "or" is missing from below "Fundable in Eight Per Cent Stock." The "For Treas." is also missing.

Printed signatures and serial numbers.

CT33/250A $5 (6) Serial letter J $45.00 $110.00

Similar to CT33/250A with printed signatures and written serial numbers (or blank).

CT33/250B $5 (5) Serial letter J $45.00 $100.00

The vertical printer's name is on the left side of the note, but the "or" is missing from below "Fundable in Eight Per Cent Stock."

Printed signatures and serial numbers.

CT33/250C $5 (5) Serial letter J $35.00 $90.00

Printed signatures and written serial numbers (or blank).

CT33/250D $5 (5) Serial letter J $35.00 $90.00

The vertical printer's name on the left side and the "or" below "Fundable..." are present on this version.

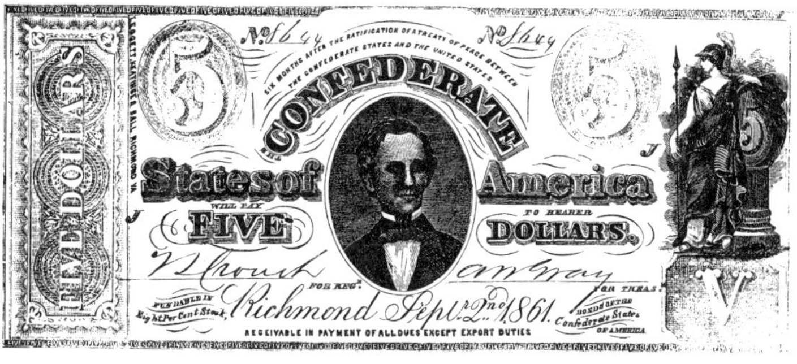

Printed signatures and serial numbers

CT33/250E $5 (5) Serial letter J $35.00 95.00

Similar to CT33/250D with printed signatures and written serial numbers (or blank).

CT33/250F $5 (5) Serial letter J $35.00 $60.00

CT-35

What is believed to be a unique specimen of a counterfeit T-35 Confederate note was discovered by Sydney C. Kerksis in 1951 in the Raphael P. Thian collection in the Manuscript Department of Duke University, Durham, N.C. Mr. Kerksis announced his discovery in the November 1951 issue of *The Numismatist.* The counterfeit is in such poor condition that it is not suitable for reproduction. The illustration below is an artist's conception of the (counterfeit) note by Brent Hughes.

Mr. Kerksis' description of the counterfeit is summarized below.

1. The note is a lithograph, printed in black on plain white paper (as is the genuine note).
2. It bears serial number 6886 written in red ink. Serial numbers on genuine notes were also written in red ink.
3. It bears printed signatures of T. Ellette and H.H. Goodloe. These two signatures were written on genuine notes in brown ink.
4. The printer's legend under the Goodloe signature reads "LITH. OF HOYER G. LUDWIGS RICHMOND, VA." (The "S" on LUDWIG being an error.)
5. The word "CONFEDERATE" in "THE CONFEDERATE STATES OF AMERICA" has a heavy cross hatched background instead of a light background as on the genuine note.
6. The figures in the left vignette are more sharply defined than on the genuine note.

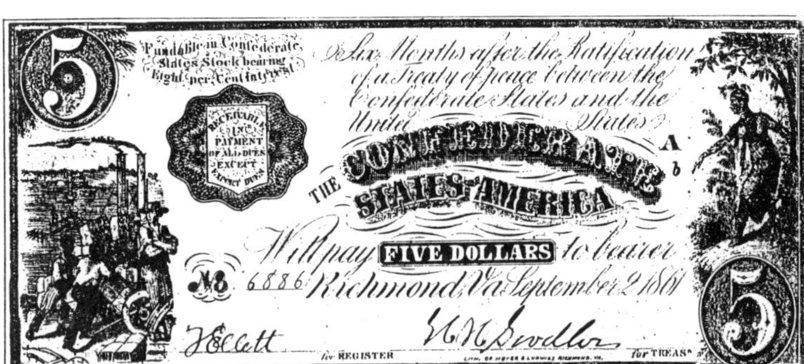

An artist's conception by Brent Hughes to show as much detail as possible.

CT35/271 $5 (11) Serial letter Ab possibly unique

CT-36

The ship's rigging line which passes behind the sailor's head on the genuine note is missing from this lithographed counterfeit.

Written signatures and serial numbers (or blank).

CT36/276	$5 (6)	Serial letter 9-A, 10-A, 11-A, 12-A, 13-A	$50.00	$85.00

"Second Series"

The ship's rigging line touches both the left and right brim of the sailor's hat on the counterfeit. On the genuine note the line on the left of the sailor stops at his right shoulder.

Printed signatures and written serial numbers (or blank.).

CT36/278	$5 (7)	Serial letters 9-A, 10-A,11-A, 12-A, 13-A	$45.00	$90.00

Written signatures and serial numbers.

CT36/278A	$5 (7)	Serial letters 9-A, 10-A,11-A, 12-A, 13-A	$45.00	$90.00

Same as above, red fiber paper

CT36/278D	$5 (10)	Serial letter 9-A	$125.00	$200.00

CT-37

Clouds over the sailor's right shoulder have a very distinct outline on genuine notes but are not distinct on this lithographed counterfeit.

Written signatures and serial numbers (or blank).

CT37/284	$5 (6)	Serial letter C	$85.00	$150.00

Printed signatures and written serial numbers (or blank).

CT37/ 284A	$5 (6)	Serial letter C	$100.00	$175.00

CT-39

The milkmaid has a very distinct apple in her left hand in this lithographed counterfeit. There are also three distinct small black clouds in the clear sky above the forward mast of the ship in the background. These so-called facsimiles were passed by the thousands as genuine.

Printed signatures and written serial numbers (or blank).

CT39/290	$100 (7)	Serial letter Ab	$60.00	$80.00

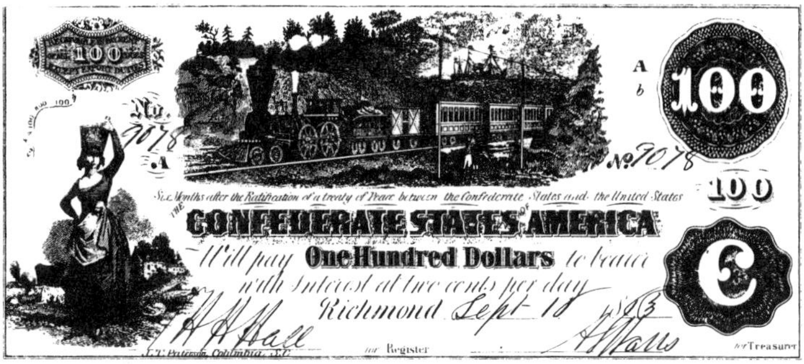

Written signatures and written serial numbers.

CT39/290A $100 (7) Serial letter Ab $50.00 $75.00

"J.T. Paterson" on right side, written serial numbers and signatures (or blank).

CT39/294 $100 (8) Serial letter A $60.00 $90.00

CT-40

The face of the milkmaid on this lithographed counterfeit is very poor. It has ugly staring eyes and a chin which is lost in blotches. Also on this counterfeit, three windows in the lower right-hand section of the building behind the milkmaid are not visible as they are on the original.

Written signatures and serial numbers (or blank).

CT40/298 $100 (9) Serial letters AB, AD, AH $75.00 $150.00

CT-41

This lithographed counterfeit has only three flourishes over the left plate letter "Z." Some have phony issue stamps from Jackson, others with fake Montgomery issue stamps.

Written signatures and serial numbers (or blank).

CT41/315 $100 (7) Serial letters X, Z $65.00 $100.00

Same as above with four flourishes above the "Z."

CT41/315A $100 (8) Serial letters W, X, Y, Z $75.00 $125.00

Calhoun's face is poorly done. The nose on *Columbia* seems broken.

Printed signatures and written serial numbers (or blank).

CT41/316 $100 (9) Serial letter X $100.00 $140.00

Calhoun's face is poorly done and the highest bird above the slaves is much clearer than on genuine notes. There is some evidence that this note may have been connected with Upham.

Printed signatures and written serial numbers.

CT41/316A $100 (7) Serial letter X $50.00 $80.00

Written signatures and serial numbers (or blank).

CT41/316B $100 (7) Serial letter X $50.00 $80.00

This note has a poor engraving of Calhoun, and Columbia has a series of horizontal marks between her nose and eye unlike the genuine note.

Printed signatures and written serial numbers (or blank).

CT41/316C $100 (7) Serial letters X, Y $60.00 $80.00

Similar to CT41/316B

Written signatures and written serial numbers (or blank).

Ct41/322C $100 (7) Serial letter Y $50.00 $80.00

CT-42

This is a lithographed counterfeit of a T-42 Confederate note. This counterfeit does not have a period after "DUNCAN" as the genuine does.

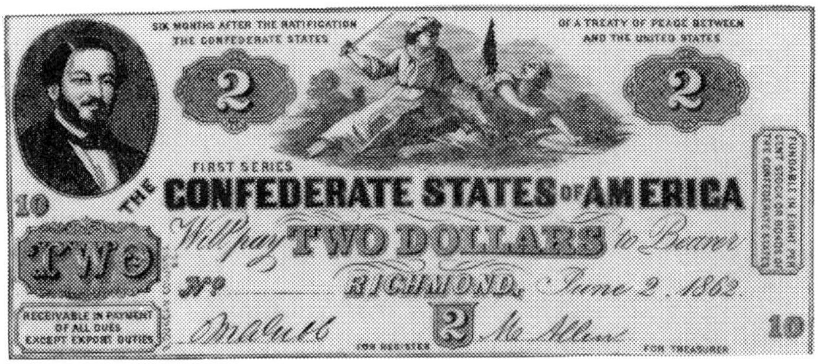

Printed signatures and written numbers (or blank).

CT42/335 $2 (9) Serial letter 10 $60.00 $175.00

CT-44

This is a woodcut facsimile of a T-44 Confederate note. This counterfeit has a period before "First Series," but the genuine does not. There is an object floating in the ocean above the "E" in "States" that is much more apparent in the facsimile than on the genuine note.

Printed signatures and written serial numbers (or blank).

CT44/339 $1 (8) Serial letter 10 $80.00 $150.00

Printed signatures and written serial numbers (or blank).

CT45/342 $1 (6) Serial letter 10 $40.00 $60.00

CT-46

This is a lithographed counterfeit of a T-46 Confederate note. This counterfeit even has the tiny engraved "LUDWIG" below the cotton bale. The "RMT HUNTER" below the portrait at lower right is much bolder on the counterfeit than on the genuine piece. The counterfeit also has the error "six Month." On some counterfeit notes the secret "LUDWIG" has almost been removed which implies that this note was printed in sheets.

Printed signatures and written serial numbers (or blank).

CT46/344 $10 (8) Serial letter K $60.00 $90.00

Written signatures and serial numbers or (blank).

CT46/344A $10 (7) Serial letters L, K $5.00 $75.00

CT-49

This is a high-quality engraved counterfeit of a T-49 Confederate note. The note has the legend "First Series" which was *not* used on any genuine notes! The counterfeit does not have the near circular lines on the top of the seated soldier's hat which are found on genuine notes. The counterfeit also is about 1/8 inch "shorter" than genuine notes. This gives the appearance of "pinching" Randolph's portrait.

Written signatures and serial numbers (or blank).

No genuine "1st Series" T-49 notes exist.

CT49/349A $100 (7) Serial letters A, B, C, D $150.00 $200.00

"2nd Series"

Written signatures (or blank) and red machine numbers.

CT49/349B $100 (7) Serial letters A, B, C, D $125.00 $200.00

CT-56

This is another high-quality engraved counterfeit. It is similar to CT-49. The note has the legend "First Series" which was *not* used on any genuine notes! The counterfeit does not have the near circular lines on the top of the seated soldier's hat which are found on genuine notes. The counterfeit also is about 1/8 inch "shorter" than genuine notes. This gives the appearance of "pinching" Randolph's portrait. Pickens nose is too large and her eye points out.

Stamped with various "issue" months.

Written signatures and printed red serial numbers.

CT56/403 $100 (8) Serial letters A, B, C, D $100.00 $125.00

CT-58

This is a lithographed counterfeit of the type 58 Confederate note. Stephens' portrait is crude and the state capitol is much darker than on genuine notes. No issuance overprints are known.

"First Series"

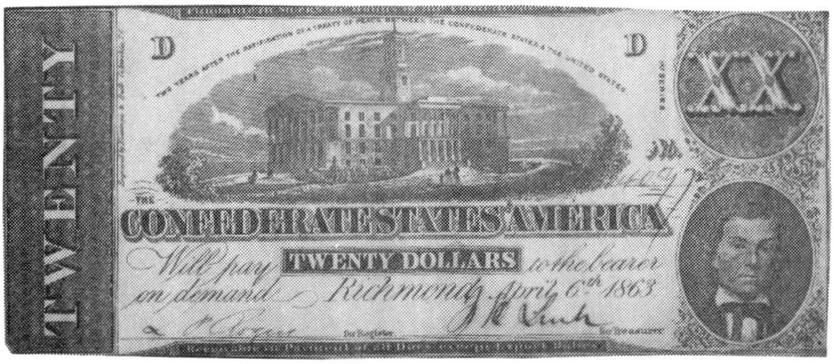

Written signatures and serial numbers.

CT58/421 $20 (9) Serial letter D $100.00 $250.00

Litho'd by Evans and Congswell."
"2nd Series"

CT58/426 $20 (9) Serial letter E, F $100.00 $250.00

Havana Counterfeits

The following counterfeits are commonly called "Havana counterfeits" because they are known to have been produced there. They are among the most interesting for study. In 1958 through personal friends, the author came very close to locating the original plates and information about the Havana operation. Unfortunately, the people in question died and the information with them.

CT-64

This is a lithographed counterfeit of type 64 Confederate notes. The overprint which is red on genuine notes is red-orange on the counterfeit. The upper and lower portions of decorative border have "blocked-in" sections. Black printing is excellent in contrast to the flawed overprint but not as detailed as the genuine. The counterfeiters laboriously had-drew the serial numbers in an attempt to copy the machine printing used on the genuine issue. Signatures are poorly forged "Miller-Baker."

Written signatures, numbers hand drawn.

CT64/489A $500 (10) Serial letters A, B, C, D $1500 $2000

CT-65

This $100 bill was the best executed of any of the Havana counterfeits. The face is virtually perfect and looks better than many of the "worn plate" productions of the government. The backs, however, were poorly done and are usually a little blurry and lighter blue than the original. Nevertheless, this note circulated readily. William West Bradbeer, in his monumental 1915 work, listed this as a genuine note.

Written signatures and machine serial numbers.

CT65/492 $100 (7) Serial letter D $75.00 $125.00

CT-66

The $50 Havana counterfeit corrected the error of the light blue, blurry back which existed on the CT-65. However, the backs are often "off center." The face colors are usually in orange-brown and the inner red circle around Davis is slightly more pronounced than on the originals, and sometime slightly off center. This note still readily passes as a genuine note!

Written signatures and machine numbers.

CT66/501 $50 (9) Serial letters Z A $175.00 $300.00

Written signatures and widely spaced machine numbers,
Davis' face appears longer and older.

CT66/501A $50 (10) Serial letters VA, XA $200.00 $350.00

THE STATE OF ALABAMA

STATE ACT OF DECEMBER 15, 1820

Dated, Cahawaba, 1820-1822

(Day written in)

Very little is known about this issue of notes.

1820 Issue.

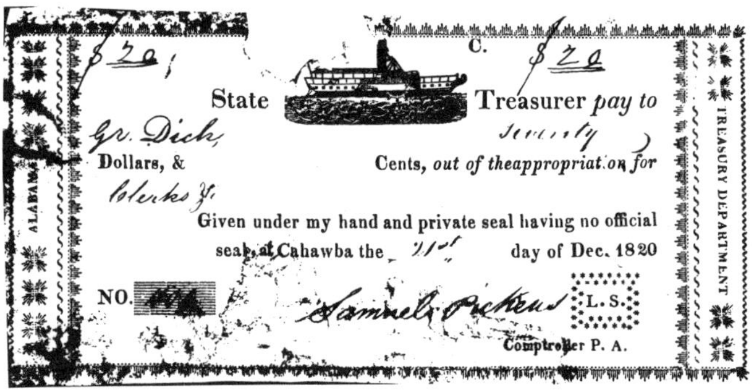

1820-A written denominations (10) very rare
1820-E $2 (11) no information available
1820-G $3 (11) no information available

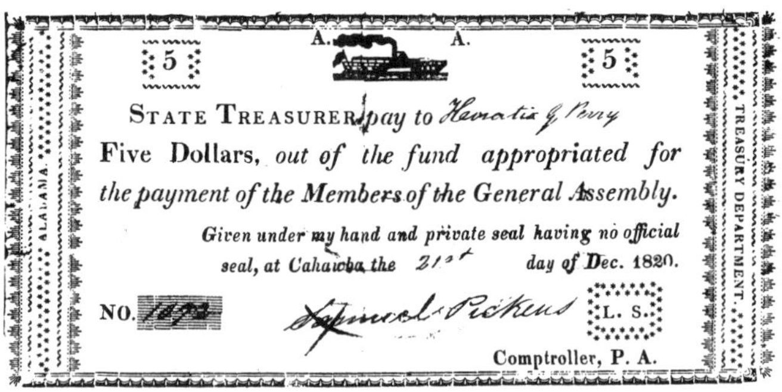

Early steamboat center, Allen and Brickell--printers.

1820-K $5 (11) A extremely rare

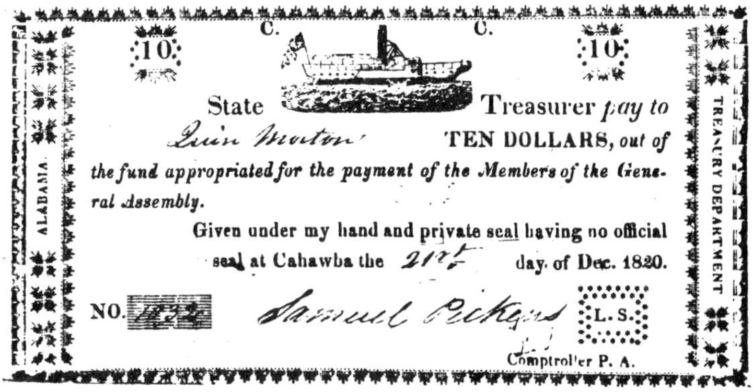

1820-M $10 (11) C extremely rare

1821 Issue

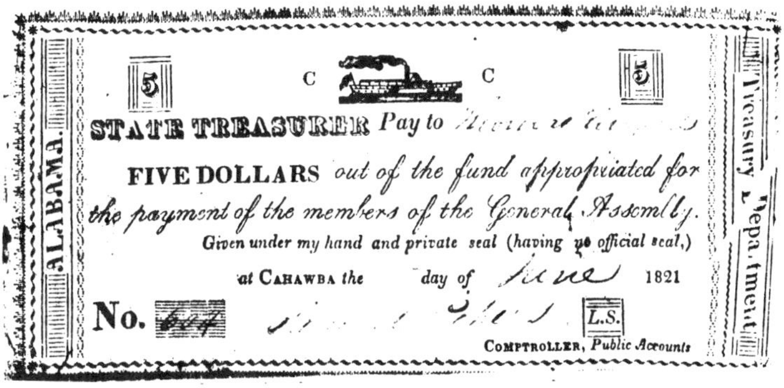

Early steamboat center.

1821-E $5 (11) C extremely rare

Sailing ship.

1821-G $10 (11) C extremely rare

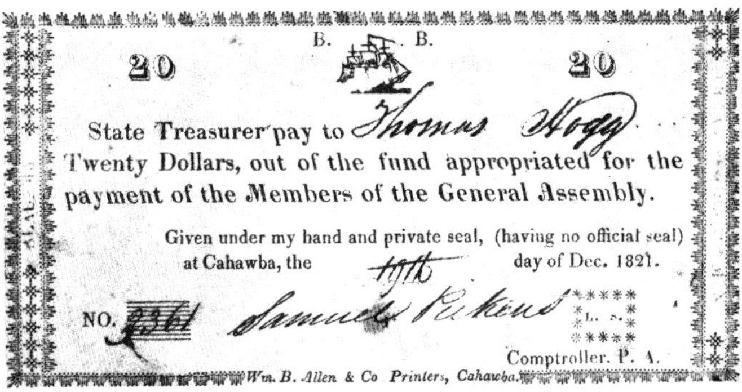

1821-N $20 (11) B extremely rare

1821-P $20 (11) extremely rare

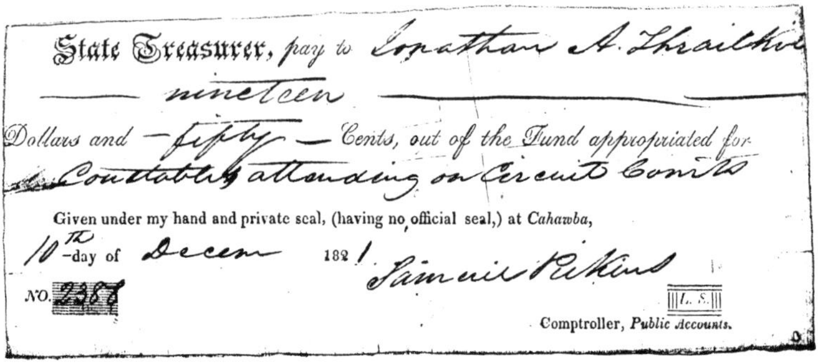

1821-S written denominations (10) very rare

March 1822 Issue

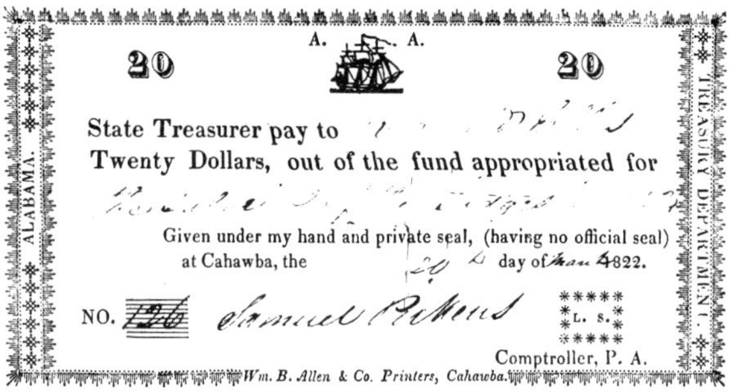

1822-K $20 (11) extremely rare

Fractional Denomination Issues

Issue of June 1, 1822 (under act of Dec. 19, 1821)

Stage coach at center.

1822-P 6.25c very rare

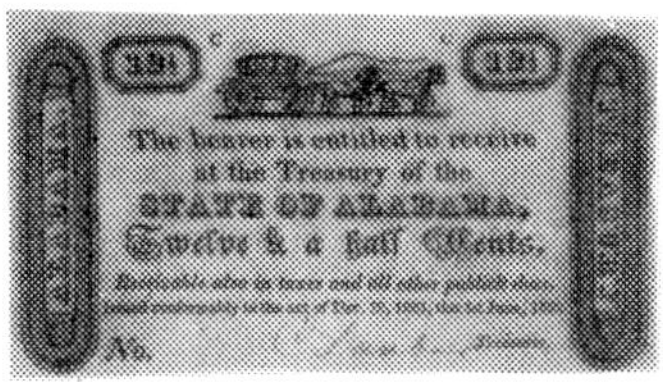

Stage coach at center.

1822-Q 12.5c (10) B very rare

Ox and plow.

1822-R 25c (10) A very rare

Steamship at center.

1822-S 37.5c (10) B very rare

Eagle and shield, sprig and arrows in talons, motto in scroll.

1822-T 50c (10) B very rare

Eagle with arrows at center.

1822-U 75c (10) very rare

Dated Montgomery, Ala. "1st. January, 1863."

"Eng'd. by J. T. Paterson & Co. Augusta, Ga."

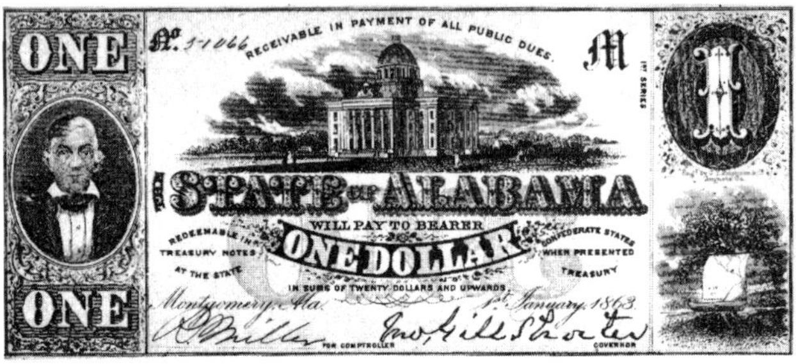

Governor at left, tree and map at right. "One," green overprint.

		"1st SERIES"		
1	$1 (3)	A B C D E F G H J K L M	$8.00	$12.00
		"One" inverted.		
1A	$1 (11)	A B C D E F G H J K L M	$100.00	$150.00
		"2nd Series" in small letters.		
2	$1 (4)	A B C D E F G H J K L M	$8.00	$12.00
		Same, "2nd Series" in large letters.		
2A	$1 (8)	A B C D E F G H J K L M	$15.00	$35.00

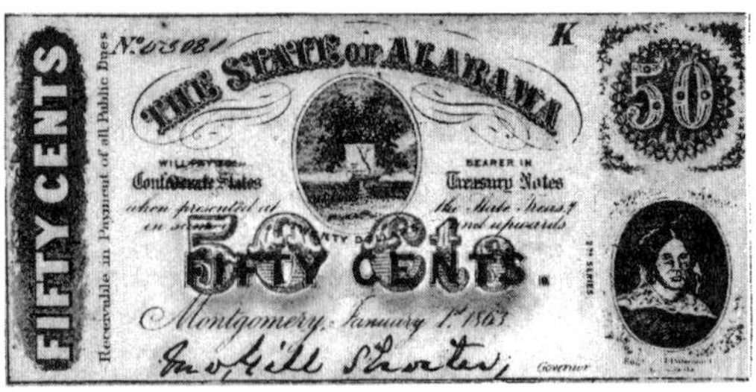

Tree and map at center, Juliett Hopkins in oval at lower right. "50 Cts" blue overprint.

		NO SERIES		
3	50c (4)	A B C D E F G H I J K L M N O	$8.00	$11.00
3A	50c (8)	with "50 cts." in green	$50.00	$100.00
		"2ND SERIES" in small letters.		
4	50c (2)	A B C D E F G H I J K L M N O	$8.00	$10.00
		Same, "2nd Series" in large letters.		
4A	50c (6)	A B C D E F G H I J K L M N O	$12.00	$40.00

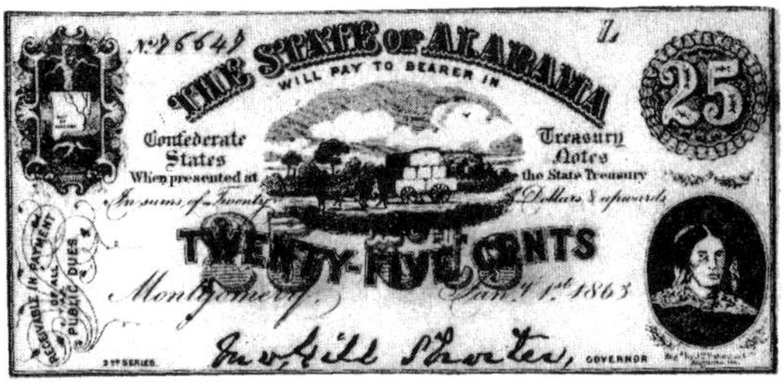

Wagon load of cotton, Juliett Hopkins in oval at lower right, "25 Cts" in red.

		NO SERIES		
5	25c (6)	A B C D E F G H I J K L M N O	$12.00	$35.00
		"2nd SERIES" in small letters.		
6	25c (2)	A B C D E F G H I J K L M N O	$6.00	$10.00
		Same, "2nd Series" in large letters.		
6A	25c (8)	A B C D E F G H I J K L M N O	$10.00	$25.00
		"3rd Series"		
7	25c (4)	A B C D E F G H I J K L M N O	$8.00	$15.00

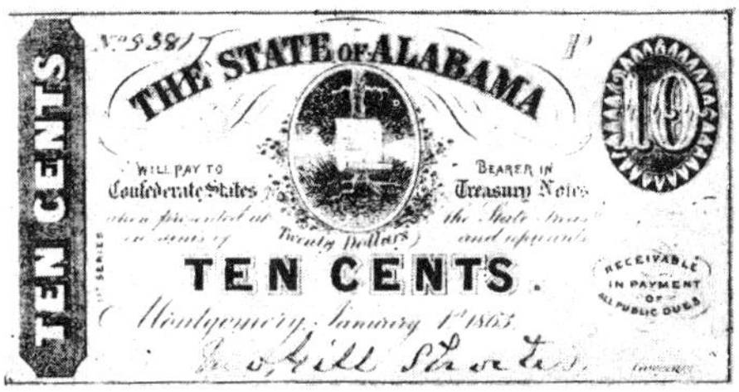

Tree and map at center.

"1st Series"

		Small serial letter.		
8	10c (7)	A B C D E F G H I J K L M N O P Q R S T U	$20.00	$40.00
		Large serial letter.		
9	10c (3)	A B C D E F G H I J K L M N O P Q R S T U	$6.00	$15.00

"1st SERIES"

Small Serial letter.

10 5c (8) A B C D E F G H I J K L M N O P Q R S T U $20.00 $40.00

Large serial letter.

11 5c (2) A B C D E F G H I J K L M N O P Q R S T U $8.00 $15.00

Dated Montgomery, Ala. 1st January 1864

"Engraved by W. Keenan & Co."
"Lith & Printed by J. T. Paterson & Co. Augusta, Ga."

Group of Indians at center, tree and map at left, fancy green back.

12 $100 (6) A B C D E F G H $40.00 $75.00

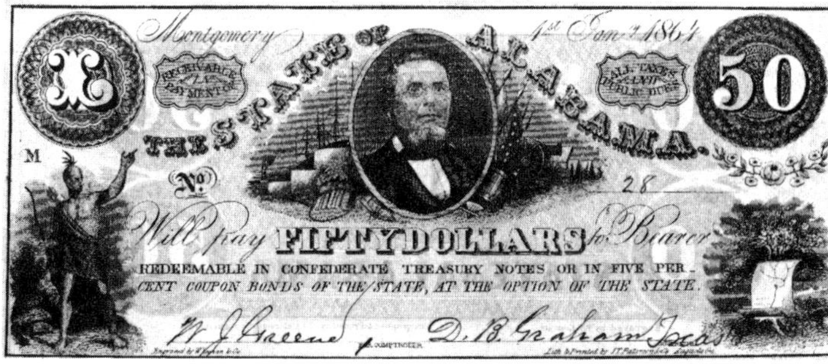

Governor Thomas N. Watts at center, Indian left, tree and map right, fancy green back.

13 $50 (6) A B C D E F G H I J K L M N O P Q R S $35.00 $65.00

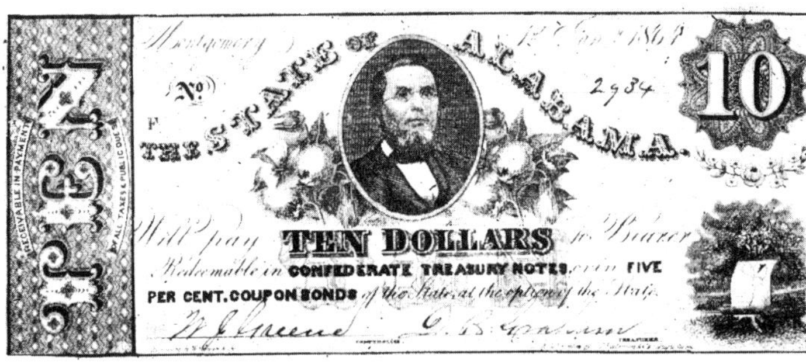

Governor Watts at center, tree and map at right, "Ten" green overprint.

14 $10 (6) A B C D E F $30.00 $50.00

Overseer watching slaves, Liberty at left, tree and map at right, "Five" green overprint.

15 $5 (6) A B C D E F $25.00 $40.00

Dated Montgomery, Ala. 17th February 1864.

"Lith & Printed by J. T. Paterson & Co. Augusta, Ga."

Governor Thomas N. Watts at center, Indian left, tree and map at right.
Black with orange overprint. Ornate green back.

20 $50 (11) A B C D E F G H $1250.00 $2000.00

THE STATE OF ARKANSAS

Issue Authorized by Acts of November 14 and 18, 1861
All war issues have written dates of 1861, 1862, 1863.

"On War Bond," Indian maiden at left.

1B	$1 (9)	White paper	very rare	
		Same, but watermarked paper		
1C	$1 (8)	Blue paper	$90.00	$150.00
2	$2 (10)	White paper	very rare	
2A	$2 (10)	Blue paper	very rare	
3	$3 (10)	White paper	very rare	
3A	$3 (10)	Blue paper	very rare	
3B	$5 (10)	White paper	very rare	

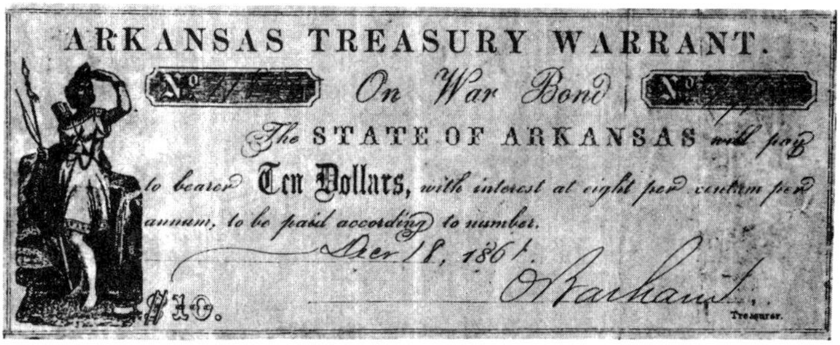

3C	$5 (10)	Blue paper	very rare
3D	$10 (10)	White paper	very rare
3E	$10 (10)	Blue paper	very rare

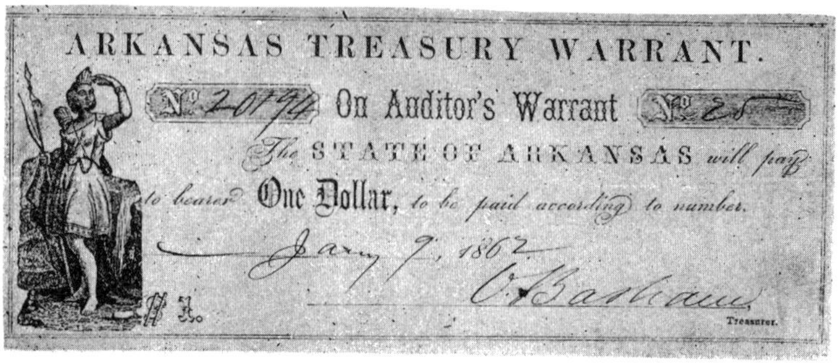

"On Auditor's Warrant," Indian maiden at left.

4 $1 (11) Blue paper very rare
4A $2 (10) Blue paper very rare
4B $3 (11) Blue paper extremely rare

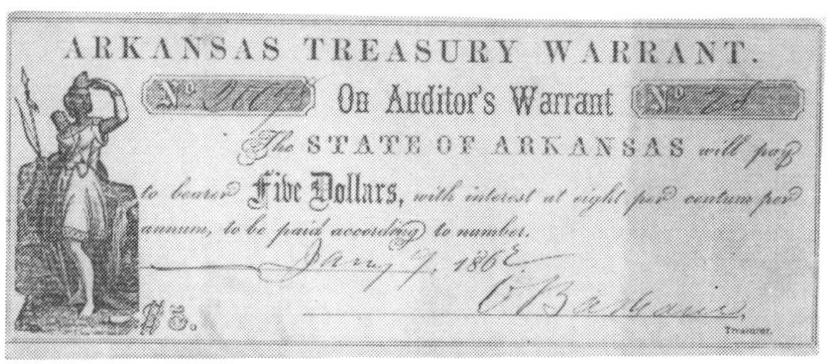

4C $5 (10) White paper very rare
4D $5 (11) Blue paper extremely rare

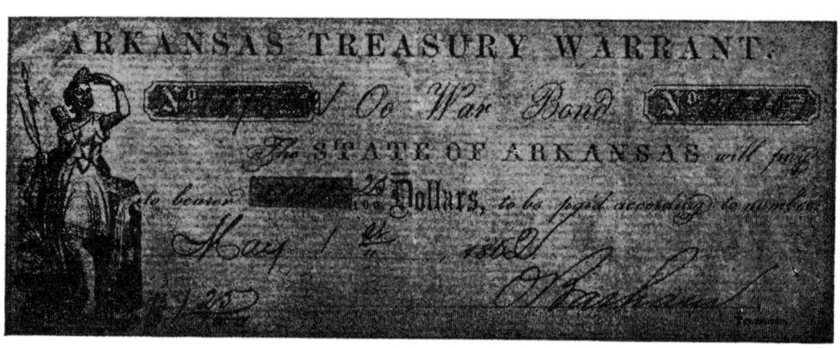

"On War Bond," Indian maiden at left.

5 written denomination (10) White paper very rare

5A written denomination (8) Blue paper $100.00 $300.00

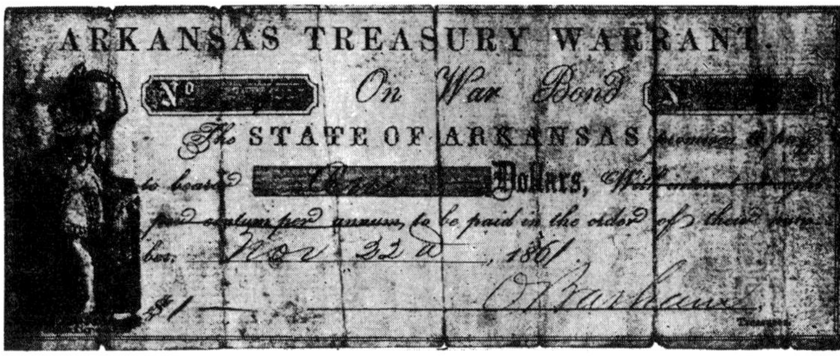

"On War Bond," Indian maiden at left.

6 written denomination (9) White paper $125.00 $275.00

6A written denomination (10) Blue paper very rare

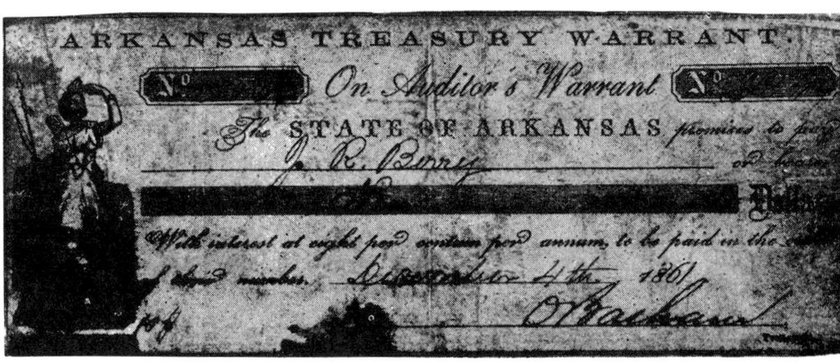

"On Auditor's Warrant," Indian maiden at left.

7 written denomination (9) White paper $125.00 $300.00

7A written denomination (10) Blue paper very rare

8	$1 (8)	White paper	$125.00	$275.00
8A	$1 (8)	Blue paper	$125.00	$275.00
9	$2 (9)	White paper	$125.00	$275.00
9A	$2 (10)	Blue paper	very rare	
10	$3 (10)	White paper	very rare	

11	$5 (10)	Blue paper	very rare
11C	$10 (10)	Blue paper	very rare
11E	$10 (10)	White paper	very rare

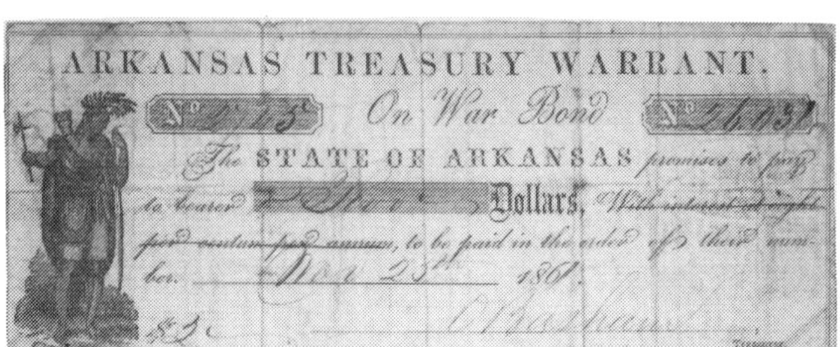

11G	written denomination (10)	White paper	very rare

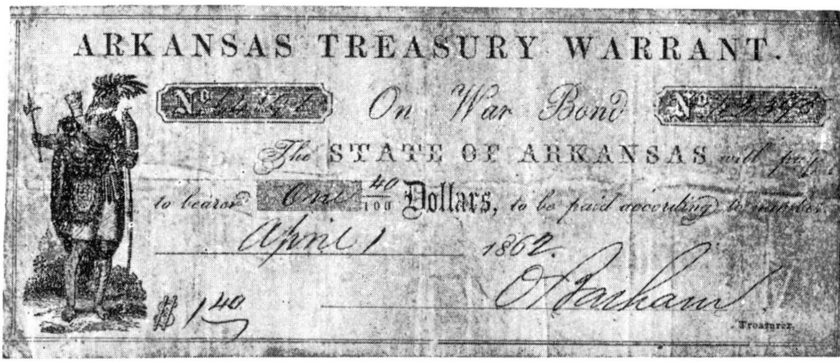

"On War Bond." Indian brave at left.

11K	written denomination (10)	White paper	very rare

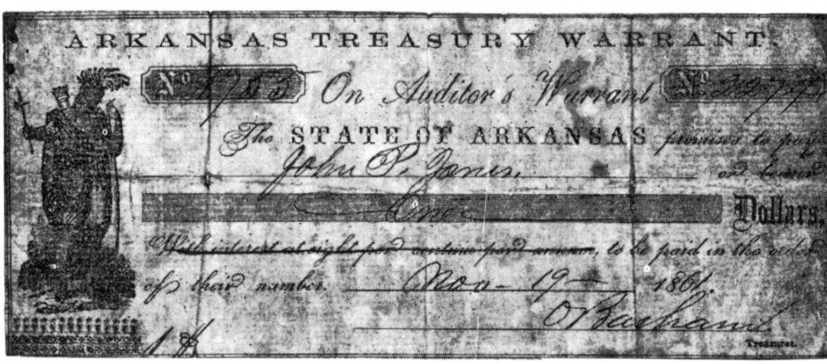

"On Auditor's Warrant," Indian brave at left.

12	$1 (9)	blue paper	$150.00	$350.00
14	written denomination (10)	blue paper	very rare	
14G	$5 (9)	blue paper	$150.00	$350.00
15	$10 (9)	white paper	$125.00	$350.00
15A	$10 (10)	white paper, watermarked	very rare	
17	written denomination (10)	blue paper	very rare	
17A	written denomination (10)	white paper	very rare	

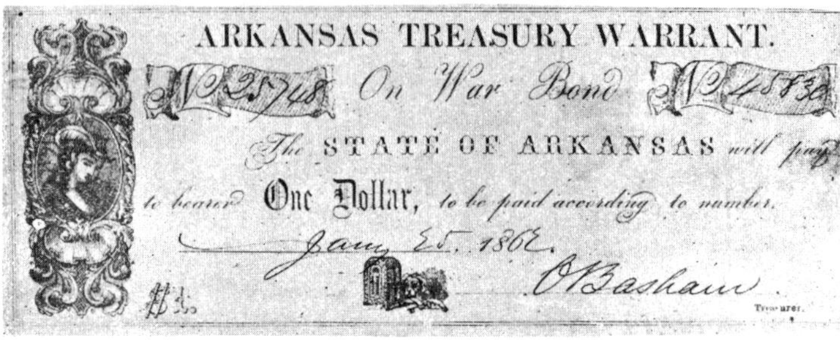

"On War Bond," bust of maiden in oval at left.

19 $1 (8) white paper $100.00 $200.00

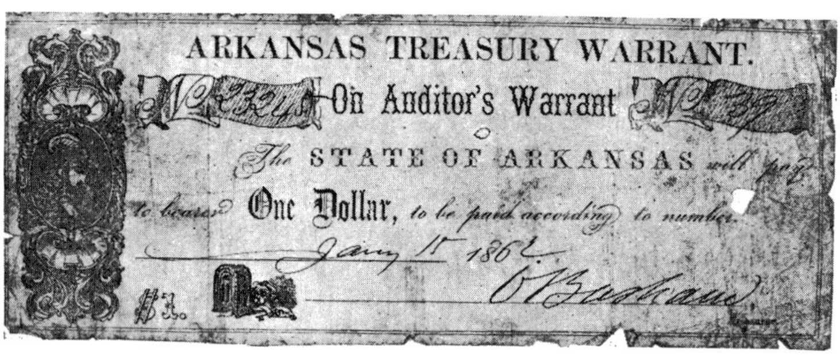

"On Auditor's Warrant," bust of maiden in oval at left.

22 $1 (11) white paper very rare

"On War Bond." Maiden in oval at left, state seal at center.

25 written denomination (10) white paper very rare

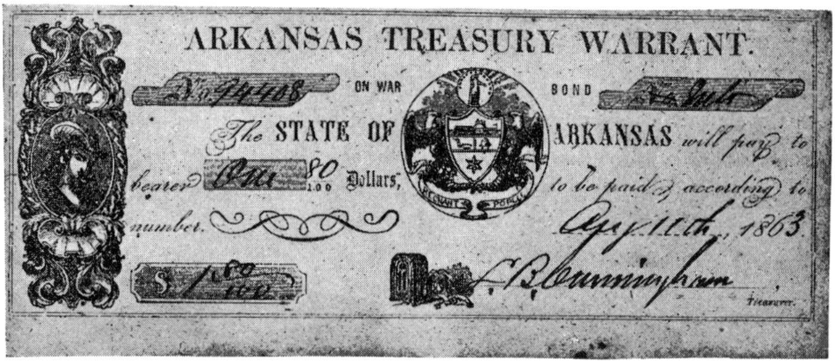

"On War Bond." Maiden in oval at left, state seal at center.

26	written denomination (7)	white paper	$50.00	$150.00
	"Arkansas Treasury Warrant" on back in green.			
26A	written denomination (10)	white paper	very rare	
	Same as above, but green overprint inverted.			
26AIB	written denomination (10)	white paper	extremely rare	

"Act of May 28, 1861"
"Redeemable Five Years After 1st July, 1861"

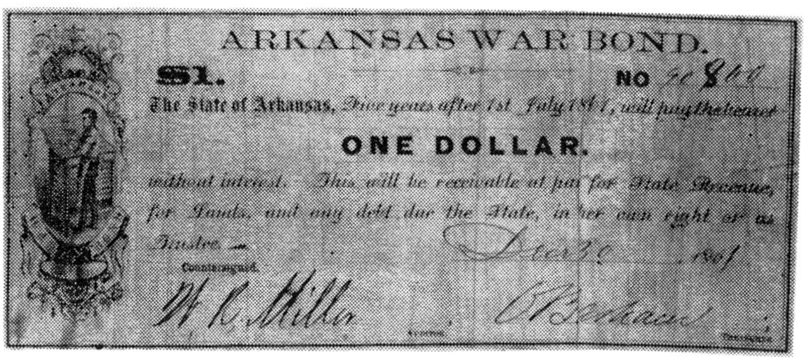

Printer in oval at left.

27	$1 (10)	very rare

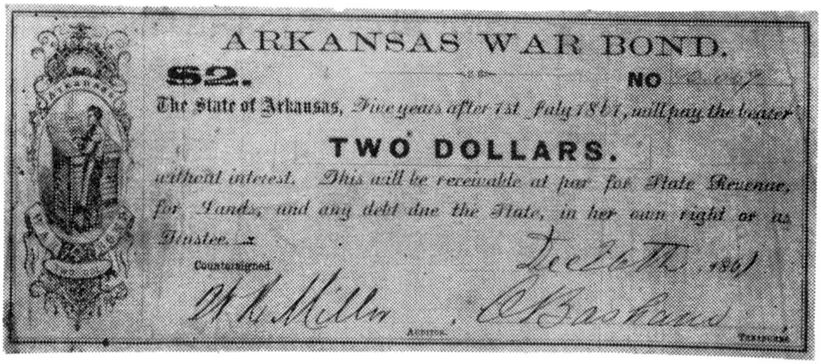

28	$2 (10)		very rare
29	$3 (10)	virtually identical to 27 and 28	very rare

Arkansas Treasury Warrants

The following five war issues were printed on both white and blue paper, and on the back of a bill of exchange. Then "Arkansas Treasury Warrant" was printed on the backs in green, blue or red. In the following listings, each color is listed as well as the word "NO" for instances where no overprint is present. This format should serve as a convenient check list for collectors.

In addition to the color varieties, three printer varieties exist. Notes may be found without an imprint, with "J.D. Butler.Print.Little Rock," or "Print.Little Rock." Listings of these notes should include an indication of the imprint:

"NP" for no imprint
"P1" for "J.D.Butler.Print.Little Rock"
"P2" for "Print.Little Rock."

A detailed listing could be 50B P2 green. This note would be a $5 denomination as listed as 50B with a green back overprint and with imprint "Print.Little Rock."

Bust of Jefferson Davis.
ALL SERIAL LETTER "A"

White paper.

30	$1 (7)	no green red blue	$25.00	$45.00
		Same as above, but "on War Bond" removed.		
30A	$1 (8)	no green red blue	$25.00	$45.00
		Same as 30 but back overprint inverted.		
31IB	$1 (8)	green red blue	$25.00	$45.00

			Same as above, but "on War Bond" removed.		
31AIB	$1 (9)		green red blue	$40.00	$65.00
			Blue paper.		
32	$1 (7)	no	green red blue	$30.00	$45.00
			Same as above, but "on War Bond" removed.		
32A	$1 (8)	no	green red blue	$45.00	$60.00
			Same as 32 but back overprint inverted.		
33IB	$1 (8)		green red blue	$45.00	$75.00
			Same as above, but "on War Bond" removed.		
33AIB	$1 (9)		green red blue	$50.00	$85.00
			Printed on back of a bill of exchange.		
34	$1 (7)	no	green red blue	$40.00	$65.00
			Same as above, but "on War Bond" removed.		
34A	$1 (9)	no	green red blue	$45.00	$70.00
			Same as 34 but back overprint inverted.		
35IB	$1 (8)		green red blue	$40.00	$60.00
			Same as above, but "on War Bond" removed.		
35AIB	$1 (9)		green red blue	$45.00	$75.00

Bust of Jefferson Davis.

ALL SERIAL LETTER "B"

			White paper.		
36	$2 (7)	no	green red blue	$35.00	$65.00
			Same as above, but "on War Bond" removed.		
36A	$2 (8)	no	green red blue	$35.00	$75.00
			Same as 36 but back overprint inverted.		
37IB	$2 (8)		green red blue	$35.00	$75.00
			Same as above, but "on War Bond" removed.		
37AIB	$2 (9)		green red blue	$65.00	$95.00
			Blue paper.		
38	$2 (7)	no	green red blue	$35.00	$65.00

			Same as above, but "on War Bond" removed.		
38A	$2 (9)	no	green red blue	$40.00	$75.00
			Same as 38 but back overprint inverted.		
39IB	$2 (8)		green red blue	$40.00	$75.00
			Same as above, but "on War Bond" removed.		
39AIB	$2 (9)		green red blue	$65.00	$95.00
			Printed on back of a bill of exchange.		
40	$2 (7)	no	green red blue	$35.00	$65.00
			Same as above, but "on War Bond" removed.		
40A	$2 (8)	no	green red blue	$35.00	$65.00
			Same as 40 but back overprint inverted.		
41IB	$2 (8)		green red blue	$40.00	$65.00
			Same as above, but "on War Bond" removed.		
41AIB	$2 (9)		green red blue	$65.00	$95.00

Bust of Jefferson Davis.

ALL SERIAL LETTER "C"

			White paper.		
42	$3 (7)	no	green red blue	$50.00	$95.00
			Same as above, but "on War Bond" removed.		
42A	$3 (8)		green red blue	$60.00	$110.00
			Same as 42 but back overprint inverted.		
43IB	$3 (8)		green red blue	$50.00	$95.00
			Same as above, but "on War Bond" removed.		
43AIB	$3 (9)		green red blue	$75.00	$125.00
			Blue paper.		
44	$3 (7)		green red blue	$65.00	$125.00
			Same as above, but "on War Bond" removed.		
44A	$3 (8)		green red blue	$70.00	$125.00
			Same as 44 but back overprint inverted.		
45IB	$3 (8)		green red blue	$75.00	$135.00
			Same as above, but "on War Bond" removed.		
45AIB	$3 (9)		green red blue	$75.00	$130.00

Printed on back of bill of exchange.

46	$3 (7) no	green red blue	$45.00	$80.00
	Same, but "on War Bond" removed.			
46A	$3 (8) no	green red blue	$75.00	$130.00
	Same as 46 but with back overprint inverted.			
47IB	$3 (8)	green red blue	$75.00	$135.00
	Same, but "on War Bond" removed, inverted overprint.			
47AIB	$3 (8)	green red blue	$75.00	$135.00

Bust of Governor H.M. Rector, slave carrying cotton at left.
ALL SERIAL LETTER "D"
white paper.

48	$5 (4) no	green red blue	$20.00	$30.00
	Same as above, but "on Auditor's Warrant" removed.			
48A	$5 (5) no	green red blue	$22.00	$35.00
	Same as 48 but "With interest at Eight Per Centum Per Annum" removed.			
48B	$5 (5) no	green red blue	$22.00	$35.00
	Same as 48A but "With interest at Eight Per Centum Per Annum" removed.			
48C	$5 (5) no	green red blue	$22.00	$35.00
	Same as 48 but only the word "Eight" removed, "six" written in.			
48D	$5 (5) no	green red blue	$25.00	$40.00
	Same as 48 but only the word "Eight" removed, "six" written in.			
48E	$5 (6) no	green red blue	$28.00	$40.00
	Same as 48, but back overprint inverted.			
49IB	$5 (6)	green red blue	$28.00	$40.00
	Same as above, but "on Auditor's Warrant" removed.			
49AIB	$5 (6)	green red blue	$28.00	$40.00
	Same as 49 but "With interest at Eight Per Centum Per Annum" removed.			
49BIB	$5 (6)	green red blue	$28.00	$40.00
	Same as 49A but "With interest at Eight Per Centum Per Annum" removed.			
49CIB	$5 (6)	green red blue	$28.00	$40.00
	Same as 49 but only the word "Eight" removed, "six" written.			
49DIB	$5 (5)	green red blue	$28.00	$40.00
	Same as 49A but only the word "Eight" removed, "six" written in.			
49EIB	$5 (4)	green red blue	$28.00	$40.00

Blue paper.

50 $5 (6) no green red blue $20.00 $30.00

Same as above, but "on Auditor's Warrant" removed.

50A $5 (4) no green red blue $20.00 $35.00

Same as 50 but "With interest at Eight Per Centum Per Annum" removed.

50B $5 (5) no green red blue $20.00 $30.00

Same as 50A but "With interest at Eight Per Centum Per Annum" removed "six" written in.

50C $5 (5) no green red blue $22.00 $40.00

Same as 50 but only the word "Eight" removed.

50D $5 (5) no green red blue $25.00 $45.00

Same as 50A but only the word "Eight" removed, "six" written in.

50E $5 (6) no green red blue $30.00 $45.00

Same as 50 but with back overprint inverted.

51IB $5 (7) green red blue $40.00 $55.00

Same as above, but "on Auditor's Warrant" removed.

51AIB $5 (7) green red blue $40.00 $60.00

Same as 51 but "With interest at Eight Per Centum Per Annum" removed.

51BIB $5 (7) green red blue $45.00 $65.00

Same as 51A but "With interest at Eight Per Centum Per Annum" removed.

51CIB $5 (7) green red blue $45.00 $65.00

Same as 51 but only the word "Eight" removed, "six" written in.

51DIB $5 (7) green red blue $45.00 $65.00

Same as 51A but only the word "Eight" removed, "six" written in.

51EIB $5 (7) green red blue $55.00 $70.00

Printed on back of a bill of exchange.

52 $5 (7) no green red blue $20.00 $3500

Same as above, but "on Auditor's Warrant" removed.

52A $5 (5) no green red blue $20.00 $35.00

Same as 52 but "With interest at Eight Per Centum Per Annum" removed.

52B $5 (6) no green red blue $20.00 $35.00

Same as 52A but "With interest at Eight Per Centum Per Annum" removed.

52C $5 (6) no green red blue $20.00 $35.00

Same as 52 but only the word "Eight" removed, "six" written in.

52D $5 (6) no green red blue $20.00 $36.00

Same as 52A but only the word "Eight" removed, "six" written in.

52E $5 (7) no green red blue $25.00 $45.00

Same as 52 but with back overprint inverted.

53IB $5 (7) green red blue $28.00 $50.00

Same as above, but "on Auditor's Warrant" removed.

53AIB $5 (7) green red blue $28.00 $50.00

Same as 53 but "With interest at Eight Per Centum Per Annum" removed.

53BIB $5 (7) green red blue $28.00 $50.00

Same as 53A but "With interest at Eight Per Centum Per Annum" removed.

53CIB $5 (7) green red blue $30.00 $55.00

Same as 53 but only the word "Eight" removed, "six" written in.

53DIB $5 (7) green red blue $30.00 $55.00

Same as 53A but only the word "Eight" removed, "six" written in.

53EIB $5 (8) green red blue $45.00 $65.00

Bust of Samuel Adams, slave carrying cotton at left.
All Serial letter "D."

White paper.

54 $10 (6) no green red blue $20.00 $35.00

Same as above, but "on Auditor's Warrant" removed.

54A $10 (6) no green red blue $20.00 $35.00

Same as 54 but "With interest at Eight Per Centum Per Annum" removed.

54B $10 (7) no green red blue $20.00 $35.00

Same as 54A but "With interest at Eight Per Centum Per Annum" removed.

54C $10 (7) no green red blue $20.00 $35.00

Same as 54 but only the word "Eight" removed, "six" written in.

54D $10 (7) no green red blue $20.00 $35.00

Same as 54A but only the word "Eight" removed, "six" written in.

54E $10 (8) no green red blue $20.00 $35.00

Same as 54, but back overprint inverted.
55 $10 (8) green red blue $20.00 $35.00
Same as above, but "on Auditor's Warrant" removed.
55AIB $10 (9) green red blue $40.00 $65.00
Same as 55but "With interest at Eight Per Centum Per Annum" removed.
55BIB $10 (9) green red blue $40.00 $65.00
Same as 55A but "With interest at Eight Per Centum Per Annum" removed.
55CIB $10 (9) green red blue $40.00 $ 65.00
Same as 55 but only the word "Eight" removed, "six" written in.
55DIB $10 (5) green red blue $50.00 $70.00
Same as 55A but only the word "Eight" removed, "six" written in.
55EIB $10 (4) green red blue $60.00 $90.00
Blue paper.
56 $10 (6) no green red blue $20.00 $35.00
Same as above, but "on Auditor's Warrant" removed.
56A $10 (6) no green red blue $20.00 $35.00
Same as 56 but "With interest at Eight Per Centum Per Annum" removed.
56B $10 (7) no green red blue $20.00 $35.00
Same as 56A but "With interest at Eight Per Centum Per Annum" removed.
56C $10 (7) no green red blue $20.00 $35.00
Same as 56 but only the word "Eight" removed, "six" written in.
56D $10 (7) no green red blue $20.00 $35.00
Same as 56A but only the word "Eight" removed, "six" written in.
56E $10 (8) no green red blue $25.00 $40.00
Same as 56 but with back overprint inverted.
57IB $10 (8) green red blue $25.00 $40.00
Same as above, but "on Auditor's Warrant" removed.
57AIB $10 (8) green red blue $25.00 $45.00
Same as 57 but "With interest at Eight Per Centum Per Annum" removed.
57BIB $10 (8) green red blue $25.00 $45.00
Same as 57A but "With interest at Eight Per Centum Per Annum" removed.
57CIB $10 (8) green red blue $25.00 $45.00
Same as 57 but only the word "Eight" removed,"six" written in.
57DIB $10 (8) green red blue $25.00 $40.00
Same as 57A but only the word "Eight" removed, "six" written in.
57EIB $10 (9) green red blue $50.00 $95.00
Printed on back of a bill of exchange.
58 $10 (6) no green red blue $20.00 $35.00
Same as above, but "on Auditor's Warrant" removed.
58A $10 (7) no green red blue $20.00 $35.00
Same as 58 but "With interest at Eight Per Centum Per Annum" removed.
58B $10 (7) no green red blue $20.00 $35.00
Same as 58A but "With interest at Eight Per Centum Per Annum" removed.
58C $10 (7) no green red blue $20.00 $30.00
Same as 58 but only the word "Eight" removed, "six" written in.
58D $10 (7) no green red blue, "six" written in $20.00 $30.00

Same as 58A but only the word "Eight" removed, "six" written in.

58E $10 (8) no green red blue $25.00 $35.00

Same as 58 but with back overprint inverted.

59IB $10 (8) green red blue $35.00 $45.00

Same as above, but "on Auditor's Warrant" removed.

59AIB $10 (9) green red blue $50.00 very rare

Same as 59 but "With interest at Eight Per Centum Per Annum" removed.

59BIB $10 (9) green red blue $50.00 very rare

Same as 59A but "With interest at Eight Per Centum Per Annum" removed.

59CIB $10 (9) green red blue $50.00 very rare

Same as 59 but only the word "Eight" removed, "six" written in.

59DIB $10 (9) green red blue $55.00 very rare

Same as 59A but only the word "Eight" removed, "six" written in.

59EIB $10 (10) green red blue extremely rare

Authorized by Act of March 16th, 1871.
"National Bank Note Co., New York."

Written dates 1871 to 1875.

Black with brown overprint, intricate brown back.
Farmer with sickle, bushel of corn left.

60 $1 (11) B extremely rare

Black with brown overprint, intricate brown back.
Three children center, hunter and dog left, mother and child at right.

62 $5 (11) no serial letter extremely rare

Black with brown overprint, intricate brown back.
Load of cotton drawn by a double team, Ceres at left.

63 $10 (9) no serial letter $500.00 $1200.00

Green and black, green back.

63A $10 (11) no serial letter extremely rare

* * * * *

Authorized by an Act of January 20th, 1875.

Fancy green network covers face of note, "One" in red.

64 $1 (11) no serial letter extremely rare

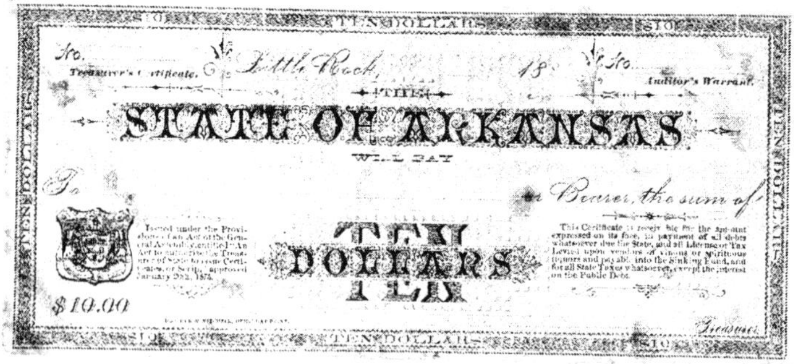

Fancy green network over face of note.

65 $10 (11) no serial letter extremely rare

Florida Republic

On June 29, 1817 the Scottish adventurer Gregor MacGregor with a force mainly recruited in Georgia and South Carolina but acting under the authorization of South American patriot representatives, seized the town of Fernandina on Amelia Island as a first step toward the liberation of Florida from Spanish rule. He proclaimed the establishment of a Republic of the Floridas and even gave it a flag, consisting of a green cross on field of white.

An obvious precedent for the Florida Republic of 1817 was the Florida Republic of 1812, which included Amelia Island and a somewhat larger swath of northeastern Florida. In 1812 however, the leaders and followers were almost without exception Anglo-Americans, and they received quite open support from the government of the United States, which expected that independence would be a brief transitional phase pending formal annexation. United States military forces even participated openly in the adventure, which collapsed when the authorities in Washington withdrew support in the face of European diplomatic pressure. In 1817, by contrast, while most members of the MacGregor expedition were United States citizens, the leader was a Venezuelan general of Scottish origin, and the idea that lay behind it was a by-product of the Spanish American movement for independence that had been raging since 1810.

While Texans still fly the Lone Star flag and revere the men who lived and fought under it, the green cross of Florida is unknown to the overwhelming majority of the state's current population. The 29th of June is not a public holiday even in Fernandina. The events of 1817 at Amelia Island are mentioned in the literature of Florida history, but hardly in a way calculated to promote state chauvinism, Texas-styled. MacGregor himself is generally portrayed as a well-intentioned if somewhat misguided figure.

At the time, MacGregor created at least the skeleton of a "national" government for the Republic of the Floridas. He established a post office and also introduced a printing press, much as any self-respecting republic had to have and Florida had not had since the end of British rule. But he did not wait for it to be set in working order to begin the stream of official proclamations and decrees for which he would perhaps be best remembered. Among other things these served to confer honors on his victorious forces, summon all right minded Floridians to assist them, and set a price on the head of George Clarke, once he made very clear that he did not intend to collaborate. There was an embryonic financial system, with levies on departing passengers (who must purchase passports for fifty cents at the Fernandina post office) and likewise on the sale of prize goods, for whose disposition an admiralty court was established under John D. Heath, a former judge from South Carolina. The land warrants that MacGregor had given out before his arrival were now supplemented by negotiable certificates--signed by MacGregor and his official secretary, Jose de Iribarren--that could be used in payment of duties at the customhouse.

By triggering the intervention of United States forces, the establishment of the Florida Republic in 1817 served as prologue to the annexation of all Florida under the terms of the Adams-Onis Treaty of 1821. The episode did not produce memorable examples of valor or self sacrifice by either insurgents of loyalist or United States occupiers, nor much less any innovative approaches to political and economic development. But certainly Amelia Island under the rule of MacGregor was something more than the piratical den of thieves that still appears in so much of the literature of Florida history. Most importantly for purposes here, paper money *was* issued!

The above information is taken nearly verbatim from "The Florida Republic: an Overview" by David Bushnell, in Publication Number 412, Pan American Institute of Geography and History, 1986. *The illustration of a $1.00 note in the listings is also from Publication 412. Permission to use this material is gratefully acknowledged.*

Issue authorized in June of 1817, with the first actual examples known dated in August of the same year. It is likely that the first design (shown below) was a hand-drawn piece. No examples of this type are reported. The picture is of a "facsimile" in "Archivo Historico National Bogota, Historia, Anexo, Tomo 25, Folio 494."

August 19, 1817
Without printers' imprint.

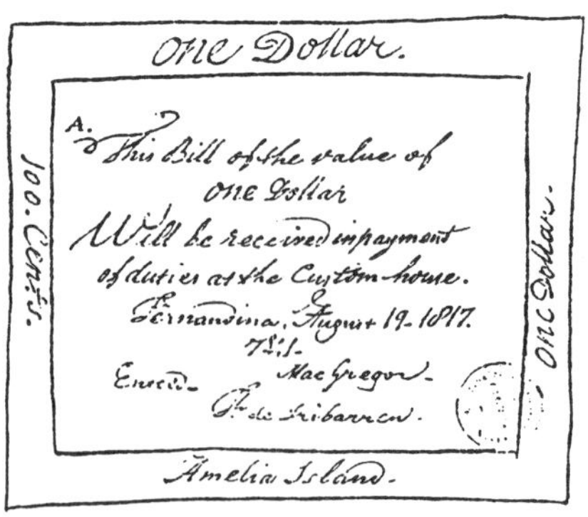

FR1 $1 no issued pieces reported

Printed piece issued August 19, 1817

Hand signed, signatures in brown ink

FR10 6 1/4 cents (11) unique

Notes: other denominations probably exist. Reports of *any* examples of these notes are needed. Credit or confidentiality is guaranteed.

THE TERRITORY OF FLORIDA

An Act of the Legislative Council of the Territory, approved November 22, 1828, directed the treasurer to issue $10,000 in notes from 12.5 cents to $5 denominations, "on good silk paper."

The pieces listed are believed to have been issued. Anyone with additional information of any kind is urged to correspond with the author.

T1	12 1/2c	no information available	
T2	25c	no information available	

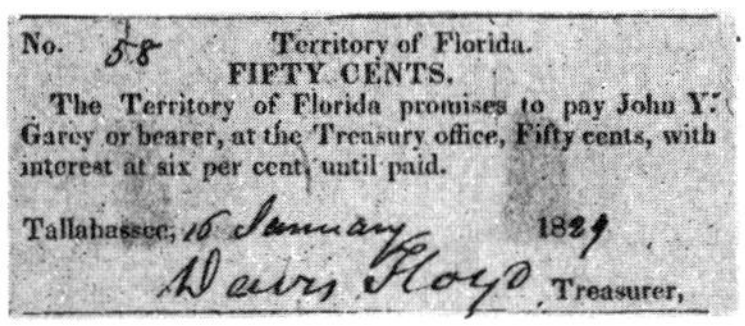

T3	50c (10)	no serial letter	very rare

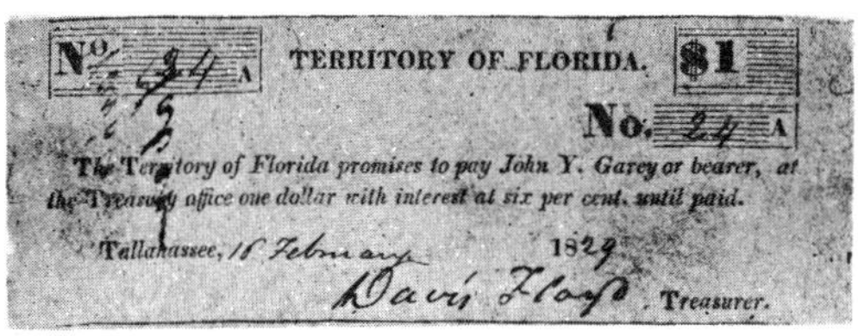

Typeset format, same for all denominatios.

T4	$1 (10)	A	very rare
T5	$2 (10)	B	very rare
T6	$3 (10)	B	very rare
T7	$5 (10)	C	very rare

"N. & S. S. Jocelyn, New Haven."

Although these notes were authorized under the same act as the preceding, they did not appear until 1829. Therefore, they have dates (written) 1829 to 1831.

Ceres and eagle, Washington at left.

T8	$1 (9)	No serial letter	$1000.00 $1500.00

Hope seated, Ceres at left.

T9 $2 (9) No serial letter $1000.00 $1500.00

Justice left, bust of Washington at center.

T10 $3 (9) no serial letter $1600.00 $2200.00

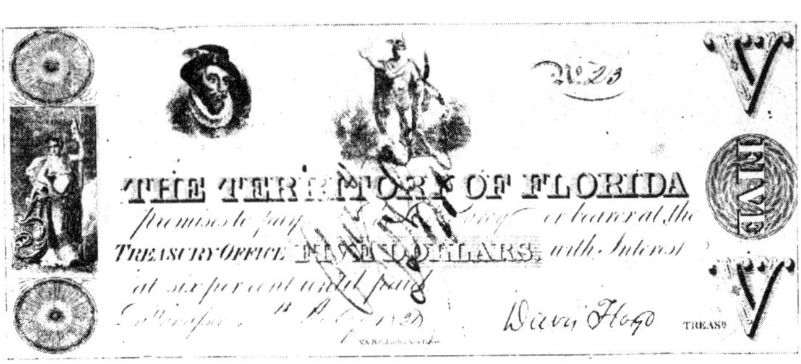

Liberty left, bust of Sir Walter Raleigh, Mercury at center.

T11 $5 (9) no serial letter $1000.00 $1500.00

THE STATE OF FLORIDA

Issue of 1861, over $1,000,000.

"Hoyer & Ludwig. Richmond, Va."

All dated "Oct. 10th, 1861."

1. $500 no information available

Ceres seated.

2 $100 (8) H $90.00 $200.00

Ceres seated.

3 $50 (8) G $75.00 $150.00

Error: same as above except "Fifty" under Florida is inverted.

3A $50 (9) G $175.00 $350.00

"L" and "50" at left have been switched in position.

3B $50 (8) G $165.00 $250.00

Ceres seated.

4 $20 (7) F $60.00 $140.00

Ceres seated.

5 $10 (7) E $60.00 $125.00

Ceres seated.

6 $5 (7) D $60.00 $125.00

Written dates ("186" Printed) of 1861

The first issue of $1, $2, and $3 notes are supposed to bear the date "Oct. 9th or 10th, 1861." Later issues bear various other monthly dates.

Washington left, Tellus seated at right, "THREE" at upper right.

7 $3 (8) C $60.00 $175.00

Washington left, Tellus seated at right, no "THREE" at upper right.

7A $3 (8) C $60.00 $150.00

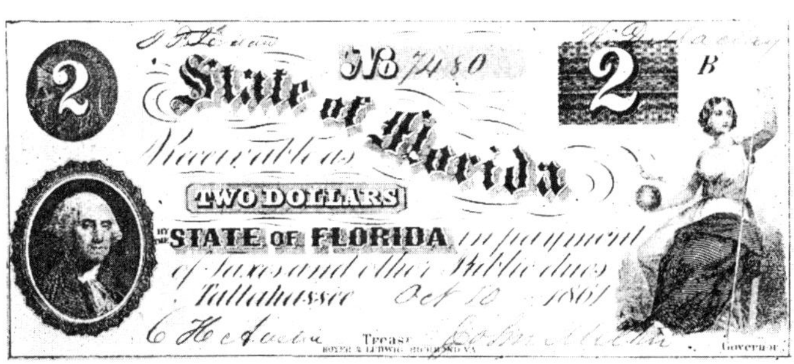

Washington left, Tellus seated at right, "TWO" at upper right.

8 $2 (8) B $40.00 $125.00

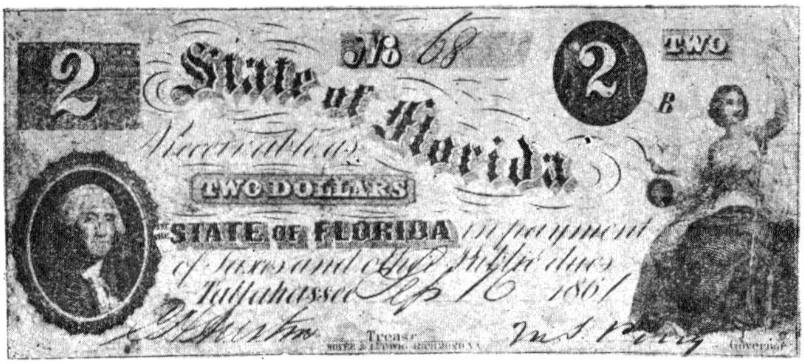

Washington left, Tellus seated at right, no "TWO" at upper right.

8A $2 (7) B $40.00 $125.00

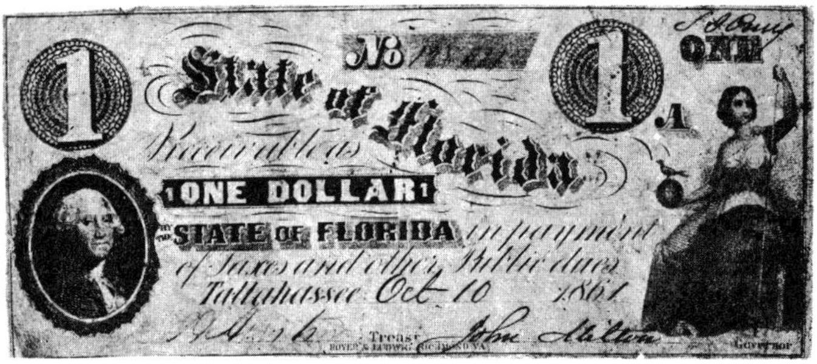

Washington left, Tellus seated at right, "ONE" at upper right.

9 $1 (8) A $40.00 $125.00

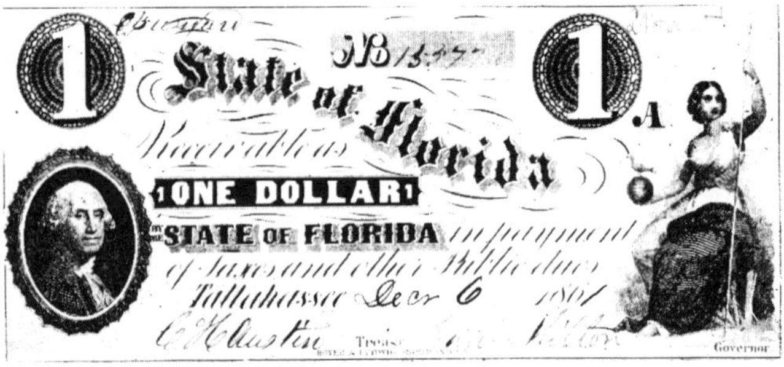

Washington left, Tellus seated at right, no "ONE" at upper right.

9A $1 (7) A $40.00 $125.00

Issue of 1862, About $1,000,000.

"Hoyer & Ludwig. Richmond, Va."
All dated "January 1, 1862."

Ceres seated between Commerce and Navigation, slaves carrying cotton at left.

10 $100 (9) H $225.00 $475.00

Serial letters are just "II" and "II"

10A $100 (10) H $260.00 $500.00

Ceres seated between Commerce and Navigation, slaves carrying cotton at left.

11 $50 (8) G $190.00 $325.00

Ceres seated between Commerce and Navigation, slaves carrying cotton at left.

12 $20 (8) F $80.00 $225.00

With fancy letter "F.".

12A $20 (8) F $80.00 $175.00

Ceres seated between Commerce and Navigation, slaves carrying cotton at left.

13	$10 (7)	E	$50.00	$165.00
13A	$10 (6)	Same as 13, but fancy letter E	$50.00	$150.00

Ceres seated between Commerce and Navigation, slaves carrying cotton at left.

14 $5 (7) A $45.00 $125.00

May 1862

Very likely a unique treasury document converted over by the state treasurer and the governor, this warrant was payable for $80,000 to the state treasurer from the assistant quartermaster at Tallahassee. The funds were to be paid by John Boston, Depository, and Collector of Customs at the Port of Savannah. The state treasurer re-endorsed the document, as a state warrant, to the governor of Florida, who then re-endorsed it to the president of the Planter's Bank of Savannah.

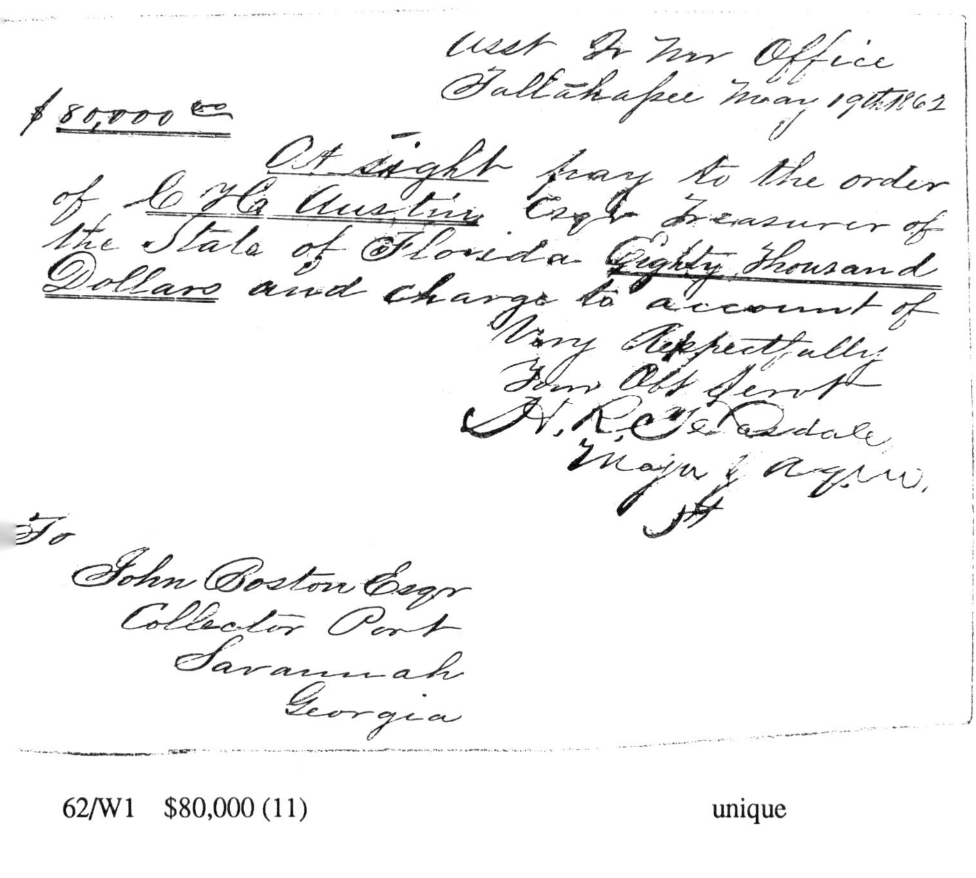

Asst Qr Mr Office
Tallahassee May 19th 1862

$80,000 00/100

At sight pay to the order of C H Austin Esqr Treasurer of the State of Florida Eighty Thousand Dollars and charge to account of

Very Respectfully
Your Obt Servt
H. R. Teasdale
Major & Asst Q.M.

To
John Boston Esqr
Collector Port
Savannah
Georgia

62/W1 $80,000 (11) unique

Issue of 1863, About $500,000.

"Keatinge & Ball. Columbia, S.C."

All dated "March 1st, 1863."

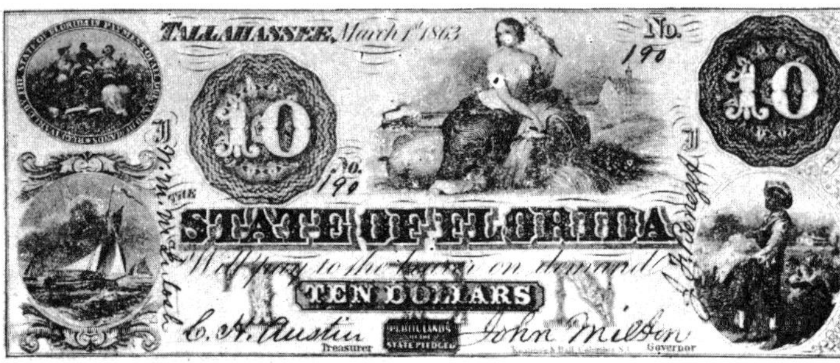

Black with red overprint.
Ceres seated, ship at left, slave with cotton right.

15 $10 (6) J $70.00 $125.00

Black with red overprint.
Moneta seated, Indian at left.

16 $5 (6) J $70.00 $125.00

Sailing ship center, hope at right, black with red overprint.

17 $3 (6) J $95.00 $150.00

Railway train at center, Ceres left, Indian maiden at right, black with red overprint.

18 $2 (6) J $70.00 $125.00

Child at left, slave with cotton center, black with red overprint.

19 $1 (6) J $70.00 $125.00

* * * * * * * * *

FRACTIONAL NOTES

No Printers' Imprint, No Serial Letters

"All Dated "Feb'y. 2nd, 1863"

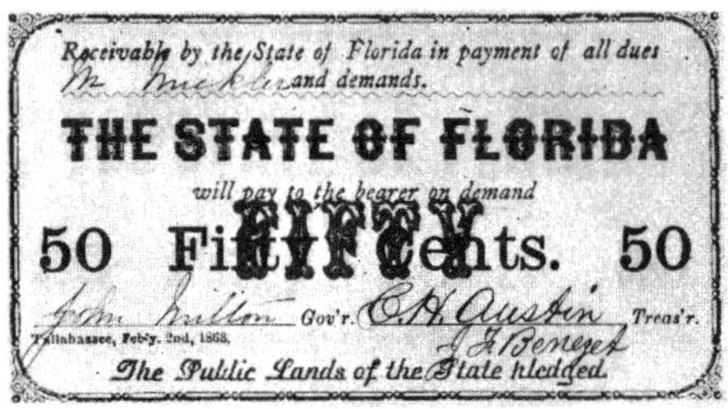

Black, red, blue, note *two* spaces for signatures.

20	50c (4)	Plain back, unwatermarked	$15.00	$25.00
20A	50c (6)	Printed on backs of Florida notes	$45.00	$90.00
20B	50c (6)	Printed on backs of Florida bonds	$45.00	$90.00
21	50c (7)	Plain back, watermarked "W.T.& Co."	$75.00	$125.00

Black, red, and blue, note *one* space for signature.

22	50c (5)	Plain back, unwatermarked	$30.00	$75.00
22A	50c (7)	Printed on backs of Florida notes	$35.00	$90.00
22B	50c (7)	Printed on backs of Florida bonds	$30.00	$85.00
23	50c (7)	Plain back, watermarked "W.T.& Co."	$100.00	$150.00
23A	50c (8)	Plain back, watermarked "Ten"	$150.00	$180.00

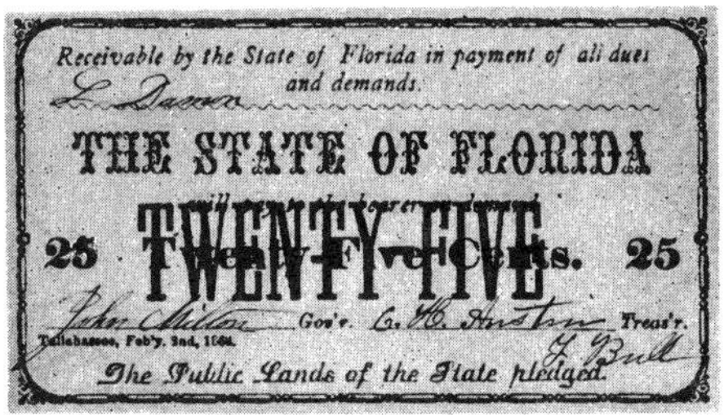

Black, red, blue, note *two* spaces for signature.

24	25c (4)	Plain back, unwatermarked	$20.00	$30.00
24A	25c (6)	Printed on backs of Florida notes	$45.00	$90.00
24B	25c (7)	Printed on backs of Florida bonds	$45.00	$90.00
25	25c (7)	Plain back, watermarked "W.T. & Co."	$75.00	$125.00

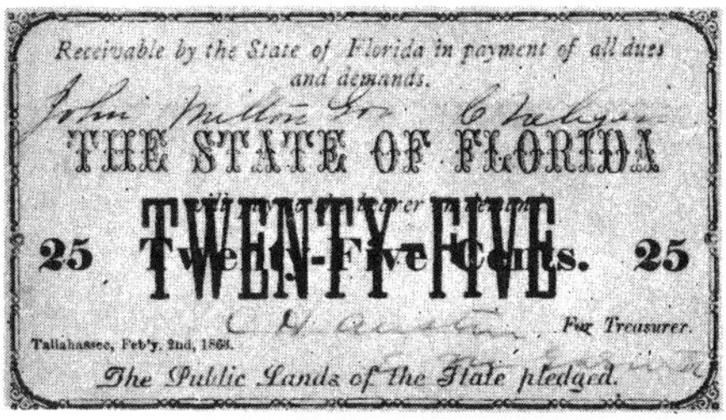

Black, red, blue, note *one* space for signatures.

26	25c (5)	Plain back, unwatermarked	$20.00	$35.00
26A	25c (7)	Printed on backs of Florida notes	$30.00	$65.00
26B	25c (7)	Printed on backs of Florida bonds	$30.00	$65.00
27	25c (7)	Plain back, watermarked "W.T.& Co."	$100.00	$150.00
27A	25c (10)	Plain back, watermarked "Ten"	$150.00	$180.00

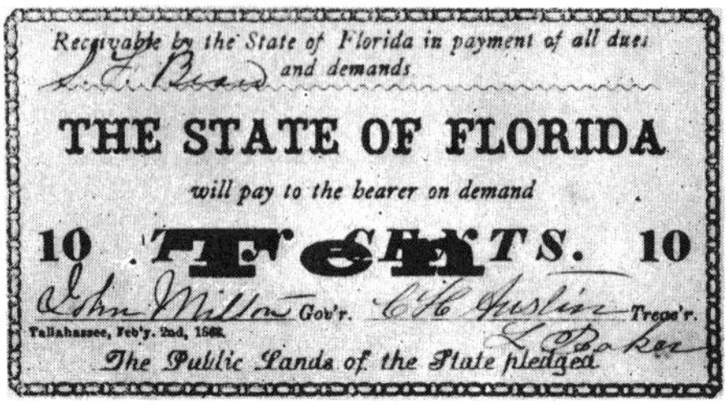

Black, red, and blue, note *two* spaces for signature.

28	10c (5)	Plain back, unwatermarked	$15.00	$30.00
28A	10c (7)	Printed on backs of Florida notes	$45.00	$80.00
28B	10c (6)	Printed on backs of Florida bonds	$45.00	$80.00
29	10c (7)	Plain back, watermarked "W.T.& Co."	$75.00	$110.00

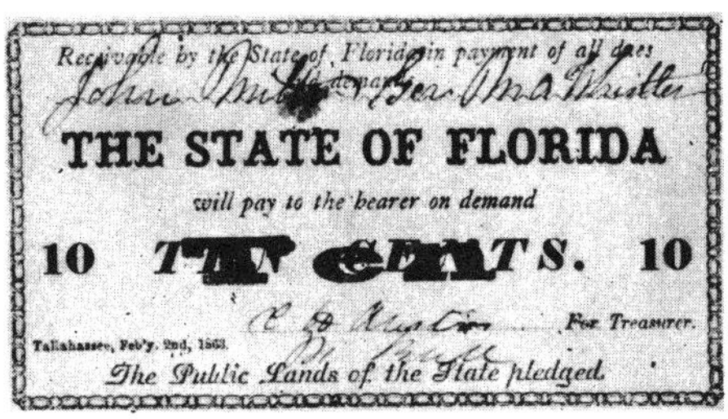

Black, red, blue, note *one* space for signatures.

30	10c (6)	Plain back, unwatermarked	$15.00	$30.00
30A	10c (7)	Printed on backs of Florida notes	$20.00	$50.00
30B	10c (7)	Printed on backs of Florida bonds	$25.00	$60.00
31	10c (7)	Plain back, watermarked "W.T.& Co."	$100.00	$150.00
31A	10c (10)	Plain back, watermarked "Ten"	extremely rare	
31B	10c (10)	Plain back, watermarked "Five"	extremely rare	

Issue of 1864, About $500,000.

"Keatinge & Ball. Columbia, S.C."

All dated "March 1st, 1864."

Ceres seated, ship at left, slave with cotton right, red and black.

32	$10 (7)	J unwatermarked	$60.00	$125.00
33	$10 (8)	J watermarked "W.T. & Co."	$80.00	$150.00

Moneta seated, Indian at left, red and black.

34	$5 (7)	J unwatermarked	$60.00	$125.00
35	$5 (8)	J watermarked "W.T. & Co."	$80.00	$150.00

Dated "Jany. 1st, 1864."

Sailing ship center, hope at right, black with red overprint.

36	$3 (10)	J	unwatermarked	very rare	
37	$3 (6)	J	watermarked "W.T. & Co."	$100.00	$150.00

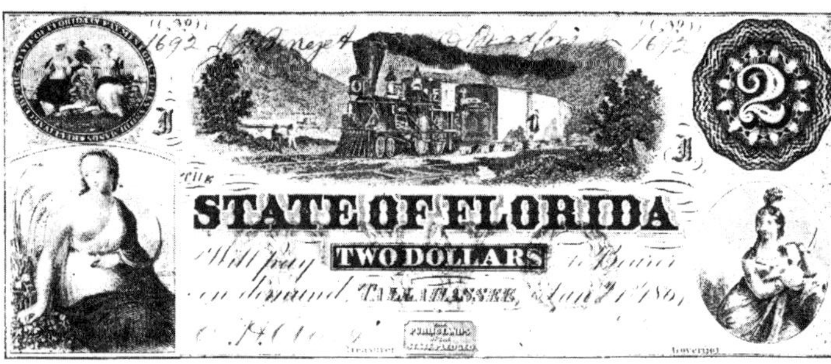

Railway train at center, Ceres left, Indian maiden at right, black with red overprint.

38	$2 (10)	J	unwatermarked	very rare	
39	$2 (6)	J	watermarked "W.T. & Co."	$60.00	$125.00

Slave carrying cotton, child at left., black with red overprint.

40	$1 (10)	J	unwatermarked	very rare	
41	$1 (6)	J	watermarked "W.T. & Co."	$60.00	$125.00

Issue of 1865, (Amount Unknown)

No Printers' Name

All dated "Jan. 1st, 1865."
Printed on the backs of Florida notes.

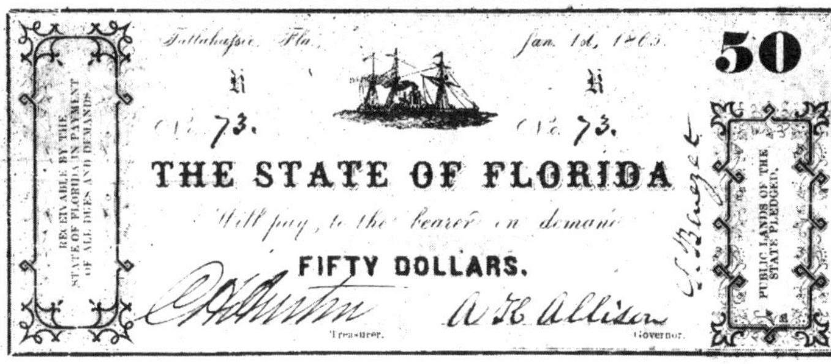

Steamship at center.

42 $50 (8) B $600.00 $1200.00

43 $100 (9) B $1000.00 $1600.00

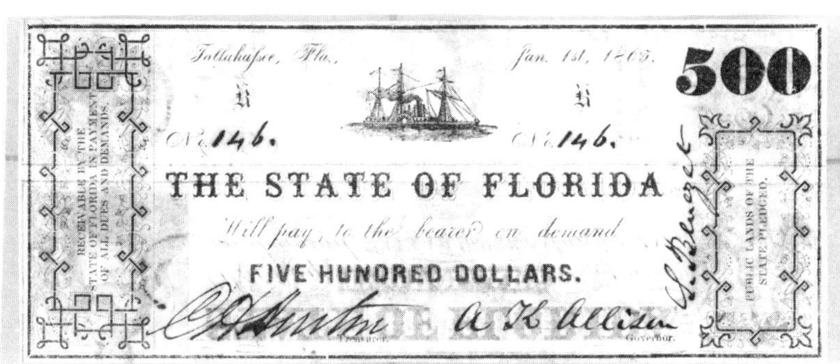

44 $500 (11) B $10,000 $20,000

$250,000 Issue
Authorized Under Acts of February and March 1870
(The amount actually issued was probably very small.)

All dated "March 1st, 1870"

"National Bank Note Co. New York."

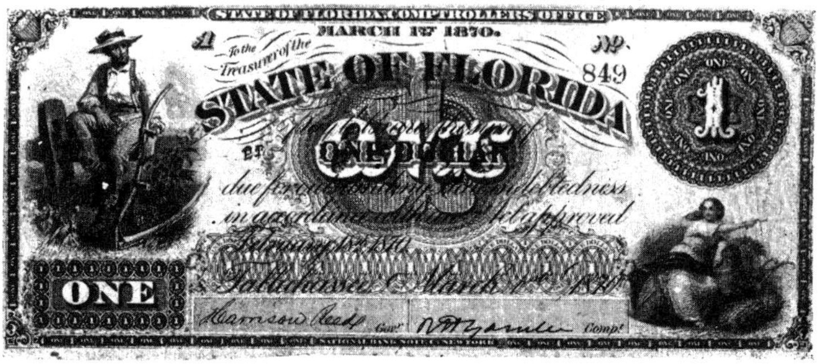

Farmer with sickle left, Ceres right. Black with green overprint. Ornate green back.

45	$1 (9)	A B C D	$800.00	$1200.00
46	$3	No information available		
47	$5	No information available		
48	$20	No information available		

"Peter Bowes, 68 Camp St, New Orleans"
186- (probably 1867) Issue

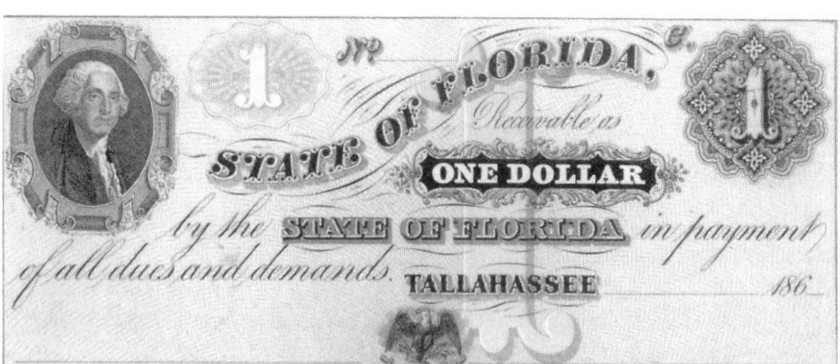

Ornate red lithograph, Washington left.

67	$1 (10)	C	very rare

Ornate green lithograph.

67F $20 (11) H extremely rare

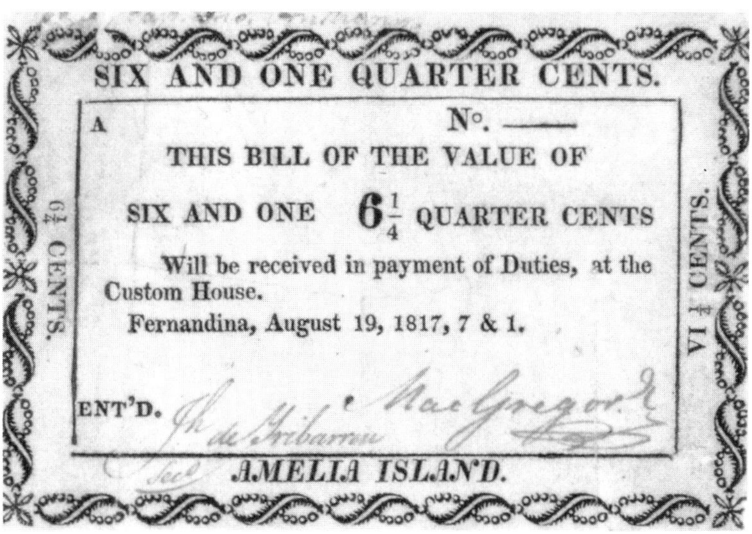

6 1/4 cents (FR10 listed on page 194)

THE STATE OF GEORGIA

$2,500,000 Authorized by Act of Dec. 5th, 1861.

"Douglas. Eng'r. N. Orleans."
Dated "January 15, 1862."

Ceres standing at center holding grain. Sailor in ovals left and right. Treasury seal on each end of face. Design printed over "ONE HUNDRED DOLLARS." Printed in red.

1	$100 (7)	serial letter A	$20.00	$45.00
1A	$100 (9)	as 1 with two seals left	$50.00	$125.00

Ceres standing at center holding grain. Justice in ovals left and right, Governor Joseph E. Brown left and right of Ceres. Treasury seal on each end of face. Design printed over "FIFTY DOLLARS." Printed in red.

2	$50 (4)	serial letter A	$20.00	$45.00
2A	$50 (9)	as 2 with two seals left	$50.00	$125.00

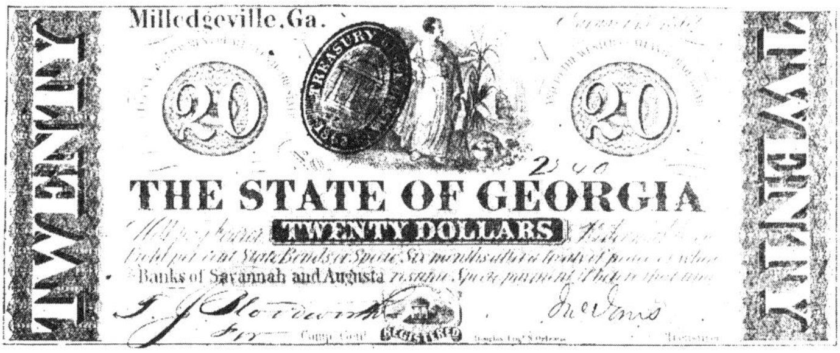

Ceres standing at center holding grain. "TWENTY" left and right, "20" left and right of Ceres. Treasury seal on face. Design printed over "TWENTY DOLLARS." Printed in red.

3	$20 (8)	serial letter A	$20.00	$55.00
3A	$20 (4)	no engraver's name	$17.50	$40.00

Ceres standing at center holding grain. "TEN" left and right, "X" left and right of Ceres. Treasury seal face. Design printed over "TEN DOLLARS." Printed in red.

4	$10 (3)	serial letter A	$12.00	$20.00

Error: red designs inverted and printed across lower part of Ceres figure.

4A	$10 (9)	serial letter A	$25.00	$35.00

James Oglethorpe in military dress, red design printed over "FIVE DOLLARS," treasury seal on back.

5	$5 (2)	serial letter A	$10.00	$18.00

Error: red design is inverted and printed across the head and shoulders.

5A	$5 (9)	serial letter A	$40.00	$65.00

Error: red overprint on back, not face.

5B	$5 (9)	A	$150.00 $200.00

Error: printed on both sides. One side is signed, the other has the red overprint and treasury seal.

5C	$5 (11)	A	extremely rare

Error: impression of a Confederate note and a block of Confederate stamps on the back.

5D	$5 (11)	serial letter A	extremely rare

$5,000,000 Authorized by Act of "Dec. 12th, 1862."

"Howell, Savannah."

Dated "February 1st, 1863."

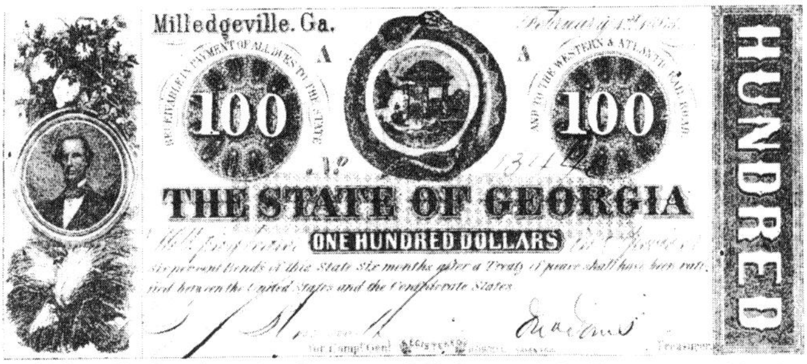

State arms within coil of rattlesnake, Governor J. E. Brown left. Treasury seal in black on back. Red design printed over "ONE HUNDRED DOLLARS."

6	$100 (5)	serial letter A with control stamp	$12.00	$35.00
		Error: red overprint on back with control stamp.		
6A	$100 (11)	serial letter A	extremely rare	
6B	$100 (8)	as 6 without control stamps	$30.00	$50.00
6C	$100 (8)	two seals on back	$35.00	$65.00

Dated "February 2d, 1863."

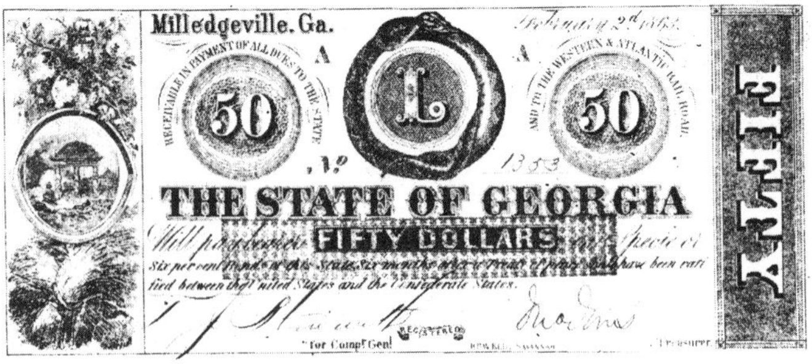

Roman numeral "L" within coil of rattlesnake. Treasury seal in black on back. Red design printed over "FIFTY DOLLARS."

7	$50 (4)	serial letter A with control stamp	$10.00	$25.00

7A	$50 (7)	as 7 without control stamps	$15.00	$35.00
7B	$50 (8)	two seals on back	$22.50	$50.00

Dated "February 2d, 1863."

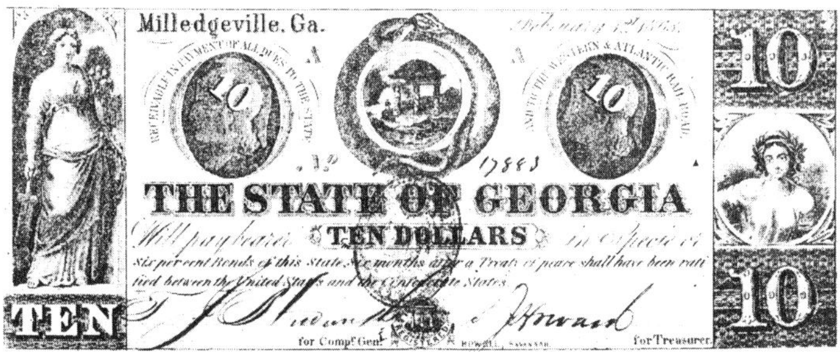

State arms within coil of rattlesnake, Minerva left, Ceres right. Treasury seal on face in red.

8	$10 (3)	Serial letter A	$8.00	$20.00

"Howell. Engraver."

Dated "January 1st, 1863."

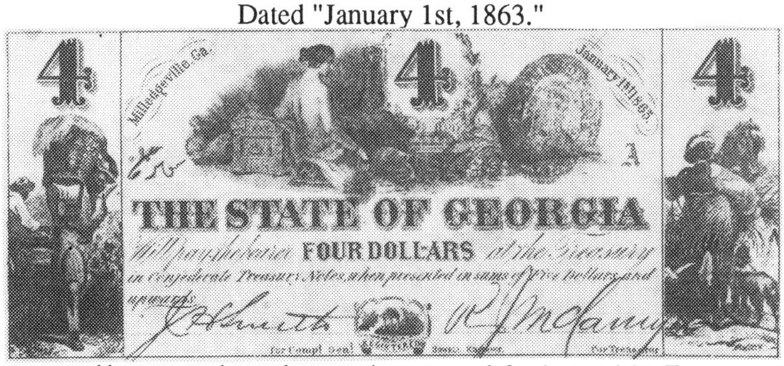

Moneta seated by treasure chests, slave carrying cotton at left, wheat at right. Treasury seal in green on face.

9	$4 (9)	serial letter A	$700.00	$2500.00

Horses drinking, Minerva left, justice right. Treasury seal on face in green.

10	$3 (9)	serial letter A	$800.00	$2750.00

Steamship at sea, treasury seal on face in green.

11	$2 (4)	serial letter A	$15.00	$40.00

Treasury seal on face in red.

11A	$2 (5)	serial letter A	$20.00	$60.00

No treasury seal.

11B	$2 (7)	serial letter A	$75.00	$175.00

Railway train, treasury seal on face in green.

12	$1 (4)	A B C D E F G H I J K	$15.00	$40.00

Treasury seal on face in red.

12A	$1 (5)	A B C D E F G H I J K	$20.00	$45.00
12B	$1 (7)	as 12 but no treasury seal	$75.00	$150.00

"Eng'd by R. H. Howell."

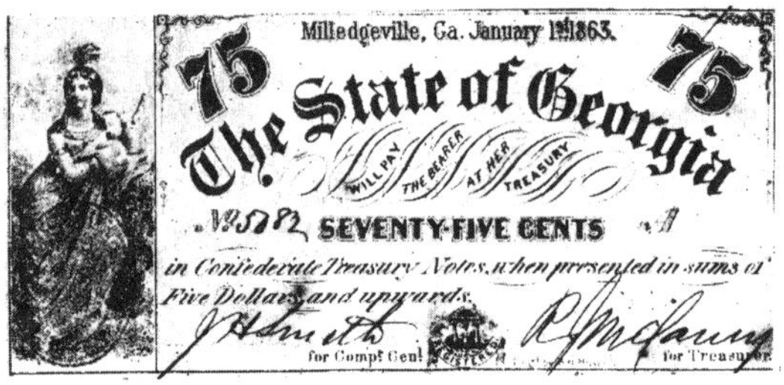

Indian maiden at left.

13	75C (6)	Serial letter A	$150.00	$475.00

"Howell. Engraver."

Group of workmen, 25 and 50-cent denominations similar.

		Treasury seal on face in green.		
14	50c (2)	A B C D E F G H I K L M N O P	$8.00	$12.00
		Treasury seal on face in red.		
14A	50c (5)	A B C D E F G H I J K L M N O P	$10.00	$25.00
		Treasury seal on face in green.		
15	25c (2)	A B C D E F G H I J K	$8.00	$12.00
		Treasury seal on face in red		
15A	25c (5)	A B C D E F G H I J K	$10.00	$25.00
15B	25c (9)	no seal at all	$75.00	$125.00

"Eng'd. by R. H. Howell."

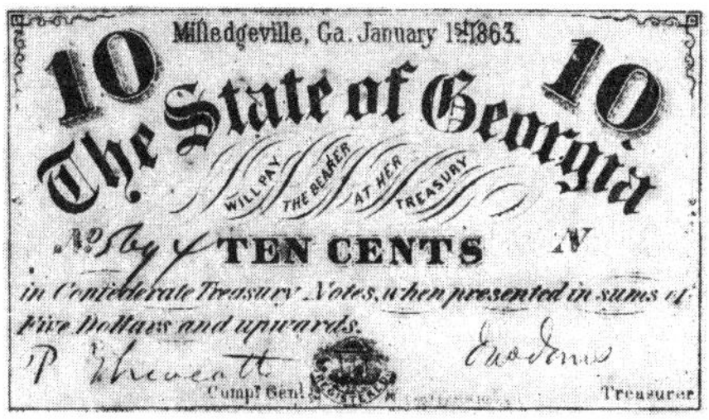

5-, 10-, 15- and 20-cent designs similar except for denomination.

16	20c (8)	serial letter A	$150.00	$350.00
17	15c (6)	A B C D E F G H I J K L M N O P Q R	$40.00	$75.00
18	10c (3)	A B C D E F G H I J K L M N O P Q R	$8.00	$12.00
19	5c (4)	A B C D E F G H I J K L M N O P Q R	$8.00	$12.00

$12,000,000 Authorized by act of Dec. 1863.

"Howell. Eng'r."

Dated "April 6th, 1864."

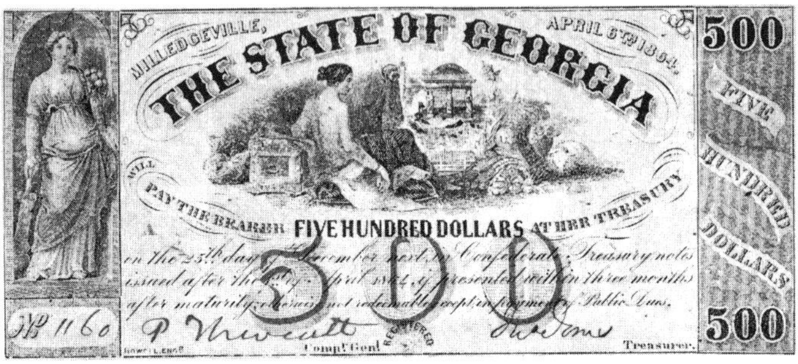

Moneta seated, state arms in background, Minerva left, "500" in red.

20	$500 (9)	serial letter A	$275.00	$1200.00

Same as above with "100" in red.

21	$100 (6)	serial letter A	$28.00	$65.00

Moneta seated, state arms in background, "50" in red.

22	$50 (5)	serial letter A	$20.00	$47.50

Treasury seal on face in green ($5, 10, 20).

23	$20 (4)	serial letter A	$15.00	$55.00

Large serial letter.

24	$10 (4)	A B C D E F G H I J K	$5.00	$20.00

Small serial letter.

25	$10 (3)	A B C D E F G H I J K	$5.00	$20.00
26	$5 (3)	A B C D E F G H I J K	$5.00	$17.50

Dated "January 1st, 1864."

The following dates are exactly the same as those illustrated for 1863, but dated "1864.

Same type as number 9.

27	$4 (7)	serial letter A	$35.00	$75.00

Same type as number 10.

28	$3 (7)	serial letter A	$35.00	$65.00

Same type as number 11.

29	$2 (6)	serial letter A	$20.00	$40.00

Same type as number 12.

30	$1 (7)	A B C D E F G I K	$20.00	$30.00

Same type as number 14 (signed).

30A	50c (9)	A B C D E F G H I K L M N O P	$75.00	$175.00

(Unsigned the above is worth about 50% less.)

Written dates, no serial letter, denomination in red.

30E	$20,000 (10)		extremely rare

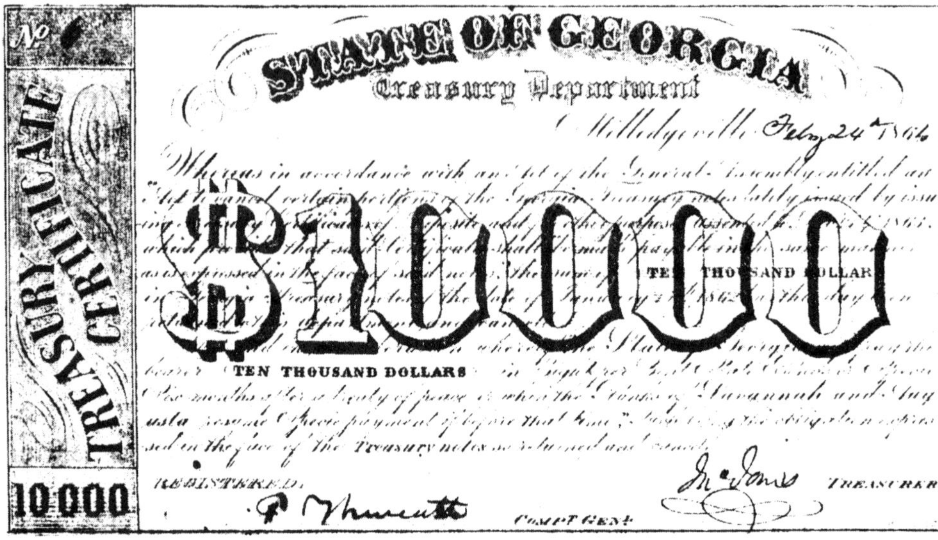

30F $10,000 (10) extremely rare

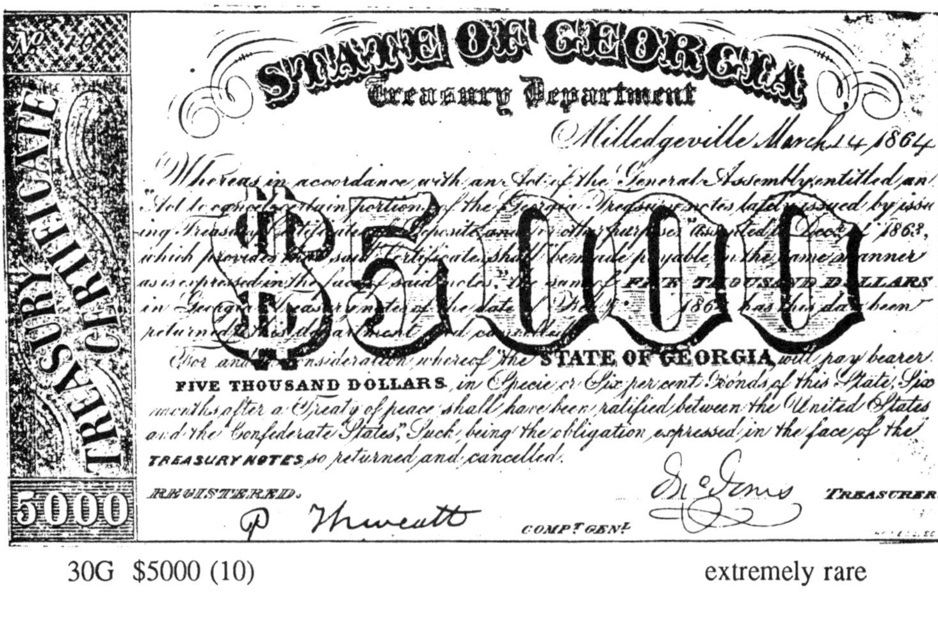

30G $5000 (10) extremely rare

The quantity of notes printed or issued in 1865 is not known.

"Howel. Eng'r. Savannah."

Dated "January 15, 1865."

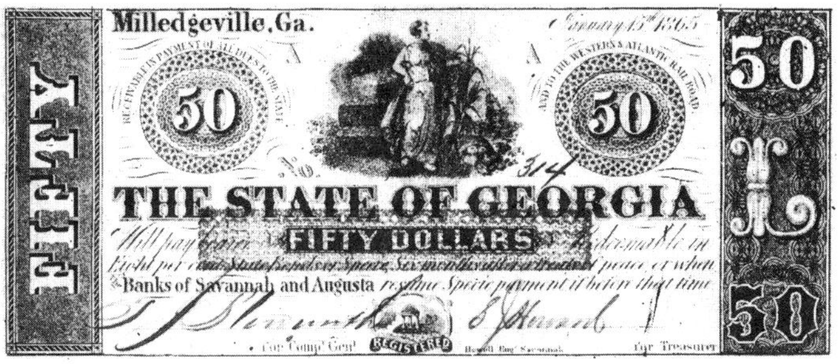

Ceres standing, holding grain. Red design printed over "FIFTY DOLLARS" and treasury seal on back in black.

31	$50 (8)	serial letter A	$30.00	$60.00

"R. H. Howell, Eng'r."

Dated "March 20th, 1865."

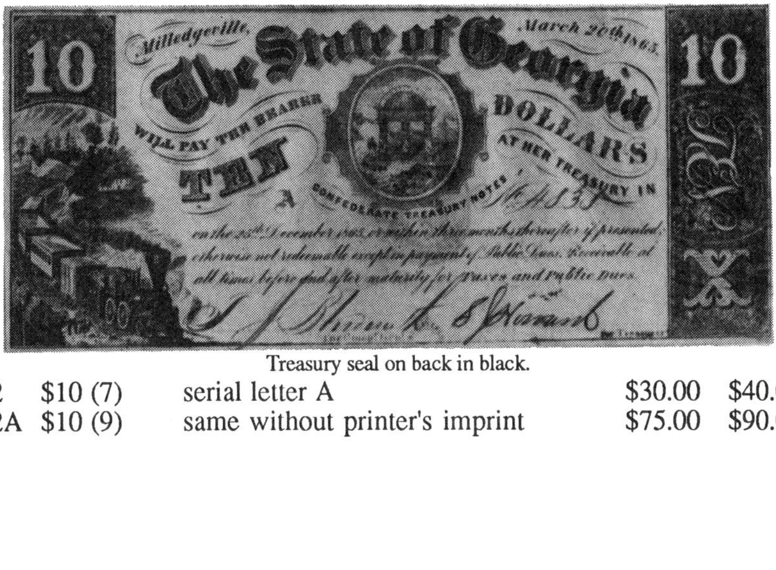

Treasury seal on back in black.

32	$10 (7)	serial letter A	$30.00	$40.00
32A	$10 (9)	same without printer's imprint	$75.00	$90.00

Same type as number 5, but:

"Howell, Eng'r. Savannah"

Dated "January 15th, 1865"

Treasury seal on back in black

33	$5 (8)	serial letter A	$26.00	$40.00

ACT OF DECEMBER 14, 1878 (redemption date: Jan 1, 1885)
Engraved by the American Bank Note Co., New York

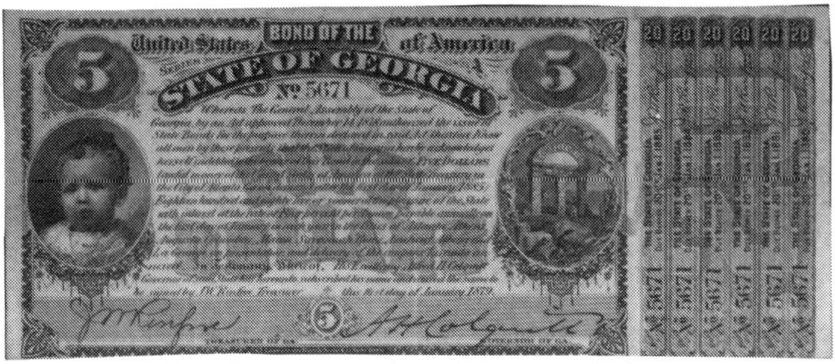

Extensive green overprint and ornate green back.

78A	$5 (11)	series A	$675.00	$1200.00
		A proof of the above, blank within oval where baby's head appears.		
78B	$5 (11)	series A	unique	

INDIAN TERRITORIES

The Cherokee, Choctaw, Creek, and Seminole Nations were definitely part of the Confederate States. The known and reported varieties of notes issued by Indian governments are listed herein for the first time. Hopefully, more information will surface and it will be included in future editions.

Graybacks and Gold by James F. Morgan is an excellent source for additional reading on Indian nations and their monetary policies and is quoted below.

I am especially indebted to J.L. Hargett of Okmulgee, Oklahoma for his assistance in locating the notes illustrated.

THE CHEROKEE NATION

Cherokee paper money in the form of warrants appeared from the early 1840s as "the Cherokee had adapted to the whiteman's culture long before the beginning of the war in 1861."

The early scrip pieces were signed by "John Ross, Principal Chief of the Cherokee," or "George Lowrey, acting principal chief of the Cherokee nation." The last issue of warrants was signed by Stand Watie, who later became principal chief as well as a general in the Confederate Army. He commanded a sizable group of Indians which fought gallantly for the Confederacy.

The warrants of the Cherokee nation were issued with various written dates, by David Vann, national treasurer, starting in the 1840s. "84" was printed. These warrants were issued at Tahlequah, C.N. in the executive department. Some of the various dates and types are show below.

Issued under "Act of Dec. 8th, 1845."

CHR 45-1	written denominations (9)	$350.00	$500.00

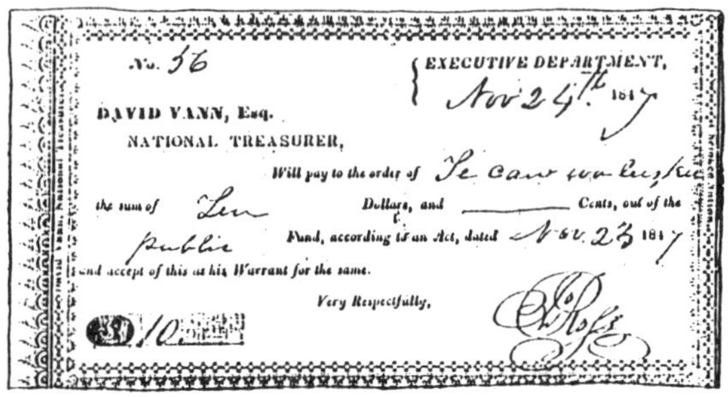
No. 56 EXECUTIVE DEPARTMENT, Nov 24th 1847
DAVID VANN, Esq.
NATIONAL TREASURER,
Will pay to the order of ____
the sum of Ten Dollars, and ____ Cents, out of the
Public Fund, according to an Act, dated Nov. 23 1847
and accept of this as his Warrant for the same.
Very Respectfully,
$10

Issued under "Act of Nov. 23, 1847"

CHR 47-1	written denominations (9)	$350.00	$500.00

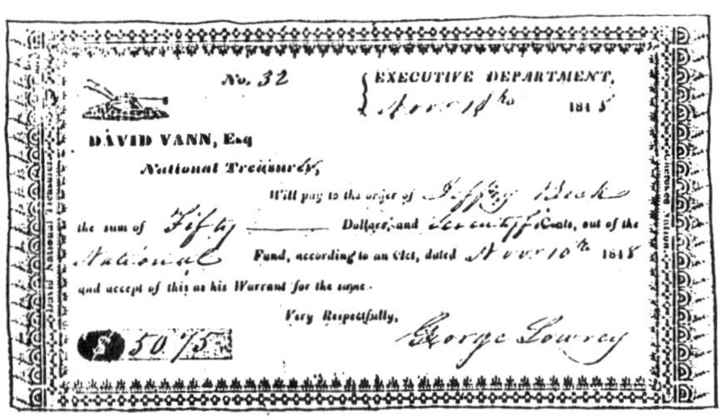
No. 32 EXECUTIVE DEPARTMENT, Nov 10th 1848
DAVID VANN, Esq
National Treasurer,
Will pay to the order of ____
the sum of Fifty Dollars and Seventy five Cents, out of the
National Fund, according to an Act, dated Nov 10th 1848
and accept of this as his Warrant for the same.
Very Respectfully, George Lowrey
$50 75

Issued under "Act of Nov. 10th, 1848"

CHR 48-1	written denominations (9)	$350.00	$500.00
CHR 60-1	written denominations (1)	$400.00	$500.00

In 1862, the Cherokee nation had firmly allied itself with the Confederacy. An issue of notes of small denominations was necessary because all coins had virtually disappeared. The act authorizing the change notes was passed in May of 1862.

Not only does the act still surve, but a receipt for printing of the money also still exists. The receipt states in part, "...that John Candy printed the twenty thousand dollars worth of notes of exchange which the Treasurer was authorized by the National Council..." This receipt is dated June 9, 1862.

The four denominations of notes authorized by May 1862 Act and printed by John Candy, are listed below. They were inscribed "Issued by authority of Law in lieu of Notes of the Confederate States...whenever the the sum of 20, 50, or 100 dollars is presented at the Office of the Treasurer." The notes were serially numbered by hand. They were signed by Josh Ross as clerk and Lewis Ross as treasurer (both brothers of John Ross, then principal chief.)

Printed on white paper.

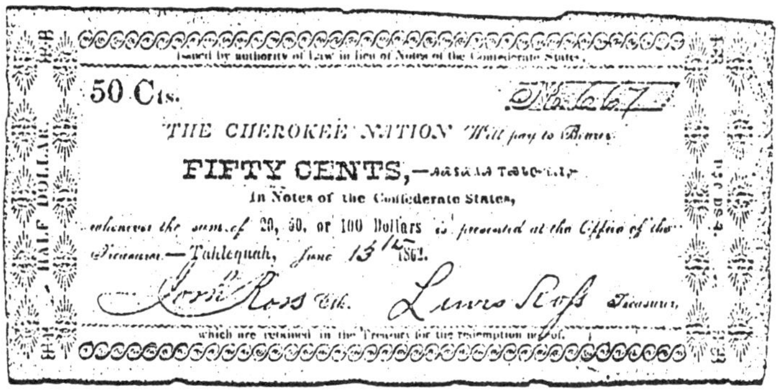

CHR N-1 50c (10) $2000 extremely rare

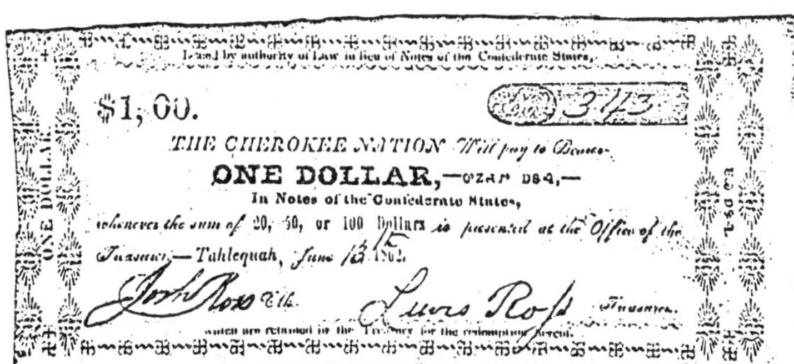

CHR N-2	$1.00 (10)	$2000	extremely rare
CHR N-3	$2.00 (10)	$2000	extremely rare
CHR N-4	$5.00 (10)	$2000	extremely rare

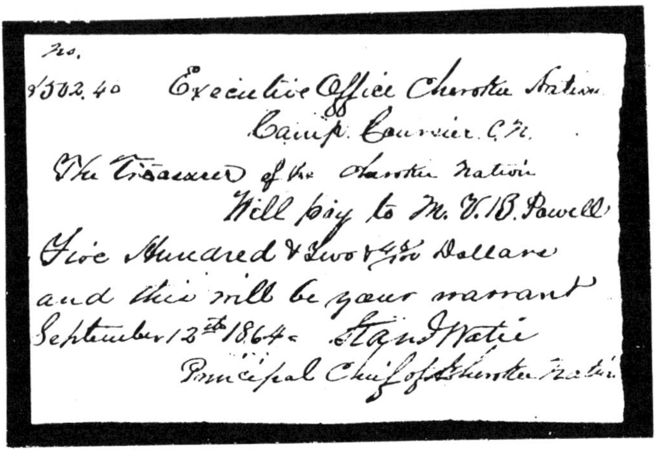
No.
$502.40 Executive Office Cherokee Nation
Camp Bourvier C.N.
The Treasurer of the Cherokee Nation
Will pay to Mr. W.B. Powell
Five Hundred & Two & 40/100 Dollars
and this will be your warrant
September 12th 1864. Stand Watie
Principal Chief of Cherokee Nation

Treasury Warrants, Stand Watic as Principal Chief.

CHR 64-1 written denominations (10) $1500 very rare

CHOCTAW NATION

The first paper money to be issued by the Choctaw nation was called "Choctaw Treasury Warrants." These warrants had written signatures of James Riley, national secretary, and were countersigned across the face "S.Garland, P.C.C.N." (Samuel Garland was the principal chief of the Choctaws during the war years.)

Issued at Armstrong Academy, Choctaw Nation
CHOCTAW TREASURY WARRANT

Most of the known pieces have been observed with the following re-issue endorsement: "Re-issued under Act Oct. 17th, 1865 with interest at five per cent. Signed Allen Wright, Nat. Treas."

Written dates of 1863 (186 printed)
Black ink, printed on deep green paper.

CHOC1 50c (10) no serial letter $1500 very rare

Black ink, printed on light green paper.

CHOC2	$1 (10)	no serial letter	$1500	very rare
CHOC2A	$1 (10)	same, "said" misspelled "sald"	$1500	very rare

Black ink, printed on yellow paper.

CHOC3	$2.50 (11)	no serial letter	$2000	very rare

Black ink, printed on light beige paper.

CHOC4	$5.00 (10)	no serial letter	$2000	very rare

CHOCTAW AUDITOR'S WARRANT

Issued at Choctaw City (Chahta Tamaha), Choctaw Nation
Written signatures of William Roebuck, auditor.

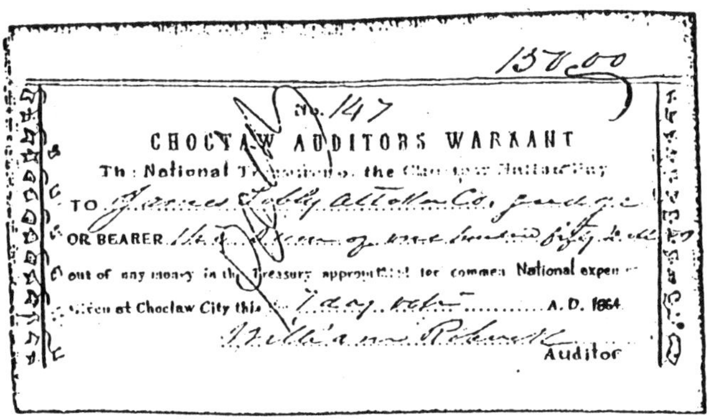

Written dates with "1864" printed.
Black ink on coarse brownish paper.

CHOC5	written denominations (9)	$600.00	very rare

Written dates with "1865" printed.

CHOC6	written denominations (10)	$600.00	very rare

Written dates, "6" written over "5" in year date.

CHOC7	written denominations (10)	$600.00	very rare

THE STATE OF LOUISIANA

Authorized by Acts of January 23, 1862.
1st issue of notes dated Baton Rouge, "Feb. 24, 1862."

"Douglas. N. Orleans."

Ceres seated at center.
"Three" red overprint printed on the back of Texas notes.

1 $3 (11) serial letter A unknown

Printed on the backs of New Orleans notes.
"THREE" overprint in blue, other figures showing in red on back.

1A $3 (11) serial letter A unknown

Same type, printed on back of Texas notes, "TWO" in red.

2 $2 (6) serial letter A $20.00 $40.00

Same type, no red "TWO" overprint.

2A $2 (10) serial letter A very rare

Same type, on backs of New Orleans notes. "TWO" in blue. Other figures showing in red.

2B $2 (8) serial letter A $20.00 $40.00

Similar to 2, but no red "TWO" overprint.

2C $2 (9) serial letter A $60.00 $110.00

Same type, printed on backs of Texas notes, "ONE" in red.

3 $1 (8) serial letter A $20.00 $35.00

Same type, printed on backs of New Orleans notes. "ONE" in blue. Other figures showing in red.

3A $1 (7) serial letter A $25.00 $45.00

Similar to 3, but no red "ONE" overprint.

3B $1 (8) serial letter A $40.00 $80.00

Same as 3, but "TWO" overprinted in red.

3C $1 (9) serial letter A $50.00 $90.00

Same as 3C, but "TWO" inverted on face.

3D $1 (10) serial letter A very rare

Printed on the backs of notes of "The Exchange Bank of Holly Springs, Mississippi."

"THREE" and "3" in green.

4	$3 (4) A B	$30.00	$40.00

Same type, "TWO" and "2" in green.

6	$2 (4) A B	$20.00	$30.00

Same type, "1" and "ONE" in green.

8	$1 (4) A B	$20.00	$30.00

Dated Baton Rouge, "Oct. 10th, 1862."
"B. Duncan, Columb."

Personification of North and South in conflict, "lazy 5" at bottom, fancy green back.

10	$5 (3) A B C D E F G H J K L M	$20.00	$35.00

10 $5 (3) A B C D E F G H J K L M $20.00 $35.00

Authorized by act of Feb. 8th, 1863.
Dated Shreveport. "March 10th, 1863."
"B. Duncan, Columbia, S.C."

State capitol. Bust of Governor Thomas O. Moore left. Liberty right. Fancy greenish-blue back.

11 $100 (7) A B C D E F G H I K $45.00 $95.00

Similar to 11, but has an inverted back.

11IB $100 (10) A B C D E F G H I J K very rare

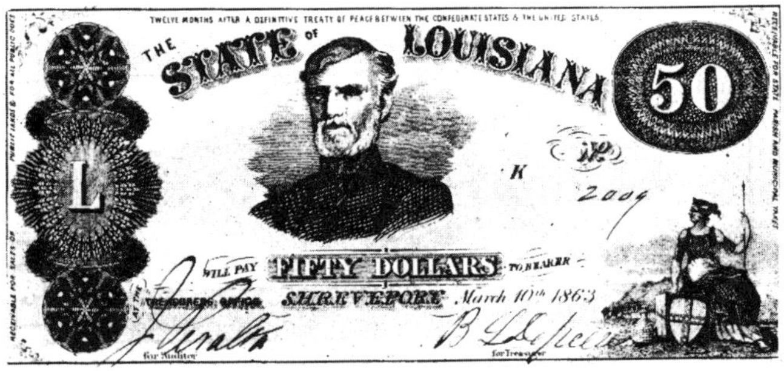

Bust of General Leonadis Polk, liberty right, fancy green back.

12 $50 (6) A B C D E F G H I K $40.00 $85.00

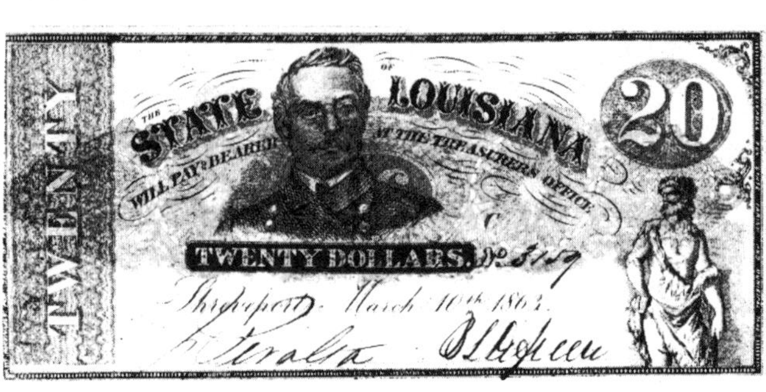

Black with red overprint. Bust of General P. G. T. Beauregard, fancy blue back.

13 $20 (5) A B C D E F G H I K $35.00 $60.00

"B. Duncan. Columb."

Personification of north and south in conflict, fancy green back.

14 $5 (4) A B C D E F G H J K L M $15.00 $35.00

Dated Shreveport. "March 1st, 1864."
"South-Western Print."

Sailing vessel at center, locomotive left.

15 $1 (4) D I M Q U $10.00 $25.00

Commerce leaning on bales of cotton, statue of Washington at left.

16 $1 (4) A E J N R $10.00 $30.00

Commerce leaning on bales of cotton, ship at left.

17 $1 (4) C G H L P T $10.00 $30.00

Steamship at center, Minerva at left.

18 $1 (4) B F K O S $10.00 $30.00

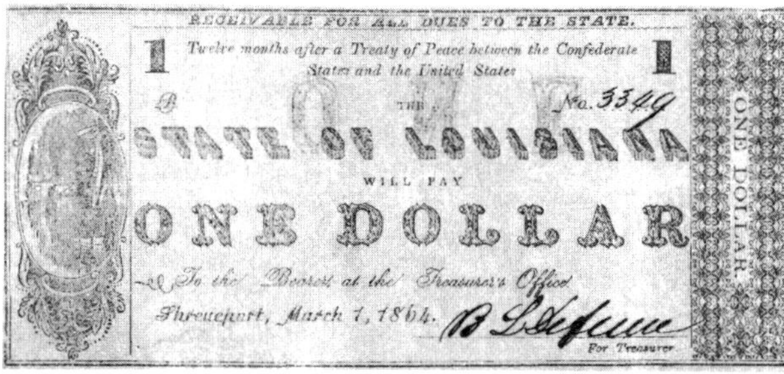

Ship in oval at left, "Two" in red on back.

19	$1 (5)	A B	$20.00	$75.00

Same type, "One" in red on back.

19A	$1 (5)	A B	$25.00	$85.00

Same type, "one" in red on face, printed on the backs of New Orleans notes.

19B	$1 (5)	A B	$20.00	$75.00
19B1	$1 (5)	A B (with blue "Two" overprint)	$20.00	$75.00
19B2	$1 (10)	A B (with both overprints)	very rare	

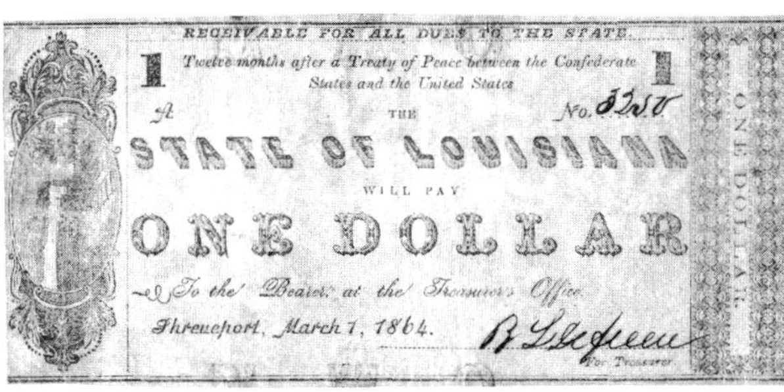

Train in oval at left, "TWO" in red on back.

19C	$1 (5)	A	$25.00	$75.00

Same type, "one" in red on back.

19D	$1 (5)	A	$18.50	$85.00

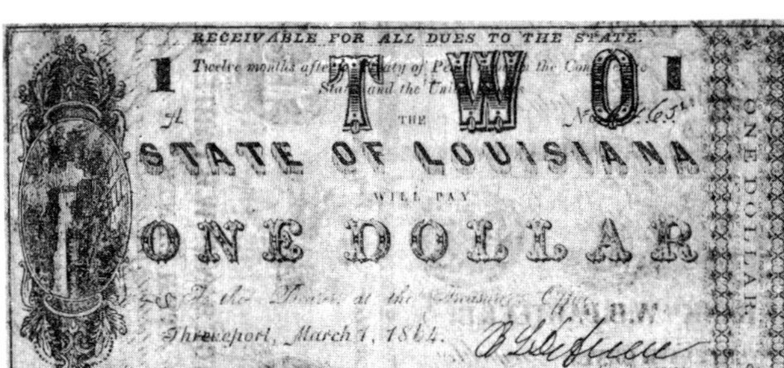

Train in oval at left.
"Two" in red on face, printed on the back of New Orleans notes.

19E	$1 (6)	A B	$30.00	$80.00

Same as 19E but parts of blue "two" showing.

19E1 $1 (8) A B $20.00 $75.00

Same but "One" in red on face inverted, and parts of blue running vertical.

19F $1 (8) A B $20.00 $75.00

Same but watermarked "T.H. Saunderson & Co."

19G $1 (10) A B very rare

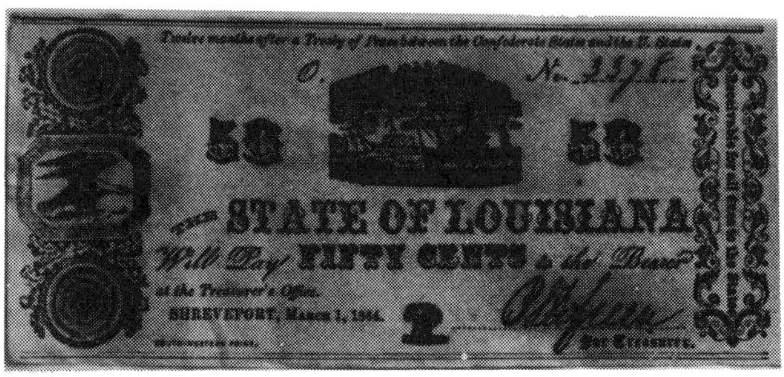

Three ships at center, eagle at left.

20 50c (5) B D F G J L O R $10.00 $25.00

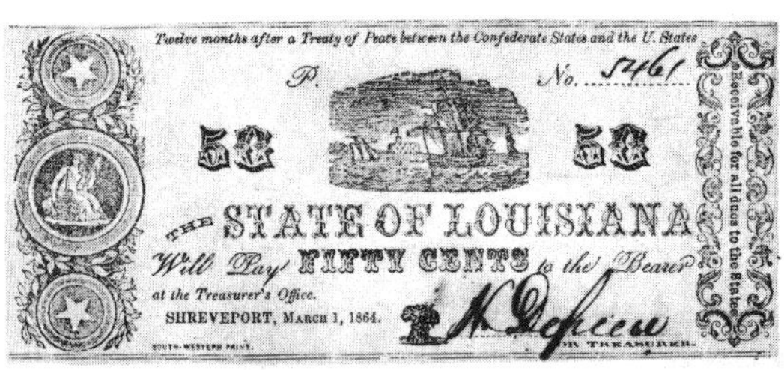

21 50c (4) A C E H K M N P Q $10.00 $25.00

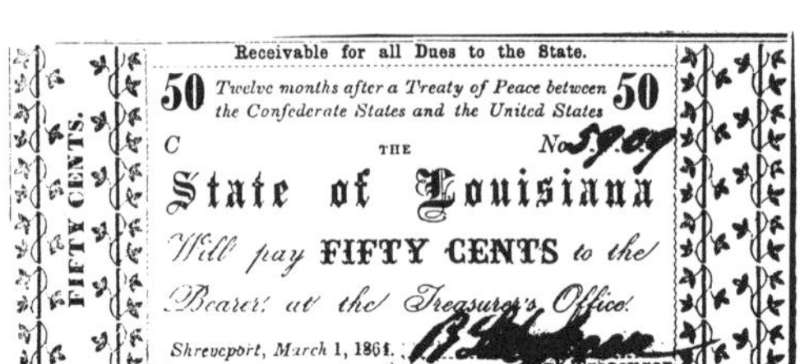

Typeset as illustrated.

21A 50c (8) A B C $20.00 $35.00

Red "one" on back.

21B 50c (8) A B C $25.00 $35.00

Red "two" on back.

21B1 50c (8) A B C $25.00 $65.00

Watermarked "T.H. Saunderson and Co."

21B2 50c (8) A B C very rare

Printed on the backs of New Orleans notes.

21C 50c (8) A B C $15.00 $40.00

On backs of New Orleans notes, parts of letters "two" on face in blue.

21D 50c (6) A B C $15.00 $38.00

Same as 21D, parts of letter "two" on face in red.

21D1 50c (6) A B C $15.00 $40.00

Printed on back of bill of exchange.

21E 50c (10) A B C $60.00 $175.00

Plain back but letters in red on back of "two."

21F 50c (6) A B C $17.00 $60.00

Same as 21C but letters of "one" on face in blue.

21G 50c (6) A B C $15.00 $55.00

As 21F and G but overprints in both colors, on New Orleans notes.

21H 50c (10) A B C very rare

Typeset as illustrated, plain paper.

22 25c (8) A B C $30.00 $75.00

Letters of "One" on back in red.

22A 25c (8) A B C $30.00 $75.00

Letters of "Two" on back in red.

22B 25c (8) A B C $25.00 $75.00

Printed on backs of New Orleans notes.

23 25c (8) A B C $30.00 $75.00

Same as 23 but "One" in red and blue on face.

23A 25c (9) A B C $34.00 $90.00

Same as 23 but "Two" in red and blue on face.

23B 25c (9) A B C $32.00 $98.00

Printed on back of bill of exchange.

24 25c (10) A B C $75.00 $175.00

Printed on back of bill of exchange, parts of letters "Two" on face in blue.

24A 25c (9) A B C $25.00 $85.00

Authorized by act of "Feb. 9th, 1866."
"American Bank Note Co. New York."

Written dates, 1866.

Heads of two maidens center, President Andrew Johnson right. Black with green overprint. Fancy green back.

25 $5 (6) A B C D $95.00 $150.00

Dog with chest center, Washington left. Black with green overprint, fancy green back.

26 $10 (10) A B $175.00 $450.00

Black with green overprint, ships at dock left, Thomas Jefferson right, fancy green back.

27 $20 (9) A B $140.00 $350.00

The warrant which was formerly listed as number 28 is actually one of a number of different pieces which are now listed at the end of this section.

Issued under constitutional provisions of the state adopted in 1879, and Act 104, approved April 10, 1880.

"Western Bank Note Co., Chicago. Fred Holyland, N.O."

Serial numbers in red, watermarked "Crane and Co. Boston, Mass. 1880," fancy blue-green back.

29	$5 (1)	B C	$5.50	$6.75

Similar to 29 but serial numbers in green.

29A	$5 (8)	B C	$6.50	$12.50

Treasurer signature written, not ink stamped.

29B	$5 (10)	B C	very rare	

Inscribed "Issued for Warrant" at upper left.

30	$5 (5)	no serial letters	$20.00	$25.00

As 30, but with "Certificate" printed in red over "Warrant."

30A	$5 (4)	no serial letters	$7.50	$9.00

Similar to 29 but bears "actual redemption" (for taxes) overprint. Dated between 1891-1901. Overprinted signature of state tax collector.

31	$5 (8)	B C	$10.00	$15.00

Similar to 30A, handwritten "Redemption by State Tax Collector."

31A	$5 (9)	B C	$20.00	$30.00

Similar to 29 but watermarked "T.H. Saunderson and Co."

32	$5 (10)	B C	very rare	

Although termed "bonds" (undoubtedly to get around Federal banking regulation), these bills were of normal currency size, and circulated as interest bearing notes, similar to the United States interest bearing notes of the 1865 period. They were issued in return for certificates of 1874 and are seldom found with all 11 coupons attached.

Various Printed Order Numbers

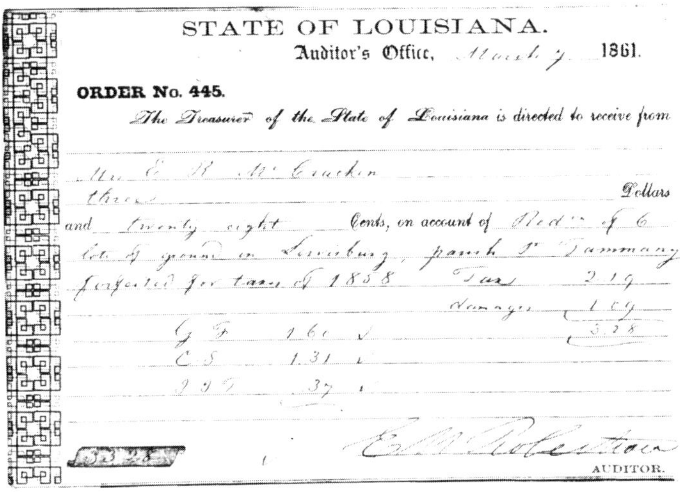

1861	written denominations (7), blue and black	$40.00	$75.00

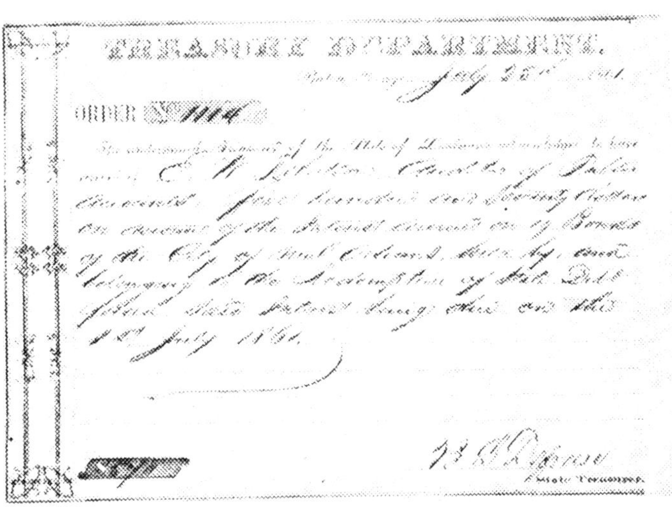

1861A	written denominations (7), similar to above, design at left with two vertical lines	$35.00	$75.00

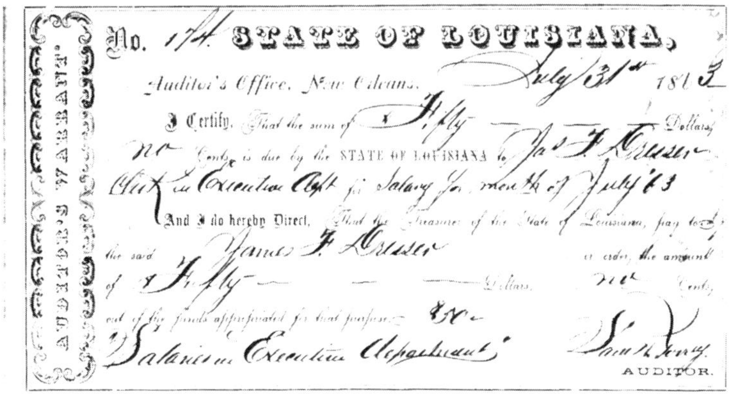

1863 written denominations (7) blue and black $30.00 $70.00

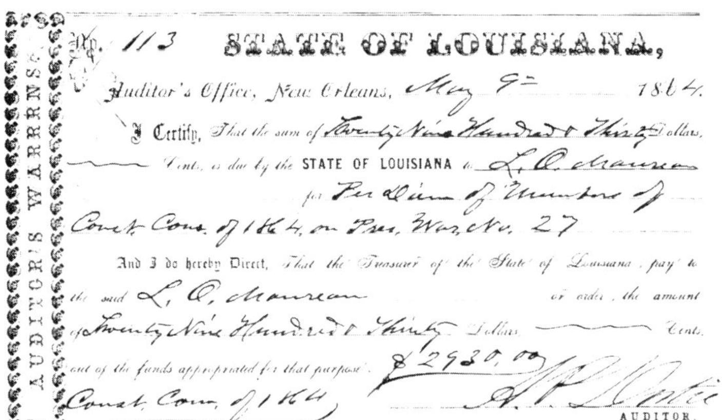

1864 written denominations (7) black and white $30.00 $70.00

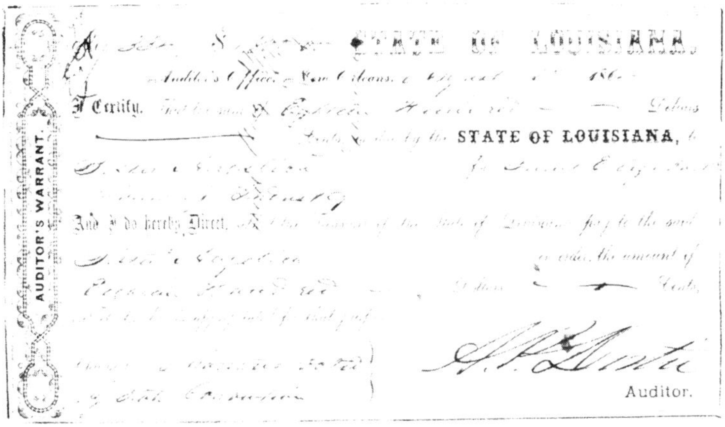

1864A written denominations (7) similar to 64 $30.00 $90.00
"AUDITOR'S WARRANT" shorter

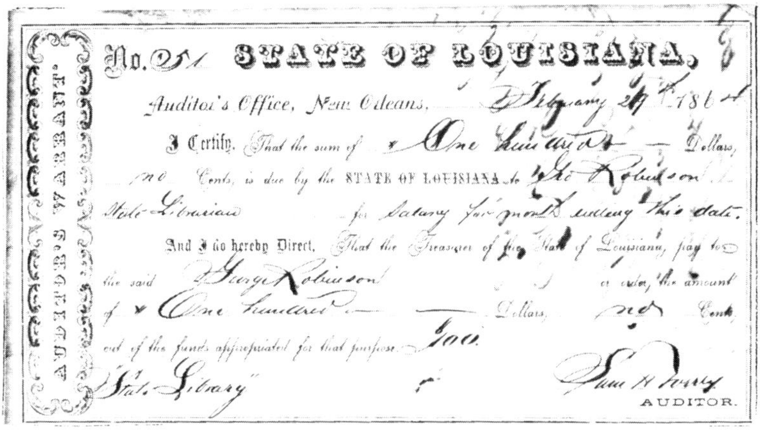

1864B written denominations (7) similar to 64 $30.00 $65.00
with different design at left, blue and black

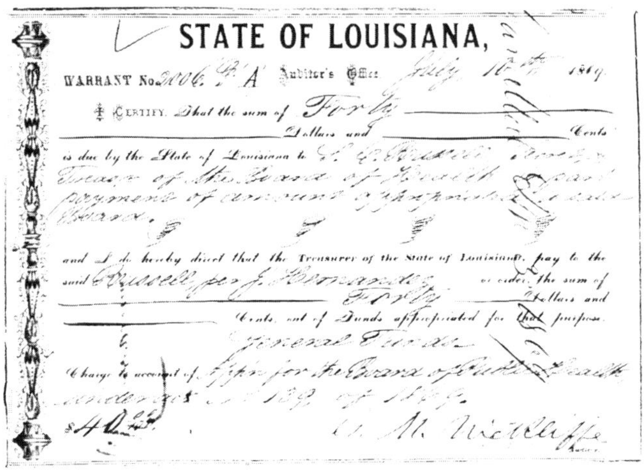
STATE OF LOUISIANA,

WARRANT No. 2006 Auditor's Office July 16th 1869.

I Certify. That the sum of Forty Dollars and Cents is due by the State of Louisiana to

and I do hereby direct that the Treasurer of the State of Louisiana pay to the said Russell per J. Hernandez or order, the sum of Forty Dollars and Cents, out of Funds appropriated for that purpose.

General Funds

Charge to account of

$40.00

1869	written denominations (7), black and white	$50.00	$65.00

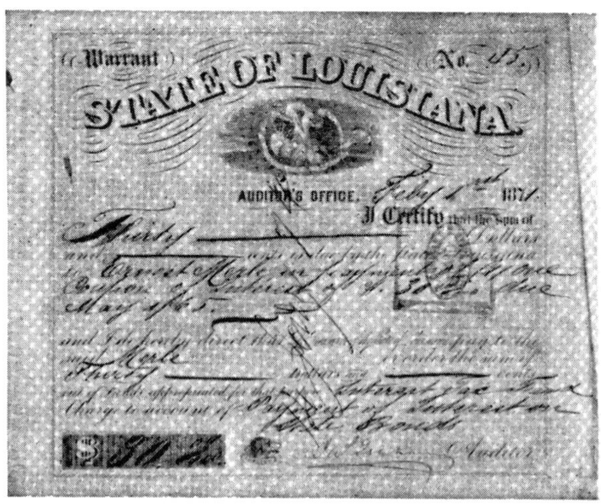
Warrant No.

STATE OF LOUISIANA.

AUDITOR'S OFFICE, 1871.

I Certify that the sum of Thirty Dollars

1871	written denominations (5), green and black more ornate with vignette at center.	$30.00	$65.00

1874 written denomination (6), similar to 74A (below) but pelican looking right, tan and orange $20.00 $60.00

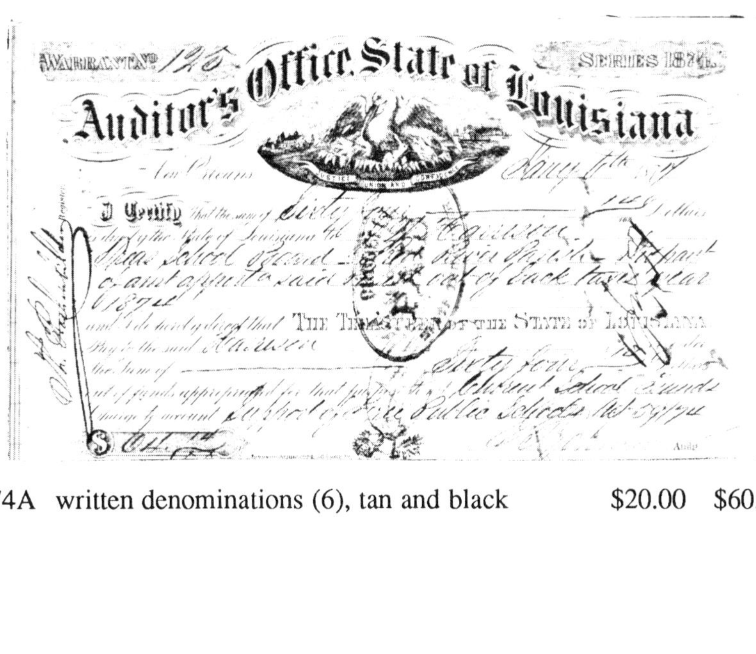

1874A written denominations (6), tan and black $20.00 $60.00

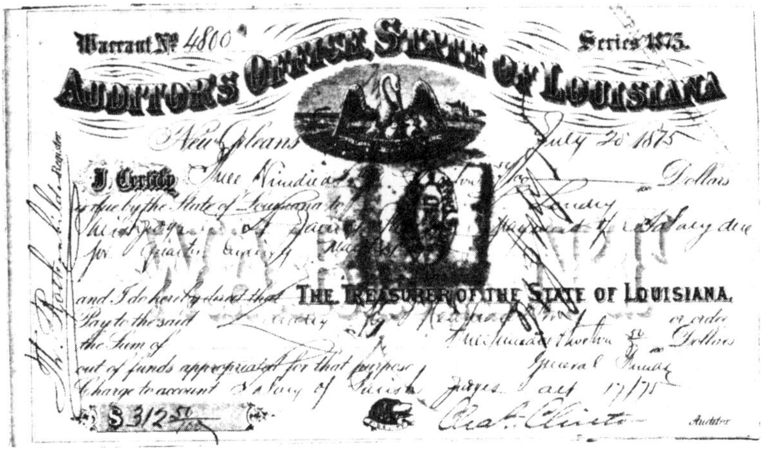

1875 written denominations (6), similar to 74A $20.00 $55.00
but pelican looking right, blue-green and black

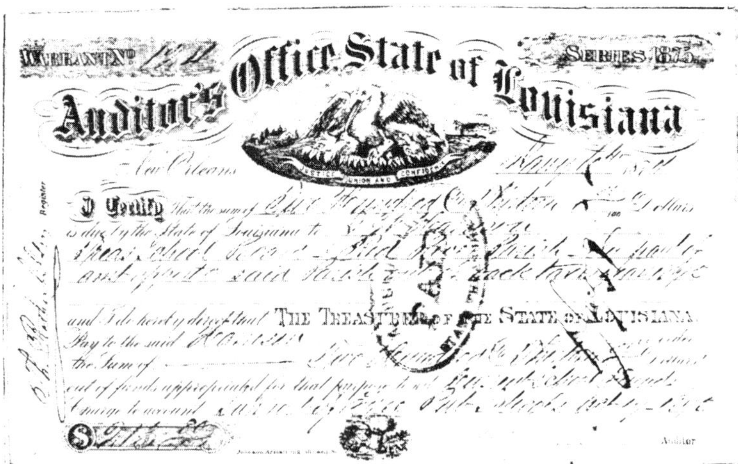

1875A written denominations (6), blue and black $20.00 $65.00
similar to 74A, pelican looking left,

1876 written denominations (6), green and black $20.00 $75.00

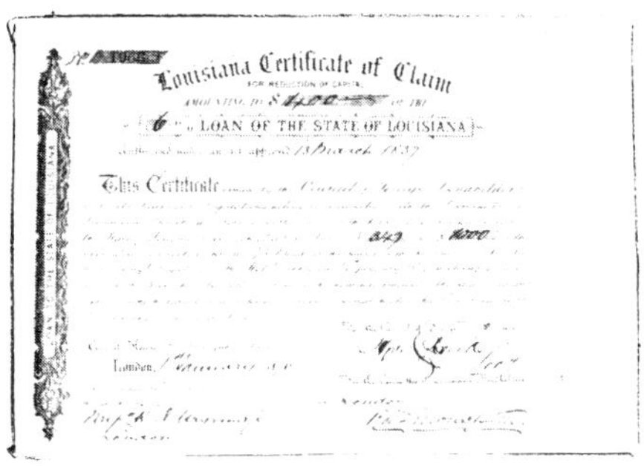

1876A written denominations (9), issued Jan. 1, 1876 $50.00 $75.00

1877 written denominations (6), green and black $25.00 $75.00

MISSISSIPPI TERRITORY AUDITOR'S WARRANTS OF 1805-1816

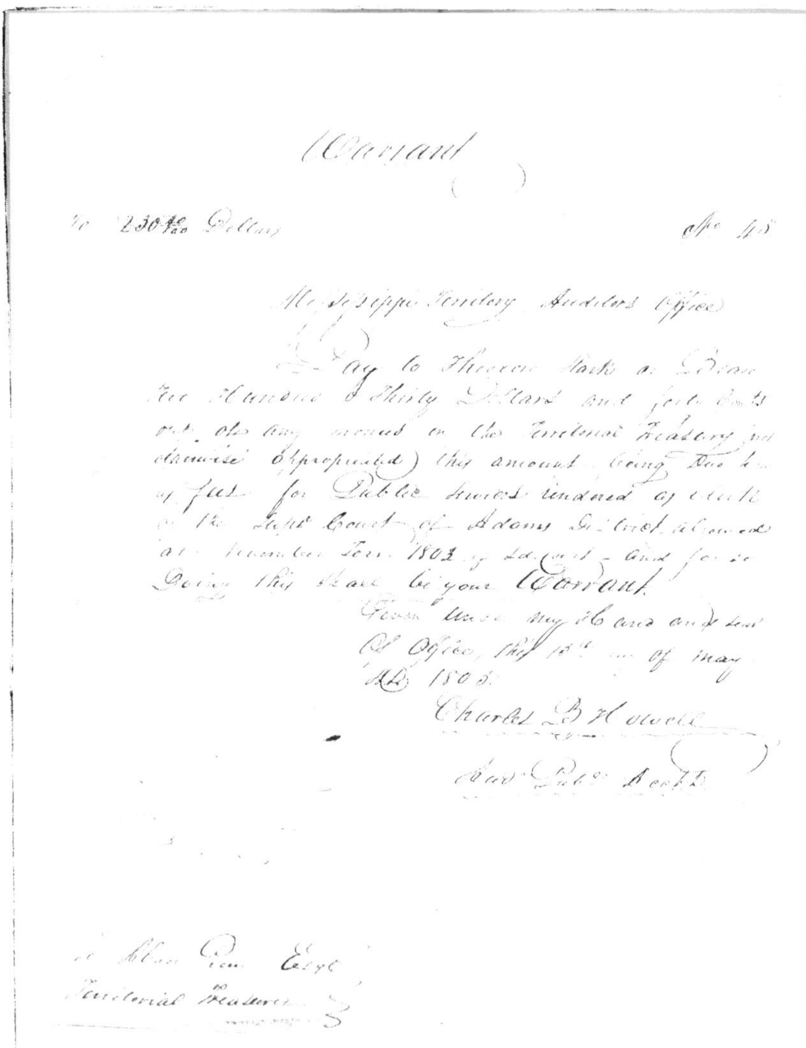

Warrant

For 230 40/100 Dollars No. 45

Mississippi Territory Auditors Office

Pay to [illegible] Two Hundred & Thirty Dollars and forty Cents out of any monies in the Territorial Treasury not otherwise appropriated this amount being due [illegible] of fees for Public services rendered as Clerk of the Supr Court of Adams District allowed at December Term 1803 [illegible] And for so doing this shall be your Warrant.

Given under my hand and seal of Office this 15th day of May AD 1805.

Charles B Howell

[illegible] Pub. Acct.

To Allen [illegible] Esqr
Territorial Treasurer

1805 written denominations (10) handwritten very rare
territorial warrant signed 1805

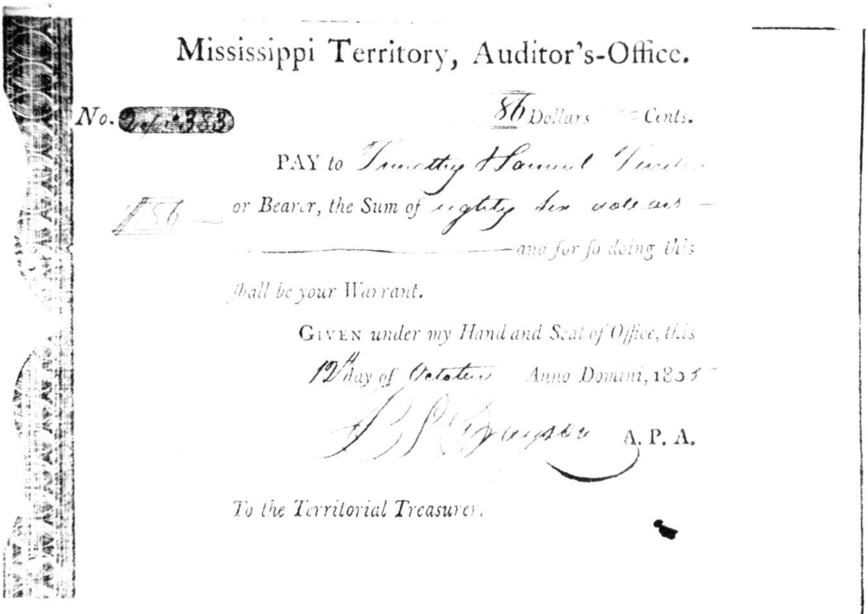

Ornate circular design left, territorial seal lower left, signed 1805-1808.

1805K written denominations (10) very rare
("shall be" on third line)

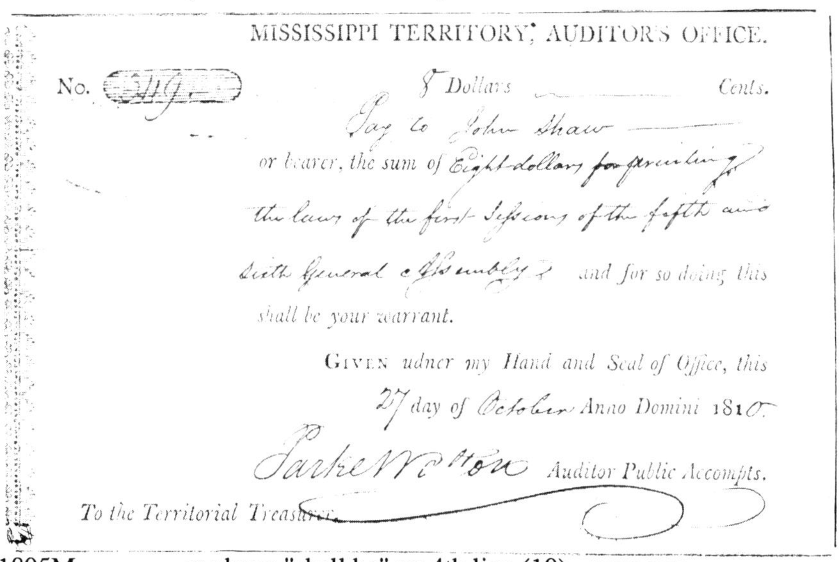

1805M as above,"shall be" on 4th line (10) very rare

Mississippi Territory, Auditor's-Office.

No.

109 Dollars — Cents.

PAY to [illegible]

or Bearer, the Sum of one hundred and nine dollars ——— and for so doing this shall be your Warrant.

GIVEN under my Hand and Seal of Office, this 12th day of July Anno Domini, 1805

[illegible] A. P. A.

To the Territorial Treasurer.

Similar to 1805K but design left end has little snowflakes rather than circular designs. Signed 1809-1810.

1809F written denominations (10) very rare

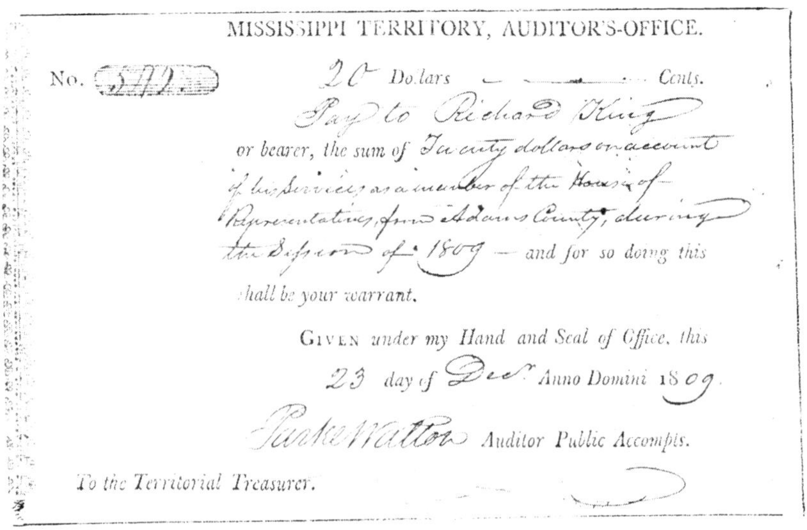

MISSISSIPPI TERRITORY, AUDITOR'S-OFFICE.

No. 540

20 Dollars — Cents.

Pay to Richard King

or bearer, the sum of Twenty dollars on account of his Services as a member of the House of Representatives, from Adams County, during the Session of 1809 — and for so doing this shall be your warrant.

GIVEN under my Hand and Seal of Office, this 23 day of Decr Anno Domini 1809.

Parke Walton Auditor Public Accompts.

To the Territorial Treasurer.

1809J as above, "UDNER" spelling (11) very rare

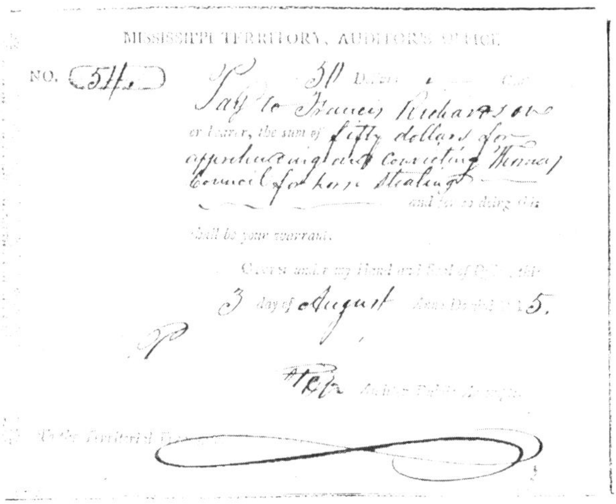

Similar to 1805K but design left end has a star at top. Signed 1811-1815.

1811H written denominations (10) very rare

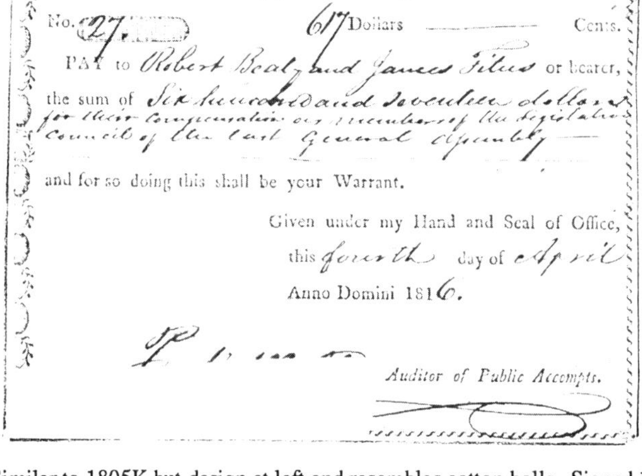

Similar to 1805K but design at left end resembles cotton bolls. Signed 1816.

1816 written denominations (10) very rare

THE STATE OF MISSISSIPPI

Authorized by acts of Jan. 24, 1861, Nov. 29, 1861, Jan. 29, 1862

"American Bank Note Co. N.Y. & N. O."

Written dates, 1861, 1862, 1863

Slaves gathering cotton, Proserpina at left, Governor J. J. Pettus right.
Black with red overprint. Serial letter A.

1	$100	dated 1861..."Payable"...		
		payable 1862 (10)	very rare	
		payable 1863 (6)	$60.00	$150.00
		payable 1864 (9)	$90.00	$250.00
1A	$100	dated 1862..."Payable"...		
		payable 1862 (10)	very rare	
		payable 1863 (6)	$60.00	$150.00
		payable 1864 (6)	$70.00	$150.00
5	$100	dated 1863..."Payable"...		
		payable 1863 (9)	very rare	
		payable 1864 (7)	$90.00	$150.00

Mules pulling a wagon, Governor J.J. Pettus left, "L" in oval left. Black with red overprint.. Serial letter "A."

2	$50	dated 1861..."Payable"...		
		payable 1862 (10)	very rare	
		payable 1863 (6)	$50.00	$125.00
		payable 1864 (9)	$95.00	$175.00
2A	$50	dated 1862..."Payable"...		
		payable 1862 (10)	very rare	
		payable 1863 (6)	$50.00	$125.00
		payable 1864 (6)	$50.00	$125.00
6	$50	dated 1863..."Payable"...		
		payable 1863 (9)	very rare	
		payable 1864 (7)	$60.00	$175.00

Mules pulling a wagon of cotton, Governor J.J. Pettus at right, maiden in oval at left. Black with red overprint, serial letter "A."

3	$20	dated 1861..."Payable"...		
		payable 1862 (10)	very rare	
		payable 1863 (6)	$40.00	$150.00
		payable 1864 (9)	$90.00	$250.00

3A	$20	dated 1862..."Payable"...		
		payable 1862 (10)	very rare	
		payable 1863 (6)	$40.00	$150.00
		payable 1864 (6)	$50.00	$150.00
7	$20	dated 1863..."Payable"...		
		payable 1863 (9)	very rare	
		payable 1864 (7)	$75.00	$150.00

Slave with two horses, Governor J.J. Pettus at left, maiden in oval at right.

Black with red overprint. Serial letter "A."

4	$10	dated 1861..."Payable"...		
		payable 1862 (10)	very rare	
		payable 1863 (6)	$45.00	$125.00
		payable 1864 (9)	$75.00	$175.00
4A	$10	dated 1862..."Payable"...		
		payable 1862 (10)	very rare	
		payable 1863 (6)	$45.00	$125.00
		payable 1864 (6)	$45.00	$125.00
8	$10	dated 1863..."Payable"...		
		payable 1863 (9)	very rare	
		payable 1864 (7)	$45.00	$150.00

Without name of engraver, no serial letter.
Written dates of 1862.

		"Cotton Pledged" on face in drab.		
9	$100 (8)	dated "March 7th, 1862," light gray background	$50.00	$130.00
9A	$100 (9)	same type, light pink background	very rare	
		"Cotton Pledged" on face in green.		
14	$100 (7)	dated "May 1st, 1862."	$50.00	$125.00
14A	$100 (8)	same type, dated "April 1st, 1862"	$65.00	$150.00
14B	$100 (9)	dated "May 1st, 1862." printed on back of bill of exchange	very rare	

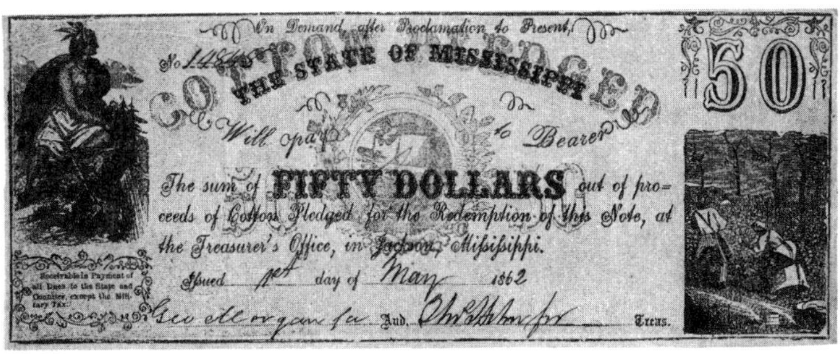

		"Cotton Pledged" on face in drab.		
10	$50 (7)	dated "March 7th, 1862," light gray background	$40.00	$100.00
10A	$50 (6)	same type, light pink background	$40.00	$90.00
		"Cotton Pledged" on face in green.		
15	$50 (6)	dated "May 1st, 1862."	$40.00	$90.00
15A	$50 (8)	same type, dated "April 1st, 1862"	$55.00	$125.00
15B	$50 (8)	dated "May 1st, 1862." printed on back of bill of exchange	rare	
15C	$50 (8)	dated "April 1st, 1862," and printed on the back of auditors bills	very rare	

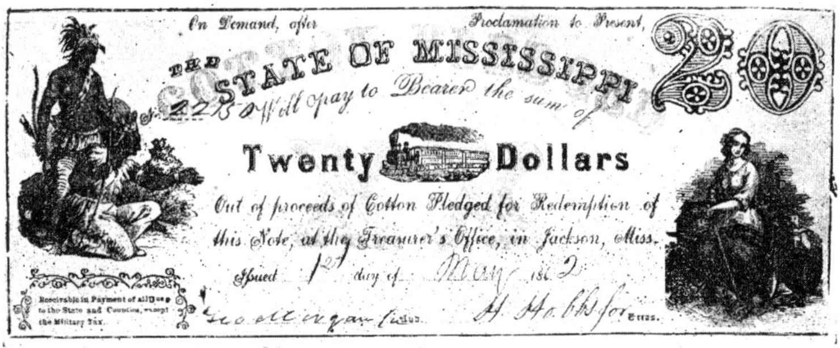

"Cotton Pledged" on face in drab.

11	$20 (8)	dated "March 7th, 1862," light gray background	$45.00	$125.00
11A	$20 (6)	same type, light pink background	$35.00	$80.00

"Cotton Pledged" on face in green.

16	$20 (5)	dated "May 1st, 1862."	$30.00	$100.00
16A	$20 (7)	same type, dated "April 1st, 1862"	$50.00	$130.00
16B	$20 (8)	dated "May 1st, 1862." printed on back of bill of exchange	$40.00	$110.00
16C	$20 (8)	dated "April 1st, 1862," and printed on the back of auditors bills	$40.00	$100.00

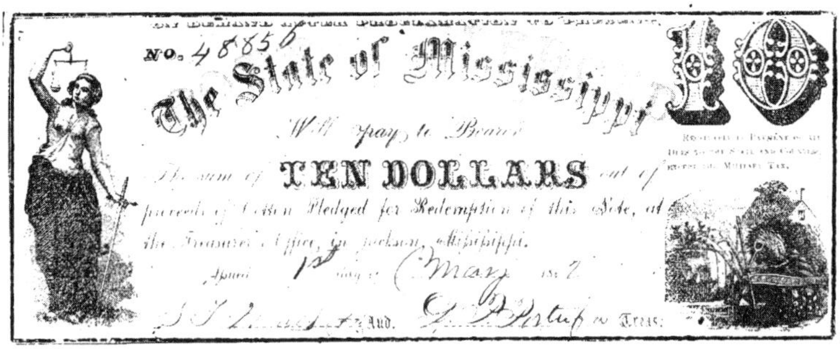

"Cotton Pledged" on face in drab.

12	$10 (9)	dated "March 7th, 1862," light gray background	$25.00	$75.00
12A	$10 (9)	same type, light pink background	$25.00	$60.00

"Cotton Pledged" on face in green.

17	$10 (4)	dated "May 1st, 1862."	$20.00	$50.00
17A	$10 (7)	same type, dated "April 1st, 1862"	$20.00	$40.00
17B	$10 (8)	dated "May 1st, 1862." printed on back of bill of exchange	$25.00	$50.00
17C	$10 (8)	dated "April 1st, 1862," and printed on the back of auditors bills	$25.00	$50.00

"Cotton Pledged" on face in drab.

13	$5 (8)	dated "March 7th, 1862," light gray background	$20.00	$65.00
13A	$5 (6)	same type, light pink background	$20.00	$65.00

"Cotton Pledged" on face in green.

18	$5 (4)	dated "May 1st, 1862."	$15.00	$30.00
18A	$5 (5)	same type, dated "April 1st, 1862"	$20.00	$35.00
18B	$5 (7)	dated "May 1st, 1862." printed on back of bill of exchange	$25.00	$50.00
18C	$5 (7)	dated "April 1st, 1862," and printed on the back of auditors bills	$25.00	$50.00

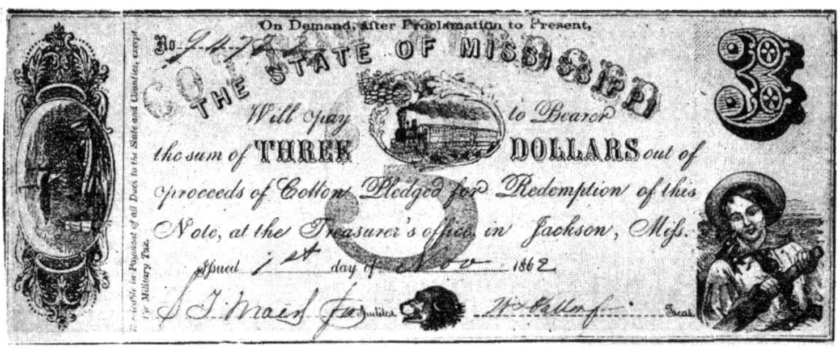

"Cotton Pledged" on face in green.

19	$3 (5)	dated "May 1st, 1862."	$30.00	$65.00
19A	$3 (6)	same type, dated "April 1st, 1862"	$30.00	$65.00
19B	$3 (9)	same type, no overprint	very rare	

"Cotton Pledged" on face in blue.

23	$3 (6)	dated "May 1st, 1862."	$25.00	$45.00
26	$3 (5)	same type, dated "Nov. 1st, 1862"	$25.00	$40.00

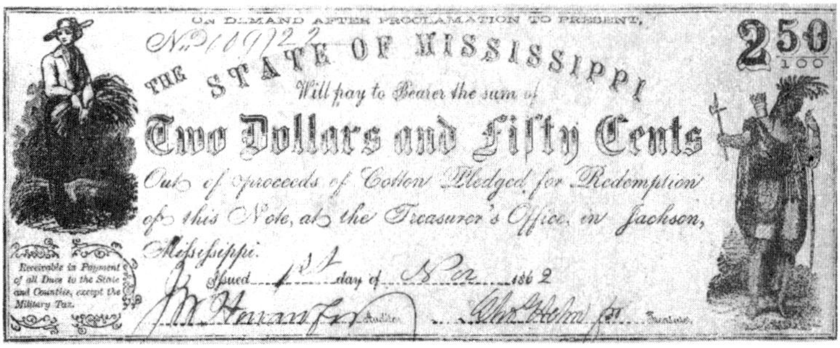

"Cotton Pledged" on face in green.

20	$2.50 (6)	dated May 1st, 1862	$20.00	$50.00
21	$2.50 (6)	same type, dated "April 1st, 1862"		

"Cotton Pledged" on face in blue.

24	$2.50 (7)	dated May 1st, 1862	$20.00	$75.00
27	$2.50 (6)	same type dated Nov. 1st, 1862	$20.00	$85.00
27A	$2.50 (11)	same as above with inverted overprint extremely rare		

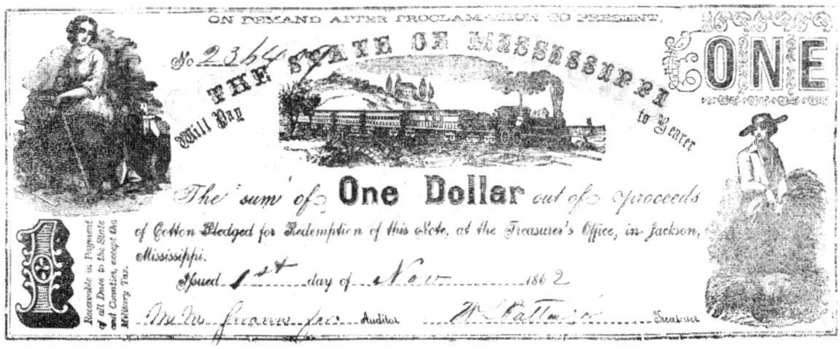

"Cotton Pledged" on face in green.

22	$1 (4)	dated "May 1st, 1862."	$6.00	$26.00
22A	$1 (6)	same type, dated "April 1st, 1862"	$10.00	$35.00
22B	$1 (9)	same type, date "March 7, 1862"	$36.00	$75.00

"Cotton Pledged" on face in blue.

25	$1 (5)	dated "May 1st, 1862"	$12.00	$25.00
28	$1 (4)	same type, dated "Nov. 1st, 1862"	$10.00	$25.00

******

Same type as number 9, except "Faith of the State Pledged" on face in red.

32	$100 (10)	dated "Nov. 1st, 1862"	very rare
32A	$100 (10)	same type, stamped "Re-Issue."	very rare

Same type, "Faith of the State Pledged" on face in blue.

37	$50 (9)	dated "Nov. 1st, 1862"	very rare
37A	$50 (10)	same type, stamped "Re-Issue"	very rare

*****

"Faith of the State Pledged" on face in red.

33	$50 (6)	dated "Nov. 1st 1862"	$35.00	$75.00
33A	$50 (7)	same type, stamped "Re-Issue"	$45.00	$90.00

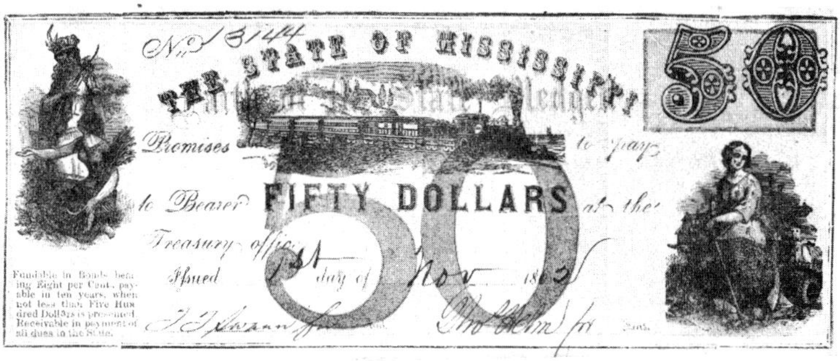

"Faith of the State Pledged" on face in blue.

38	$50 (6)	dated "Nov. 1st, 1862"	$35.00	$110.00
38A	$50 (7)	same type, stamped "Re-Issue"	$45.00	$130.00

******

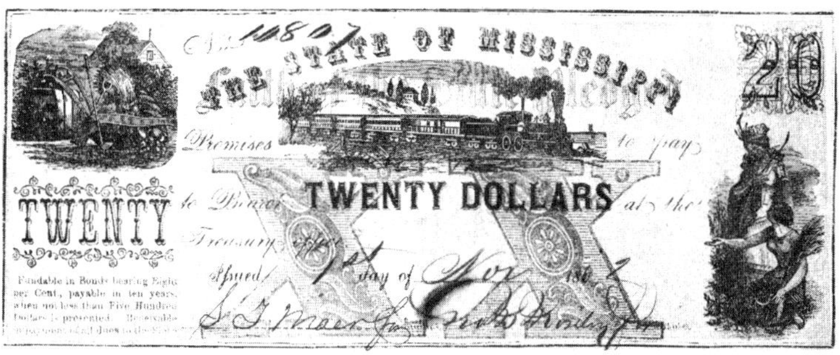

"Faith of the State Pledged" on face in red.

29	$20 (6)	dated "July 1st, 1862"	$25.00	$50.00
29A	$20 (7)	same type, stamped "Re-Issue"	$30.00	$55.00
34	$20 (4)	dated "Nov. 1st, 1862"	$25.00	$50.00
34A	$20 (6)	same type, but printed on backs of "Mississippi Cotton Company" fractional notes	$25.00	$50.00
34B	$20 (6)	same as 34, stamped "Re-Issue"	$35.00	$65.00
34C	$20 (7)	same as 34A, stamped "Re-Issue"	$40.00	$65.00

"Faith of the State Pledged" on face in blue.

39	$20 (5)	dated "Nov. 1st, 1862"	$20.00	$50.00
39A	$20 (6)	same type, stamped "Re-Issue"	$35.00	$65.00

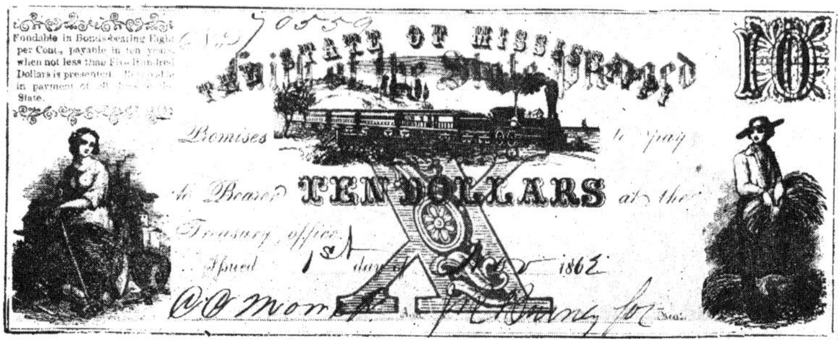

"Faith of the State Pledged" on face in red.

30	$10 (5)	dated "July 1st, 1862"	$15.00	$35.00
30A	$10 (6)	same type, stamped "Re-Issue"	$15.00	$35.00
35	$10 (4)	dated "Nov. 1st, 1862"	$15.00	$35.00
35A	$10 (6)	same type, but printed on backs of "Mississippi Cotton Company" fractional notes	$30.00	$55.00
35B	$10 (6)	same as 35, stamped "Re-Issue"	$35.00	$75.00
35C	$10 (7)	same as 35A, stamped "Re-Issue"	$35.00	$80.00

"Faith of the State Pledged" on face in blue.

40	$10 (5)	dated "Nov. 1st, 1862"	$20.00	$55.00
40A	$10 (6)	same type, stamped "Re-Issue"	$20.00	$60.00
40B	$10 (9)	as 40, but on back of Mississippi Cotton Company notes	$50.00	$100.00

****

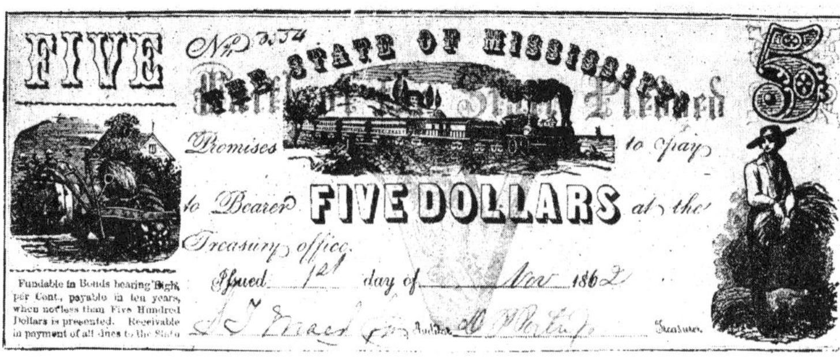

"Faith of the State Pledged" on face in red.

31	$5 (4)	dated "July 1st, 1862"	$16.00	$35.00

31A	$5 (6)	same type, stamped "Re-Issue"	$25.00	$60.00
36	$5 (4)	dated "Nov. 1st, 1862"	$16.00	$50.00
36A	$5 (6)	same type, but printed on backs of "Mississippi Cotton Company" fractional notes	$20.00	$60.00
36B	$5 (5)	same as 36, stamped "Re-Issue"	$20.00	$45.00
36C	$5 (7)	same as 36A, stamped "Re-Issue"	$45.00	$100.00
		"Faith of the State Pledged" on face in blue.		
41	$5 (4)	dated "Nov. 1st, 1862"	$25.00	$35.00
41A	$5 (6)	same type, stamped "Re-Issue"	$45.00	$95.00
42B	$5 (10)	similar to 41 but dated Jan. 1, 1863		very rare

Lithographic Date "May 1st, 1864"

"Three" in red.
Sentinel on duty, Indian at left.
No printer's name.

42	$3 (5)	A B C D E	$30.00	$50.00
		"Lith. & Printed by J. T. Paterson & Co., Augusta, Ga." (On lower edge.)		
42A	$3 (6)	A B C D E	$35.00	$60.00

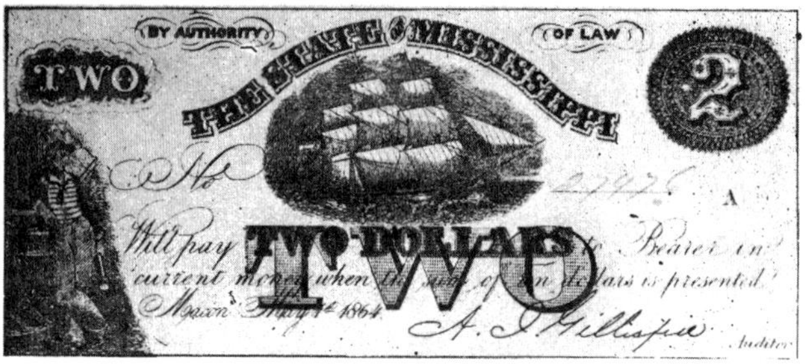

"Two" in red.
Sailing vessel, sailor left.

No printer's name.

43 $2 (5) A B C D E F G $20.00 $35.00

"Lith. & Printed by J. T. Paterson & Co., Augusta, Ga."
(On lower edge.)

43A $2 (6) A B C D E F G $20.00 $35.00

****

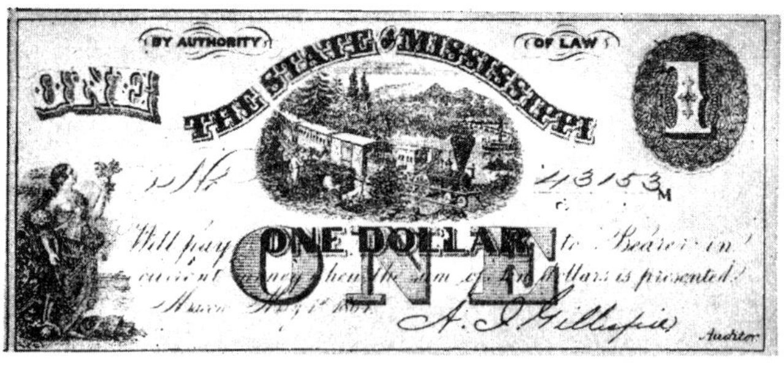

"One" in red.
Railway train, Ceres left.

No printer's name.

44 $1 (5) A B C D E F G H I J K L M $20.00 $30.00

"Lith. & Printed by J. T. Paterson & Co., Augusta, Ga."
(On lower edge.)

44A $1 (6) A B C D E F G H I J K L M $20.00 $30.00

"J. T. Paterson & Co., Augusta, Ga."

"50 Cts" in red
Slave hoeing.

45 50c (5) A B C D E F G H J K L M N O P $15.00 $25.00

"25 Cts" in red.
Cotton bolls left.

46 25c (5) A B C D E F G H J K L M N O P $15.00 $30.00

"25Cts" in red inverted!

46A 25c (11) A B C D E F G H J K L M N O P extremely rare

Similar to 48, but "50" in red, fancy green back.

47 $50 (11) No information available

******

"J. T. Paterson & Co., Augusta, Ga."
Notes without dates, and unsigned.

Watermarked "Ten."

"20" in red, fancy green back.
Eagle and shield, Indian right.

48	$20 (9)	A B C D E F G H	$150.00 $300.00
		Same, but plain paper.	
48A	$20 (10)	A B C D E F G H	$250.00 $450.00
		Same, but overprint reversed on face and back.	
48B	$20 (11)	A B C D E F G H	extremely rare

Same, but green overprint on face, in additon to red "20."

48C	$20 (11)	A B C D E F G H	extremely rare

"J. T. Paterson, & Co. Lithographers, Augusta, GA."
Written date "April 1st, 1865"

Black with green overprint, fancy orange back.
Commerce and Ceres seated, Indian left.

49 $50 (9) A B C D E F G H $125.00 $200.00

"J. T. Paterson, & Co. Engravers and Lithographers, Augusta, GA."
Written dates of 1867

Black with orange overprint. Harbor scene.
Fancy green back.

49A $100 (11) A B C D E F G H $500.00 $1200.00

Engraved by "Continental Bank Note Co., New York."
Lithographic date "Sept. 1st, 1870"

Notes 50 -53 generally come with a large punch cancel. Notes without the cancel are worth six times more.

Black with green overprint, fancy green back.
Gov. J. L. Alcorn, maiden left, cotton boll right.

50	$5 (5)	serial letter A	$40.00	$100.00

Green and black, fancy green back.
Steamship center, Gov. J. L. Alcorn left, eagle right.

51 $3 (5) serial letter A $75.00 $150.00

Black with green overprint, fancy green back.
Slaves loading cotton, Gov. J. L. Alcorn left, train right. Back similar to $3 above.

52 $2 (5) serial letter A $50.00 $100.00

Black with green overprint, fancy green back similar to $5 number 50.
Man with horse and plow, Gov. J. L. Alcorn left, locomotive right.

53 $1 (6) serial letter A $30.00 $150.00

Note: contrary to previously published information, numbers 50 through 53 are seldom found in sheets although the notes are almost all cut out cancelled.

"Hosford & Sons, 56 Cedar St., N. Y."
Written dates ("187" of date printed)

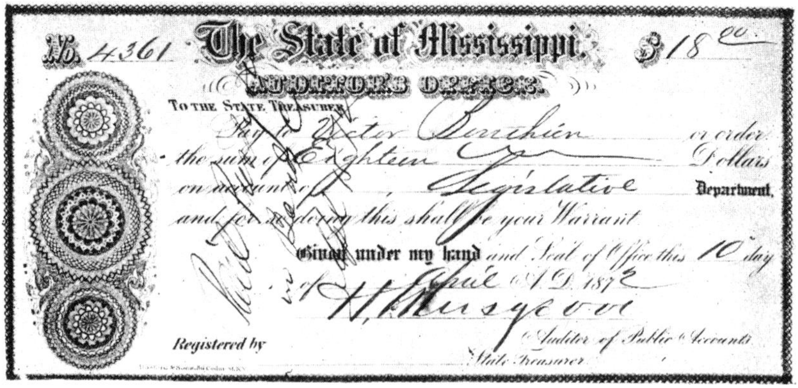

State seal impressed into paper.

54 written denominations (9) no serial letter $60.00 $88.00

Written date of 1888 ("18" of date printed).
State capitol with horse drawn streetcar in oval left, eagle below center.

60 written denominations (10) very rare

Authorized by Act of February 10, 1894

"St. Louis Bank Note Company."
Written dates of "1894"

Notes 94-94B come with large punch cancellations, notes without are worth six times more.

Fancy green back.

94 $5 (5) no serial letter $30.00 $80.00

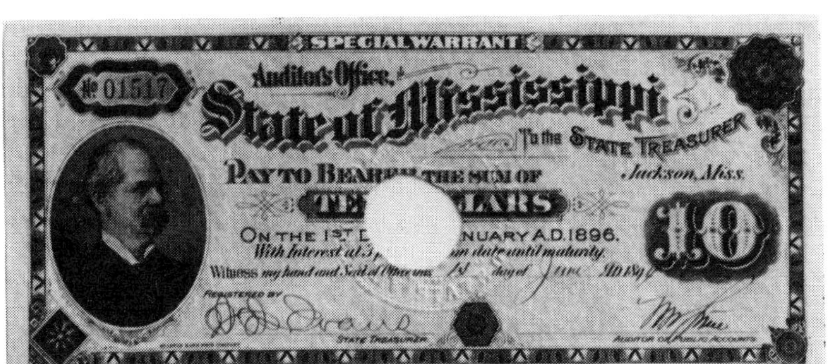

Fancy brown back similar to above.

94A $10 (7) no serial letter $90.00 $150.00

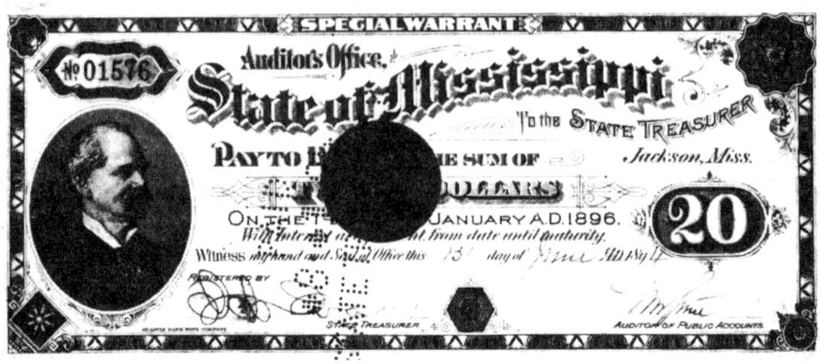

Fancy green back similar to $5 number 94.

94B $20 (9) no serial letter $175.00 $275.00

Authorized by Act of February 10th, 1895

"S. C. Toof & Co. Memphis."
Printed date "June 15th, 1895."

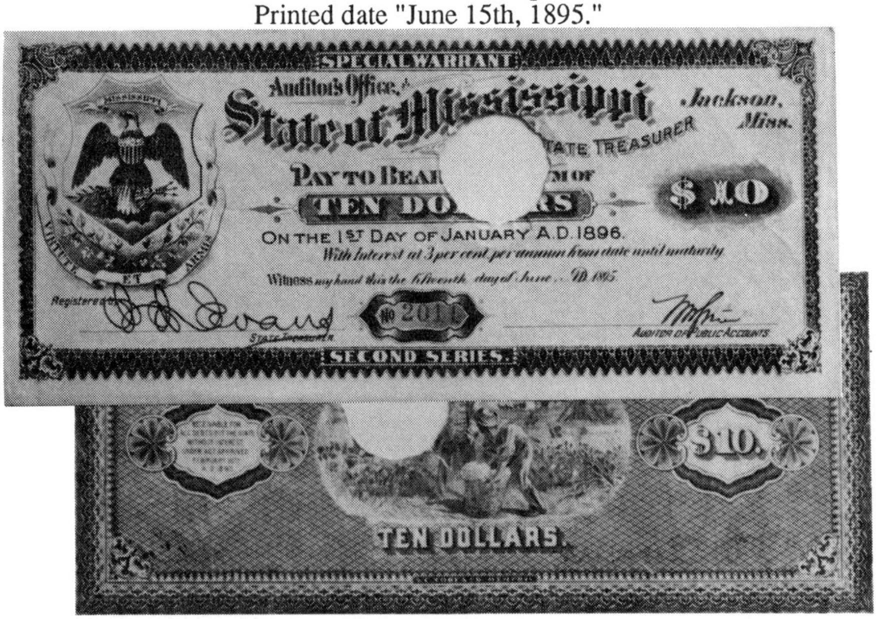

Fancy brown back.

95 $10 (8) no serial letter $75.00 $150.00

THE STATE OF MISSOURI

The earliest known issues of any notes of the state of Missouri are those dated 1821. Three of the five different denominations are illustrated below, but the exact quantities produced of each denomination are not known.

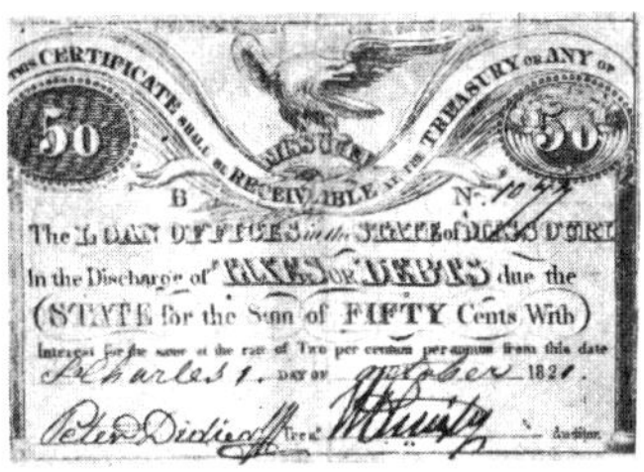

Eagle at center.

01	50c (11)	A B	extremely rare

02	$1 (11)	A B	extremely rare
03	$3	no information available	
04	$5	no information available	

05	$10 (11)	A B	extremely rare

Missouri Confederate Government Issues

On October 21, 1861 C. F. Jackson, who had retired from Jefferson City into Southern Missouri, called an extra session of the state legislature to convene at Neosho, Newton County, Missouri. That legislature adjourned from day to day for want of a quorum until October 28, when it passed an act of secession, voted ten million dollars for defense and authorized the issuance of defense bonds for that amount.

This act did not become a law until November 5, at which time the legislature had removed to Cassville, Barry Country. Governor Jackson signed this bill in Cassville on November 5, 1861. This bill provided for three commissioners, any one of whom might sign the defense bonds when issued.

* * * * * *

Dated Jefferson City, "JAN'Y 1st, 1862"
Engraved by "A. Malus, N. O."

No serial letter, Ceres Volante center, Liberty left.

		PAYABLE "THREE YEARS AFTER DATE."		
1	$20 (6)	cream colored paper	$30.00	$65.00
2	$20 (8)	same type, blue tinted paper	$40.00	$75.00
2A	$20 (8)	same as above, date changed by hand to "1863"	$50.00	$85.00
		PAYABLE "FIVE YEARS AFTER DATE."		
2C	$20 (9)	cream colored paper	very rare	
2D	$20 (6)	same type, blue tinted paper	$75.00	$125.00
2E	$20 (9)	same as above, date changed by hand to "1863"	extremely rare	

"D. Weil Eng."

No serial letters, Ceres seated on horn of plenty.

3	$10 (7)	cream colored paper, with engravers name	$35.00	$75.00
3A	$10 (5)	same as above but engravers name removed	$20.00	$50.00
4	$10 (6)	blue colored paper, with engravers name	$25.00	$60.00
4A	$10 (6)	same as above but engravers name removed	$30.00	$65.00
4B	$10 ((7)	same but date of issue changed in red pen to "Aug. 1, 1863"	$50.00	$85.00

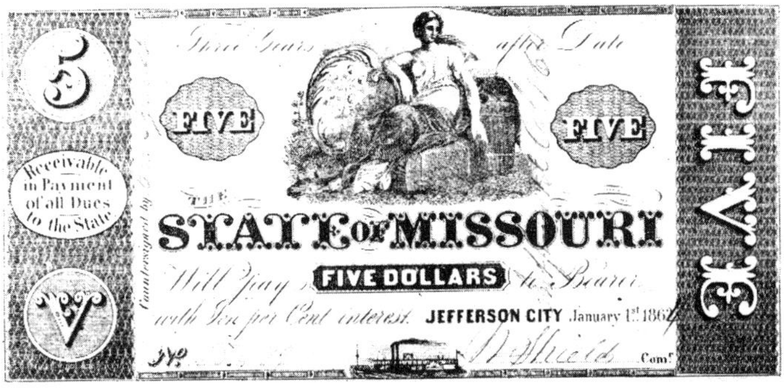

No serial letter, Commerce seated on bale of cotton.

5	$5 (6)	cream colored paper, with engravers name	$25.00	$50.00
5A	$5 (5)	same but no engravers name	$20.00	$45.00
5B	$5 (6)	same but date of issue changed in red pen to "Aug. 1, 1863"	$25.00	$50.00
5C	$5 (5)	same as 5A but date of issue changed in red pen to "Aug. 1, 1863"	$20.00	$45.00
5D	$5 (8)	same as 5 but date of issue changed in red to "Oct. 1, 1864" and at bottom Jan. 1, 1862 changed to 1864	$75.00	$125.00
6	$5 (7)	blue tinted paper, with engravers name	$30.00	$55.00
6A	$5 (6)	same but no engravers name	$25.00	$50.00

6B	$5 (8)	same as 6A but date of issue changed in red to "Oct. 1, 1864" and at bottom Jan. 1, 1862 changed to 1864 "A. Malus. Eng. N. O."	$75.00	$125.00

No serial letter, "THREE" in green. Gov. C. F. Jackson at center, Liberty left, hunter right.

7	$3 (10)	cream colored plain paper	very rare	
7A	$3 (9)	cream colored paper on back of bill of exchange	$55.00	$100.00
8	$3 (8)	blue tinted paper	$40.00	$75.00
8C	$3 (8)	same as 8 but date at bottom changed with pen from Jan. 1, 1862 to 1864.	$75.00	$125.00
9	$3 (6)	blue tinted paper, on back of bill of exchange	$35.00	$70.00
9A	$3 (11)	as above, but no "THREE" in green	extremely rare	

No serial letter. "TWO" in green. Farmer with horses and plow at center, girl left, state arms at right.

10	$2 (6)	cream colored paper	$35.00	$55.00
10A	$2 (8)	cream colored paper, on back of bill of exchange	$35.00	$65.00
10B	$2 (10)	same as 10 but "TWO" overprint is at extreme right of note	$200.00	$250.00

10C	$2 (8)	same as 10 but date at bottom changed with pen from Jan. 1, 1862 to 1864.	$75.00	$100.00
11	$2 (9)	blue tinted paper	extremely rare	
11A	$2 (8)	blue tinted paper on back of bill of exchange	extremely rare	

No serial letter, "ONE" in red (in multiple shades).
Jefferson Davis at center, Liberty left, hunter right.

12	$1 (8)	blue tinted paper	$30.00	$50.00
13	$1 (7)	blue tinted paper, on back of bill of exchange	$25.00	$45.00
13A	$1 (8)	same as 12 but date at bottom changed with pen from Jan. 1, 1862 to 1864.	$75.00	$100.00
14	$1 (8)	cream colored paper	$35.00	$50.00
14A	$1 (8)	cream colored paper, on back of bill of exchange	$35.00	$60.00

MISSOURI CONFEDERATE DEFENSE BOND CURRENCY

Authorized by Act of "Nov. 5th, 1861." $10,000,000

Engraved by "Keatinge & Ball. Columbia, S.C."

Paper watermarked with "W.T.& Co.," "T. C. C. & Co.," or unwatermarked.

Note: although it is generally supposed that the following notes exist unsigned only, several signed piece are confirmed. Such pieces, if genuinely signed are very rare. Due to this rarity, the listings below are for unsigned pieces. Collectors should beware of fake signatures.

Red and black with Ceres seated between Commerce and Navigation.

Watermarked "W. T. & Co."

15	$4.50 (7)	A B	$65.00	$100.00
15A	$4.50 (11)	A B same with overprint inverted	extremely rare	

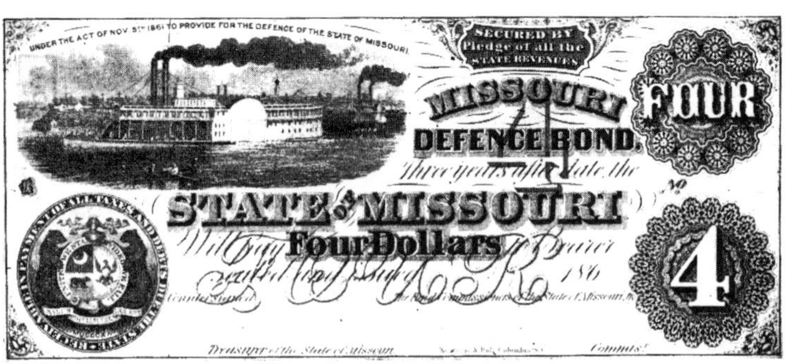

Red and black with Mississippi river boat.

16	$4 (6)	A B	$50.00	$85.00
16A	$4 (11)	A B same with overprint inverted	extremely rare	

Red "THREE," Ceres Volante, maiden right.
Watermarked "W.T. & Co." (vertically)

17 $3 (6) A $25.00 $50.00

Unwatermarked (red fibre paper).

17A $3 (6) A $30.00 $60.00

Watermarked "T. C. C. & Co."

17B $3 (7) A $40.00 $65.00

Red "ONE," cattle in pasture, maiden at right.

Watermarked "W.T. & Co."

18 $1 (4) A B C $12.00 $25.00

Unwatermarked

18A $1 (6) A B C $15.00 $35.00

Watermarked "T. C. C. & Co."

18B $1 (6) A B C $15.00 $35.00

Watermarked "T. C. C. & Co."

18B	$1 (6)	A B C	$15.00	$35.00

Requisitions for Missouri Defense Bonds.

Jefferson Davis, red "100," fancy green back.

Unwatermarked

19	$100 (5)	A B	$55.00	$100.00

Slaves gathering cotton, Ceres left, red "50," fancy green back.

20	$50 (5)	A B	$40.00	$75.00

Steamship center, Liberty seated at left, red "TWENTY," fancy green back.

			Watermarked "W. T. C. C. & Co."		
21	$20 (8)	A B C D		$35.00	$75.00
			Unwatermarked		
21A	$20 (4)	A B C D		$30.00	$60.00

* * * * * *

Missouri Union Government Issues
"DEFENCE WARRANTS"

Issued under authorization of an ordinance passed October 18, 1862. These notes were secured by stock in the Bank of the State of Missouri, and were all redeemed ($5, $10, $20, $50, $100, and $1,000 denominations were authorized).

"A. McLean Lith. St. Louis."

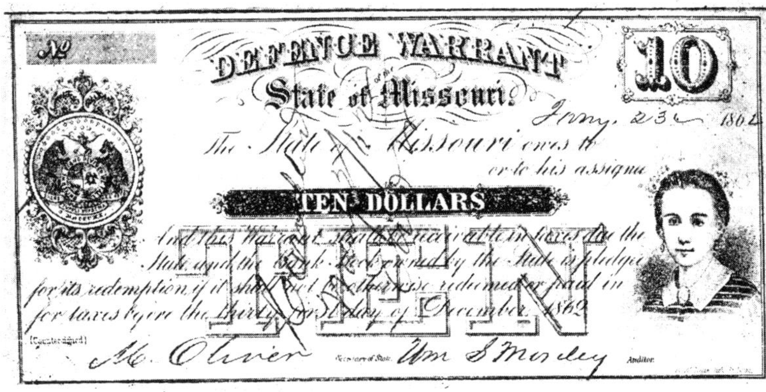

State seal and girl's face, "TEN" in green.

UG1 $10 (9) written dates, no serial letter very rare

State seal and girl's face, "TEN" in green.

UG2 $10 (10) printed or stamped dates, no serial letter very rare

"R. P. Studley & Co. Lith. St. Louis."

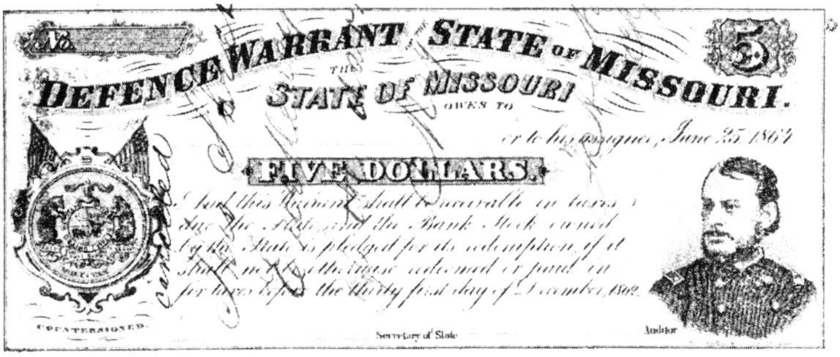

State seal and unidentified Union officer.

UG3 $5 (11) serial letter C extremely rare

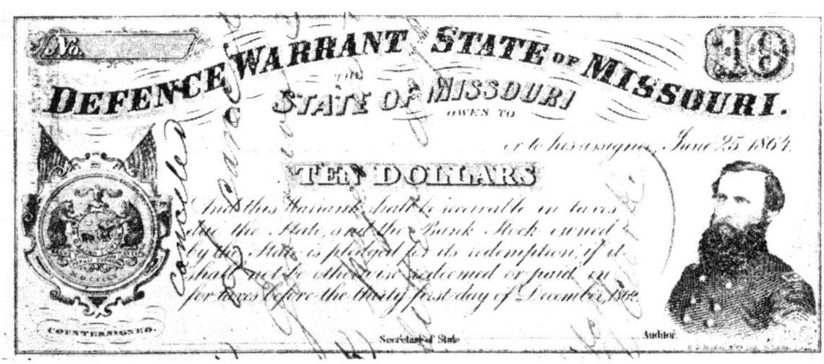

State seal and unidentified Union officer.

UG4 $10 (11) serial letter C extremely rare

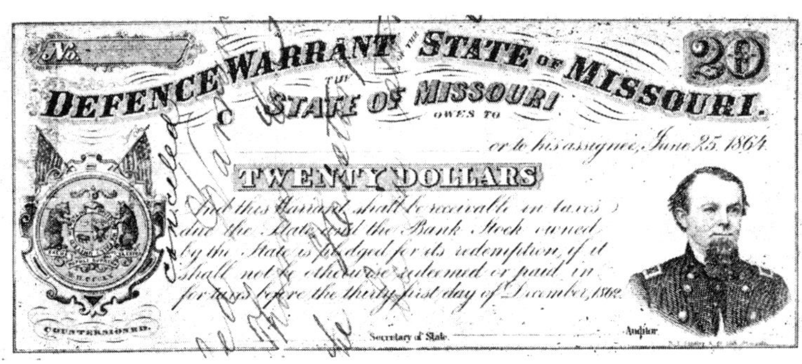

State seal and unidentified Union officer.

UG5 $20 (11) serial letter C extremely rare

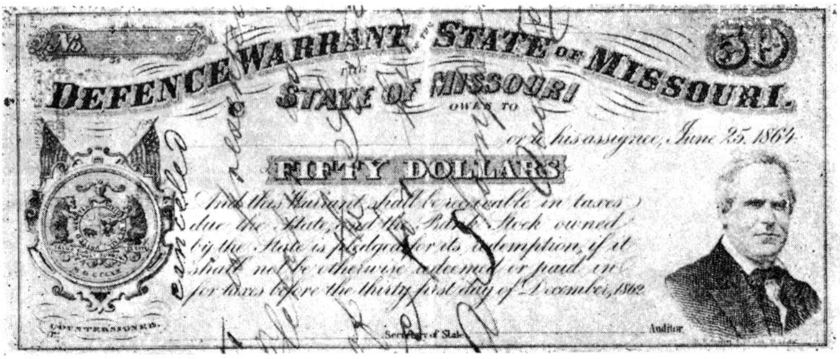

State seal and Willard Preble Hall (governor 1864-65).

UG6 $50 (11) serial letter C extremely rare

"UNION MILITARY BONDS"

Issued under an act approved March 9, 1863. "1863" of date is printed. "American Bank Note Co. Philada."

General Lyons left, Liberty, globe and eagle right, ornate green back.

UG11 $1 (9) A C F G very rare

Portrait of unidentified man, ornate green back.

UG12 $3 (11) A C extremely rare

UG13 $5 (11) D (as UG33 except date) extremely rare

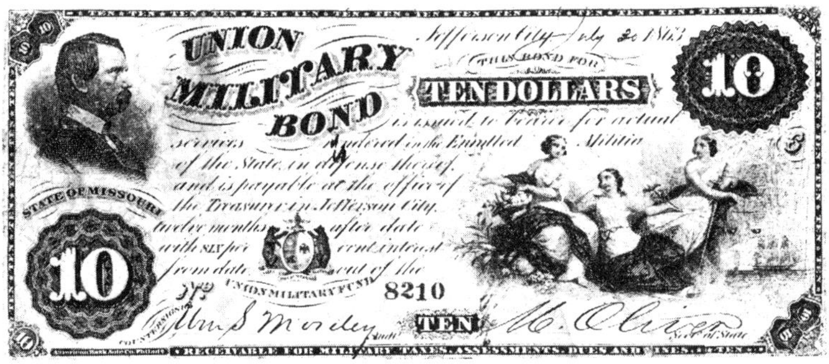

Brig. General Francis P. Blair, Jr. and three women, ornate green back.

UG14 $10 (10) A B C extremely rare

UG15 $20 no information available

Reissue, authorized under act approved Feb. 20, 1865.
"1865" of date is printed.
"American Bank Note Co. Philada."

UG21 $1 (11) A C G (as UG11 except date) extremely rare

Unidentified man, Liberty, ornate green back.

UG22 $3 (11) C extremely rare

UG23 $5 (11) D (as UG33 except date) extremely rare

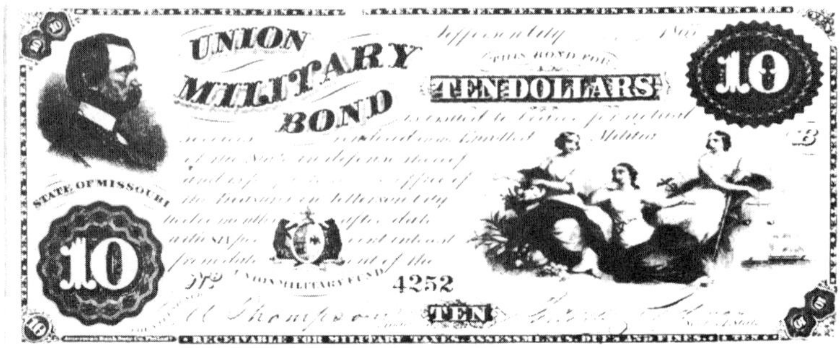

Brig. General Francis P. Blair, Jr. and three women, ornate green back.

UG24 $10 (11) B C extremely rare
UG25 $20 no information available

Reissue, authorized under same act as 1865 issue.
"American Bank Note Co. Philada."

UG31 $1 (11) A C G (as UG11 except date) extremely rare
UG32 $3 (11) C extremely rare

UG33 $5 (11) D extremely rare
UG34 $10 (11) B C (as UG24 except date) extremely rare
UG35 $20 no information available
UG36 $50 no information available

"WAR CLAIM CERTIFICATES"

At the close of the Civil War the Missouri defense fund was exhausted. No provision was made for the payment of these claims until the year 1874, when the Missouri legislature passed a law entitled "An act to audit and adjust the war debt of the state." This act was approved March 19th, 1874. By an agreement with the federal government, claims were to be filed with and passed by the state, and then forwarded with proof to Washington, D.C. Upon proper proof, the federal government remitted to the state, and the state made settlement with the claimant.

Later, the federal government uncovered many irregularities and frauds in connection with claims, and refused to make further payments. This put an end to payment of Missouri war claims.

In 1875 when the people adopted a new constitution, in article four section fifty-two, thereof, the following repudiation of all war time obligations became a part of the state constitution.

"...War Debt, Payment of: The General Assembly shall have no power to make any appropriation of money, or to issue any bonds or other evidences of indebtedness for the payment, or on account or in recognition of any act entitled 'An act to audit and adjust the war debt of the State,' approved March 19, 1874, or any act of a similar nature, until after the claims so audited shall have been presented to and paid by the Government of the United States to the State of Missouri."

"The R. P. Studley Co. Lith. St. Louis."
Written dates of 1874.

Military Service
Payment was made in "State of Missouri War Claim Certificates.

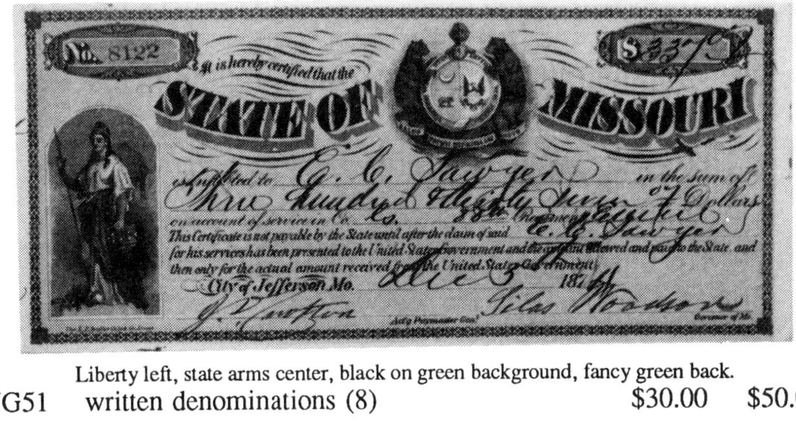

Liberty left, state arms center, black on green background, fancy green back.

UG51 written denominations (8) $30.00 $50.00

UG51A written denominations (3) as above but litho is very crude, green on back is darker $45.00 $65.00

No. 8122
It is hereby certified that the
STATE OF MISSOURI
is indebted to E. C. Sawyer in the sum of
Dollars
on account of services in Co.
Regiment
This Certificate is not payable by the State until after the claim of said E. C. Sawyer
for his services has been presented to the United States Government and the amount allowed and paid to the State, and then only for the actual amount received from the United States Government.
City of Jefferson, Mo. 187
Act'g Paymaster Gen'l
Silas Woodson
Governor of Mo.

stars above seal and bears are slimmer

UG51B written denominations (9) $85.00 $110.00

Civil Service

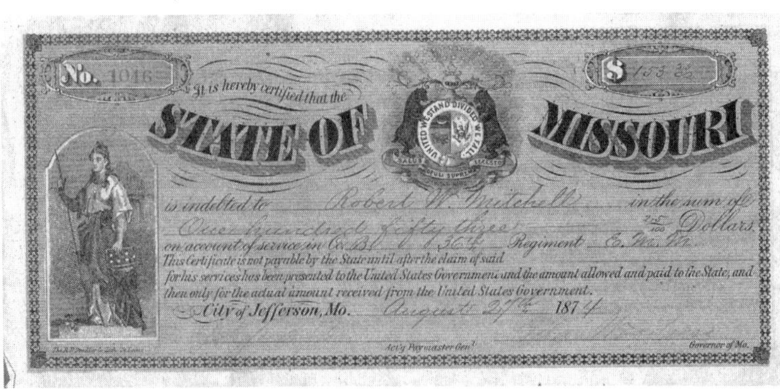
No. 1046
It is hereby certified that the
STATE OF MISSOURI
is indebted to Robert W. Mitchell in the sum of
One hundred fifty three Dollars
on account of services in Co.
Regiment
This Certificate is not payable by the State until after the claim of said
for his services has been presented to the United States Government and the amount allowed and paid to the State, and then only for the actual amount received from the United States Government.
City of Jefferson, Mo. August 27th 1874
Act'g Paymaster Gen'l
Governor of Mo.

Liberty left, state arms center, black on brown background, fancy green back.

UG52 written denominations (10) $75.00 $175.00

THE STATE OF NORTH CAROLINA

The issues of notes in 1815, 1817 and 1824 by North Carolina State Treasurer John Haywood are interesting and rare, and also probably an illegal state issue. They are listed below.

Act of 1814
Written dates 1814-16 ("181" printed, or "1815" printed).

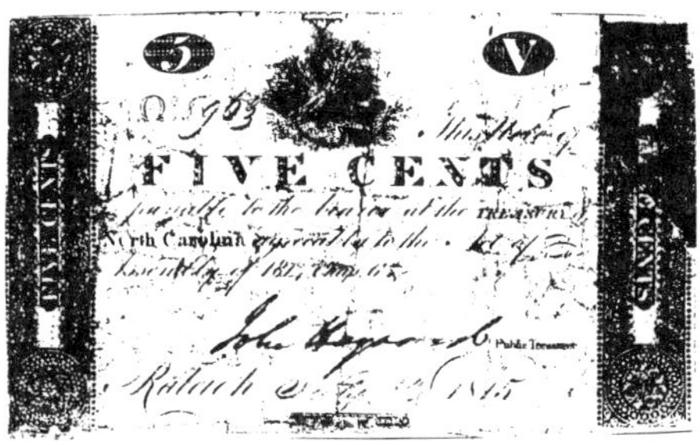

Vignette at top center, "5" at top left in oval, "V" at top right in oval.

01 5c (11) extremely rare

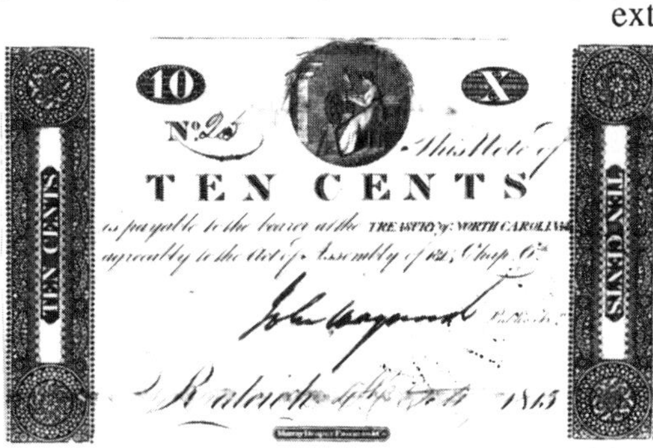

02 10c (11) extremely rare

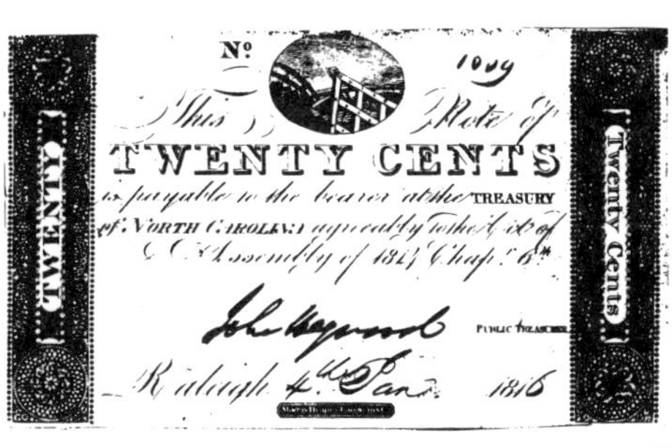

03 20c (11) extremely rare

04 25c no information available

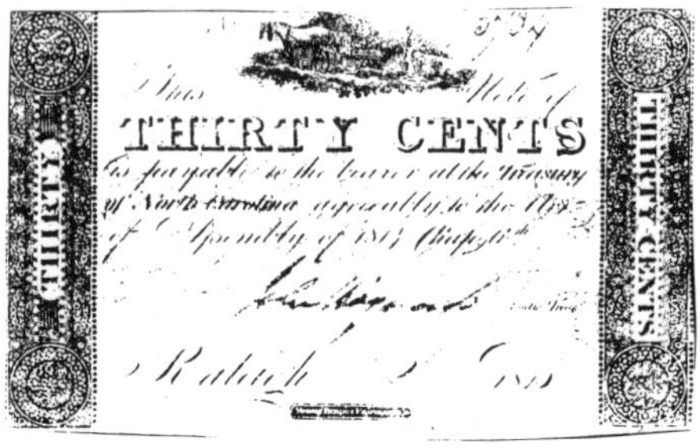

05 30c (11) extremely rare

06 40c (11) extremely rare

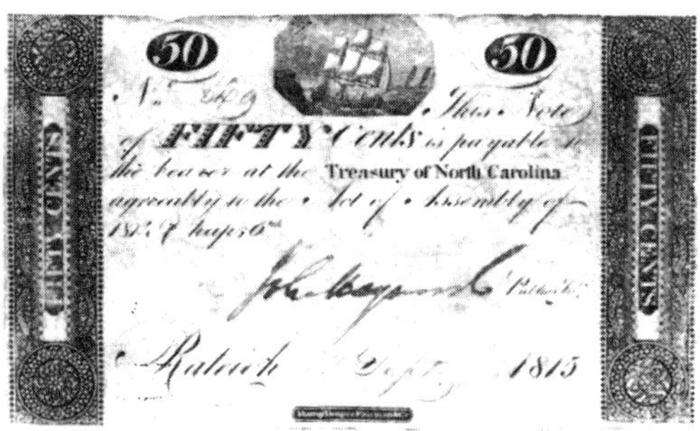

07 50c (11) extremely rare

Act of 1816
Written Dates (1817 Printed.)

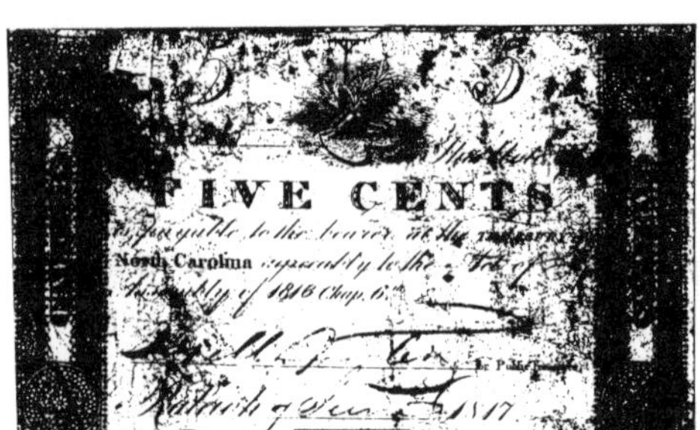

08 5c (11) extremely rare

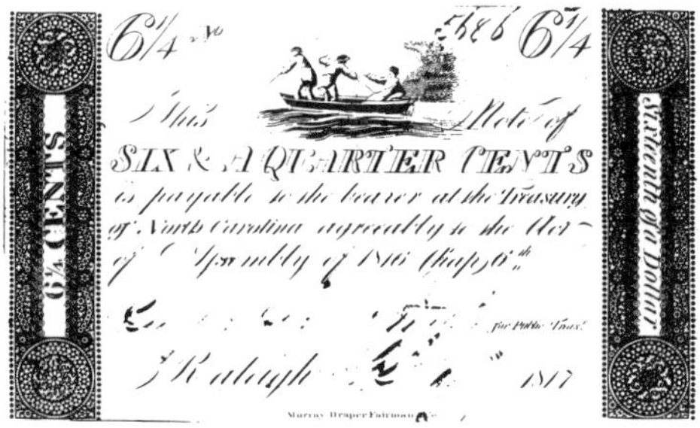

09 6 1/4c (11) extremely rare

010 10c (11) as 02 except dates extremely rare

011 12.5c (11) extremely rare

012 20c (11) as 03 except dates extremely rare

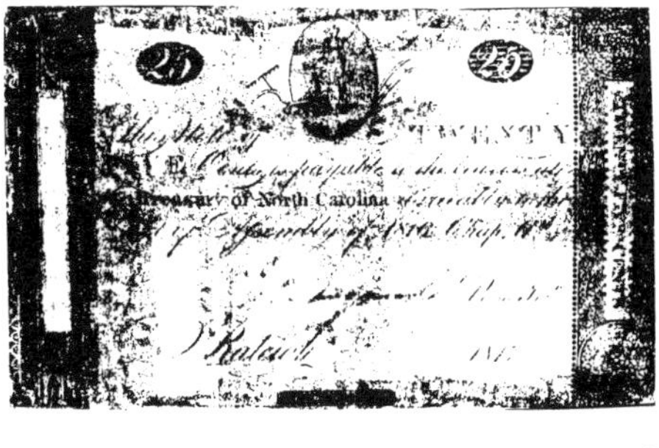

013 25c (11) extremely rare

014 30c (11) as 05 except dates extremely rare

015 40c no information available

016 50c no information available

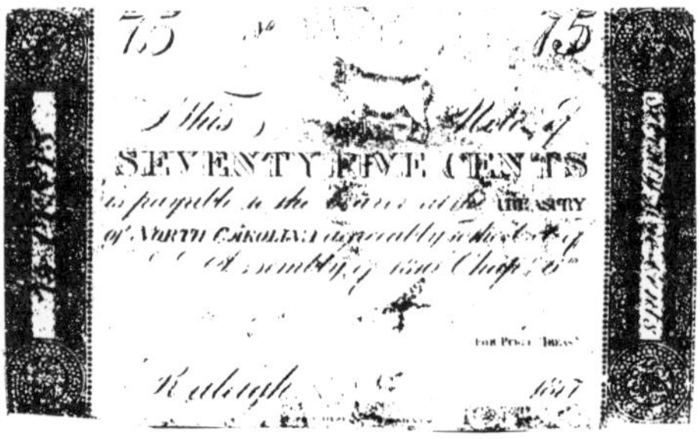

017 75c (11) extremely rare

Act of 1823
Written dates (1824 printed).

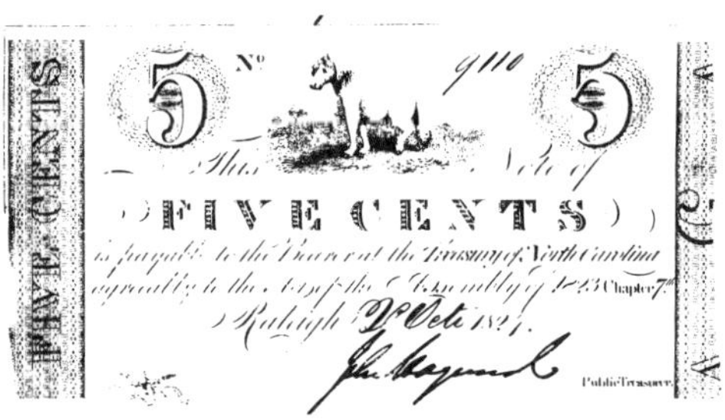

018 5c (11) extremely rare
018A 5c proof of above note extremely rare

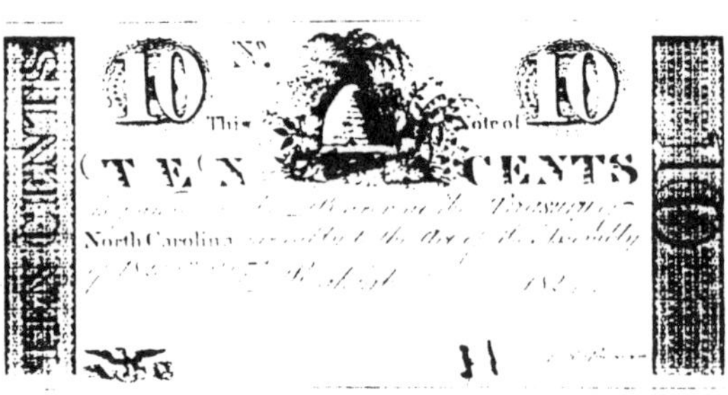

019 10c (11) extremely rare
019A 10c proof of above note extremely rare

020 20 cents extremely rare
020A 20 cents proof of above note extremely rare

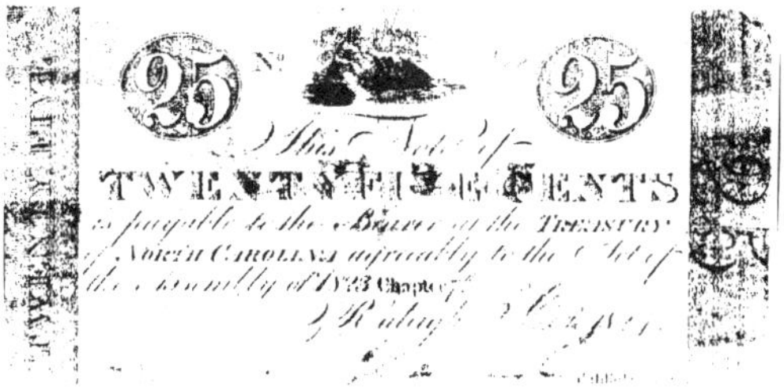

021 25 cents (11) extremely rare
021A 25 cents proof of above note extremely rare

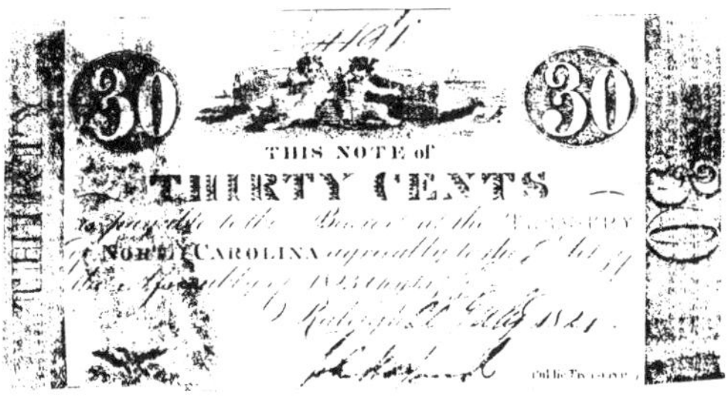

022 30 cents (11) extremely rare
022A 30 cents proof of above note extremely rare

023 40 cents (11) extremely rare
023A 40 cents proof of above note extremely rare

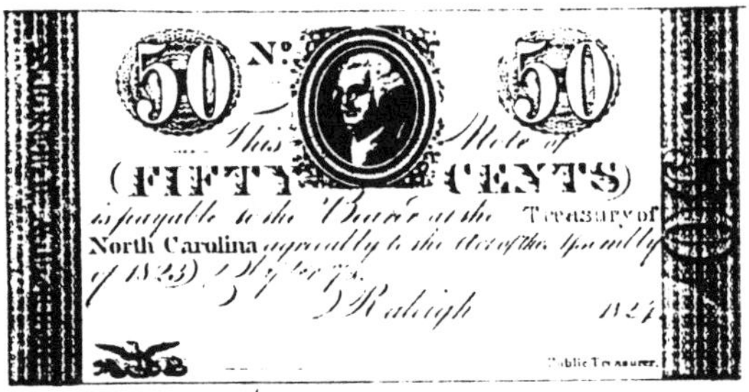

024 50 cents extremely rare
024A 50 cents proof of above note extremely rare

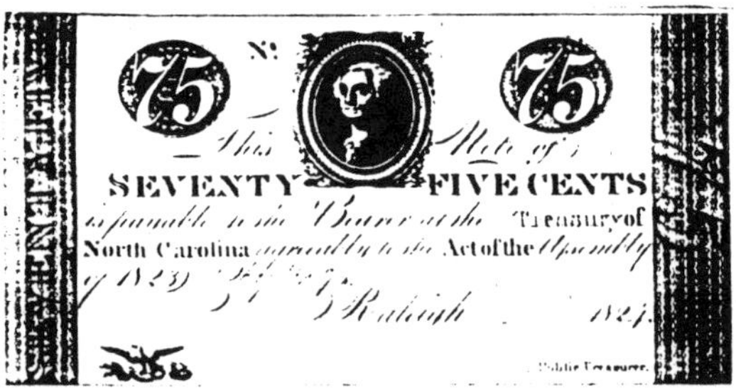

025 75 cents (11) extremely rare
025A 75 cents proof of above note extremely rare

$3,250,000 Authorized by Act of May 11th, 1861
Printed by "F.W. Bornemann, Charleston, S.C."

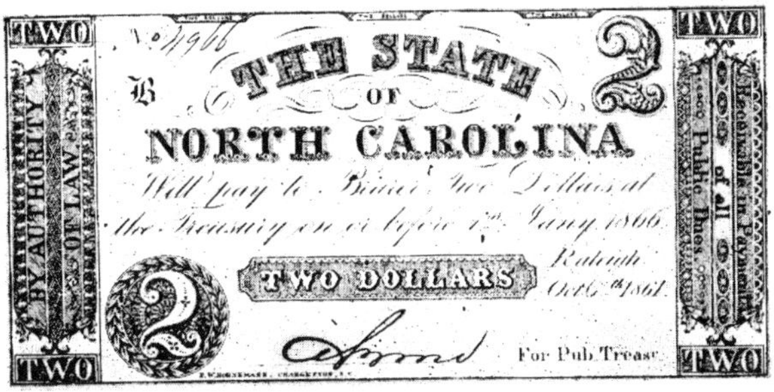

Printed on backs of N.C. broken bank notes of various denominations.
"Two dollars" on back in red.

Dated "Oct. 1st, 1861."

1	$2 (3)	A B C D	$14.00	$20.00

Dated "Oct. 2nd, 1861."

5	$2 (7)	A B C D	$15.00	$30.00

"Two Dollars" on back inverted.

5IB	$2 (10)	A B C D	very rare	

Printed on back of North Carolina $1000 bond.

"Two Dollars" in red on back.

9	$2 (8)	A B C D	$25.00	$45.00

Plain paper, plain back.

13	$2 (5)	A B C D	$12.00	$20.00

Plain paper, "Two Dollars" in red on back.

17	$2 (6)	A B C D	$15.00	$24.00

Dated "Oct. 4th, 1861."

Plain paper, plain back.

21	$2 (3)	A B C D E	$12.00	$20.00

Paper watermarked "FIVE."

21A	$2 (8)	A B C D E	$45.00	$65.00

Dated "Oct. 6th, 1861."
Plain paper, plain back.

22	$2 (5)	A B C D E	$12.00	$20.00

"N.C. Inst. Deaf & Dumb Print."
Dated "Oct. 2nd, 1861."

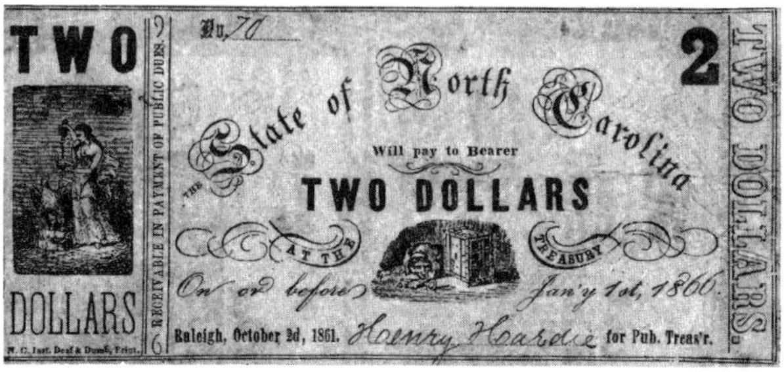

Watchdog and safe, Liberty at left, printed on the back of North Carolina broken bank notes.
"Two Dollars" in red on back.

23	$2 (9)	No serial letter	$8000.00 ex rare

"N.C. Inst. Deaf & Dumb Print."

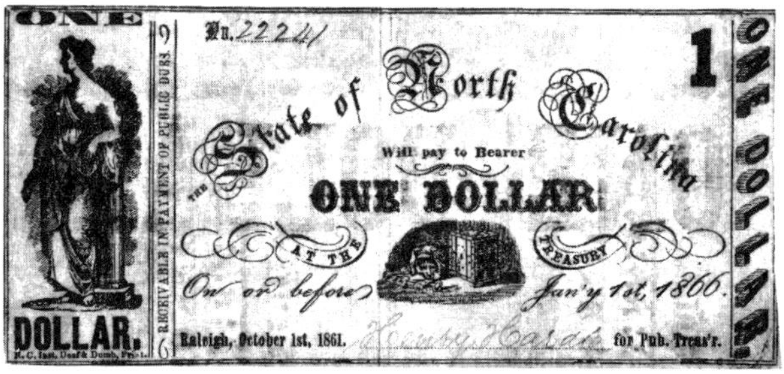

Watchdog and safe, Minerva at left, printed on the back of North Carolina broken bank notes.
"One Dollars" in red on back.

Dated "Oct. 1st 1861."

24	$1 (5)	No serial letter	$15.00	$40.00
24A	$1 (10)	Similar to 24 but "one dollar" twice on back	very rare	

No serial letter.

24B	$1 (10)	No "for" before "treasurer"	very rare	

Dated "Oct. 2nd 1861."

25	$1 (5)	No serial letter	$15.00	$40.00
25B	$1 (10)	No "for" before "treasurer"	very rare	

Dated "Oct. 3rd 1861."

26	$1 (5)	No serial letter	$15.00	$40.00
26A	$1 (10)	Watermarked T.C.C. and Co.	very rare	
		Dated "Oct. 4th 1861."		
27	$1 (5)	No serial letter	$15.00	$40.00
		Dated "Oct. 5th 1861."		
28	$1 (10)	No serial letter	very rare	
		Printed on back of N.C. bond. (Oct.5th 1861.)		
29	$1 (5)	No serial letter	$20.00	$60.00
		"One Dollar" in red inverted on back		
29IB	$1 (9)	No serial letter	$115.00	$175.00

No printers' imprint.

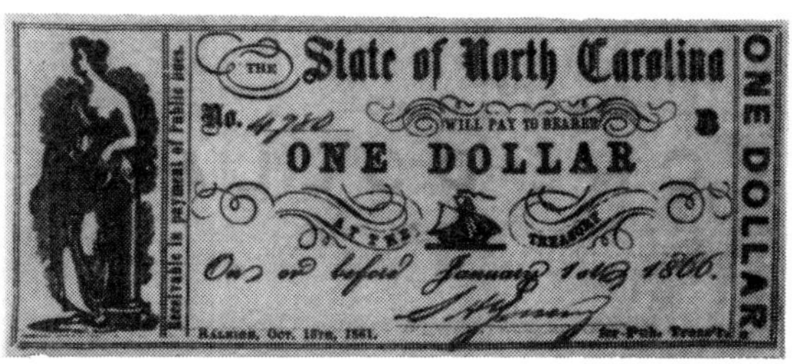

Minerva at left, small ship at center. Plain paper, ornate red back. The red ink was made of a berry substance and washes of easily.

Dated "Oct. 10th, 1861."

32	$1 (2)	A B	$12.00	$30.00
32IB	$1 (10)	A B Back is inverted	very rare	
		Dated "Oct. 11th, 1861."		
32A	$1 (2)	A B	$12.00	$30.00
		Dated "Oct. 12th, 1861."		
32B	$1 (2)	A B	$12.00	$30.00
		Dated "Oct. 13th, 1861."		
32C	$1 (2)	A B	$12.00	$30.00
		"One Dollar" in red inverted on back.		
32CIB	$1 (9)	A B	$80.00	$120.00

No.	Value	Description	Price 1	Price 2
CT32	$1 (9)	A B counterfeit Brown note, numbers in black. Line under signature is not broken but a thin sold line. "J" in January is in lower case. Poor quality engraving of Minerva.	rare	
		Dated "Oct. 14th, 1861."		
32D	$1 (2)	A B	$12.00	$30.00
		Dated "Oct. 15th, 1861."		
32E	$1 (2)	A B	$12.00	$30.00
		Dated "Oct. 16th, 1861."		
32F	$1 (2)	A B	$12.00	$30.00
32F1	$1 (10)	A B January misspelled "Jonuary"	very rare	
		Dated "Oct. 17th, 1861."		
32G	$1 (2)	A B	$12.00	$30.00
		"One Dollar" in red inverted on back.		
32IB	$1 (9)	A B	$75.00	$125.00
		Double printed "one dollar on back.		
32G2	$1 (10)	A B	very rare	
		Dated "Oct. 18th, 1861."		
32H	$1 (2)	A B	$12.00	$30.00
		Dated "Oct. 19th, 1861."		
32I	$1 (2)	A B	$12.00	$30.00
		Dated "Oct. 20th, 1861."		
32J	$1 (2)	A B	$12.00	$30.00
		"One dollar" on back twice.		
32J1	$1 (2)	A B	very rare	
		Dated "Oct. 21st, 1861."		
32K	$1 (2)	A B	$12.00	$30.00

"ONE DOLLAR" IN RED ON BACK, WATERMARKED "TEN."

No.	Value	Description	Price 1	Price 2
		Dated "Oct. 16th, 1861."		
38	$1 (4)	A B	$15.00	$45.00
		Dated "Oct. 17th, 1861."		
38A	$1 (4)	A B	$15.00	$45.00
		Dated "Oct. 18th, 1861."		
38B	$1 (4)	A B	$15.00	$45.00
		Dated "Oct. 19th, 1861."		
38C	$1 (4)	A B	$15.00	$45.00
		Dated "Oct. 20th, 1861."		
38D	$1 (4)	A B	$15.00	$45.00
		Dated "Oct. 21st, 1861."		
38E	$1 (4)	A B	$15.00	$60.00

SAME TYPES, WATERMARKED "FIVE."

Dated "Oct. 16th, 1861."

39	$1 (5)	A B	$25.00	$60.00

Dated "Oct. 17th, 1861."

39A	$1 (5)	A B	$25.00	$60.00

Dated "Oct. 18th, 1861."

39B	$1 (5)	A B	$25.00	$60.00

Dated "Oct. 19th, 1861."

39C	$1 (5)	A B	$25.00	$60.00

Dated "Oct. 20th, 1861."

39D	$1 (5)	A B	$25.00	$60.00

Dated "Oct. 21st, 1861."

39E	$1 (5)	A B	$25.00	$60.00

SAME TYPES, WATERMARKED "T.C.C. and Co."

Dated "Oct. 16th, 1861."

40	$1 (4)	A B	$24.00	$60.00

Dated "Oct. 17th, 1861."

40A	$1 (4)	A B	$24.00	$60.00
40A1	$1 (10)	A B January misspelled "Jonuary"	very rare	

Dated "Oct. 18th, 1861."

40B	$1 (4)	A B	$24.00	$60.00

Dated "Oct. 19th, 1861."

40C	$1 (4)	A B	$24.00	$60.00

Dated "Oct. 20th, 1861."

40D	$1 (4)	A B	$24.00	$60.00

Dated "Oct. 21st, 1861."

40E	$1 (4)	A B	$24.00	$60.00

$200,000.00 Authorized by Act of June 28th, 1861.

"J. Spelman. Public Printer."
Dated "Oct. 1st, 1861."

The fractional denominations are of the same type as illustrated.

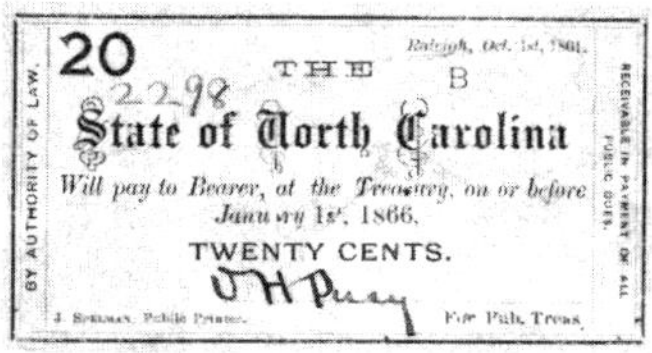

Unwatermarked, plain paper.

42	50c (4)	No serial letter.	$24.00	$30.00
43	25c (4)	No serial letter.	$24.00	$30.00
		No serial leter.		
43A	25c (10)	On blue paper.	very rare	
44	20c (4)	No serial letter.	$25.00	$60.00
		Plain paper, tinted blue.		
45	20c (5)	No serial letter.	$40.00	$90.00
		Printed on back of North Carolina bond.		
46	20c (4)	No serial letter.	$27.50	$45.00
		Plain paper.		
47	10c (4)	No serial letter.	$6.00	$15.00
CT47	10c (10)	No serial letter. Counterfeit. "J. Conway, Pub. Pr." Letters and numbers different from genuine note.	very rare	
		Plain paper.		
48	5c (4)	No serial letter.	$6.00	$12.00
CT48	5c (10)	No serial letter. Counterfeit Similar to CT47.	rare	
		Printed on back of N.C. bond.		
48A	5c (7)	No serial letter.	$55.00	$80.00
		Plain blue paper.		
48B	5c (8)	No serial letter.	$70.00	$110.00

SAME TYPES. WATERMARKED "TEN."

49	50c (4)	No serial letter.	$35.00	$60.00
50	25c (4)	No serial letter.	$22.50	$50.00
51	20c (5)	No serial letter.	$40.00	$100.00
52	10c (4)	No serial letter.	$20.00	$60.00
53	5c (4)	No serial letter.	$20.00	$60.00

SAME TYPES. WATERMARKED "FIVE."

49A	50c (6)	No serial letter.	$35.00	$60.00
50A	25c (6)	No serial letter.	$35.00	$60.00
51A	20c (6)	No serial letter.	$40.00	$200.00
52A	10c (6)	No serial letter.	$20.00	$60.00
53A	5c (6)	No serial letter.	$20.00	$60.00

SAME TYPES. WATERMARKED "T.C.C. and Co."

49B	50c (8)	No serial letter.		rare
50B	25c (8)	No serial letter.		rare
51B	20c (8)	No serial letter.		rare
52B	10c (8)	No serial letter.		rare
53B	5c (8)	No serial letter.		rare

SAME TYPES (WITH SERIAL LETTERS "A" & "B") PLAIN PAPER.

54	50c (4)	A B	$12.00	$35.00
CT54	50c (10)	B Counterfeit. All are signed O.H. Perry. Style of note slightly different from genuine note.	very rare	
55	25c (4)	A B	$15.00	$35.00
CT55	25c (8)	B Counterfeit.	$25.00	$30.00
56	20c (5)	A B	$35.00	$60.00
CT56	20c (5)	B Counterfeit.	$27.50	$42.50
57	10c (4)	A B	$15.00	$30.00
CT57	10c (10)	B	very rare	
58	5c (4)	A B	$15.00	$30.00

SAME TYPES. WATERMARKED "TEN."

64	50c (5)	A B	$35.00	$75.00
65	25c (5)	A B	$35.00	$75.00
66	20c (6)	A B	$60.00	$100.00
67	10c (5)	A B	$35.00	$75.00
68	5c (6)	A B	$35.00	$75.00

		SAME TYPES. WATERMARKED "FIVE."		
69	50c (5)	A B	$35.00	$75.00
70	25c (5)	A B	$35.00	$75.00
71	20c (6)	A B	$75.00	$200.00
72	10c (5)	A B	$35.00	$75.00
73	5c (6)	A B	$35.00	$75.00

$300,000.00 Authorized by Act of Dec. 1st, 1861.

Engraved by "J. Manouvrier. N. Orls. La."
Written dates of 1861 & 1862.

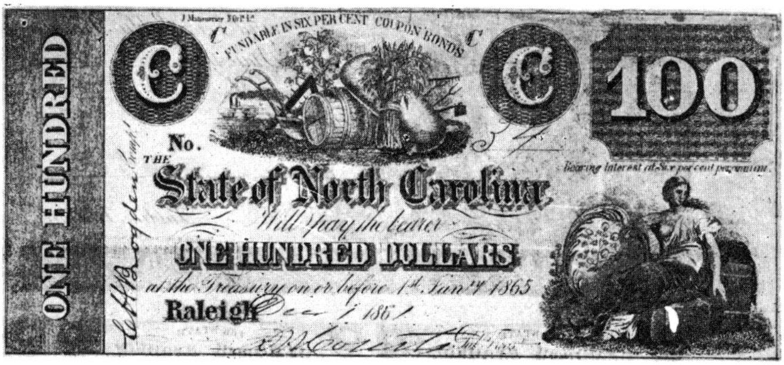

Agricultural tools and products, Commerce seated at right.
Printed on back of North Carolina bonds.

74	$100 (10)	A B C D	$400.00	$1200.00
		Plain back.		
74A	$100 (11)	A B C D	$500.00	$1500.00

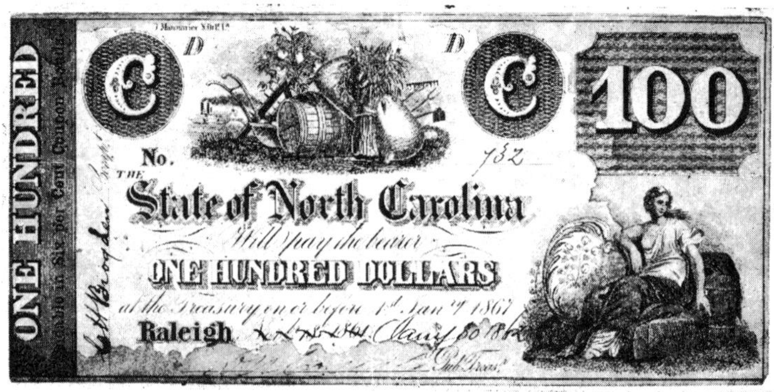

Printed on back of North Carolina bond.

74B	$100 (11)	A B C D	extremely rare

Liberty standing, Ceres seated at center, "FIFTY DOLLARS" in red on back.

Printed on back of North Carolina bond.

74C $50 (10) A B C D $500.00 $1300.00

Same as above, but "fundable" overprint in red.

74D $50 (11) A B C D $700.00 $1500.00

Trimmed to eliminate "Bearing interest at the rate of..."

74E $50 (11) A B C D $700.00 $1500.00

Note: Many 1862 notes, numbers 75 through 87 exist with and without a red "FUNDABLE" overprint as illustrated on note below.

Ceres Volant.

Written date "Feb. 15th, 1862."

"Fundable in six per cent bonds" on upper and lower edge.
Plain paper, no "FUNDABLE" overprint.

75 $20 (5) A B C D $35.00 $90.00

Same. Printed on back of bill of exchange.

76 $20 (5) A B C D $35.00 $90.00

Same type, but with "Fundable" overprint in red.

76A $20 (6) A B C D $35.00 $50.00

Similar to 76A but oval overprint.

76A1 $20 (9) A B C D $100.00 $250.00

Same, but printed on backs of bonds.

76B $20 (9) A B C D $40.00 $90.00

Same as 76B but with oval overprint.

76C $20 (9) A B C D $100.00 $250.00

Printed on back of fill of exchange.

"Fundable in six per cent bonds" on upper edge only.

77 $20 (6) A B C D $75.00 $125.00

Same as 77, but "Fundable" statement at top cut off.

77A $20 (6) A B C D $75.00 $125.00

With oval overprint.

77B $20 (9) A B C D very rare

Same as 77B, but "fundable" statement on top edge cut off.

77C $20 (9) A B C D very rare

Written date "March 1st, 1862."

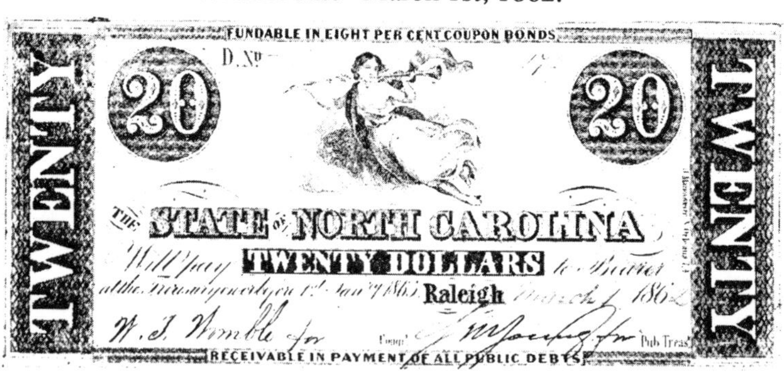

"Fundable in eight per cent coupon bonds" on upper edge.

78 $20 (5) A B C D $35.00 $80.00

Same type, but with "fundable" overprint in red.

78A $20 (6) A B C D $45.00 $100.00

Same, but "fundable" overprint is vertical in two lines.

78B $20 (7) A B C D $45.00 $100.00

Printed on back of bill of exchange. "Fundable in eight per cent bonds" on upper edge.

79 $20 (5) A B C D $40.00 $90.00

Same type, but with"Fundable" overprint in red.

79A $20 (6) A B C D $40.00 $90.00

"Fundable" ...etc. cut off top edge.

79B $20 (6) A B C D $40.00 $55.00

Similar to 79B, but overprinted like 78B.

79C $20 (9) A B C D very rare

Similar to 78B, but trimmed like 79B.

79D $20 (8) A B C D very rare

Engraved by "J.T. Paterson & Co. Augusta, Ga."
Written date "May 1st, 1862."

Railway train at center.
Narrow note. (Edges are trimmed to eliminate "Fundable in eight per cent coupon bonds.)
With "Fundable" overprinted in red.

80	$20 (6)	A B C D	$40.00	$110.00

Same as above, but with untrimmed edges.

80A	$20 (8)	A B C D	$125.00	$250.00

(Same type as above, dated "Jan. 1st, 1863." See 121.)

Engraved by "J. Manouvrier. N. Orls. La."
Written dates of "Jan'y.--1862."

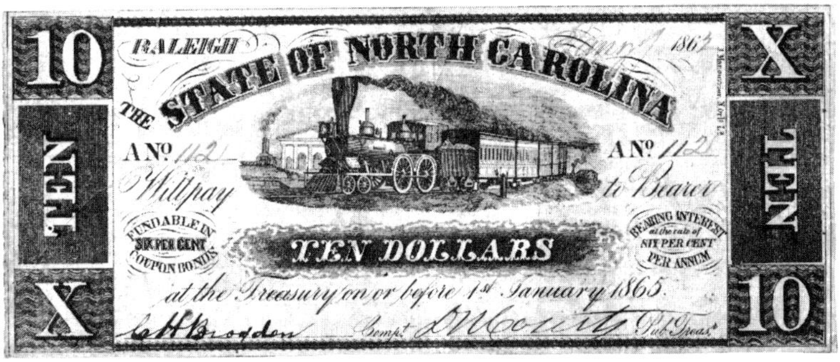

Railway train. Printed on back of North Carolina bond. "Ten dollars" in red on back. "Bearing interest at the rate of six per cent per annum."

81	$10 (7)	A B C D	$75.00	$150.00

Written date "Feb. 15th, 1862."

Railway train, "Fundable in six per cent bonds."

Plain paper, plain back.

82 $10 (5) A B C D $25.00 $75.00

Same, but oval "Fundable" overprint at right end.

82A $10 (7) A B C D $50.00 $125.00

Same as 82 but oval 'Fundable" overprint at left end.

82B $10 (8) A B C D $60.00 $140.00

Printed on back of bill of exchange

83 $10 (5) A B C D $25.00 $65.00

Printed on back of N.C. bonds.

83A $10 (5) A B C D $25.00 $65.00

Red overprint at right end.

83B $10 (8) A B C D $90.00 $175.00

Written date "March 1st, 1862."

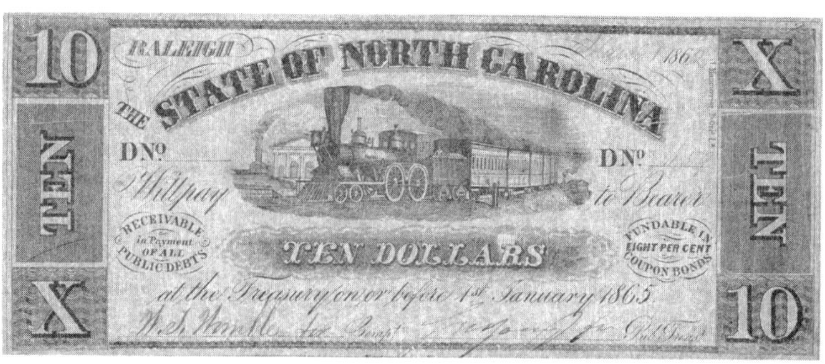

Railway train. Fundable in eight per cent bonds, paper watermarked "Ten."

84 $10 (7) A B C D $35.00 $100.00

"Fundable" overprint in red.

84A $10 (7) A B C D $35.00 $100.00

With oval overprint vertically at right end.

84A1 $10 (10) A B C D $150.00 $275.00

With oval overprint vertically at left end.

84A2 $10 (10) A B C D $60.00 $125.00

Same as 84, but on plain paper.

84B $10 (9) A B C D $60.00 $125.00

Same as 84A, but on plain paper.

84C $10 (9) A B C D $80.00 $150.00

With oval overprint vertically at right end.

84D $10 (10) A B C D $150.00 $275.00

With oval overprint vertically at left end.

84E $10 (10) A B C D $150.00 $300.00

Written date "Feb. 15th, 1862."

Ceres seated at center; train at far right end.

Plain paper.

85 $5 (8) A B C D $50.00 $90.00

Same, but "fundable" overprint in red.

85A $5 (8) A B C D $60.00 $100.00

Same as 85, but on back of bill of exchange.

85B $5 (9) A B C D $75.00 $150.00

Same as above, but with "fundable" overprint.

85C $5 (9) A B C D $75.00 $150.00

Written date "March 1st, 1862."

Liberty standing, Ceres seated at center. Train at far right end. Plain paper.

86 $5 (4) A B C D $30.00 $65.00

Same, but "fundable" overprint in red.

86A $5 (8) A B C D $50.00 $90.00

Dated May 1, 1862.

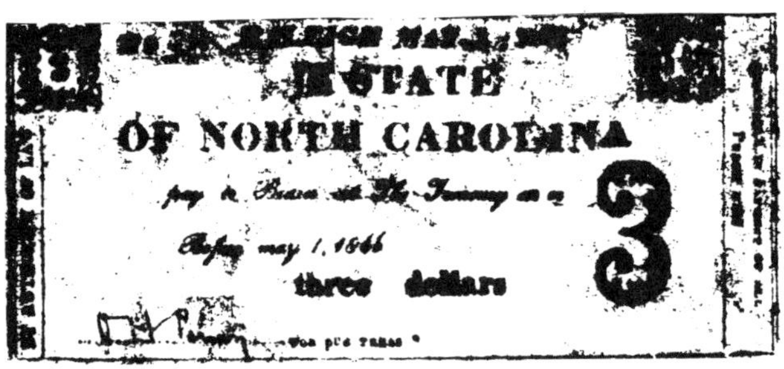

86G $3 (11) extremely rare

Dated June 8th, 1862.

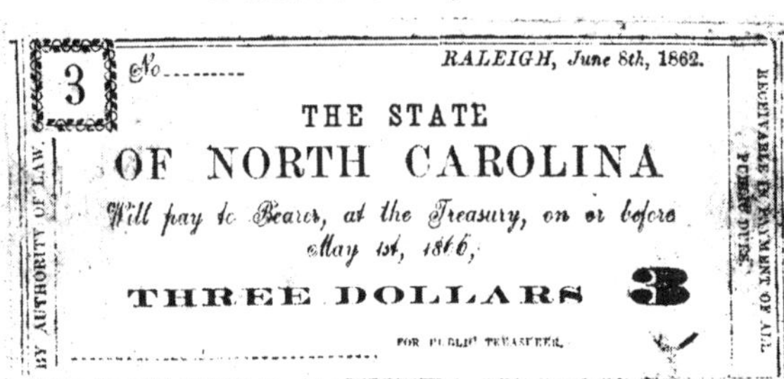

86H $3 (11) extremely rare

Dated August 1, 1862.

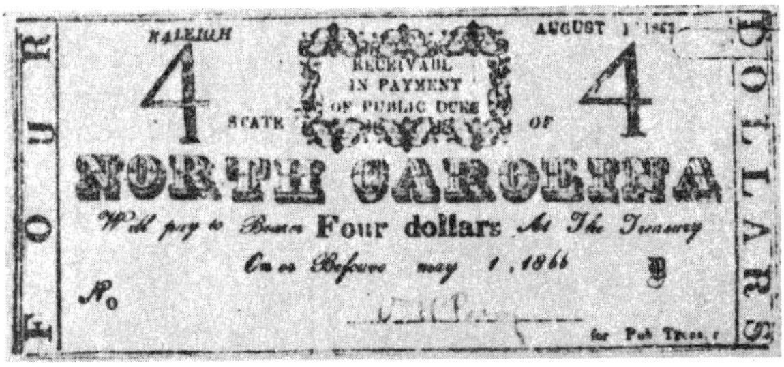

86M $4 (11) extremely rare

Written date "July 1st, 1862."

(Similar note to below but with different red overprint and dated 1863, see no. 124.)

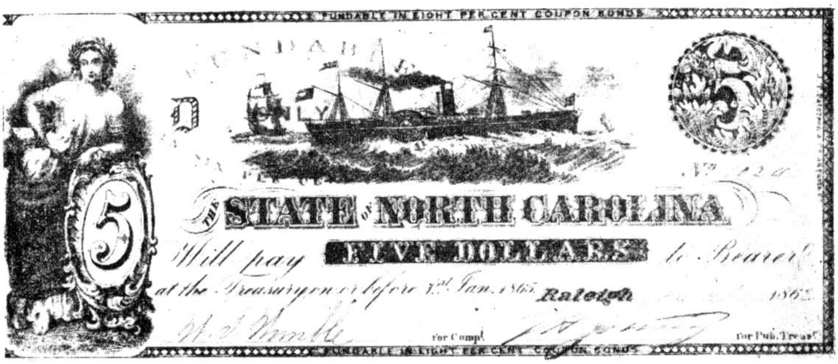

Ceres standing at left, steamship at center. "Fundable" overprint in red.

87	$5 (5)	A B C D	$20.00	$40.00

Narrow note. (Edges trimmed to eliminate "fundable..." line).

87A	$5 (4)	A B C D	$15.00	$30.00

Full edges, but no "fundable" overprinting.

87B	$5 (9)	A B C D	$50.00	$90.00

Oval "fundable..." overprint at top left and inverted at bottom right also.

87C $5 (11) A B C D extremely rare

Written date "Aug. 1" with "fundable" overprint.
87D $5 (9) A B C D $80.00 $125.00

Trimmed as 87A.
87E $5 (9) A B C D $75.00 $120.00

As 87B.
87F $5 (10) A B C D very rare

Lithographic date "Sep. 1st, 1862."

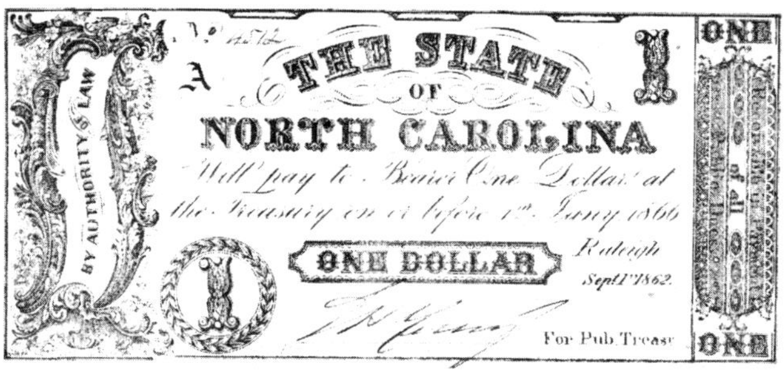

Small serial letter.
88 $1 (3) A B C D E $8.00 $20.00
Large serial letter.
89 $1 (7) A B C D E F G H I J K $25.00 $40.00
Same as above, watermarked "FIVE."
89A $1 (10) A B C D E F G H I J K $85.00 $125.00
Red fiber paper.
89B $1 (10) A B C D E F G H I J K $85.00 $125.00

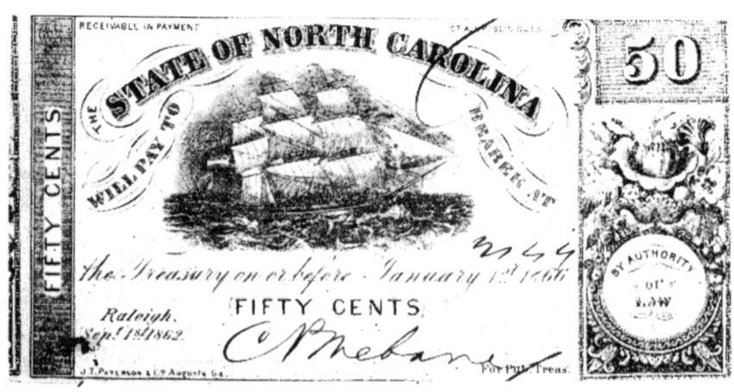

Sailing ship at sea.
"No" written at left end. Serial number right center. Plain paper.
90 50c (4) No serial letter. $9.00 $18.00
Same, but printed on back on N.C. bond.
91 50c (7) No serial letter. $18.00 $50.00

Same type, without "No" at left. Serial number right center, plain paper.

92 50c (3) No serial letter. $9.00 $15.00

Same, but printed on back of N.C. bond.

92A 50c (3) No serial letter. $9.00 $16.00

Same, but printed on back of an Albemarle & Chesapeake Canal Co. bond.

92B 50c (3) No serial letter. $9.00 $15.00

Without "No" written. Serial number under "1862." Printed on back of N.C. bond.

93 50c (3) No serial letter. $9.00 $15.00

Same, but "No" written in front of serial number.

93A 50c (3) No serial letter. $9.00 $15.00

Same, without "No" at left. Serial number under "1862." Plain paper.

94 50c (3) No serial letter. $10.00 $20.00

Same, but serial number to right of "1862."

94A 50c (3) No serial letter. $10.00 $20.00

Same, but printed on back of N.C. bond.

95 50c (3) No serial letter. $10.00 $10.00

Serial number under "1866." without "No" at left. Plain paper.

96 50c (4) No serial letter. $10.00 $20.00

Same, but printed on back of Albemarle & Chesapeake Canal Co. bond.

96A 50c (4) No serial letter. $10.00 $20.00

Same, but printed on back of N.C. bond.

97 50c (4) No serial letter. $10.00 $20.00

Without "no" written. Serial number at left center. Plain paper.

97A 50c (4) No serial letter. $10.00 $20.00

Same, but serial number in upper right hand corner.

97B 50c (4) No serial letter. $10.00 $20.00

"No" written at left. Serial letter at right center. Serial number over "January."

98 50c (5) A B C D E F G H I J K L M N O $12.00 $20.00

Without "no" at left. Serial letter at right center. Serial number at left center.

99 50c (9) A B C D E F G H I J K L M N O $30.00 $50.00

Same,but serial letter is a very small dark black block letter.

99A 50c (4) A B C D E F G H I J K L M N O $10.00 $20.00

Same, but serial letter is written in.

99B 50c (4) A B C D E F G H I J K L M N O $10.00 $20.00

Without "No." Serial letter above "1866." Serial number below "1866."

99C 50c (4) A B C D E F G H I J K L M N O $10.00 $20.00

Without "No" at left. Serial letter right center. Serial number above "1866."

99D 50c (5) A B C D E F G H I J K L M N O $10.00 $20.00

Serial letter written right center. Serial number below "1862."

99E 50c (5) A B C D E F G H I J K L M N O $10.00 $20.00

Serial letter printed right center. Serial number below "1862."

99F 50c (5) A B C D E F G H I J K L M N O $10.00 $20.00

Without "No" at left. Serial number at right center. Large serial letter at left center.

100 50c (5) A B C D E F G H I J K L M N O P $10.00 $20.00

Same, but serial letter is written in, plain paper.

100A 50c (5) A B C D E F G H I J K L M N O $10.00 $20.00

Same, but printed on back of North Carolina bonds.

100B 50c (5) A B C D E F G H I J K L M N O $10.00 $20.00

Same, but small printed serial letter at left.

101 50c (5) A B C D E F G H I J K L M N O $10.00 $20.00

Without "No" written in. Serial number at left center. Serial number below "1866."

101A 50c (5) A B C D E F G H I J K L M N O $10.00 $20.00

Small letter at left. Serial number to right of letter.

101B 50c (5) A B C D E F G H I J K L M N O $10.00 $20.00

Ceres at left.

Large serial letter at left of "25 cents."

102 25c (5) A B C D E F G H I J K L M N O $9.00 $15.00

Small serial letter at let of "25 Cts."

103 25c (5) A B C D E F G H I J K L M N O $9.00 $15.00

Serial letter at upper right corner. Serial number under Raleigh.

104 25c (5) A B C D E F G H I J K L M N O $9.00 $15.00

Same, but serial number right of "1866."

104A 25c (5) A B C D E F G H I J K L M N O $9.00 $15.00

Same, but no serial number.

104B 25c (5) A B C D E F G H I J K L M N O very rare

Serial letter at right.

105 25c (5) A B C D E F G H I J K L M N O $9.00 $15.00

Same, but printed on back of N.C. bond.

106 25c (5) A B C D E F G H I J K L M N O $9.00 $15.00

Same, but printed on back of N.C. note.

106A 25c (5) A B C D E F G H I J K L M N O $9.00 $15.00

Same, but printed on back of Wilmington, Charlotte & Rutherford Railroad bond.

107 25c (5) A B C D E F G H I J K L M N O $9.00 $15.00

Same, but printed on back of Albemarle & Chesapeake Canal Co. bond.

107A 25c (5) A B C D E F G H I J K L M N O $9.00 $15.00

Plain paper. No serial letter, number below "Raleigh."

108 25c (7) No serial letter. $20.00 $35.00

Same, but printed on back of N.C.bond.

108A 25c (8) No serial letter. $15.00 $25.00

Plain paper, serial number at right of "1866."

109 25c (8) No serial letter. $15.00 $25.00

Same, but printed on back of N.C. bond.

109A 25c (9) No serial letter. $20.00 $40.00

Same, but printed on back of N.C. bonds.

110 25c (10) No serial letter. $25.00 $50.00

Same, but printed on back of Albemarle & Chesapeake Canal Co. bond.

110A 25c (10) No serial letter. $25.00 $50.00

Plain back, number at right of "1862."

111 25c (7) No serial letter. $12.00 $22.00

Same, but printed on back of N.C. bond.

112 25c (7) No serial letter. $12.00 $22.00

Same as above, but serial number left of "25 Ct."

112A 25c (11) No serial letter. $50.00 $90.00

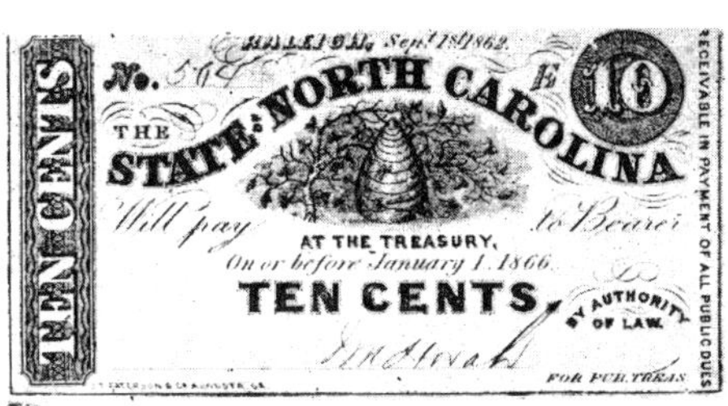

Hornet's nest.

113 10c (4) A B C D E F G H I J K L M N O P Q R S T U $9.00 $20.00

Similar to 113 but "3" shows after "1862" date.

113A 10c (11) A B C D E F G H I J K L M N O P Q R S T U very rare

Slave plowing.

Serial letter printed at left end.

114	10c (7)	A B C D E F G H I J K L M N O P Q R S T U	$12.00	$35.00

Serial letter written at left end.

115	10c (10)	A	very rare	
116	10c (6)	No serial letter.	$12.00	$30.00

$4,500,000.00 Authorized by Act of Dec. 20th, 1862.

"Eng'd and Litho'd by J. T. Paterson & Co. Augusta, Ga."
Lithographic date, "1st Jan. 1863."

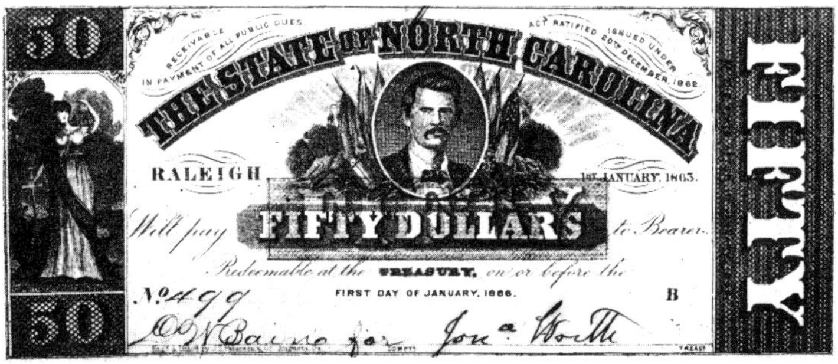

Governor Zebulon Vance center, Justice left. Black with red overprint.

Plain paper.

117 $50 (10) A B C D E F G H I J K L very rare

Paper watermarked "J. Whatman, 1861," and/or horizontal lines and/or coat of arms or parts.

118 $50 (7) A B C D E F G H I J K L $40.00 $75.00

Similar to 118 but watermarked "1862."

118A $50 (9) A B C D E F G H I J K L very rare

Governor Vance center, beehive at right. Black with red overprint.

Plain paper.

119 $20 (5) A B C D E F G H I J K L $40.00 $75.00

Paper watermarked "J. Whatman, 1861," and/or horizontal lines and/or coat of arms or parts.

120 $20 (6) A B C D E F G H I J K L $36.00 $55.00

Similar to 120 but watermarked "1862."

120A $20 (10) A B C D E F G H I J K L very rare

Same as 120 but red "Twenty" inverted.

120B $20 (10) A B C D E F G H I J K L extremely rare

"Eng'd by J. T. Paterson & Co. Augusta, Ga."

Written date, "Jan. 1st, 1863."

Railway train at center. Same as 80 except date.

"Fundable..." overprint in two horizontal lines.

121 $20 (7) A B C D $45.00 $110.00

"Fundable..." statement is not trimmed from the bottom. With "Fundable..." overprint in two horizontal lines.

121A $20 (10) A B C D very rare

Printed Date "Jan. 1st, 1863."

State capitol at Raleigh. D. W. Courts at right. "X" and "Ten" in red.

122 $10 (5) A B C D E F $25.00 $45.00

Same, but no "Fundable" overprint in red.

122A $10 (10) A B C D E F extremely rare

View of harbor and city of Wilmington, N.C., Liberty at left, D. W. Courts right. "Five" in red.

123 $5 (4) A B C D E $25.00 $40.00

Without red "Five" overprint.

123A $5 (10) A B C D E F G H very rare

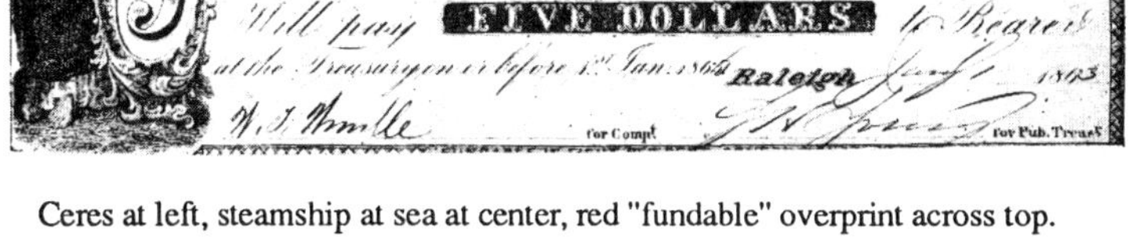

Ceres at left, steamship at sea at center, red "fundable" overprint across top.

124 $5 (5) A B C D $18.00 $45.00

Same, but "fundable" statement written in red ink.

124A $5 (8) A B C D $60.00 $140.00

The word "only" included in the "Fundable..." statement.
"Fundable only..." in two straight lines as 124.

124B $5 (10) A B C D $100.00 $175.00

Liberty standing, ceres seated.

SERIAL LETTER AT RIGHT.

Plain paper.

125 $3 (4) A B C D E F G H $25.00 $40.00

With oval "fundable" overprint in upper center of note.

125A $3 (10) A B C D E F G H very rare

Similar to number 125 but serial letter is written by hand.

125B $3 (10) A B C D E F G H very rare

Paper watermarked "Ten."

126 $3 (6) A B C D E F G H $45.00 $65.00

Similar to number 126 but serial letter is written by hand.

126A $3 (10) A B C D E F G H very rare

Paper watermarked "Five."

127 $3 (6) A B C D E F G H $45.00 $65.00

Paper watermarked "T.C.C. & Co."

127A $3 (9) A B C D E F G H $50.00 $85.00

Watermarked "Five" with written serial letters at right.

127B $3 (10) A B C D E F G H very rare

SERIAL LETTER AT LEFT.

Plain paper.

128 $3 (6) A B C D E F G H $40.00 $65.00

Paper watermarked "Ten."

129 $3 (7) A B C D E F G H $40.00 $65.00

Paper watermarked "Five."

130 $3 (7) A B C D E F G H $45.00 $65.00

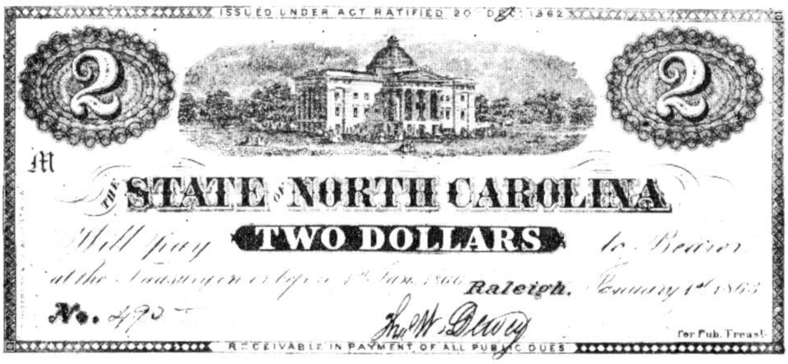

State capitol at Raleigh.

131 $2 (3) A B C D E F G H I K L M $9.00 $12.00

Commerce and Industry holding figure "1."

132 $1 (2) A B C D E F G H I K L M $9.00 $12.00

133 $1 (4) AB BB CB DB EB FB GB HB $9.00 $12.00
IB KB LB MB

Error with top left fancy "1" leans noticeably inward.

133A $1 (9) AB BB CB DB EB FB rare
GB HB IB KB LB MB

Industry beside beehive.

134 75c (4) A B C D E F G H I J K L M N O $25.00 $35.00

Same as above, but left border trimmed up to design.

134A	75c (4)	A B C D E F G H I J K L M N O	$15.00	$25.00

SERIAL LETTER AT UPPER LEFT

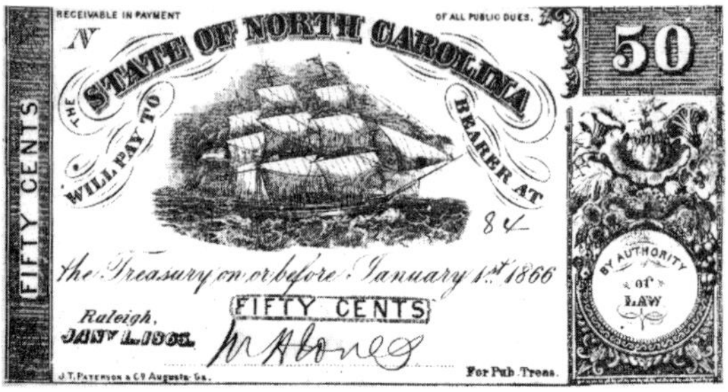

		Serial number at right center.		
135	50c (4)	A B C D E F G H I J K L M N O	$9.00	$12.00
		Serial number under "1866."		
135A	50c (40)	A B C D E F G H I J K L M N O	$9.00	$12.00
		Serial number upper right corner.		
135B	50c (4)	A B C D E F G H I J K L M N O	$9.00	$12.00
		Serial number at left center		
136	50c (5)	A B C D E F G H I J K L M N O	$9.00	$12.00
		Serial number under "Jan'y 1, 1863."		
136A	50c (5)	A B C D E F G H I J K L M N O	$9.00	$12.00

SERIAL LETTER AT RIGHT CENTER

		Serial number at right center.		
137	50c (5)	A B C D E F G H I J K L M N O	$10.00	$16.00
		Serial number below "1866."		
137A	50c (5)	A B C D E F G H I J K L M N O	$10.00	$16.00
		Serial number under letter. "No" at left center.		
137B	50c (5)	A B C D E F G H I J K L M N O	$10.00	$16.00
		Serial number at left center.		
138	50c (5)	A B C D E F G H I J K L M N O	$10.00	$16.00
		Serial number under "Jan'y 1, 1863."		
138A	50c (6)	A B C D E F G H I J K L M N O	$12.00	$20.00
		Serial number and serial letter at left center.		
138B	50c (6)	A B C D E F G H I J K L M N O	$12.00	$20.00

As above but serial number is written.

138C	50c (4)	A B C D E F G H I J K L M N O	$9.00	$15.00

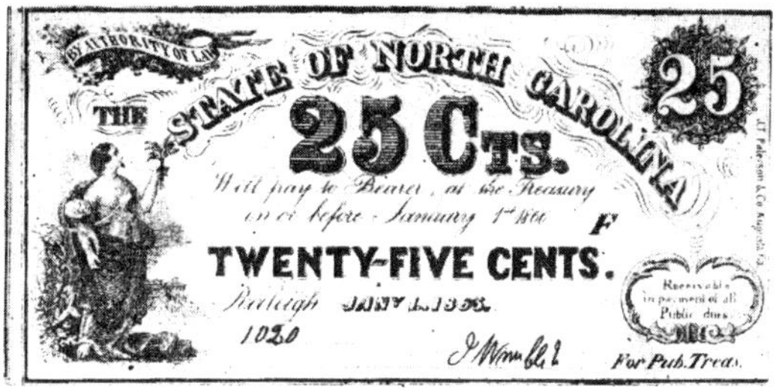

Ceres standing at left.

		Plain back.		
139	25c (3)	A B C D E F G H I J K L M N O	$9.00	$15.00
		"25c" in red on back.		
139A	25c (9)	A B C D E F G H I J K L M N O	$20.00	$35.00
		As 139 but printed on the back of notes.		
139B	25c (7)	A B C D E F G H I J K L M N O	$15.00	$25.00
		Printed on back of N.C. $50.00 of 1863.		
140	25c (8)	A B C D E F G H I J K L M N O P Q R S T U	$25.00	$48.00
		As above but watermarked "Whatman."		
140A	25c (10)	A B C D E F G H I J K L M N O P Q R S T U	very rare	
		Printed on back of N.C. $20.00 of 1863.		
141	25c (5)	A B C D E F G H I J K L M N O P Q R S T U	$25.00	$50.00
		Printed on back of N.C. $3.00 of 1863.		
142	25c (5)	A B C D E F G H I J K L M N O	$20.00	$30.00
		Printed on back of 5-cent Mechanics Bank of Augusta, Georgia notes.		
143	25c (7)	A B C D E F G H I J K L M N O	$20.00	$35.00
		Same type, but figure "5" in red below "Mechanics Bank."		
144	25c (5)	A B C D E F G H I J K L M N O	$15.00	$25.00
		Printed on back of 25-cents Mechanics Bank of Augusta, Ga. notes.		
144A	25c (5)	A B C D E F G H I J K L M N O	$18.00	$30.00
		"One" or parts thereof printed in green on back.		
145	25c (7)	A B C D E F G H I J K L M N O	$20.00	$40.00
		"25 Cts." in red on back.		
146	25c (5)	A B C D E F G H I J K L M N O	$20.00	$40.00
		As above, but with inverted "25 Cts." in red.		
146IB	25c (10)	A B C D E F G H I J K L M N O	$150.00	$225.00

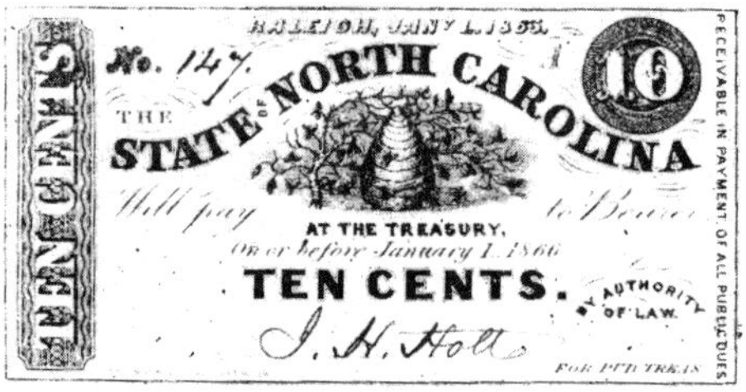

Hornet's nest

147 10c (2) A B C D E F G H I J K L M N O P Q R S T U $9.00 $12.00

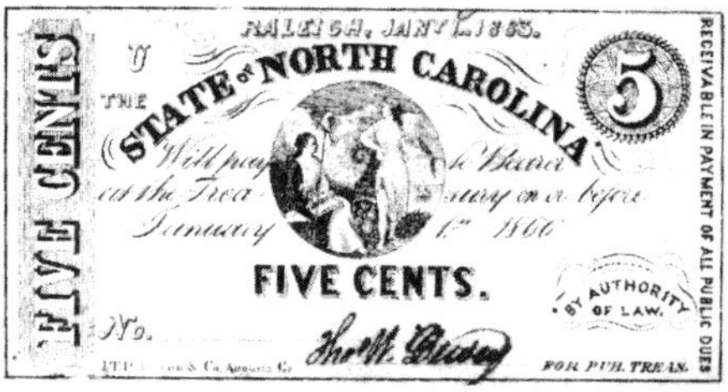

Liberty and Peace within circle.

148 5c (2) A B C D E F G H I J K L M N O P Q R S T U $9.00 $11.00

$400,000 Authorized by Act of Dec. 12th, 1863.
Dated "Jan'y 1st, 1864.

Ship at sea. "50 cts" overprint in red.
Serial number at right center directly above 1870.

149 50c (2) A B C D E F G H I J K L M N O P $10.00 $15.00

Same as above, but serial number at left center.

149A 50c (8) A B C D E F G H I J K L M N O P $20.00 $35.00

Same, but serial number at lower left below "1864."

149B 50c (4) A B C D E F G H I J K L M N O P $10.00 $15.00

Same, but serial number at left and right in center.

149C 50c (10) A B C D E F G H I J K L M N O P rare

Note number at top right corner at left of "50."

149D 50c (9) A B C D E F G H I J K L M N O P rare

Number at right center just below front sail of ship.

149E 50c (9) A B C D E F G H I J K L M N O P rare

"50c" in red inverted.

149H 50c (10) A B C D E F G H I J K L M N O P very rare

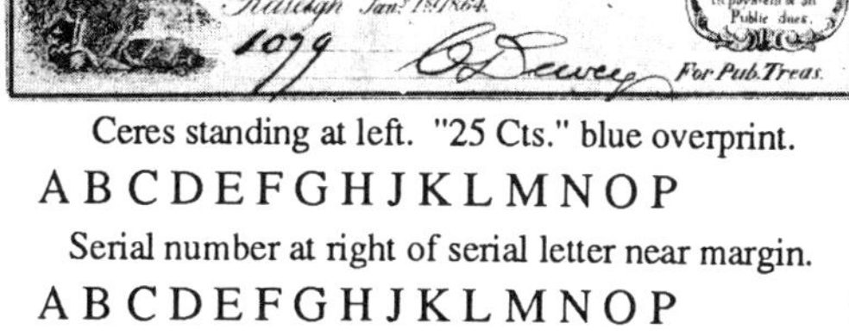

Ceres standing at left. "25 Cts." blue overprint.

150 25c (3) A B C D E F G H J K L M N O P $9.00 $12.00

Serial number at right of serial letter near margin.

150A 25 c (9) A B C D E F G H J K L M N O P $25.00 $35.00

Similar to number 150 but "25c." in green.

150B 25 c (9) A B C D E F G H J K L M N O P $100.00 $200.00

THE STATE OF SOUTH CAROLINA

The Criswell numbers given here are entirely different from the old Bradbeer numbers, because the notes issued by The Bank of the State of South Carolina were not state notes. The first known state notes appeared in January of 1866, having been authorized under act of the legislature in December of 1865. These notes have the word "January" and "1866" printed with the actual date entered by hand.

AMERICAN BANK NOTE COMPANY

Oxen pulling cart, two children in oval, maiden right.
Green and black, with fancy green back.

01 $1 (11) A B extremely rare

Harbor scene, gathering grain left, girl right.
Green and black with fancy green back.

02 $2 (11) A B extremely rare

General Francis Marion's "sweet-potato dinner,"
General Thomas Sumter left, General William Moultrie right.
Green and black with fancy green back.

03 $5 (11) A B extremely rare

Sergeants Jasper and Newton free captives.
General Daniel Morgan at left, a young girl at right.
Green and black with fancy green back.

04 $10 (11) A B extremely rare

Notes of the 1872 issue were "issued under an act to relieve the State of South Carolina of all liability for its guarantee of the bonds of the Blue Ridge Railroad Company, by providing for the securing and destruction of the Same."

No printer's name.
All bear the act date, "March 2, 1872."

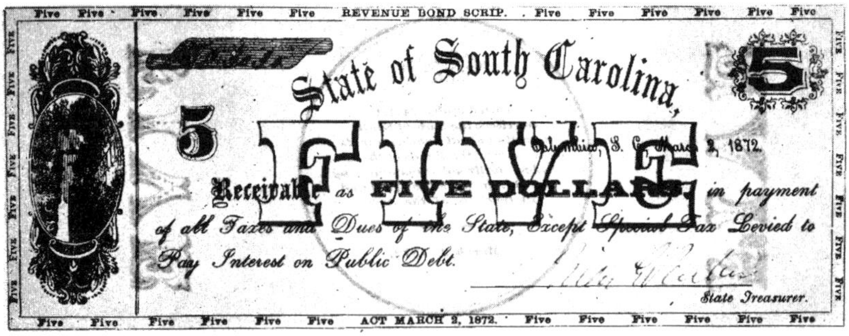

"FIVE" and "5" in green, train in oval at left. Type set back.

1 $5 (8) no serial letter $30.00 $35.00

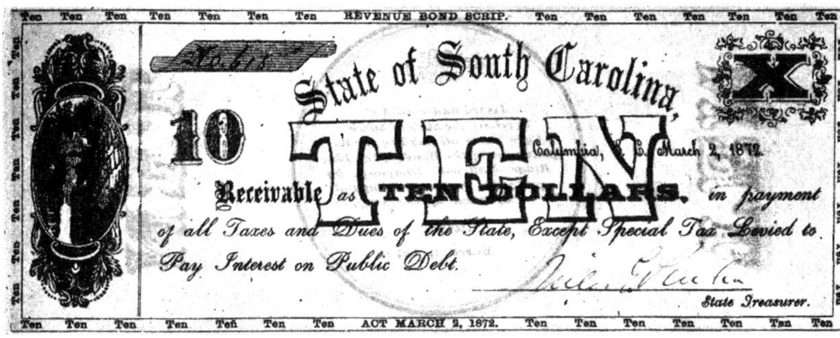

"TEN" and "10" in green, train in oval at left. Type set back.

2 $10 (8) no serial letter $30.00 $35.00

Printed by "American Bank Note Company, New York."
Oxen pulling cart, two children in oval, maiden right, green and black. Fancy green back.

3 $1 (4) A B $30.00 $35.00

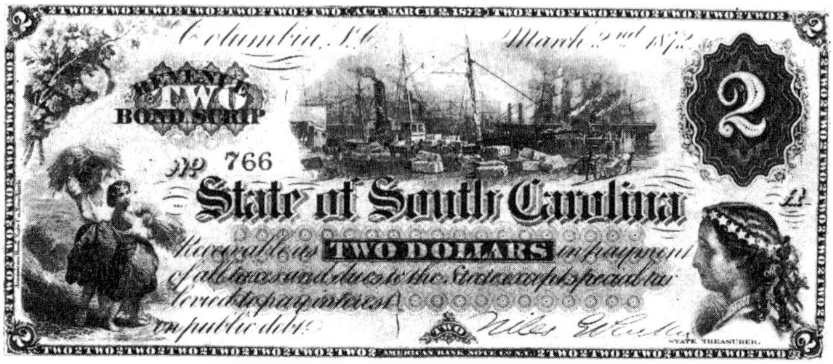

Green and black Harbor scene, gathering grain left, girl right. Fancy green back.

4 $2 (4) A B $30.00 $35.00

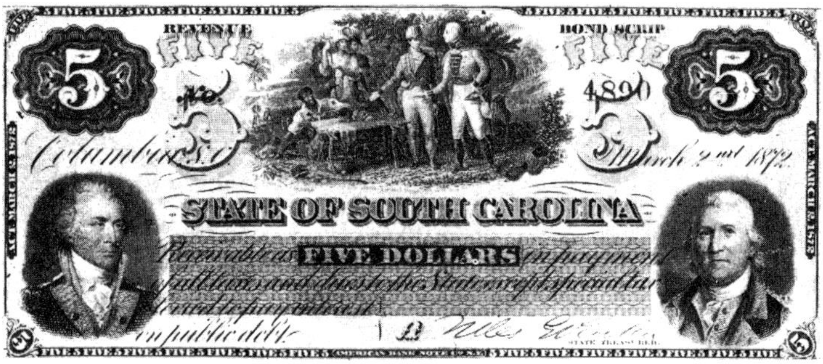

Green and black; General Francis Marion's "sweet-potato dinner," General Thomas Sumter left, General William Moultrie right. Fancy green back.

5 $5 (5) A B $30.00 $35.00

Green and black; Sergeants Jasper and Newton freeing captives, General Daniel Morgan at left, a young girl at right. Fancy green back.

6 $10 (5) A B $30.00 $35.00

Green and black; Liberty, soldier and angel guarding state seals. Fancy green back.

7 $20 (5) A B $30.00 $35.00

Green and black; George Washington, horses pulling cart left, slave carrying cotton right. Fancy green back.

8 $50 (5) A B $30.00 $35.00

Written dates of 1872.

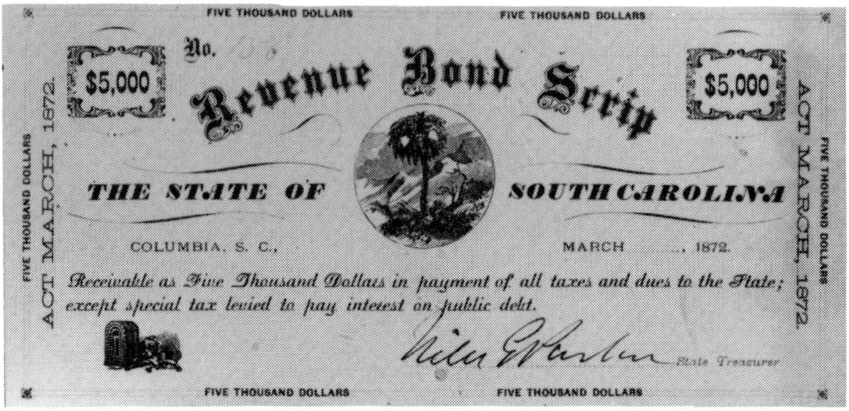

No printers name.

Palmetto tree within circle, dog and safe at left.

9	$100 (8)	no serial letter	$65.00	$90.00
11	$1000 (11)	no serial letter	extremely rare	
12	$5000 (11)	no serial letter	extremely rare	

Issue of "December 1st, 1873"

These are similar to 3, through 8 except for date.

13	$1 (10)	A B	very rare

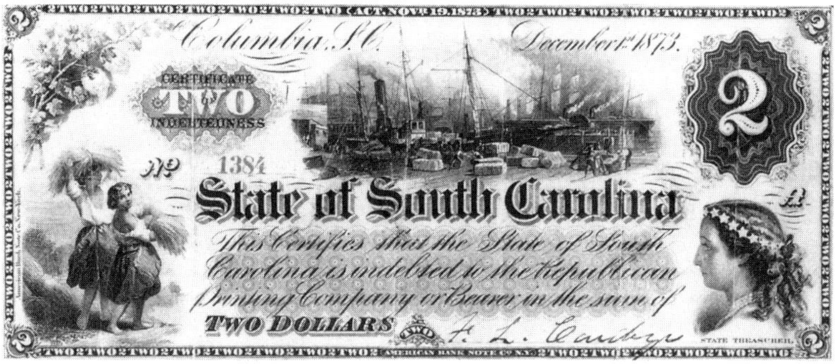

14 $2 (10) A B very rare

15 $5 (10) A B very rare

16 $10 (10) A B very rare

17 $20 (11) A B very rare

18 $50 (11) A B very rare

THE STATE OF TENNESSEE

In previous editions of this catalog, Cherry Valley, Smithville, and Kingston notes of 1863 were listed. After considerable consultation with well-known scholars, and in the absence of any signatures of known state officials on the notes, the conclusion is that these were not official Tennessee government issues.

Thus the first official issue would be that of 1875.

"American Bank Note Co. N.Y."
Dated "May 1st, 1875."

NOTE: Numbers 5-10 are almost always found punch cancelled.

Green and black; wagonload of cotton, children at left, Ceres right, intricate green back.

5 $1 (10) no serial letter $200.00 $500.00

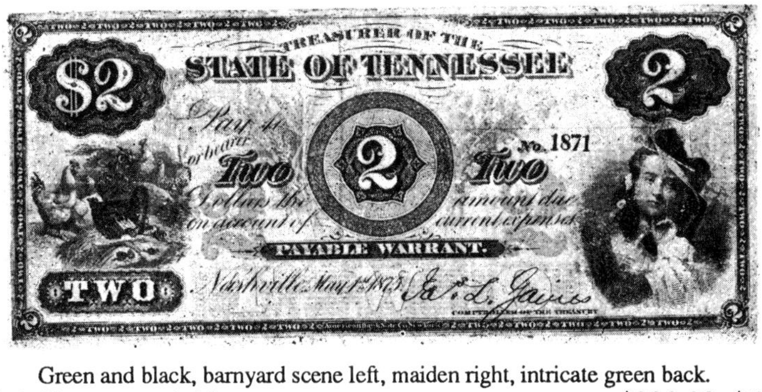

Green and black, barnyard scene left, maiden right, intricate green back.

6 $2 (10) no serial letter $200.00 $500.00

Green and black; agricultural implements center, slave left picking cotton, James Polk at right.

7 $5 (9) no serial letter $200.00 $500.00

Green and black; Andrew Jackson, boy gathering corn left, dog and safe at right; green back.

8 $10 (10) no serial letter $200.00 $500.00

Slave picking cotton left, Agriculture right.

9 $20 (10) no serial letter $350.00 $600.00

Green and black; two horses, plow and boy at center, girl left, Indian princess right.

10 $50 (9) no serial letter $200.00 $500.00

Louisville Lithographing Co.

Certificates issued July 1, 1883 entitled an act to provide for the redemption of the notes March 29, 1883. The actual quantity issued is uncertain.

Green and black; portrait of Governor William B. Bates at left, "ONE" dark green. Back with vignette of state capitol.

Redeemable Oct. 1883.

20 $1 (10) series A very rare

Same as number 20 but redeemable October 1884.

21 $1 (10) series B very rare

Same as number 20 but redeemable October 1885.

22 $1 (10) series C very rare

Same as number 20 but redeemable October 1886.

23 $1 (10) series D very rare

Same as number 20 but redeemable October 1887.

24 $1 (10) series E very rare

Green and black; portrait of Governor William B. Bates at left, "FIVE" dark green, back with vignette of state capitol.

Redeemable Oct. 1883.

25 $5 (10) series A very rare

Same as number 25 but redeemable October 1884.

26 $5 (10) series B very rare

Same as number 25 but redeemable October 1885.

27 $5 (10) series C very rare

Same as number 25 but redeemable October 1886.

28 $5 (10) series D very rare

Same as number 25 but redeemable October 1887.

29 $5 (10) series E very rare

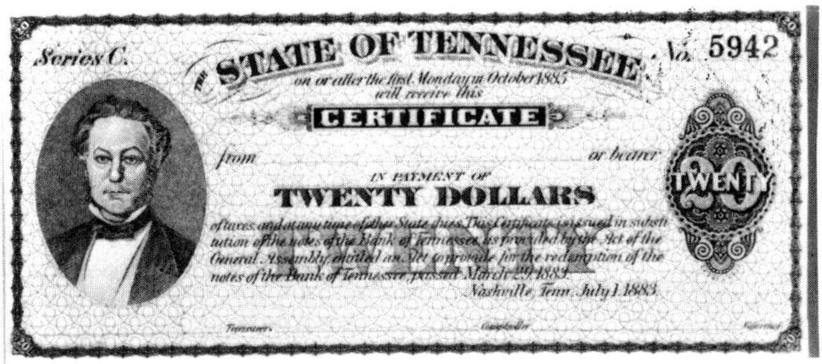

Green and black; portrait of Governor William B. Bates at left, "TWENTY" dark green.
Back with vignette of state capitol.

Redeemable Oct. 1883.

30 $20 (10) series A very rare

Same as number 30 but redeemable October 1884.

31 $20 (10) series B very rare

Same as number 30 but redeemable October 1885.

32 $20 (10) series C very rare

Same as number 30 but redeemable October 1886.

33 $20 (10) series D very rare

Same as number 30 but redeemable October 1887.

34 $20 (10) series E very rare

Certificates issued October 1, 1885 by act of the general assembly to provide for the redemption of the notes of the Bank of Tennessee, passed March 31, 1885 and approved April 2, 1885.

Green and black, "ONE" dark green, ornate blue back with vignette of state capitol.

Redeemable Oct. 1883.

40 $1 (10) series F very rare

Same as number 40 but redeemable October 1884.

41 $1 (10) series G very rare

Same as number 40 but redeemable October 1885.

42 $1 (10) series H very rare

Same as number 40 but redeemable October 1886.

43 $1 (10) series I very rare

Same as number 40 but redeemable October 1887.

44 $1 (10) series J very rare

Green and black, "FIVE" dark green, ornate blue back with vignette of state capitol.

Redeemable Oct. 1883.

45 $5 (10) series F very rare

Same as number 45 but redeemable October 1884.

46 $5 (10) series G very rare

Same as number 45 but redeemable October 1885.

47 $5 (10) series H very rare

Same as number 45 but redeemable October 1886.

48 $5 (10) series I very rare

Same as number 45 but redeemable October 1887.

49 $5 (10) series J very rare

Green and black, "TWENTY" dark green, ornate blue back with vignette of state capitol.

Redeemable Oct. 1883.

50 $20 (10) series F very rare

Same as number 50 but redeemable October 1884.

51 $20 (10) series G very rare

Same as number 50 but redeemable October 1885.

52 $20 (10) series H very rare

Same as number 50 but redeemable October 1886.

53 $20 (10) series I very rare

Same as number 50 but redeemable October 1887.

54 $20 (10) series J very rare

THE REPUBLIC AND GOVERNMENT OF TEXAS

A SPECIAL FOREWORD

This section is a complete listing on the notes and Warrants used in the republic. The Criswell numbering system employed herein uses letter prefixes to divide the republic and government into places of issue thus allowing flexibility to encompass new varieties that might turn up. A few general hints on Texana, including a special index of this chapter follows.

PAPER

Many types of paper exist in these early issues. The author has noted over 20 minor paper varieties, and there are undoubtedly many more.

PRINTERS

An unknown number of persons performed services for the new republic government in various places, thus creating many minor varieties, particularly in warrants.

REASONS FOR ISSUE

The author has not attempted to list the different reasons of issue. It should be remembered that, with a young government, the regulating policies would not be too strict, nor were they.

NEW VARIETIES

Persons discovering new varieties are urged to correspond with the author in order that varieties may be listed in future works.

Provisional Government of Texas.

The first known Texas currency, in the form of warrants, appeared even before her declaration of independence from Mexico on March 2nd, 1836. It was issued, obviously from Washington on the Brazos, in the name of the Provisional Government of Texas.

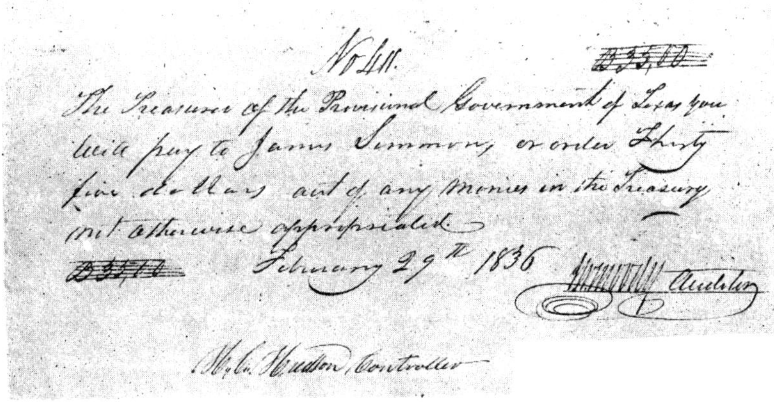
No 411. $35,00
The Treasurer of the Provisional Government of Texas you will pay to James Simmons or order Thirty five dollars out of any monies in the Treasury not otherwise appropriated
$35,00 February 29th 1836 [illegible] Auditor
M. C. Hudson, Controller

Handwritten on pink, buff,yellow or white paper.

P1 written denominations (9) $600.00 $800.00

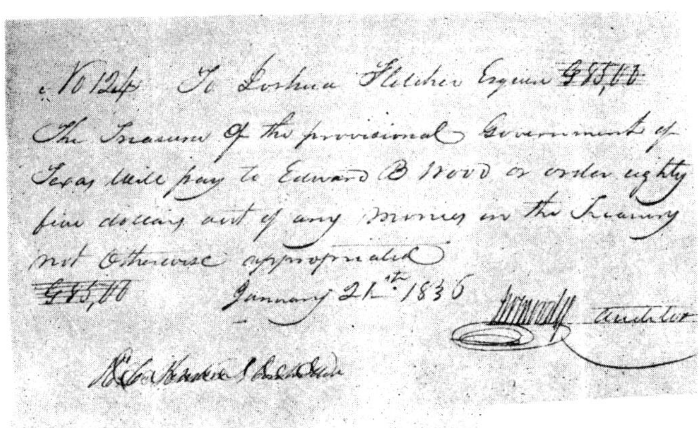
No 124 To Joshua Fletcher Esquire $85,00
The Treasurer of the provisional Government of Texas will pay to Edward B Wood or order eighty five dollars out of any monies in the Treasury not otherwise appropriated
$85,00 January 21st 1836 [illegible] Auditor
[illegible]

P2 written denominations (10) $600.00 $800.00

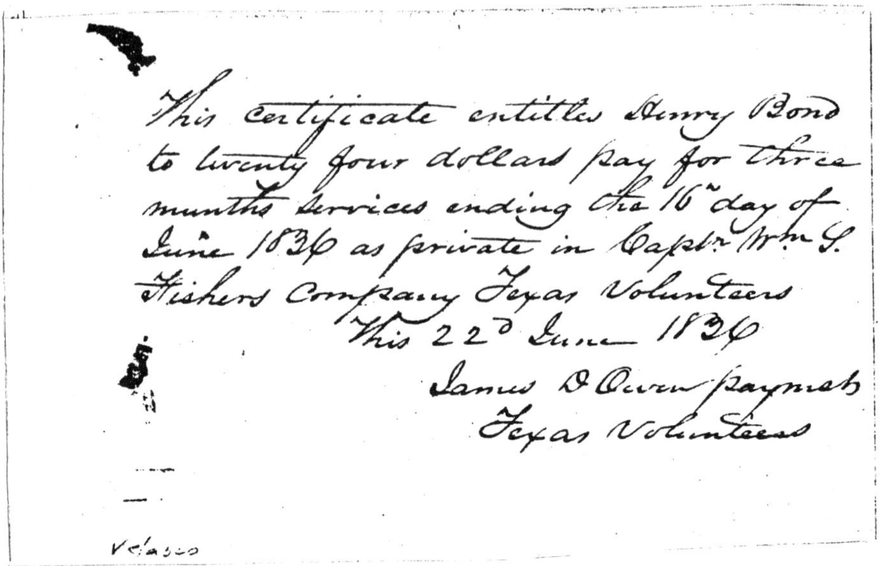

This certificate entitles Henry Bond
to twenty four dollars pay for three
months services ending the 16th day of
June 1836 as private in Captn Wm S.
Fishers Company Texas Volunteers
This 22d June 1836
James D Owen paymstr
Texas Volunteers

Velasco

P3 written denominations (10) extremely rare

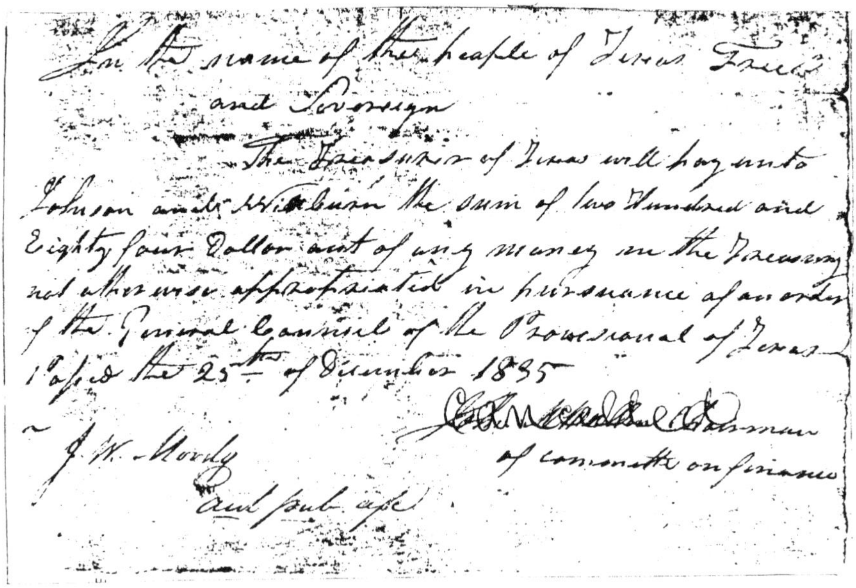

In the name of the people of Texas Free
and Sovereign
The Treasurer of Texas will pay unto
Johnson and Whitburn the sum of two Hundred and
Eighty four Dollars out of any money in the Treasury
not otherwise appropriated in pursuance of an order
of the General Council of the Provisional of Texas
Passed the 25th of December 1835
[illegible] Chairman
of committee on finance
J. W. Moody
Aud pub. acc.

P4 written denominations (10) extremely rare

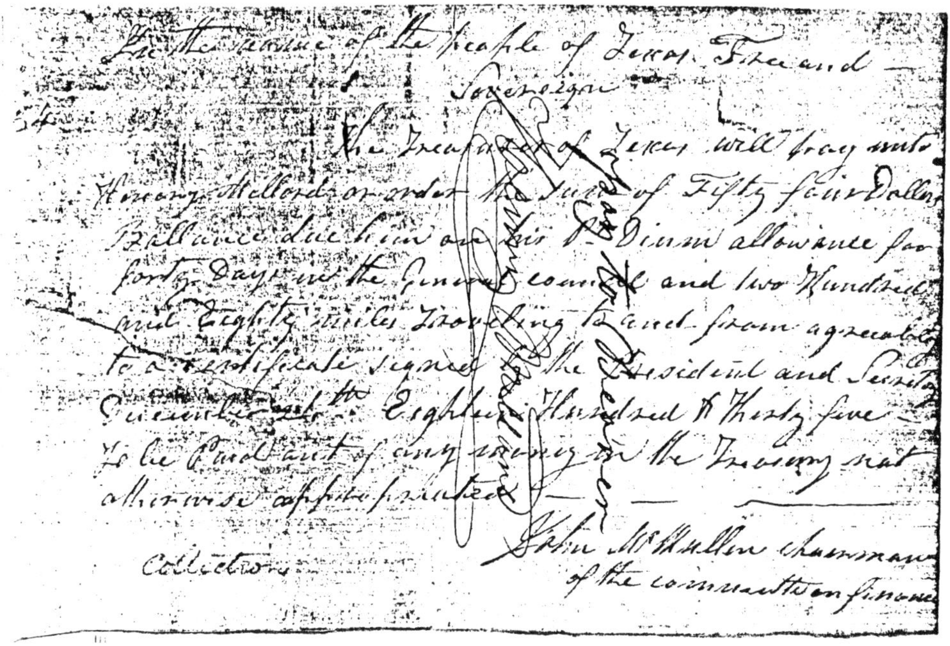
The Treasurer of the People of Texas Free and Sovereign

The Treasurer of Texas will pay unto Henry Millard or order the sum of Fifty four Dollars Ballance due him on his Per Diem allowance for forty Days in the General council and two Hundred and Eighty miles Traveling to and from agreeable to a certificate signed by the President and Secretary December ... Eighteen Hundred & Thirty five To be Paid out of any money in the Treasury not otherwise appropriated

John McMullen chairman of the committee on finance

Collector

P5 written denominations (11) extremely rare

Gonzales, Texas 1835

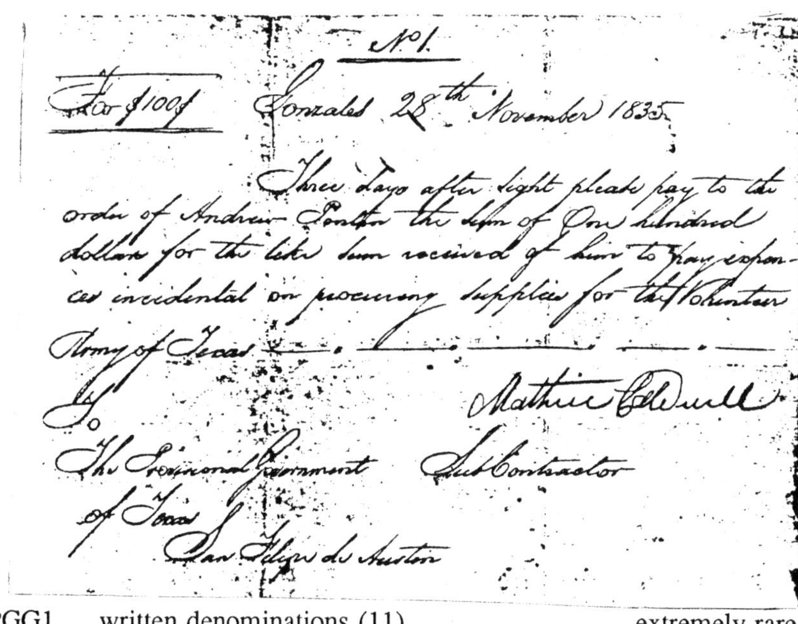
No 1.

For $100 Gonzales 28th November 1835.

Three days after sight please pay to the order of Andrew Ponton the sum of One hundred dollars for the like sum received of him to pay expences incidental on procuring supplies for the Volunteer Army of Texas

Mathew Caldwell
Sub Contractor

To
The Provisional Government
of Texas
San Felipe de Austin

PGG1 written denominations (11) extremely rare

Second issue of warrants, in the name of

THE GOVERNMENT OF TEXAS

Issued from
VELASCO

These bear a date of 1836 only.

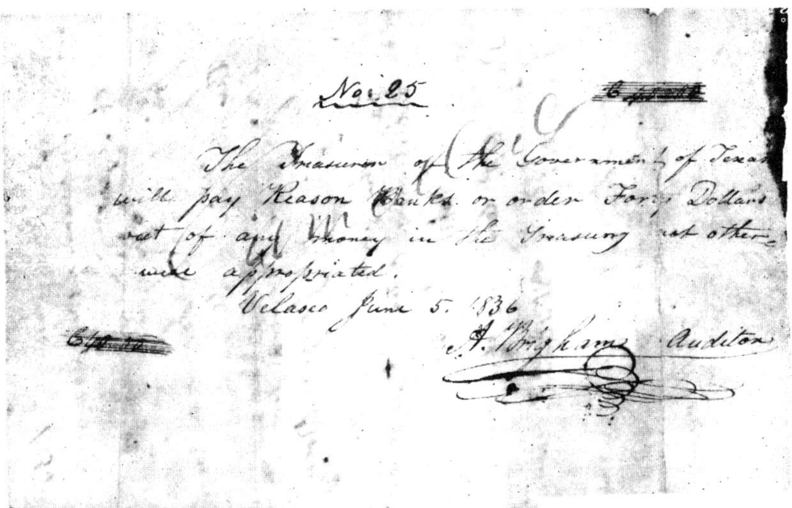

V1 written denominations (10) $200.00 rare

With a controller signature at left lower corner.

V1A written denominations (10) $200.00 rare

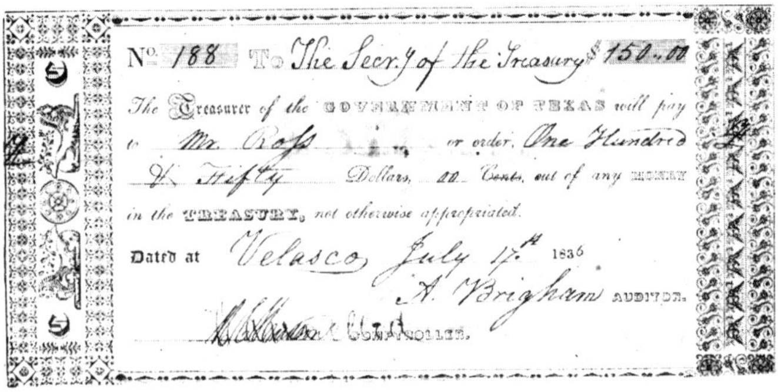

Printed blanks with "183" of date printed.

V2 written denominations (8) A B C D $150.00 $225.00

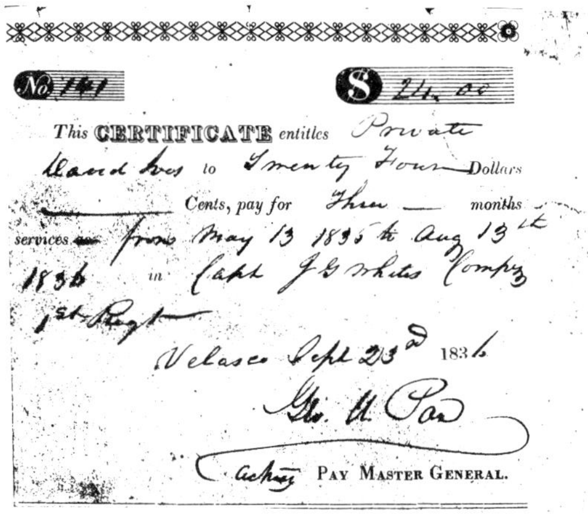

V3 written denominations (10) $85.00 $120.00

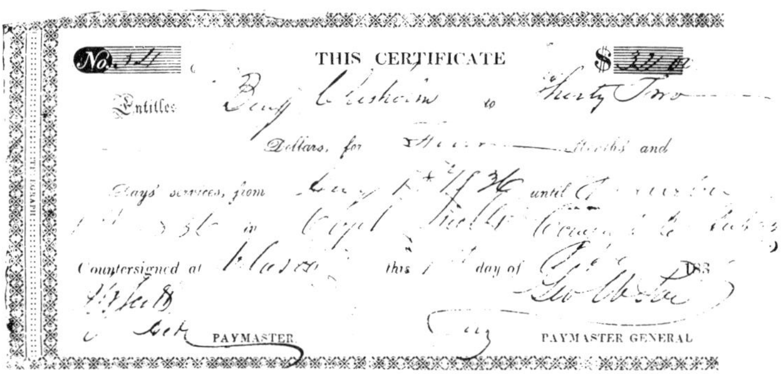

V4 written denominations (10) $90.00 $125.00

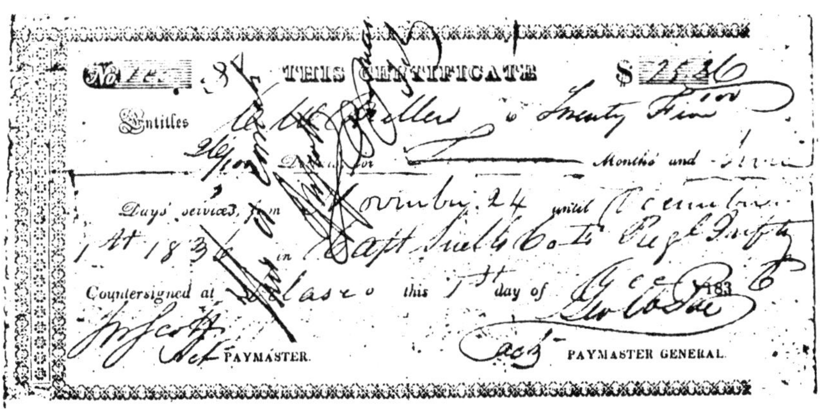

V5 written denominations (9) $150.00 rare

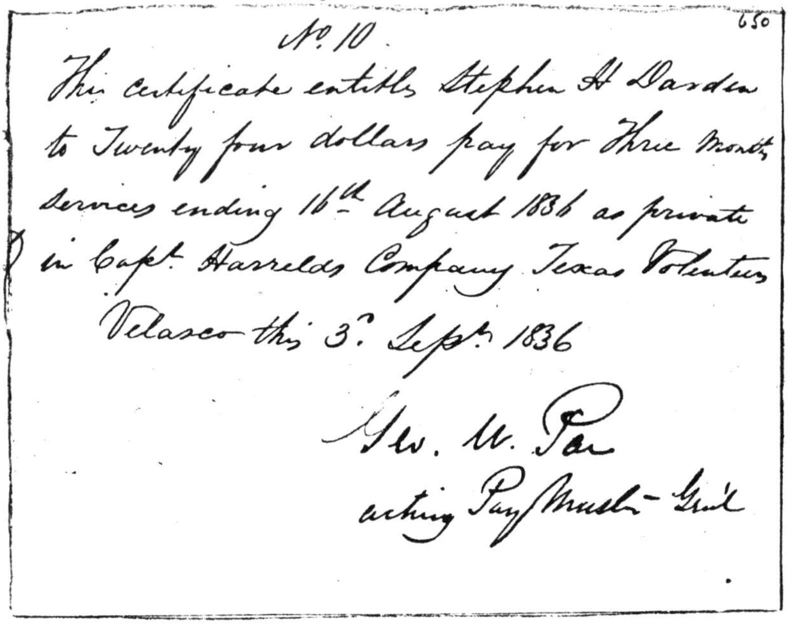

650

No. 10.

This certificate entitles Stephen H Darden to Twenty four dollars pay for Three Months services ending 16th August 1836 as private in Capt. Harrelds Company Texas Volunteers

Velasco this 3d Sept. 1836

Geo. W. Poe
acting Pay Master Genl

V7 written denominations (9) $150.00 rare

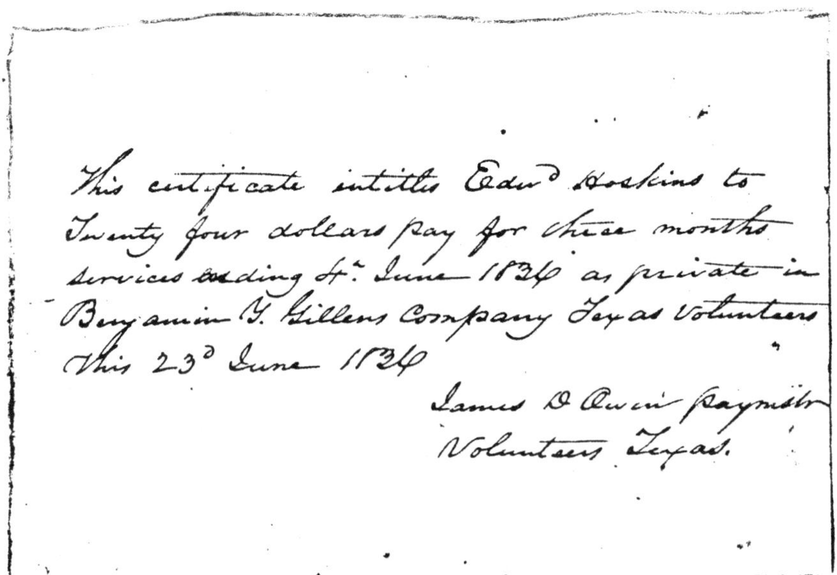

This certificate intitles Edwd Hoskins to Twenty four dollars pay for three months services ending 4th June 1836 as private in Benjamin Y. Gillens Company Texas Volunteers this 23d June 1836

James D Owen Paymaster
Volunteers Texas.

V7A written denominations (9) $150.00 rare

Third issue of warrants, in the name of

THE REPUBLIC OF TEXAS

Issued from
COLUMBIA

These may bear dates of 1836 or 1837.

Written dates with "183" of date printed.

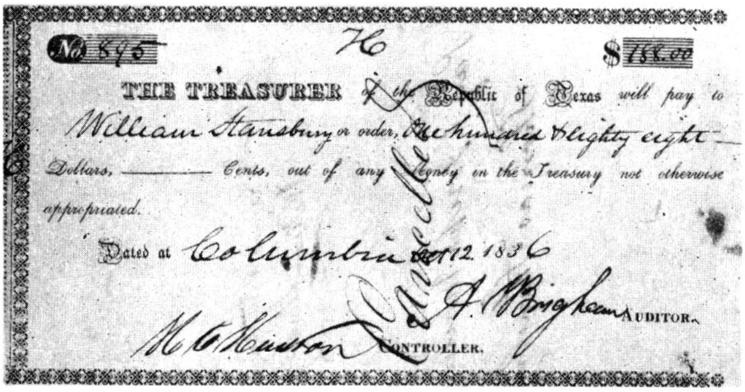
No. 875 $188.00
THE TREASURER of the Republic of Texas will pay to
William Stansbury or order, One hundred & eighty eight
Dollars, ——— Cents, out of any Money in the Treasury not otherwise appropriated.
Dated at Columbia Oct 12 1836
A. Brigham Auditor.
Controller.

C1 written denominations (9) $100.00 $150.00

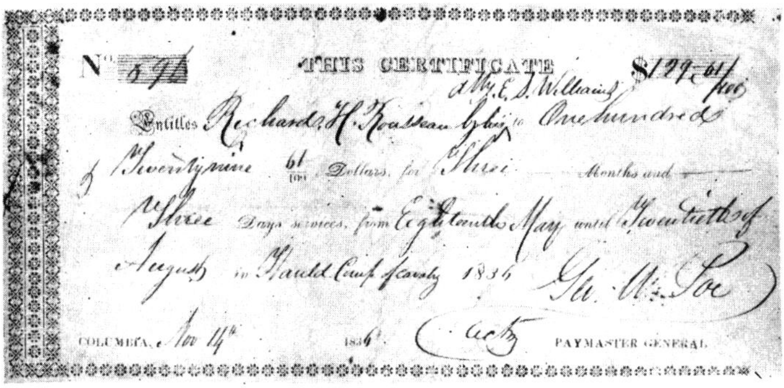
No. 591 THIS CERTIFICATE $129 61/100
Entitles Richard H. Rousseau to One hundred & Twentynine 61/100 Dollars, for Three Months and Three Days services, from Eighteenth May until Twentieth of August in 1836
Columbia, Nov 14th 1836. Paymaster General.

C2 written denominations (9) $100.00 $150.00

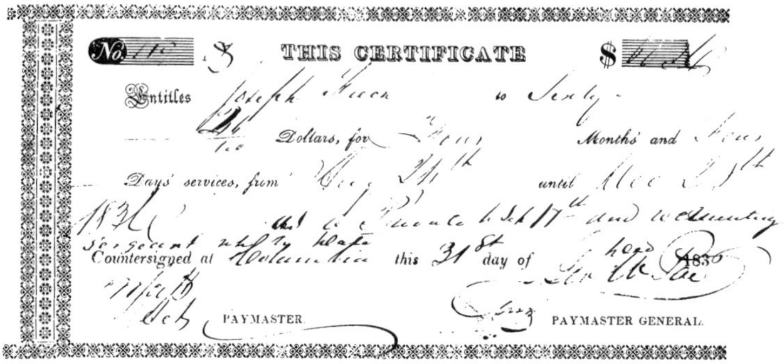
No. THIS CERTIFICATE $
Entitles Joseph to Sixty
Dollars, for Months' and
Days' services, from until
1836
Countersigned at this 31st day of 1836
PAYMASTER PAYMASTER GENERAL.

C2A written denominations (9) $140.00 $160.00

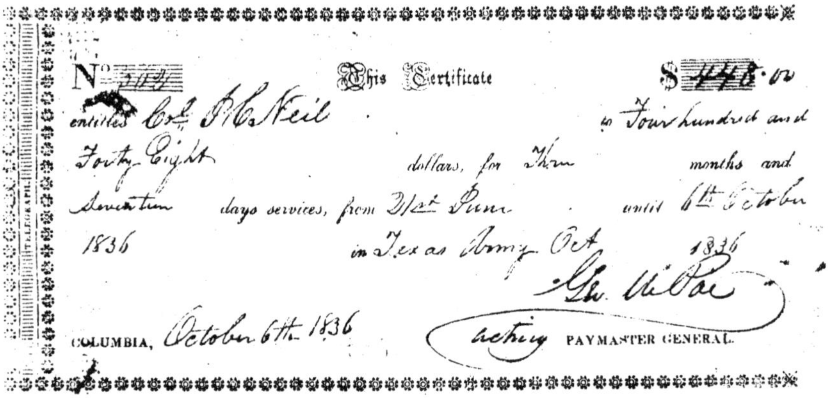
No. 204 This Certificate $448.02
entitles Col. P. C. Neil to Four hundred and
Forty-Eight dollars, for Three months and
Seventeen days services, from 21st June until 6th October
1836 in Texas Army Oct. 1836
Geo. W. Poe
COLUMBIA, October 6th 1836 acting PAYMASTER GENERAL.

C2Al written denominations (10) $140.00 $160.00

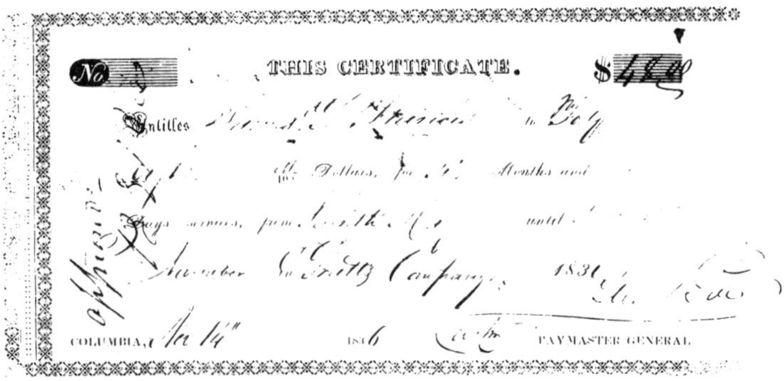
No. THIS CERTIFICATE. $48.00
Entitles
Dollars, for Months and
Days services, from until
1836
COLUMBIA, 1836 PAYMASTER GENERAL.

C2B written denominations (9) $140.00 $160.00

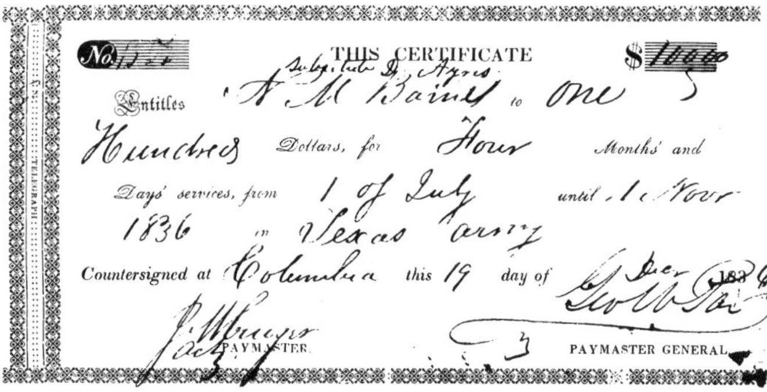
THIS CERTIFICATE $100
Entitles N. M. Bains to One Hundred Dollars, for Four Months' and Days' services, from 1 of July until 1 Nov 1836 in Texas army
Countersigned at Columbia this 19 day of Dec 1836
PAYMASTER. PAYMASTER GENERAL.

C2C written denominations (9) $140.00 $160.00

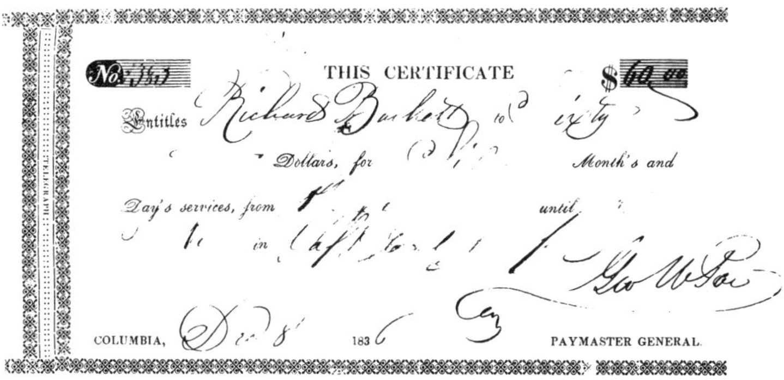
THIS CERTIFICATE $60
Entitles Richard Barker to Sixty Dollars, for Month's and Day's services, from until in
COLUMBIA, Dec 8 1836 Geo W Poe PAYMASTER GENERAL.

C2D written denominations (10) $110.00 $150.00

Printed form, "18" of date printed.

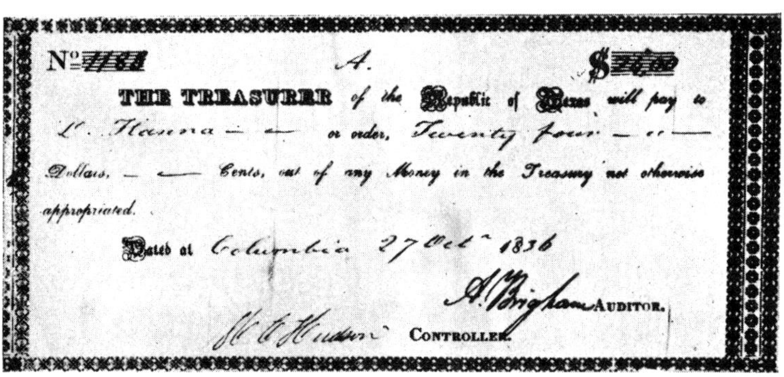
Nº A.
THE TREASURER of the Republic of Texas will pay to L. Hanna or order, Twenty four Dollars, Cents, out of any Money in the Treasury not otherwise appropriated.
Dated at Columbia 27 Oct 1836
A. Brigham AUDITOR.
CONTROLLER.

C3 written denominations (8) A B C D $100.00 $125.00

Printed form, "183" of date printed.

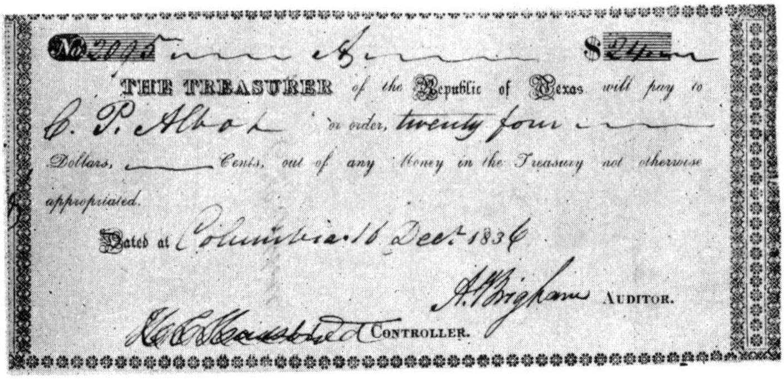

No. 2095 $24

THE TREASURER of the Republic of Texas will pay to C. P. Albot or order, twenty four Dollars, Cents, out of any Money in the Treasury not otherwise appropriated.

Dated at Columbia 16 Decr 1836

A. Brigham AUDITOR.

CONTROLLER.

C4 written denominations (8) A $100.00 $125.00

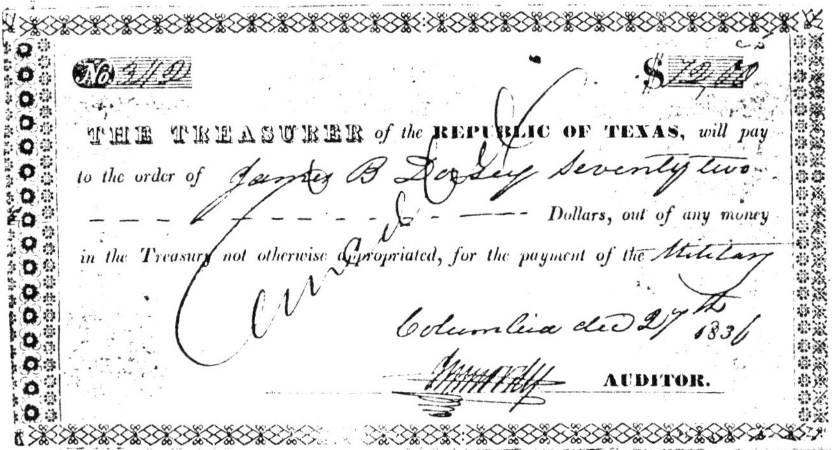

No. 319 $72

THE TREASURER of the REPUBLIC OF TEXAS, will pay to the order of James B Dorsey Seventy two Dollars, out of any money in the Treasury not otherwise appropriated, for the payment of the Military

Columbia dec 27th 1836

AUDITOR.

C4A written denominations (9) $80.00 $110.00

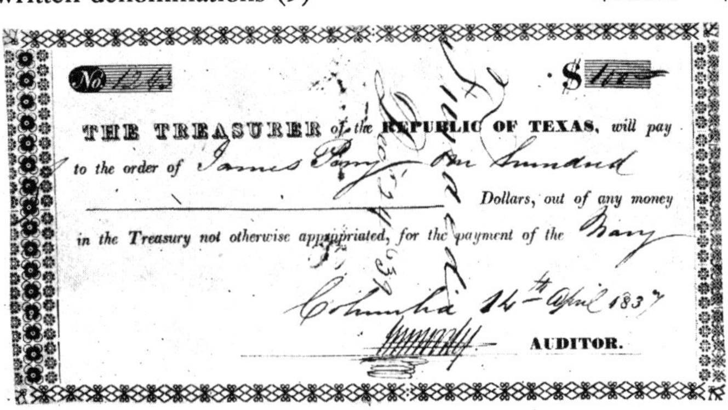

No. 124 $100

THE TREASURER of the REPUBLIC OF TEXAS, will pay to the order of James Perry One hundred Dollars, out of any money in the Treasury not otherwise appropriated, for the payment of the Navy

Columbia 14th April 1837

AUDITOR.

C5 written denominations (8) $100.00 $125.00

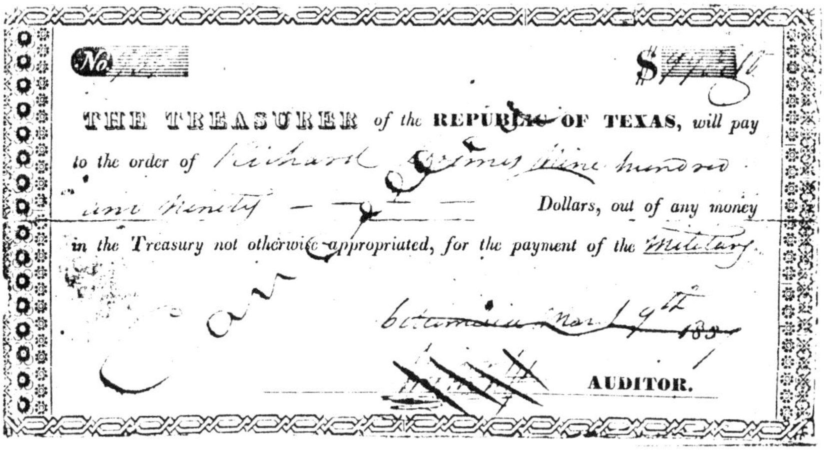

C5A written denominations (9) $100.00 $150.00

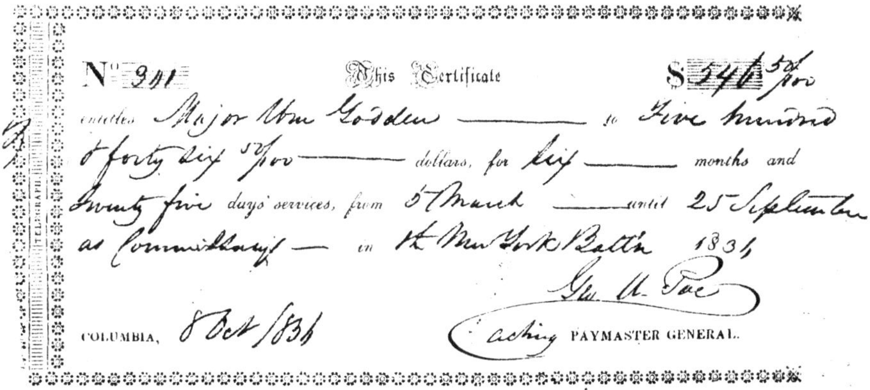

C7 written denominations (9) $100.00 $150.00

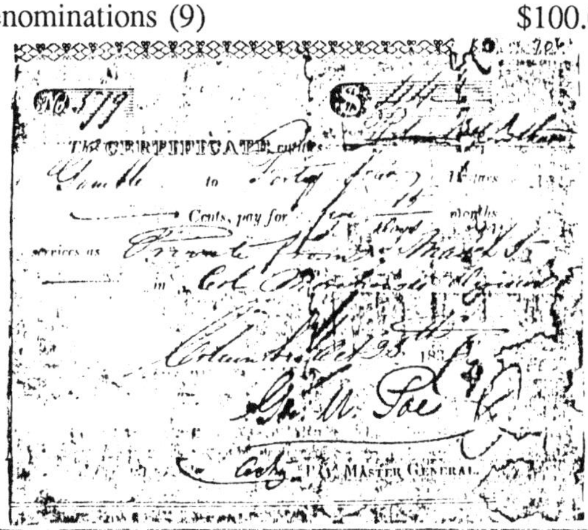

C8 written denominations (9) $100.00 $150.00

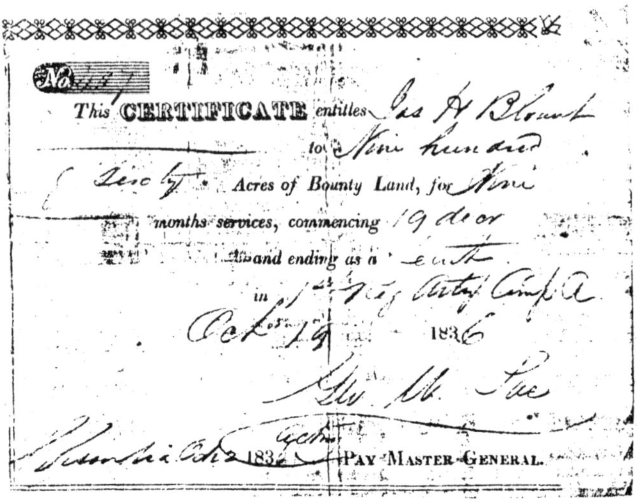
This CERTIFICATE entitles
to
Acres of Bounty Land, for
months services, commencing
and ending
in
1836
183
PAY MASTER GENERAL.

C9 written denominations (9) $100.00 $150.00

"Texian Army" Warrant
Written dates ("183" of date printed)

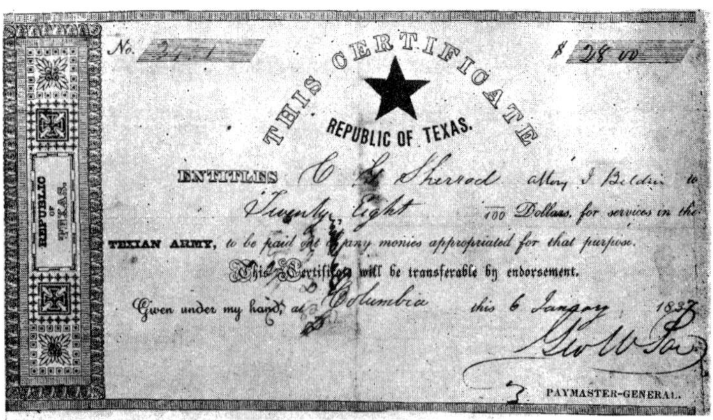
No.
$
THIS CERTIFICATE
REPUBLIC OF TEXAS.
ENTITLES to
100 Dollars, for services in the
TEXIAN ARMY, to be paid out of any monies appropriated for that purpose.
This Certificate will be transferable by endorsement.
Given under my hand, at Columbia this 6 January 1837
PAYMASTER-GENERAL.
REPUBLIC OF TEXAS.

C16 written denominations (9) $250.00 $350.00

"Quartermaster" written in over "Texian Army."

C16A written denominations (10) $400.00 $600.00

GALVESTON ISSUE (actually also third issue)

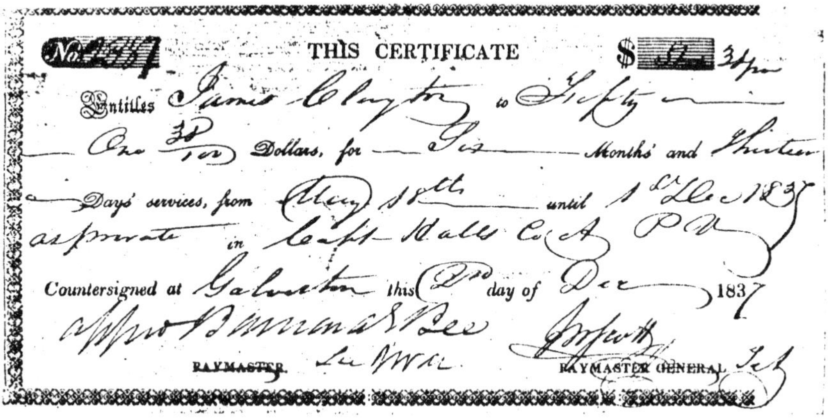
No. 2587 THIS CERTIFICATE $ 51 38/100
Entitles James Clayton to Fifty One 38/100 Dollars, for Six Months' and Thirteen Days' services, from May 18th until 1st Dec 1837 as private in Capt Halls Co A P V
Countersigned at Galveston this 2nd day of Dec 1837
PAYMASTER. PAYMASTER GENERAL.

G1 written denominations (11) very rare

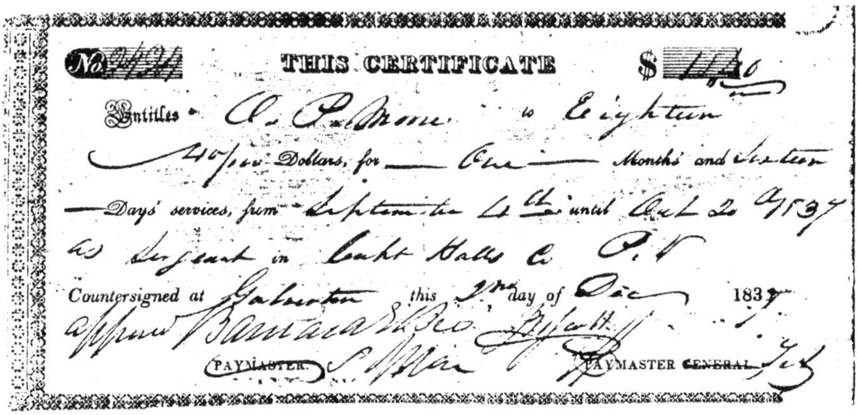
No. 2424 THIS CERTIFICATE $ 18 40/100
Entitles A. Palmore to Eighteen 40/100 Dollars, for One Months' and Sixteen Days' services, from September 16th until Oct 2d 1837 as Sergeant in Capt Halls Co P V
Countersigned at Galveston this 2nd day of Dec 1837
PAYMASTER. PAYMASTER GENERAL.

G2 written denominations (11) very rare

Fourth issue of warrants, in the name of

THE REPUBLIC OF TEXAS

Issued from
HOUSTON

These bear dates of 1837 or 1838.

Entirely hand written.

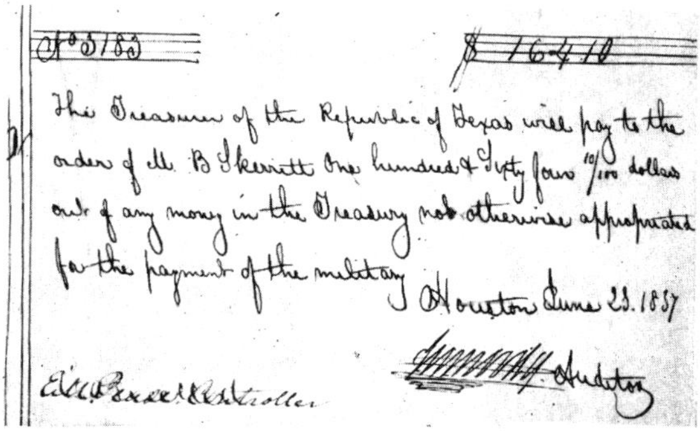

No 3183 $ 164 10

The Treasurer of the Republic of Texas will pay to the order of M. B. Skerrett One hundred & Sixty four 10/100 dollars out of any money in the Treasury not otherwise appropriated for the payment of the military

Houston June 23. 1837

Auditor

Controller

HW1	written denominations (8)	$125.00	$150.00
	Same, but without controller signature.		
HW1A	written denominations (9)	$125.00	$150.00

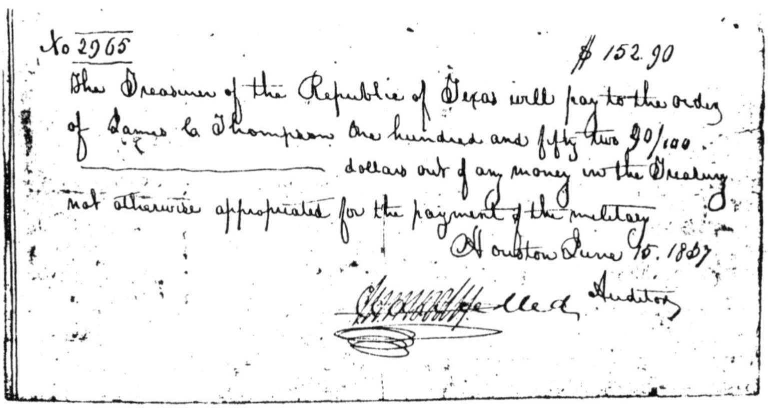

No 2965 $ 152.90

The Treasurer of the Republic of Texas will pay to the order of James C Thompson One hundred and fifty two 90/100 dollars out of any money in the Treasury not otherwise appropriated for the payment of the military

Houston June 15. 1837

Auditor

HW1B	written denominations (10)	$150.00	very rare

Printed blanks with "183" of date printed.

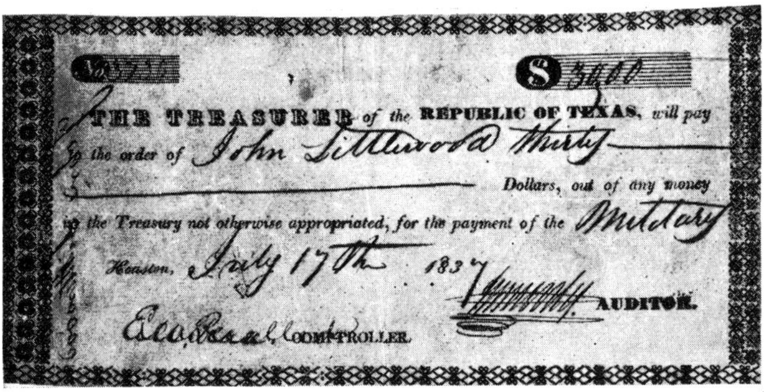

HW2 written denominations (8) $125.00 $150.00

Same, except roseates at left and right of flowers on left. "To" on line one.

4W2A written denomination (9) $140.00 $200.00

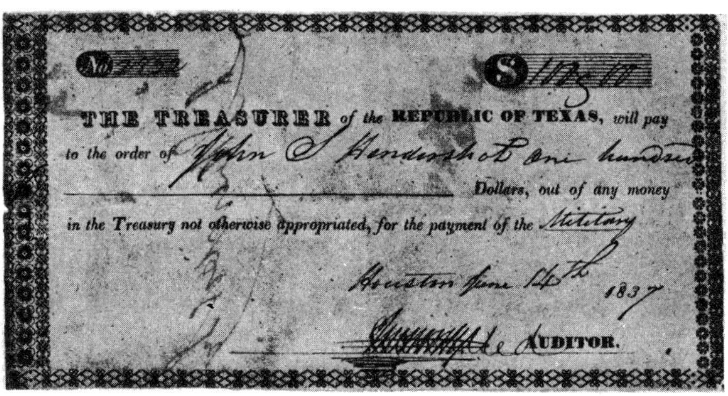

HW3 written denominations (8) $125.00 $150.00

Same, except roseates at both left and right of flowers on left, and at right in two columns.

HW3A written denomination (9) $135.00 $190.00

HW4 written denominations (8) $125.00 $150.00

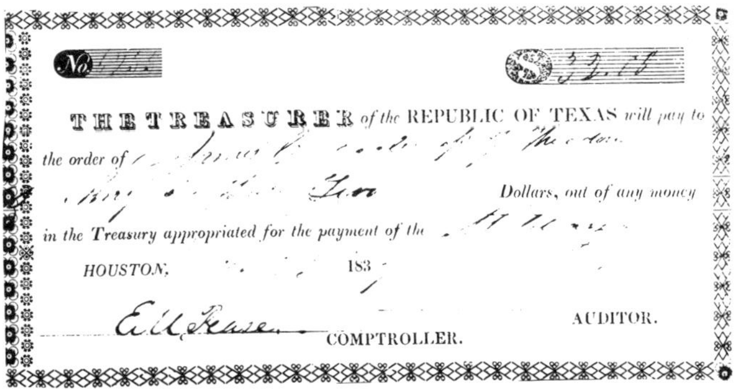

HW4A written denominations (9) $125.00 $150.00

HW4B written denominations (9) $125.00 $150.00

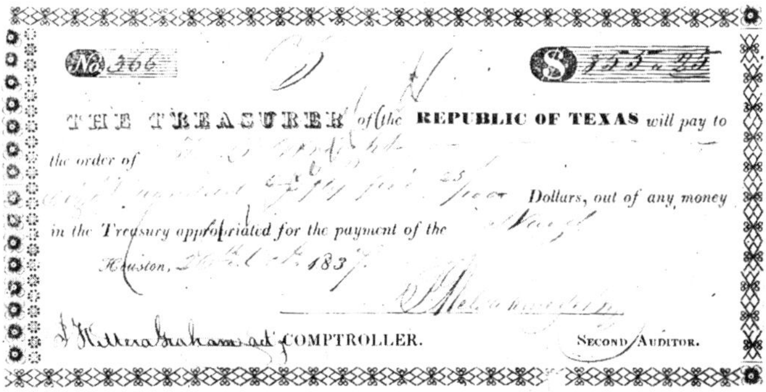

HW5 written denominations (9) $125.00 $150.00

Different border at left, two rows of emblems at right.

HW5A written denominations (9) $125.00 $150.00

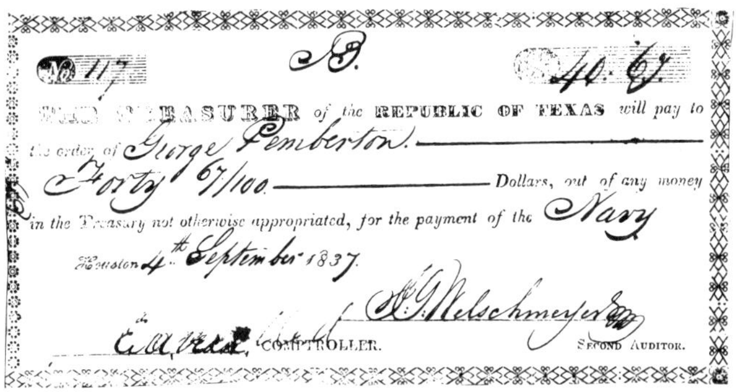

HW5B written denominations (9) $125.00 $150.00

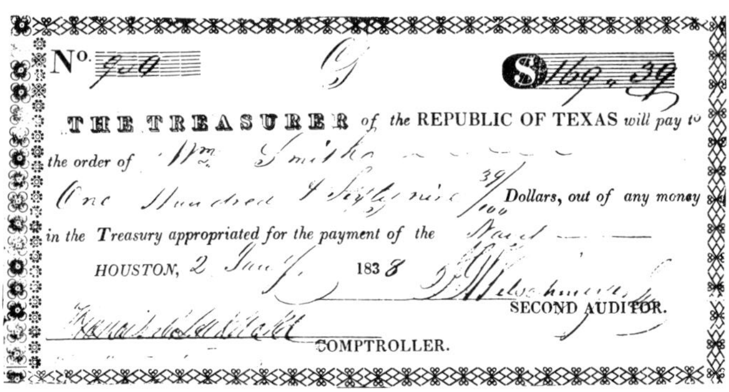

HW5C written denominations (9) $125.00 $150.00

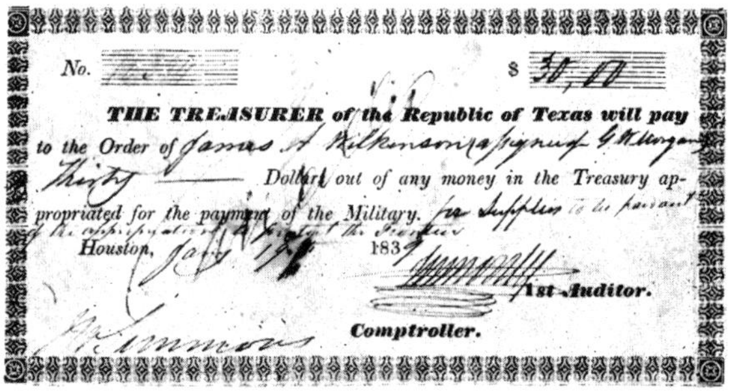

HW10	written denominations (8)	$45.00	$90.00

"18__" of date printed

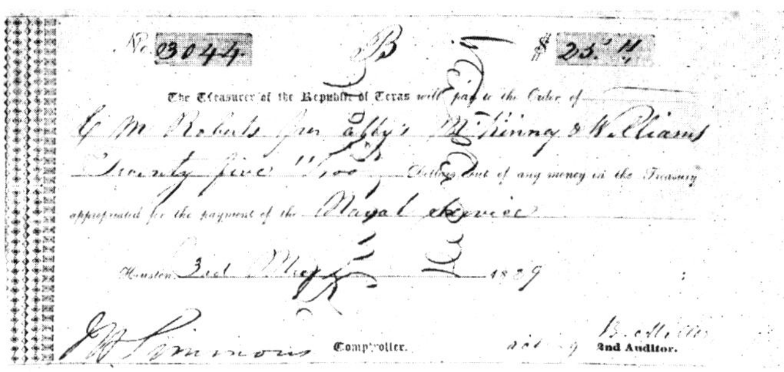

HW11	written denominations (9)	$50.00	$110.00

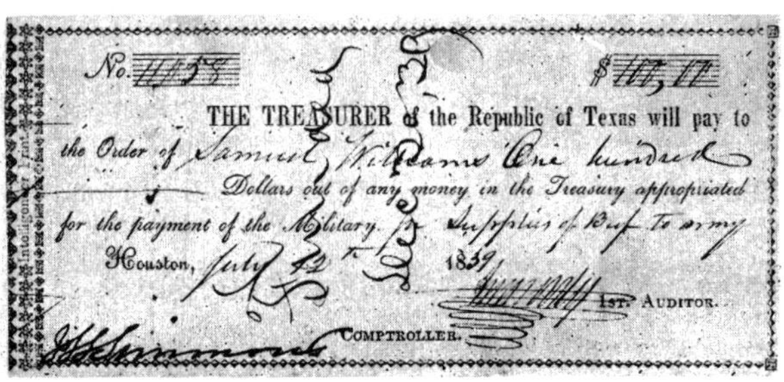

HW12	written denominations (8)	$37.50	$67.50

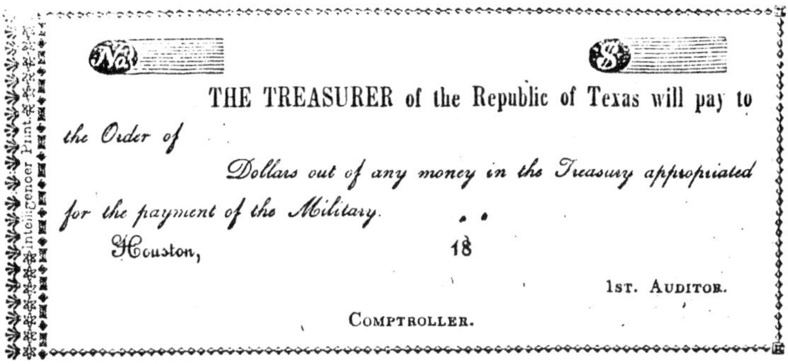

HW12A written denominations (8) $35.00 $55.00

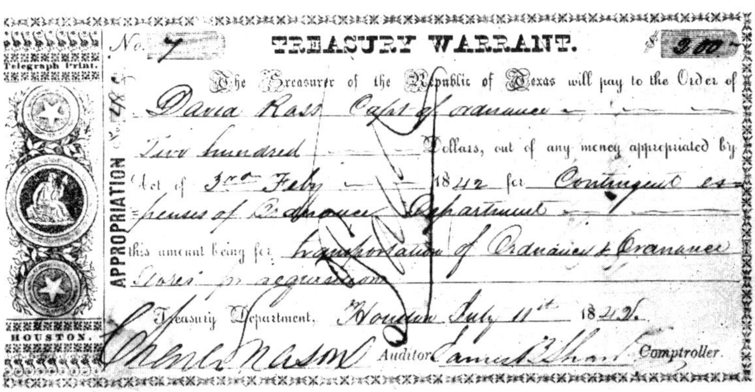

HW13 written denominations (8) $35.00 $55.00

Similar, leafy designs on borders.

HW14 written denominations (9) $45.00 $75.00

First issue of notes, in the name of

THE REPUBLIC OF TEXAS

Issued from
HOUSTON

These bear dates of 1837 and 1838

"Star" note issue, authorized by act of Congress "June 9th, 1837."
(At least eight different types of paper have been observed.)

"1837," inscribed "Sec. of Treas'y," "Five Dollars"

H1 $5 (8) $400.00 $1200.00

Inscribed "Sec of the Treas'y," "Five Dollras."

H2 $5 (9) $400.00 $1200.00

"1837," inscribed "Sec of Treas'y." Above "TEN DOLLARS" at right are four emblems (alternating rosette and X emblems).

H3 $10 (8) $350.00 $1000.00

With only three emblems above "TEN DOLLARS."

H3A $10 (8) $350.00 $1000.00

Inscribed "Sec of the Treas'y.'

H4 $10 (9) $350.00 $1000.00

"1837," inscribed "Sec. of Treas'y," "Twenty Dollars"

H5 $20 (8) $350.00 $1000.00

As above except amount across the center of the note is not as tall and "Republic of Texas" on the left border does not fill the full space.

H5A $20 (9) $350.00 $1000.00

Inscribed "Sec of the Treas'y," "Twenty Dollras."

H6 $20 (9) $350.00 $1000.00

"1837," inscribed "Sec of Treas'y," the inside vertical border at left of "L" is entirely of rosettes.

H7 $50 (8) $350.00 $1000.00

Inscribed "Sec of Treas'y.'
Inside vertical border at left of "L" has an "X" at the bottom instead of a rosette.

H7A $50 (9) $400.00 $700.00

Inscribed "Sec of the Trras'y." Inside vertical border at left of "L" has an "X" at the bottom instead of a rosette.

H7B $50 (9) $400.00 $1200.00

"1838," Inscribed "Sec of the Trras'y.'

H8 $50 (9) $400.00 $1200.00

Large "ONE HUNDRED DOLLARS"

"1837"

H9 $100 (9) $400.00 $1200.00

Same but inside lower border emblem around "C" changed to match.

H9A $100 (9) $400.00 $1200.00

Small "One Hundred Dollars."

"1837," the two rosettes on each side of the "C" are in a vertical alignment with the top and bottom rosettes.

H10 $100 (8) $350.00 $1000.00

The two rosettes are close to the "C" and not in alignment with the top and bottom rosettes.

H10A $100 (8) $350.00 $1000.00

Inscribed "Sec. of the Trras'y."

H10B $100 (8) $350.00 $1000.00

"1838," inscribed "Sec. of the Trras'y."

H11 $100 (10) $600.00 $1500.00

"1838"

H12 $500 (9) $1200.00 $4500.00

Second issue of notes, in the name of

THE GOVERNMENT OF TEXAS

Issued from
HOUSTON

These bear dates of 1838 and 1839 ("18" of date printed).

Issue authorized by act of Congress "June 9th, 1837."

Engraved by "Draper, Toppan, Longacre & Co. Philad. & N.Y."

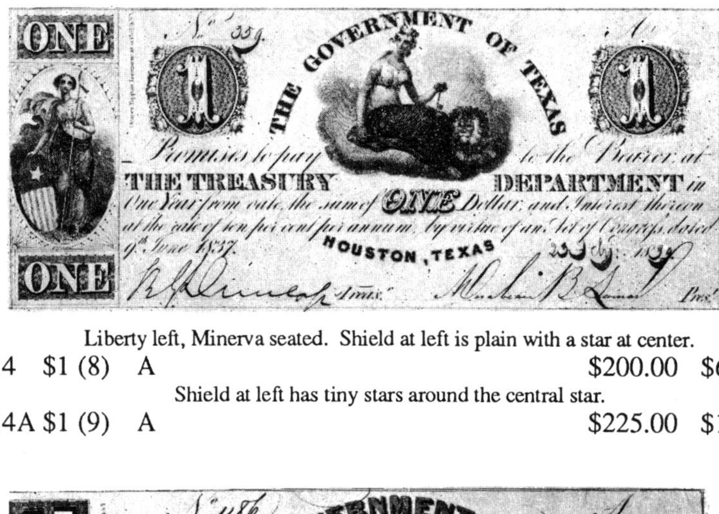

Liberty left, Minerva seated. Shield at left is plain with a star at center.

H14 $1 (8) A $200.00 $600.00

Shield at left has tiny stars around the central star.

H14A $1 (9) A $225.00 $1000.00

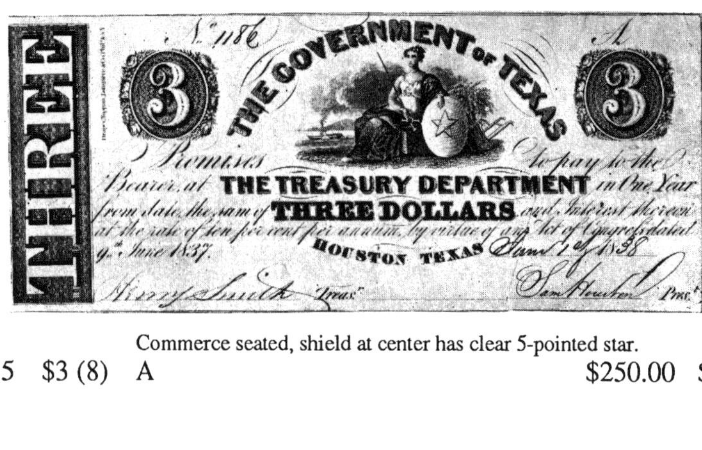

Commerce seated, shield at center has clear 5-pointed star.

H15 $3 (8) A $250.00 $1200.00

Shield has 5-pointed star with line across base of left point.

H15A $3 (8) A $250.00 $1200.00

Shield is heavily shaded and star is almost indistinct.

H15B $3 (8) A $250.00 $750.00

Indian on horseback chasing bison, Commerce left.

H16 $5 (7) A B $175.00 $350.00

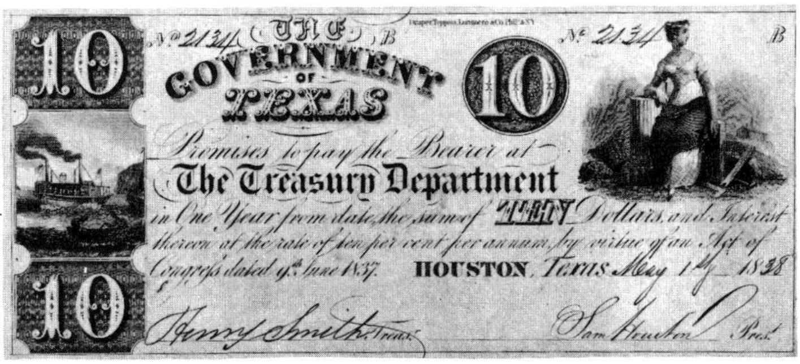

Ship at left, Industry seated at right.

Tops of letters in "Government" are white, with dot.

H17 $10 (5) A B $60.00 $100.00

Tops of letters in "Government" are shaded, with dot.

H17A $10 (5) A B $60.00 $100.00

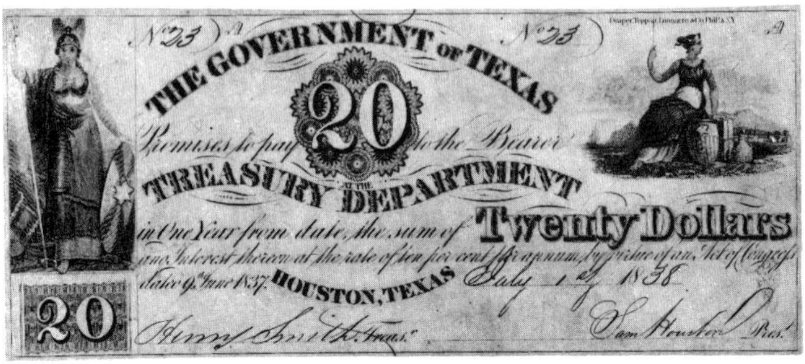

Liberty at left, Minerva right.

Five-pointed star on shield at left.

H18	$20 (6)	A	$60.00	$100.00

Six-pointed star on shield at left, star on shield at right.

H19	$20 (5)	A	$60.00	$100.00

Six-pointed star on shield at left, eagle on shield at right.

H20	$20 (6)	A	$60.00	$100.00

Justice seated, sailor and flag at left.

Star on flag at left is small with points even.

H21	$50 (6)	A	$75.00	$125.00

Star on flag at left is large with points uneven.

H21A	$50 (6)	A	$75.00	$125.00

Third issue of notes, in the name of

THE REPUBLIC OF TEXAS

Issued from
HOUSTON

Change note issues, authorized by act of Congress "Dec. 14th, 1837."
These bear written dates of 1838 (with "18" printed).

All engraved by "Childs, Clark & Co. N. Orleans."

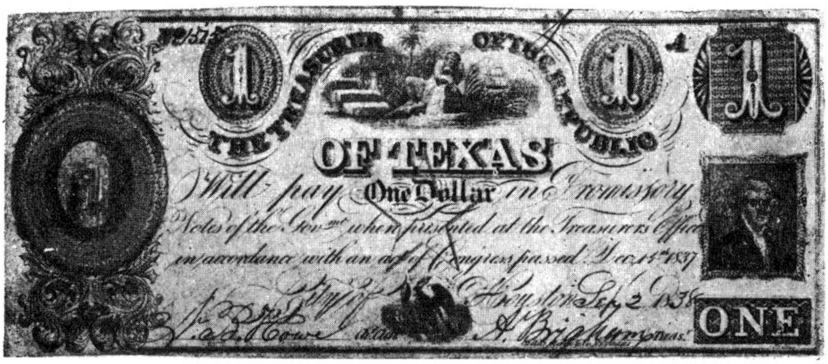

Man asleep at center, portrait of Thomas Jefferson at right.

"Niles Print. Houston," under left signature.

H22 $1 (9) A $450.00 $2500.00

Printer's name omitted.

H23 $1 (9) A $450.00 $2500.00

Liberty, shield and eagle.

"Niles Print. Houston," under left signature.

H24 $2 (9) A $450.00 $3500.00

Printer's name omitted.

H25 $2 (9) A $450.00 $3500.00

Man asleep at center, portrait of Thomas Jefferson right.

"Niles Print. Houston," under left signature.

H26 $3 (9) A $500.00 $4500.00

Printer's name omitted.

H27 $3 (9) A $500.00 $4500.00

"CONSOLIDATED FUND OF TEXAS"

Consolidated fund of Texas notes were authorized by act of Congress on the "7th of June, 1837 to consolidate and fund the public debt."

1837 HOUSTON ISSUE

All bear the printed date "September 1, 1837," but other dates are frequently also written on the notes.

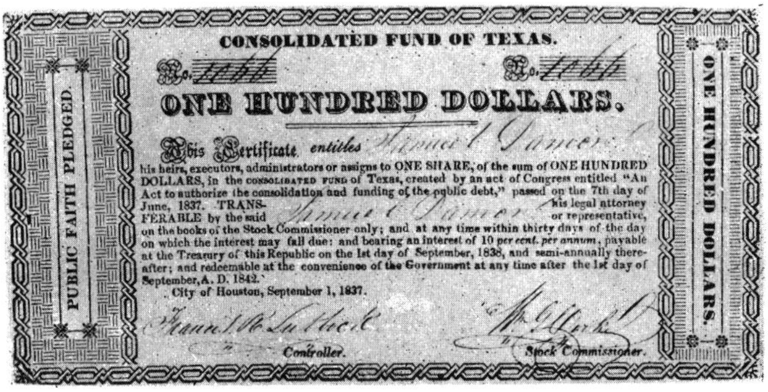

All notes are the same except for denomination.

CF1	$100 (7)	$55.00	$125.00
CF2	$500 (11)		unknown
CF3	$1000 (11)		unknown

All notes are the same except for denomination.

CF4	$100 (11)		unknown
CF5	$500 (8)	$80.00	$150.00

CF6	$1000 (9)	$120.00	$225.00
CF6A	$5000 (10)	very rare	
CF6B	$10,000 (11)	extremely rare	

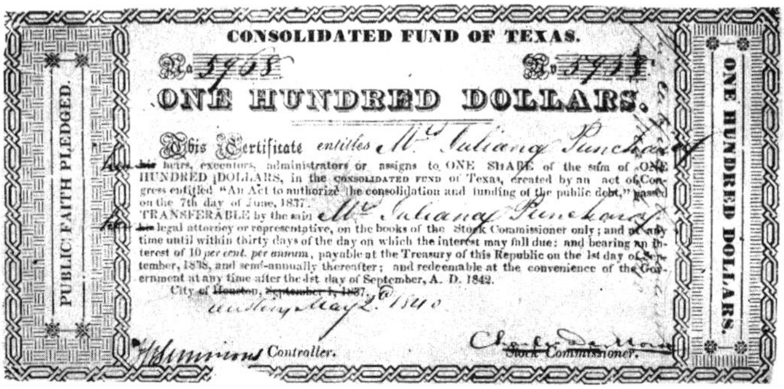

All the same except denominations.

CF7	$100 (7)	$70.00	$125.00

Same but "JUNE" spelled "JUND."

CF7A	$100 (8)	$90.00	$200.00

Same as CF7 but "His" omitted in both places

CF7B	$100 (9)	$125.00	$250.00
CF8	$500 (8)	$75.00	$125.00
CF9	$1000 (9)	$125.00	$275.00

All the same except denomination.

CF10	$100 (7)	$85.00	$125.00
CF11	$500 (8)	$90.00	$150.00
CF12	$1000 (9)	$300.00	$1200.00
CF12A	$5000 (11)	$1500.00	$2800.00

1839 HOUSTON ISSUE

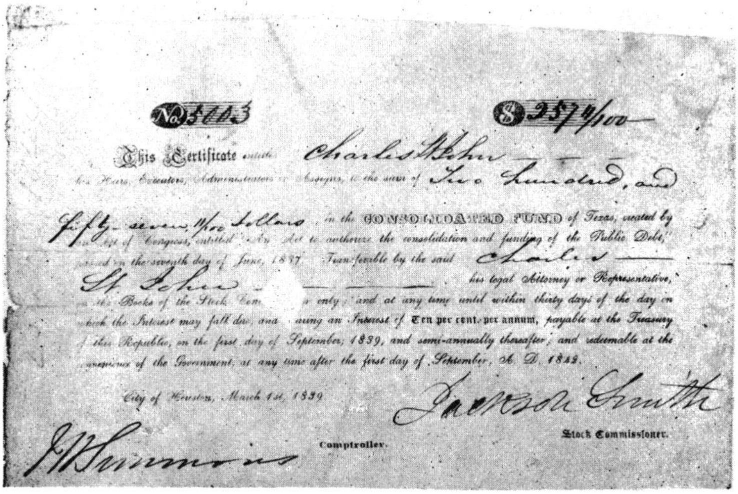

CF13 written denominations (9) $200.00 $450.00

AUSTIN ISSUE

Written dates.

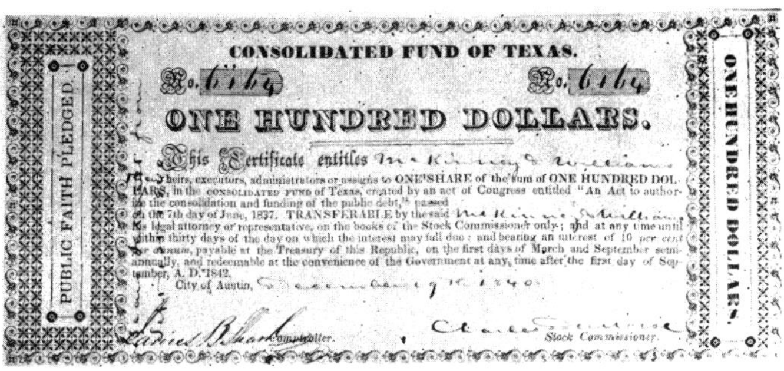

CF14 $100 (9) $250.00 $275.00

Fourth issue of notes, in the name of

THE REPUBLIC OF TEXAS

Issued from
AUSTIN

$150,000 authorized by an act of Congress,
December 14, 1838, in $1, $2, and $3 denominations only.

Written dates of 1839-1841 ("18" of date printed.)
All engraved by "Endicott & Clark. New Orleans."

Ceres seated at center, Indian brave at left.

A1 $1 (5) A B $100.00 $200.00

Cowboy roping steer, stag at left.

A2 $2 (5) A $150.00 $250.00

Ceres seated by lone star.

A3 $3 (7) A $250.00 $450.00

5th issue of notes, in the name of

THE REPUBLIC OF TEXAS

Issued from
AUSTIN

Rawdon, Wright, Hatch & Edson, New Orleans
Rawdon, Wright, & Hatch, New York

Authorized by act of Congress, January 19th, 1839.

Written dates of 1839-1841 ("18" of date printed)

All denominations have a rather ornate red-orange back picturing a large star in the center.

Indian brave seated. Portrait "Deaf" Smith at right.

A4 $5 (6) A $125.00 $250.00

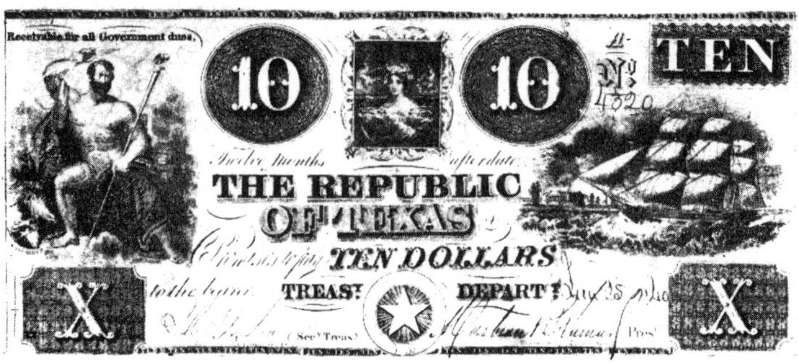

Hercules at left, ship at right.

A5 $10 (4) A $80.00 $150.00

Indian and maiden by shield with star, Indian left.

A6 $20 (4) A $80.00 $150.00

Steamship and nude maiden. Portrait of Stephen Austin at right.

A7 $50 (4) A $80.00 $125.00

Minerva seated, mercury flying at center.

A8 $100 (6) A B C $325.00 $700.00

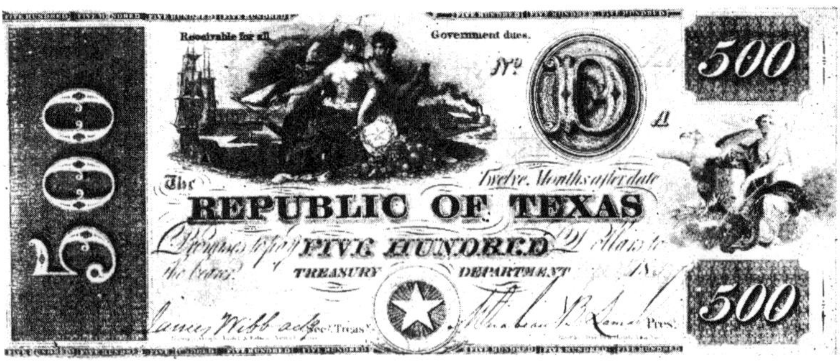

Commerce and Industry seated.

A9 $500 (8) A $750.00 $2000.00

Sixth issue of notes, in the name of

THE REPUBLIC OF TEXAS

Issued from
AUSTIN

This is the famous and extremely rare "Exchequer Series" of notes. Very little information is available on any of these notes. They are very rare with only about five pieces reported. Reports of additional pieces and any other information is needed.

Engraved and printed by "Rawdon, Wright, Hatch & Edson. New York."
Authorized by act of Congress, January 29, 1842.
$150,000 was issued in the below listed denominations.

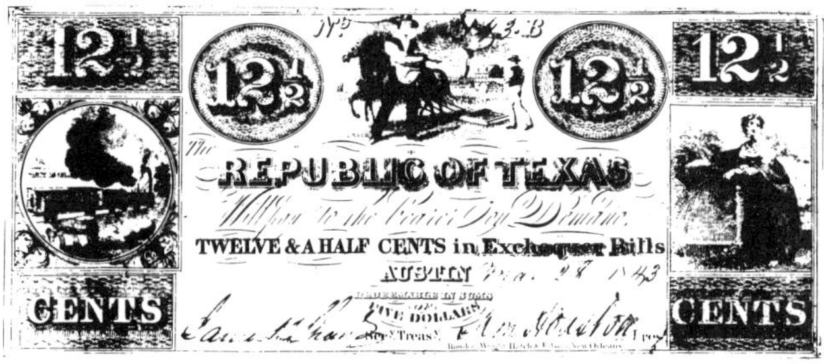

Horse pulling plow left at center, train at left.

A10 12.5c (11) extremely rare

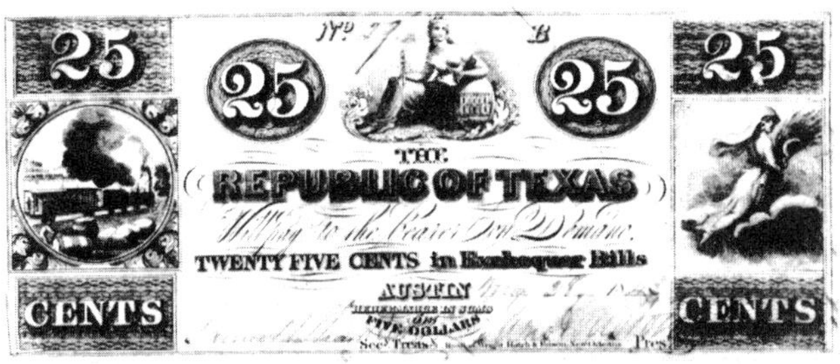

Liberty seated replaces horse with plow.

A11 25c (11) A B extremely rare

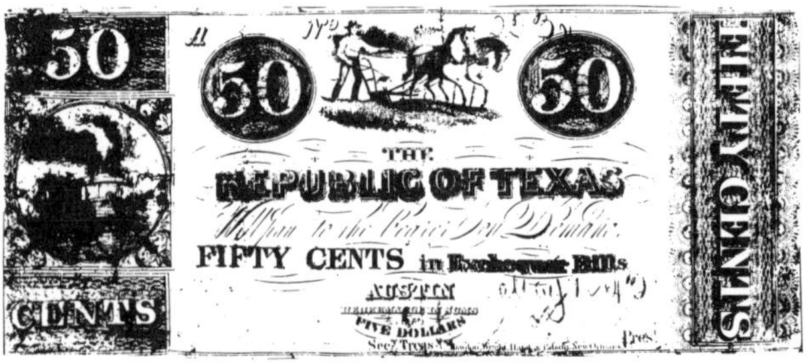

Horse pulling plow to right.

A12 50c (11) A B extremely rare
A13 75c no information available

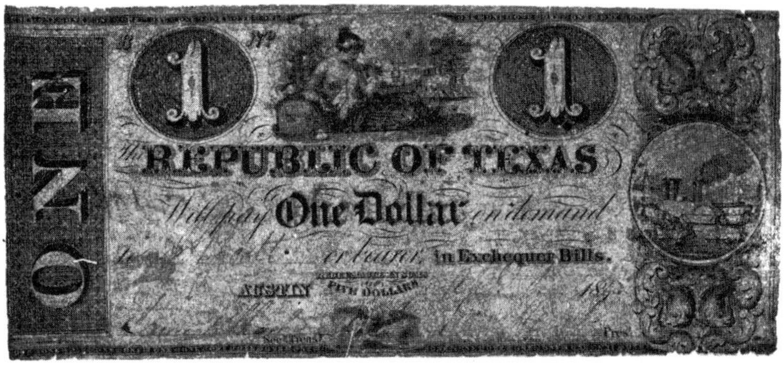

Ceres seated beside bale of cotton, steamship at right.

A14 $1 (11) A B extremely rare
A15 $2 no information available
A16 $3 no information available

Sailor in oval, ship at left.

A17 $5 (11) extremely rare
A18 $10 no information available
A19 $20 no information available
A20 $50 no information available
A21 $100 no information available

Fifth issue of warrants, in the name of

THE REPUBLIC OF TEXAS

Issued from
AUSTIN

These may bear dates from 1839 to 1845.

Written dates ("18" of date printed).

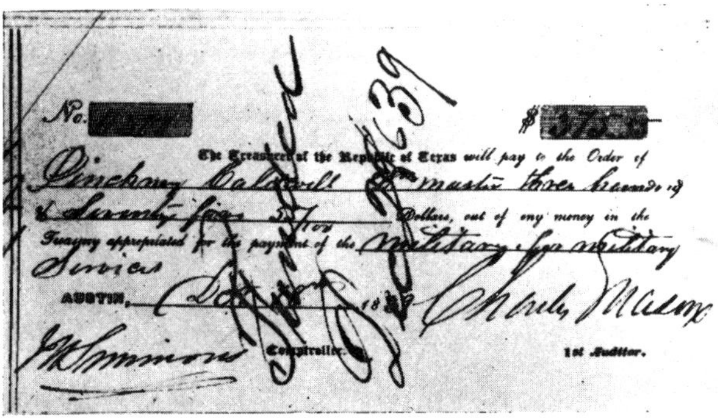
No. $

The Treasurer of the Republic of Texas will pay to the Order of Pinckney Caldwell ... three hundred & seventy five ... Dollars, out of any money in the Treasury appropriated for the payment of the Military for military Services

AUSTIN, 18

Comptroller. 1st Auditor.

AW1 written denominations (8) $75.00 $200.00

"Whiting's Press. Austin."

Written dates ("18" of date printed).

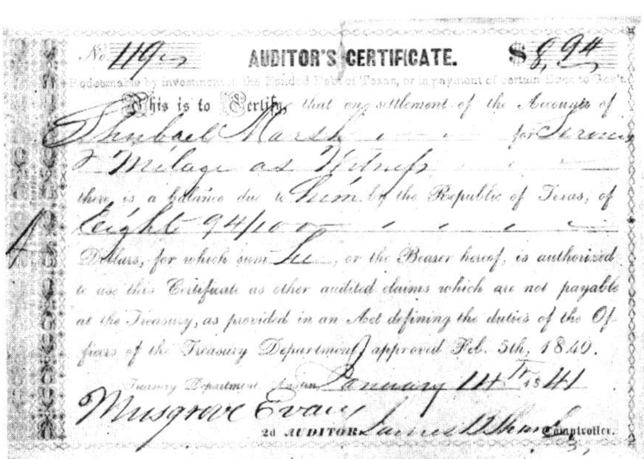
No. 119 AUDITOR'S CERTIFICATE. $8.94

Redeemable by investment in the Funded Debt of Texas, or in payment of certain Dues to Gov't.

This is to Certify, that on settlement of the Accounts of Shubael Marsh for Services & Milage as Witness there is a balance due to him by the Republic of Texas, of Eight 94/100 Dollars, for which sum he, or the Bearer hereof, is authorized to use this Certificate as other audited claims which are not payable at the Treasury, as provided in an Act defining the duties of the Officers of the Treasury Department, approved Feb. 5th, 1840.

Treasury Department Austin January 11th 1841

Musgrove Evans 2d AUDITOR Comptroller.

AW2 written denominations (9) $90.00 $250.00

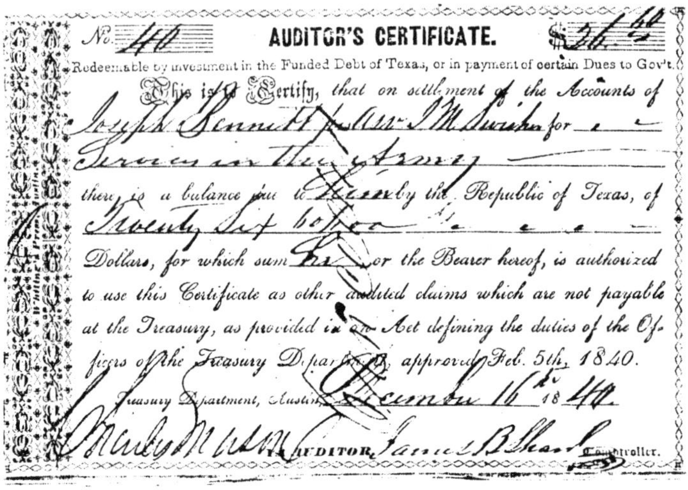

No. 40 AUDITOR'S CERTIFICATE. $26 60/100

Redeemable by investment in the Funded Debt of Texas, or in payment of certain Dues to Gov't.

This is to Certify, that on settlement of the Accounts of Joseph Bennett for Services in the Army there is a balance due to by the Republic of Texas, of Twenty Six 60/100 Dollars, for which sum or the Bearer hereof, is authorized to use this Certificate as other audited claims which are not payable at the Treasury, as provided in an Act defining the duties of the Officers of the Treasury Department, approved Feb. 5th, 1840.

Treasury Department, Austin, December 16th 1840.

Auditor. James B. Shaw Comptroller.

AW2A written denominations (10) $90.00 $275.00

Special naval payment warrant.

Known dated "April 23" (23 hand written), "1841," only.

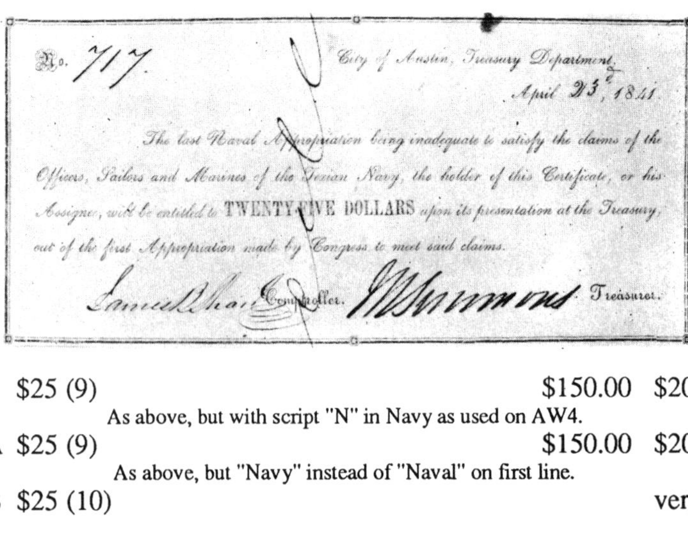

No. 717. City of Austin, Treasury Department, April 23d, 1841.

The last Naval Appropriation being inadequate to satisfy the claims of the Officers, Sailors and Marines of the Texian Navy, the holder of this Certificate, or his Assignee, will be entitled to TWENTY-FIVE DOLLARS upon its presentation at the Treasury, out of the first Appropriation made by Congress to meet said claims.

James B. Shaw Comptroller. Treasurer.

AW3 $25 (9) $150.00 $200.00

As above, but with script "N" in Navy as used on AW4.

AW3A $25 (9) $150.00 $200.00

As above, but "Navy" instead of "Naval" on first line.

AW3B $25 (10) very rare

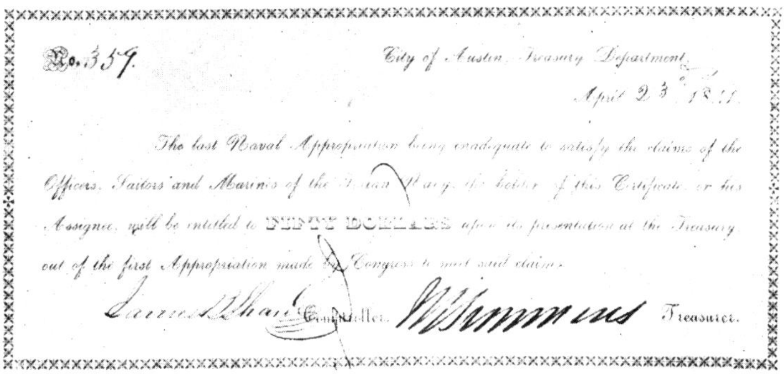
No. 359. City of Austin Treasury Department, April 23rd 18..

The last Naval Appropriation being inadequate to satisfy the claims of the Officers, Sailors and Marines of the Texian Navy, the holder of this Certificate or his Assignee, will be entitled to FIFTY DOLLARS upon its presentation at the Treasury out of the first Appropriation made by Congress to meet said claims.

Comptroller. Treasurer.

AW4 $50 (10) $150.00 $225.00

"Whiting's Press. Austin."

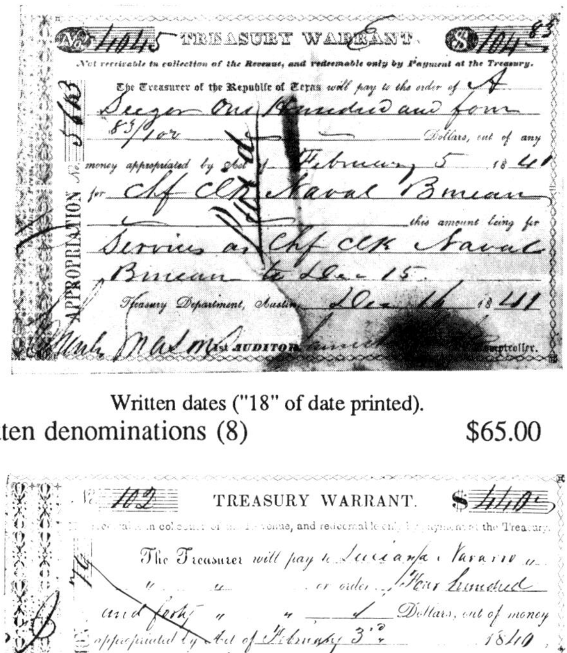
No. 1045 TREASURY WARRANT. $104 83/100

Not receivable in collection of the Revenue, and redeemable only by Payment at the Treasury.

The Treasurer of the Republic of Texas will pay to the order of A. Seeger One Hundred and four 83/100 Dollars, out of any money appropriated by Act of February 5 1841 for Chf Clk Naval Bureau this amount being for Services as Chf Clk Naval Bureau to Dec 15.

Treasury Department, Austin, Dec 16 1841

APPROPRIATION No.

1st AUDITOR. Comptroller.

Written dates ("18" of date printed).

AW5 written denominations (8) $65.00 $100.00

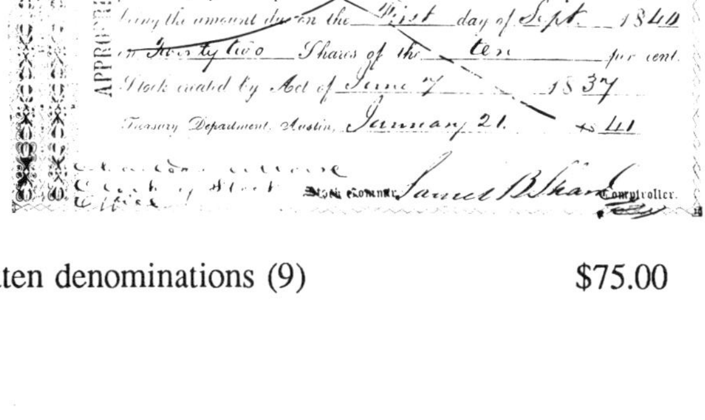
No. 102 TREASURY WARRANT. $440

Not receivable in collection of the Revenue, and redeemable only by payment at the Treasury.

The Treasurer will pay to Luciana Navarro or order, Four hundred and forty Dollars, out of money appropriated by Act of February 3rd 1840, for the payment of Interest on the Funded Debt of Texas, this being the amount due on the first day of Sept. 1840 on Forty two Shares of the ten per cent. Stock created by Act of June 7 1837

Treasury Department, Austin, January 21. 1841

APPROPRIATION

Stock Commr. Comptroller.

AW5A written denominations (9) $75.00 $100.00

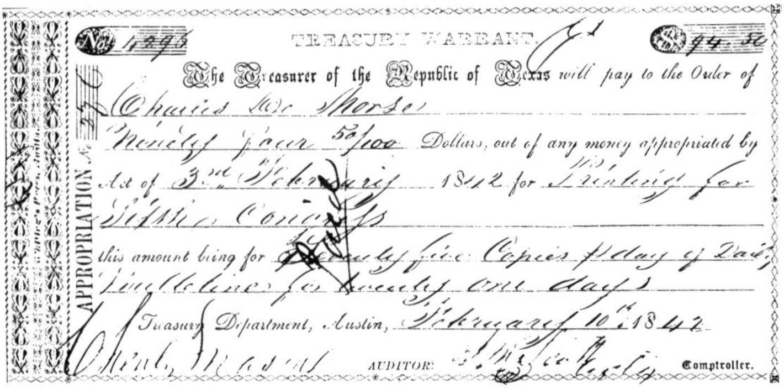

AW5B written denominations (9) $75.00 $85.00

Written dates ("18" of date printed)

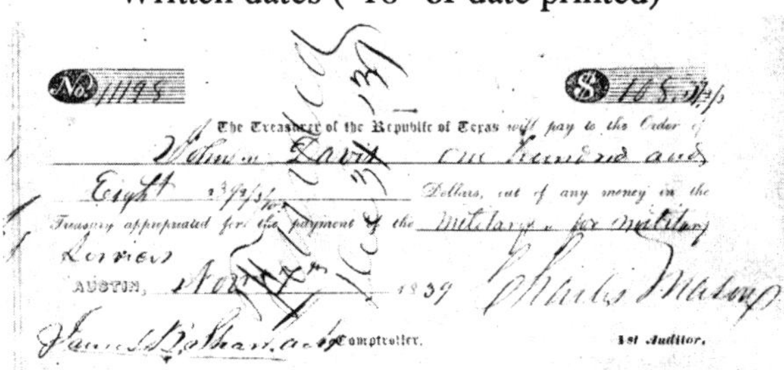

"The Treasurer of the Republic of Texas" in small letters.

AW6 written denominations (8) $60.00 $125.00

"The Treasurer of the Republic of Texas" in large letters.

AW7 written denominations (8) $60.00 $130.00

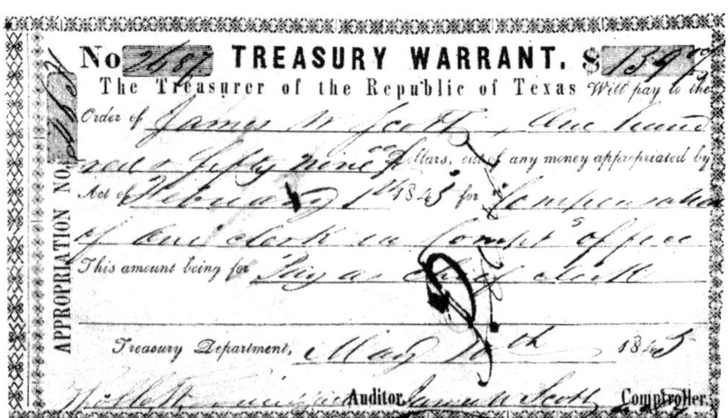

Written dates ("184" of date printed).

AW8 written denominations (8) $55.00 $70.00

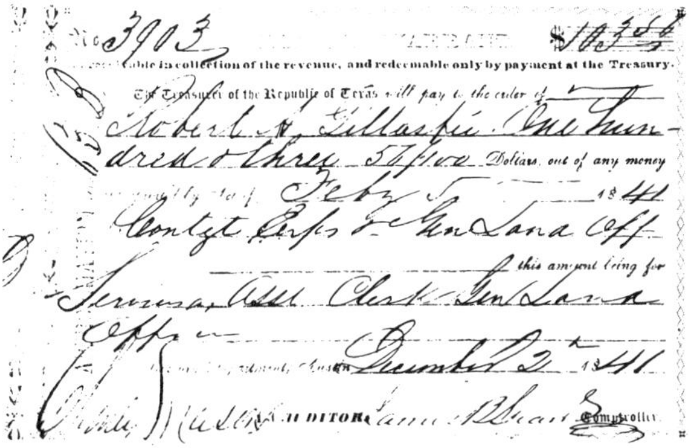

AW8A written denominations (9) $55.00 $70.00

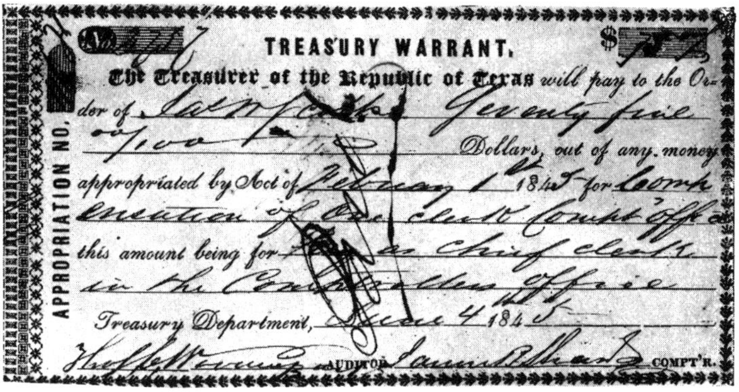

Written dates ("184" of date printed).

AW9 written denominations (8) $55.00 $80.00

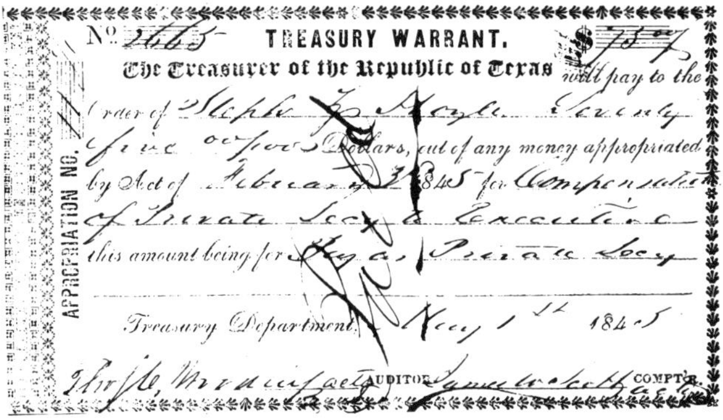

AW9A written denominations (9) $65.00 $80.00

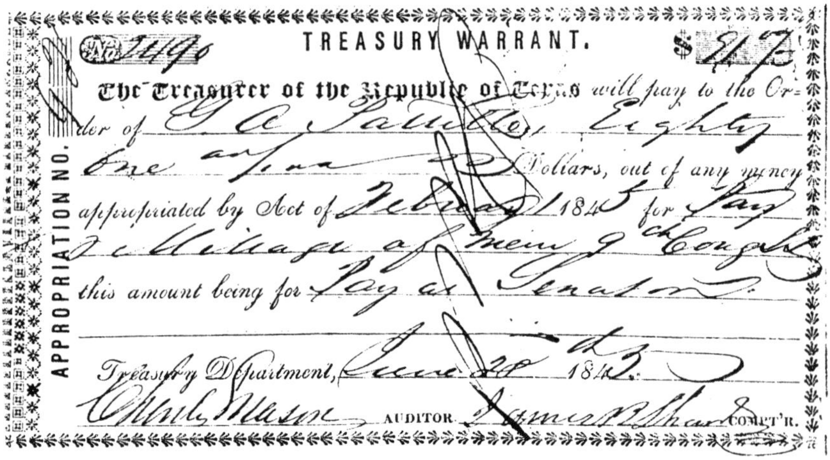

No. 1496 TREASURY WARRANT. $ 81

The Treasurer of the Republic of Texas will pay to the Order of G. A. Pattillo Eighty one and Dollars, out of any money appropriated by Act of February 1843 for Pay & Milage of mem 9th Congress

this amount being for Pay as Senator

Treasury Department, June 28 1843.

Charles Mason AUDITOR. James B. Shaw COMPT'R.

APPROPRIATION NO.

AW9B written denominations (10) $150.00 $250.00

Written dates ("18" of date printed).

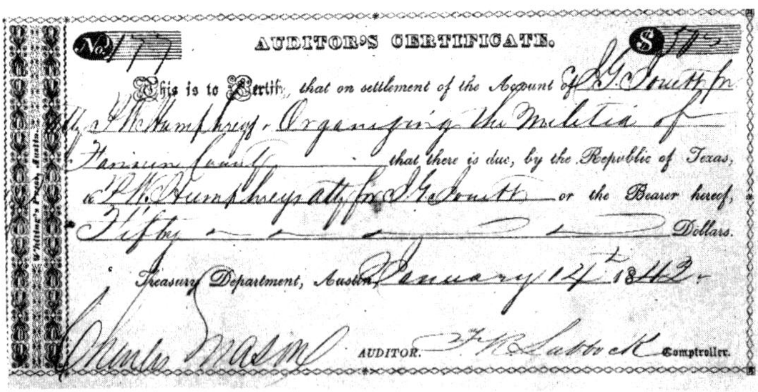

No. 177 AUDITOR'S CERTIFICATE. $ 50

This is to Certify, that on settlement of the Account of S. G. Jouett for W. Humphrey - Organizing the Militia of Fannin County that there is due, by the Republic of Texas, to J. W. Humphreys atty for S. G. Jouett or the Bearer hereof, Fifty Dollars.

Treasury Department, Austin, January 14th 1842.

Charles Mason AUDITOR. F. R. Lubbock Comptroller.

AW10 written denominations (9) $65.00 $110.00

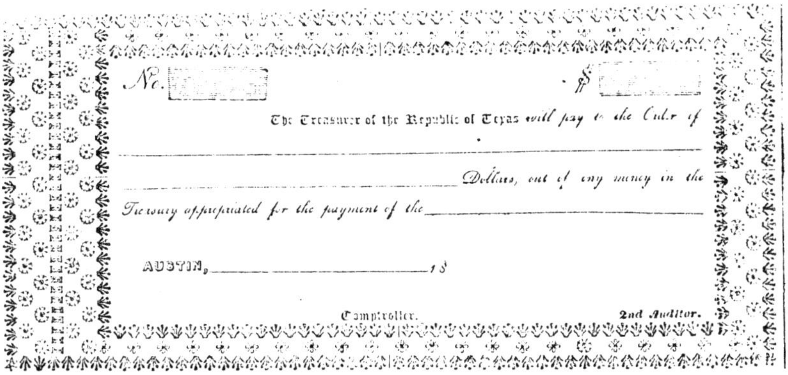

No. $

The Treasurer of the Republic of Texas will pay to the Order of

Dollars, out of any money in the

Treasury appropriated for the payment of the

AUSTIN, 18

Comptroller. 2nd Auditor.

AW11	written denominations (or blank) (9)	$65.00	$110.00
AW11A	written denominations (or blank) (9)	$65.00	$110.00

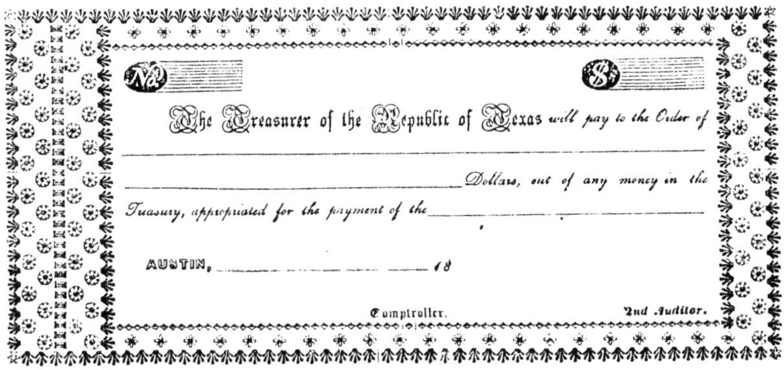

No. $

The Treasurer of the Republic of Texas will pay to the Order of

Dollars, out of any money in the

Treasury, appropriated for the payment of the

AUSTIN, 18

Comptroller. 2nd Auditor.

AW12	written denominations (or blank) (9)	$65.00	$110.00

Sixth issue of warrants, in the name of

THE REPUBLIC OF TEXAS

Issued from
WASHINGTON

These bear dates of 1842 to 1843.

"Texian Print. Washington."
"January, (written day) 1843."

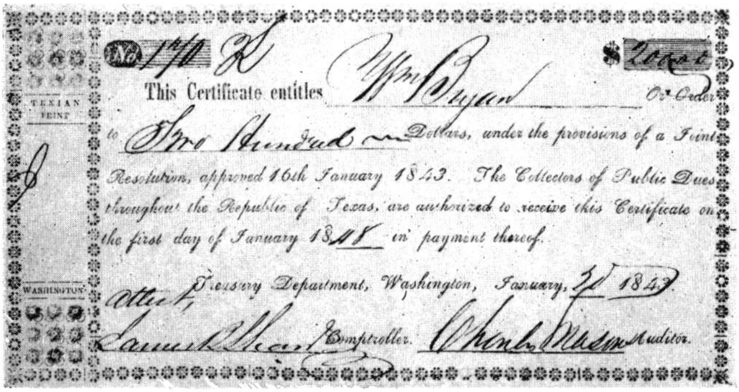

TEXIAN PRINT

No 170 $200

This Certificate entitles Wm Bryan Or Order

to Two Hundred Dollars, under the provisions of a Joint Resolution, approved 16th January 1843. The Collectors of Public Dues throughout the Republic of Texas, are authorized to receive this Certificate on the first day of January 1848 in payment thereof.

WASHINGTON

Treasury Department, Washington, January 20 1843.

Attest, Comptroller. Charles Mason Auditor.

W1 written denominations (9) $100.00 $150.00

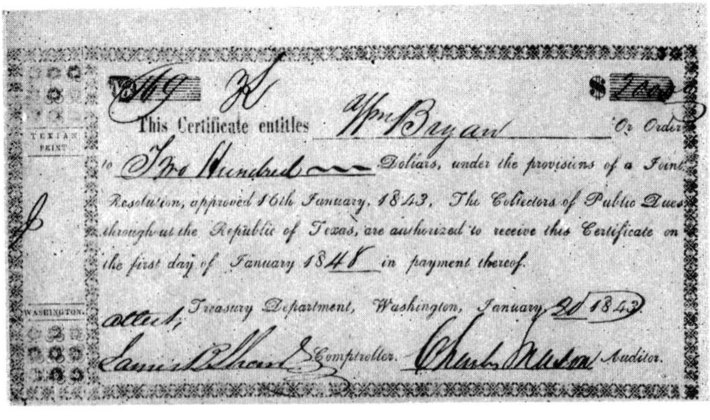

TEXIAN PRINT

No 149 $200

This Certificate entitles Wm Bryan Or Order

to Two Hundred Dollars, under the provisions of a Joint Resolution, approved 16th January, 1843. The Collectors of Public Dues throughout the Republic of Texas, are authorized to receive this Certificate on the first day of January 1848 in payment thereof.

WASHINGTON

Treasury Department, Washington, January 20 1843.

Attest, Comptroller. Charles Mason Auditor.

W2 written denominations (9) $100.00 $150.00

"Telegraph Print. Houston."

Written dates ("18" of date printed).

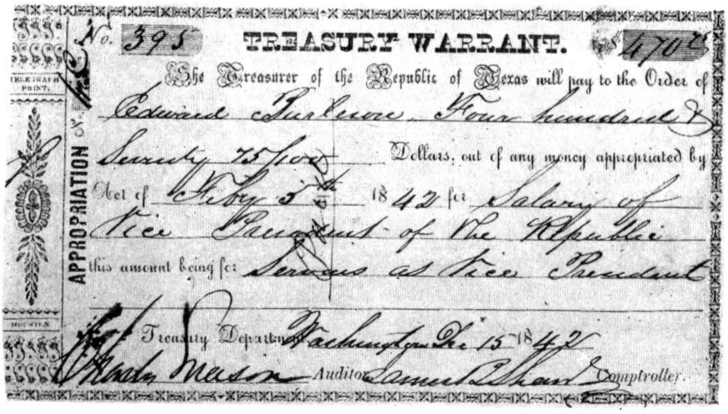
TELEGRAPH PRINT. HOUSTON. APPROPRIATION No.

No. 395 TREASURY WARRANT. $470 75/100

The Treasurer of the Republic of Texas will pay to the Order of Edward Burleson Four hundred & Seventy 75/100 Dollars, out of any money appropriated by Act of Feby 5th 1842 for Salary of Vice President of the Republic

this amount being for Services as Vice President

Treasury Department, Washington Dec 15 1842

Auditor Comptroller.

W3 written denominations (9) $80.00 $100.00

"Texian Print. Washington."

Written dates ("184" printed).

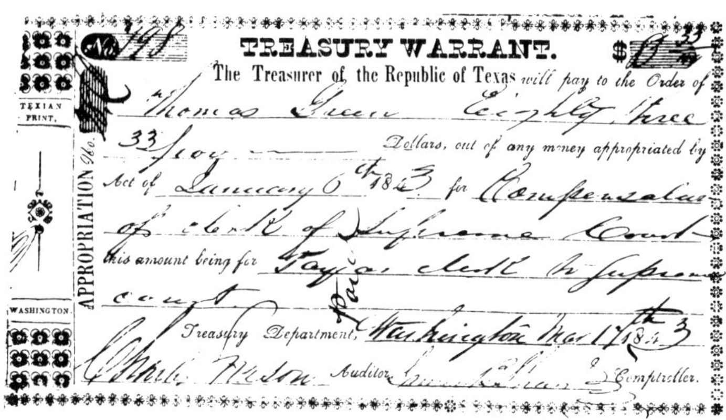
TEXIAN PRINT. WASHINGTON. APPROPRIATION No.

No. 498 TREASURY WARRANT. $83 33/100

The Treasurer of the Republic of Texas will pay to the Order of Thomas Green Eighty Three 33/100 Dollars, out of any money appropriated by Act of January 6th 1843 for Compensation of clerk of Supreme Court

this amount being for Pay as clerk of Supreme court

Treasury Department, Washington Mar 17th 1843

Auditor Comptroller.

W4 written denominations (9) $80.00 $100.00

W9	written denominations (9)	$85.00	$95.00
W10	hand written (10)	$150.00	rare

THE STATE OF TEXAS

The treasury warrants issued by the State of Texas during its alliance with the Confederacy are extremely difficult to list, since state records do not show what type of bill was used to draw money from each of the separate appropriations. We do know the 12 military and 11 civil (hereinafter called "M" and "C") Service Act dates, and it is conceivable that each type bill could have been used for each act date. Every "M" or "C" number is listed under each type. The table below indicates the dates for the respective issues. It should be understood that some "M" and "C" numbers may be much rarer than the rarity given for the type note, which is the rarity of the most common variety known.

If "military" is written over "civil," the standard number for it would be M/C and the "Military" or "M" number. Vice versa for a "civil" over "military" issue. In general, the "military" use of a "civil" warrant increases the rarity by 1. The "civil" use of a "military" warrant is extremely rare, and will yield an increase of 3 to 4 in rarity.

Act dates other than those listed in the standard list below are simply man-made "errors" of the pen. Examples dated 1852 have been seen.

Master list of all authorized military and civil act dates.

Military Service		Civil Service	
M1	Feb 3, 1860	C1	Feb 11, 1860
M2	Feb 8, 1861	C2	Apr. 8, 1861
M3	Apr 5, 1861	C3	Jan. 8, 1862
M4	Apr. 8, 1861	C4	Jan. 13, 1862
M5	Jan. 4, 1862	C5	Mar. 2, 1863
M6	Jan. 12, 1862	C6	Mar. 3, 1863
M7	Jan. 13, 1862	C7	Mar. 5, 1863
M8	Jan. 14, 1862	C8	Dec. 15, 1963
M9	Mar. 5, 1863	C9	Dec. 16, 1863
M10	Mar. 6, 1863	C10	May 28, 1864
M11	Apr. 11, 1863	C11	Nov. 15, 1864
M12	Dec. 16, 1863		

No printers' names.

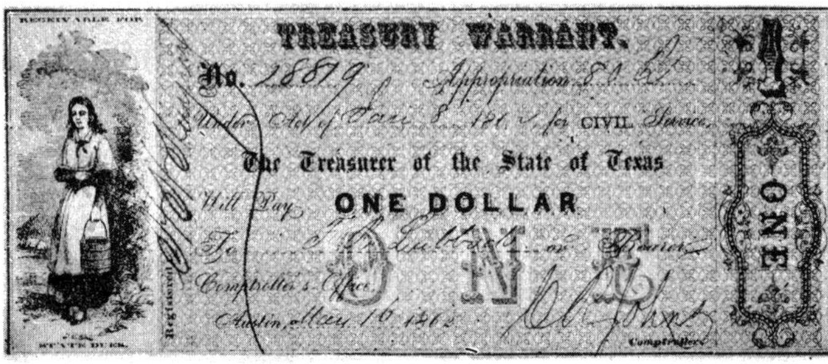

Milkmaid at left, black with orange lace overprint covering most of the note.

		Military Service		
1	$1 (6)	M1 M2 M3 M4 M5 M6 M7 M8 M9 M10 M11 M12	$25.00	$50.00
		Civil Service		
2	$1 (5)	C1 C2 C3 C4 C5 C6 C7 C8 C9 C10 C11	$25.00	$50.00

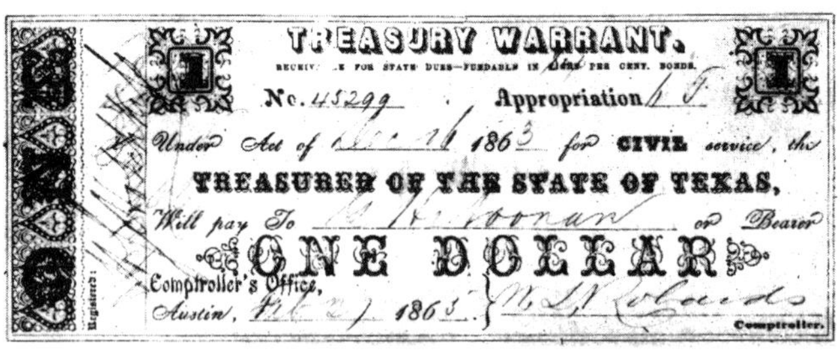

Green and black.

		Military Service		
3	$1 (6)	M1 M2 M3 M4 M5 M6 M7 M8 M9 M10 M11 M12	$25.00	$50.00
		Civil Service		
4	$1 (6)	C1 C2 C3 C4 C5 C6 C7 C8 C9 C10 C11	$25.00	$50.00

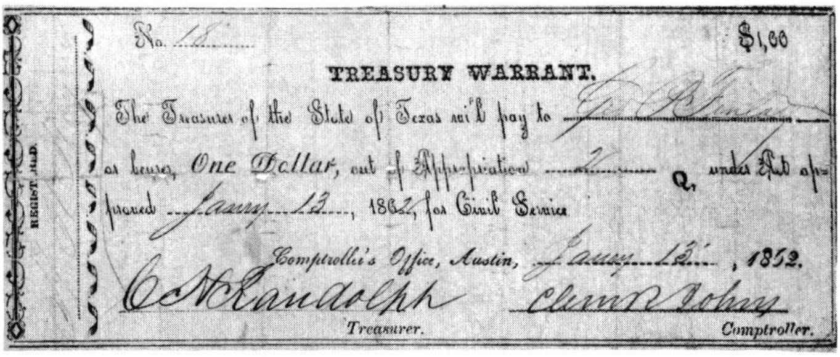

Typeset. This note exists *with* and *without* a printed "Q" serial letter after the appropriation number.

Military service

		"Approved" is on second line, without "Q."		
5	$1 (8)	M1 M2 M3 M4 M5 M6 M7 M8 M9 M10 M11 M12	$35.00	$75.00
		As above with "Q."		
5A	$1 (8)	M1,Q M2,Q M3,Q M4,Q M5,Q M6, Q M7,Q M8,Q M9,Q M10,Q M11,Q M12,Q	$35.00	$75.00
		"Approved" is hyphenated, without "Q."		
5B	$1 (10)	M1 M2 M3 M4 M5 M6 M7 M8 M9 M10 M11 M12	$60.00	$100.00
		As above with "Q."		
5C	$1 (10)	M1,Q M2,Q M3,Q M4,Q M5,Q M6, Q M7,Q M8,Q M9,Q M10,Q M11,Q M12,Q	$60.00	$100.00
		"Approved" is on third line without "Q."		
5D	$1 (10)	M1 M2 M3 M4 M5 M6 M7 M8 M9 M10 M11 M12	$60.00	$100.00
		As above with "Q."		
5E	$1 (10)	M1,Q M2,Q M3,Q M4,Q M5,Q M6, Q M7,Q M8,Q M9,Q M10,Q M11,Q M12,Q	$60.00	$100.00
		Civil service		
		"Approved" is on second line, without "Q."		
6	$1 (9)	C1 C2 C3 C4 C5 C6 C7 C8 C9 C10 C11	$60.00	$100.00
		As above with "Q."		
6A	$1 (8)	C1,Q C2,Q C3,Q C4,Q C5,Q C6, Q C7,Q C8,Q C9,Q C10,Q C11,Q	$60.00	$100.00
		"Approved" is hyphenated, without "Q."		
6B	$1 (10)	C1 C2 C3 C4 C5 C6 C7 C8 C9 C10 C11	$75.00	$100.00

As above with "Q."

6C $1 (10) C1,Q C2,Q C3,Q C4,Q C5,Q C6,Q C7,Q C8,Q C9,Q C10,Q C11,Q $75.00 $100.00

"Approved" is on third line without "Q."

6D $1 (10) C1 C2 C3 C4 C5 C6 C7 C8 C9 C10 C11 $75.00 $100.00

As above with "Q."

6E $1 (10) C1,Q C2,Q C3,Q C4,Q C5,Q C6,Q C7,Q C8,Q C9,Q C10,Q C11,Q $75.00 $100.00

Printed on buff brown paper.

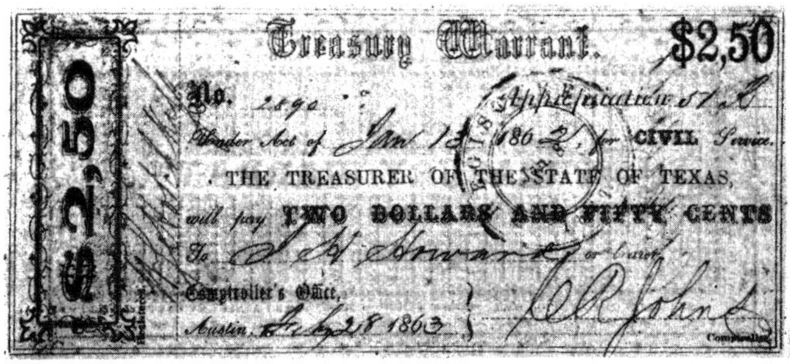

Military service

Solid blue network on back.

7 $2.50 (8) M1 M2 M3 M4 M5 M6 M7 M8 M9 M10 M11 M12 $40.00 $80.00

As above but with a window for a signature in the network.

7A $2.50 (7) M1 M2 M3 M4 M5 M6 M7 M8 M9 M10 M11 M12 $35.00 $75.00

Civil service

Solid red network on back.

8 $2.50 (6) C1 C2 C3 C4 C5 C6 C7 C8 C9 C10 C11 $35.00 $70.00

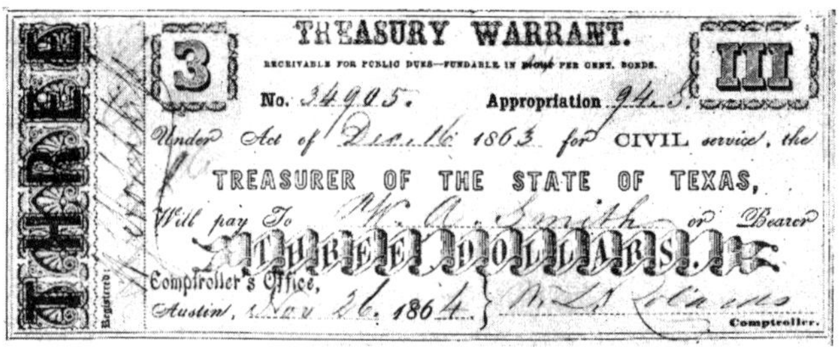

Military service, green and black.

9 $3 (6) M1 M2 M3 M4 M5 M6 M7 M8 M9 M10 M11 M12 $40.00 $75.00

Civil service

10 $3 (5) C1 C2 C3 C4 C5 C6 C7 C8 C9 C10 C11 C12 $40.00 $75.00

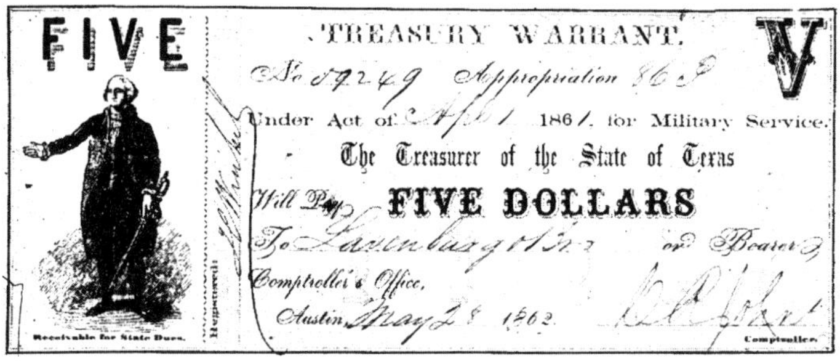

Black with green lace overprint covering most of the note.
Statue of Washington at left.

Military service.
Blue gray paper, single scroll to "N" of "No."

11 $5 (4) M1 M2 M3 M4 M5 M6 M7 M8 M9 M10 M11 M12 $25.00 $50.00

Same, double scroll to "N" of "No."

11A $5 (5) M1 M2 M3 M4 M5 M6 M7 M8 M9 M10 M11 M12 $25.00 $50.00

White paper, single scroll to "N" of "No."

12 $5 (4) M1 M2 M3 M4 M5 M6 M7 M8 M9 M10 M11 M12 $25.00 $50.00

Same, double scroll to "N" of "No."

12A $5 (8) M1 M2 M3 M4 M5 M6 M7 M8 M9 M10 M11 M12 $25.00 $50.00

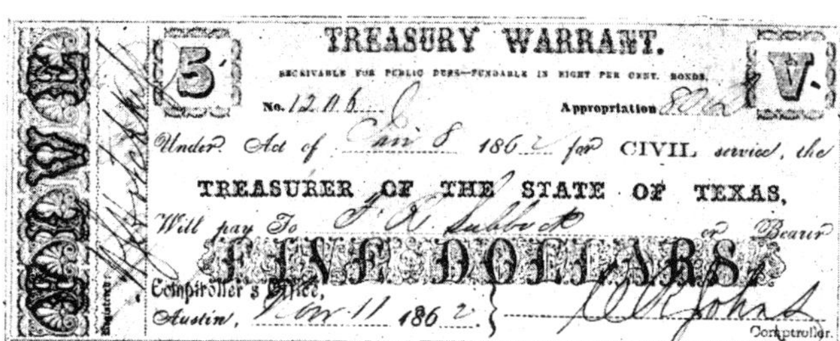

Military service, green and black.

13 $5 (5) M1 M2 M3 M4 M5 M6 M7 M8 M9 M10 M11 M12 $20.00 $40.00

Civil service.

14 $5 (5) C1 C2 C3 C4 C5 C6 C7 C8 C9 C10 C11 $22.00 $45.00

Same as above, "dues" spelled "deus."

14A $5 (9) C4 very rare

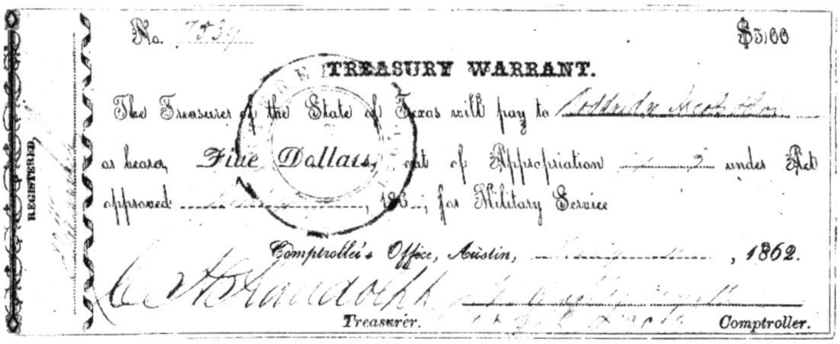

Typeset. This note exists *with* and *without* a printed "Q" serial letter after the appropriation number.

Military Service

"Approved" is on second line, without "Q."

15	$5 (9)	M1 M2 M3 M4 M5 M6 M7 M8 M9 M10 M11 M12	$40.00	$80.00

As above with "Q."

15A	$5 (10)	M1,Q M2,Q M3,Q M4,Q M5,Q M6, Q M7,Q M8,Q M9,Q M10,Q M11,Q M12,Q	$60.00	$100.00

"Approved" is hyphenated, without "Q."

15B	$5 (10)	M1 M2 M3 M4 M5 M6 M7 M8 M9 M10 M11 M12	$60.00	$100.00

As above with "Q."

15C	$5 (10)	M1,Q M2,Q M3,Q M4,Q M5,Q M6,Q M7,Q M8,Q M9,Q M10,Q M11,Q M12,Q	$60.00	$100.00

"Approved" is on third line without "Q."

15D	$5 (10)	M1 M2 M3 M4 M5 M6 M7 M8 M9 M10 M11 M12	$60.00	$100.00

As above with "Q."

15E	$5 (10)	M1,Q M2,Q M3,Q M4,Q M5,Q M6,Q M7, M8,Q M9,Q M10,Q M11,Q M12,Q	$60.00	$100.00

Civil Service

"Approved" is on second line, without "Q."

16	$5 (9)	M1 M2 M3 M4 M5 M6 M7 M8 M9 M10 M11 M12	$60.00	$80.00

As above with "Q."

16A	$5 (8)	M1,Q M2,Q M3,Q M4,Q M5,Q M6,Q M7,Q M8,Q M9,Q M10,Q M11,Q M12,Q	$50.00	$200.00

"Approved" is hyphenated, without "Q."

16B $5 (10) M1 M2 M3 M4 M5 M6 M7 M8 M9 M10 M11 M12 $65.00 $200.00

As above with "Q."

16C $5 (10) M1,Q M2,Q M3,Q M4,Q M5,Q M6,Q M7,Q M8,Q M9,Q M10,Q M11,Q M12,Q $65.00 $200.00

"Approved" is on third line without "Q."

16D $5 (10) M1 M2 M3 M4 M5 M6 M7 M8 M9 M10 M11 M12 $65.00 $200.00

As above with "Q."

16E $5 (10) M1,Q M2,Q M3,Q M4,Q M5,Q M6,Q M7,Q M8,Q M9,Q M10,Q M11,Q M12,Q $65.00 $200.00

Black with red lace overprint covering entire note. Sailing ship at left.

Military Service

17 $10 (4) M1 M2 M3 M4 M5 M6 M7 M8 M9 M10 M11 M12 $30.00 $65.00

Civil Service

18 $10 (5) C1 C2 C3 C4 C5 C6 C7 C8 C9 C10 C11 $30.00 $65.00

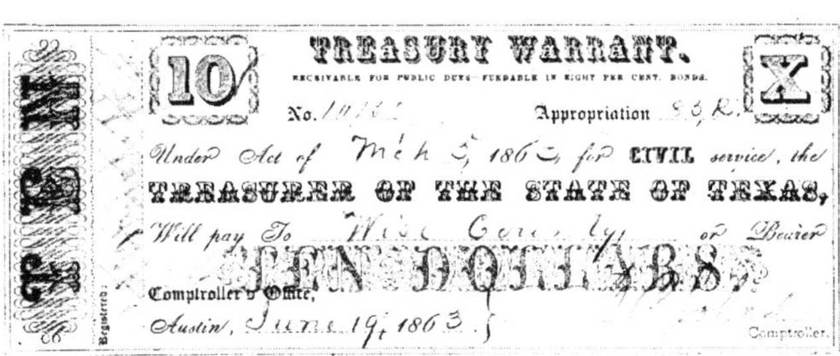

Green and Black.

Military Service

19 $10 (6) M1 M2 M3 M4 M5 M6 M7 M8 M9 M10 M11 M12 $30.00 $60.00

		Civil Service		
20	$10 (6)	C1 C2 C3 C4 C5 C6 C7 C8 C9 C10 C11	$30.00	$60.00

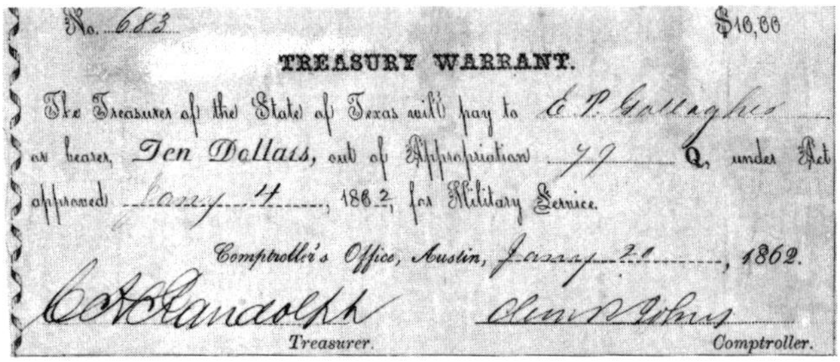

No. 683 $10,00

TREASURY WARRANT.

The Treasurer of the State of Texas will pay to E. P. Gallagher or bearer, Ten Dollars, out of Appropriation 79 Q, under Act approved Jany 4, 1862, for Military Service.

Comptroller's Office, Austin, Jany 21, 1862.

Treasurer. Comptroller.

Typeset. *with* and *without* a printed "Q" serial letter after the appropriation number.

		Military Service		
		"Approved" is on second line, without "Q."		
21	$10 (9)	M1 M2 M3 M4 M5 M6 M7 M8 M9 M10 M11 M12	$85.00	$150.00
		As above with "Q."		
21A	$10 (10)	M1,Q M2,Q M3,Q M4,Q M5,Q M6,Q M7,Q M8,Q M9,Q M10,Q M11,Q M12,Q	$100.00	$200.00
		"Approved" is hyphenated, without "Q."		
21B	$10 (10)	M1 M2 M3 M4 M5 M6 M7 M8 M9 M10 M11 M12	$100.00	$200.00
		As above with "Q."		
21C	$10 (10)	M1,Q M2,Q M3,Q M4,Q M5,Q M6,Q M7,Q M8,Q M9,Q M10,Q M11,Q M12,Q	$100.00	$200.00
		"Approved" is on third line without "Q."		
21D	$10 (10)	M1 M2 M3 M4 M5 M6 M7 M8 M9 M10 M11 M12	$100.00	$200.00
		As above with "Q."		
21E	$10 (10)	M1,Q M2,Q M3,Q M4,Q M5,Q M6,Q M7,Q M8,Q M9,Q M10,Q M11,Q M12,Q	$100.00	$200.00
		Civil Service		
		"Approved" is on second line, without "Q."		
22	$10 (9)	C1 C2 C3 C4 C5 C6 C7 C8 C9 C10 C11	$85.00	$150.00
		As above with "Q."		
22A	$10 (8)	C1,Q C2,Q C3,Q C4,Q C5,Q C6,Q C7,Q C8,Q C9,Q C10,Q C11,Q C12,Q	$85.00	$130.00

"Approved" is hyphenated, without "Q."

22B $10 (10) C1 C2 C3 C4 C5 C6 C7 C8 C9 C10 C11 C12 $100.00 $200.00

As above with "Q."

22C $10 (10) C1,Q C2,Q C3,Q C4,Q C5,Q C6,Q C7,Q C8,Q C9,Q C10,Q C11,Q C12,Q $100.00 $200.00

"Approved" is on third line without "Q."

22D $10 (10) C1 C2 C3 C4 C5 C6 C7 C8 C9 C10 C11 C12 $100.00 $200.00

As above with "Q."

22E $10 (10) C1,Q C2,Q C3,Q C4,Q C5,Q C6,Q C7,Q C8,Q C9,Q C10,Q C11,Q C12,Q $100.00 $200.00

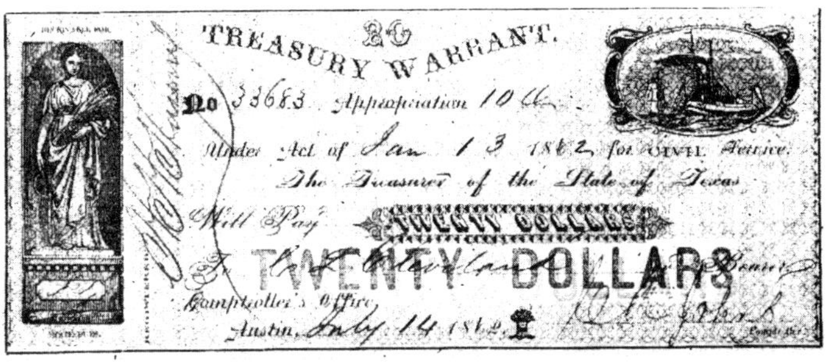

Ceres on pedestal at left. Steamboat in oval at right.
Black with red lace overprint covering entire note.

Military Service

23 $20 (9) M1 M2 M3 M4 M5 M6 M7 M8 M9 M10 M11 M12 $40.00 $80.00

Civil Service

24 $20 (10) C1 C2 C3 C4 C5 C6 C7 C8 C9 C10 C11 $40.00 $80.00

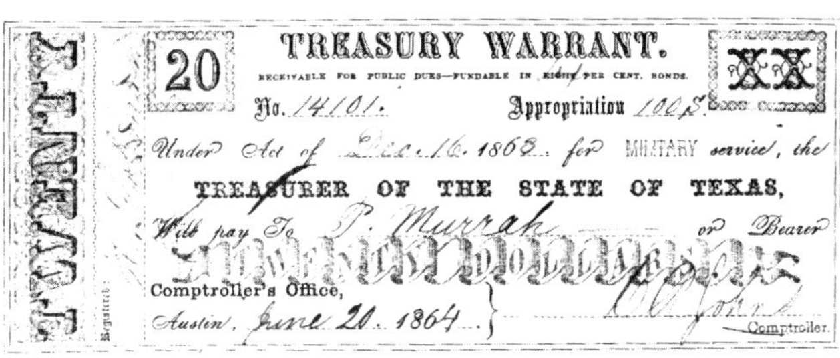

Green and black.

Military Service

25 $20 (6) M1 M2 M3 M4 M5 M6 M7 M8 M9 M10 M11 M12 $25.00 $45.00

Civil Service

26 $20 (6) C1 C2 C3 C4 C5 C6 C7 C8 C9 C10 C11 $25.00 $45.00

As above but the back of the note is printed with blue-green design. "Treasury Warrant" across the entire notes. "Treasurer" in small type, also "Twenty" repeated six times vertically. This type is unknown for military service.

26A $20 (7) C1 C2 C3 C4 C5 C6 C7 C8 C9 C10 C11 $60.00 $90.00

Error: as above, but "TWENTY" misspelled "WNETY" on back.

26B $20 (10) C1 C2 C3 C4 C5 C6 C7 C8 C9 C10 C11 $75.00 $110.00

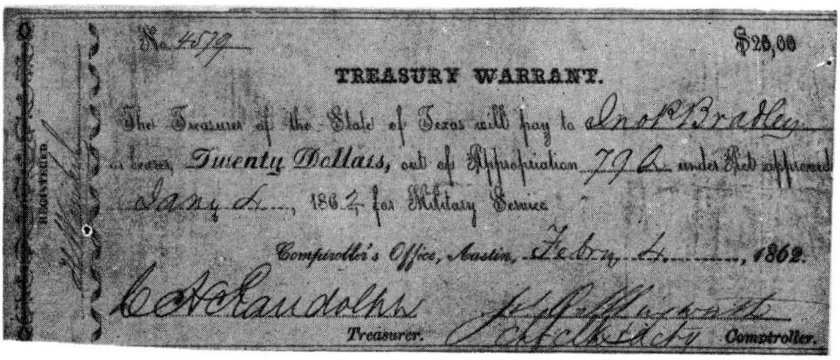

Military Service

Typeset. This note exists *with* and *without* a printed "Q" serial letter after the appropriation number as does the $5 type.

27 $20 (9) M1 M2 M3 M4 M5 M6 M7 M8 M9 M10 M11 M12 $150.00 $200.00

As above with "Q."

27A $20 (10) M1,Q M2,Q M3,Q M4,Q M5,Q M6,Q M7,Q M8,Q M9,Q M10,Q M11,Q M12,Q $150.00 $250.00

"Approved" is hyphenated, without "Q."

27B $20 (10) M1 M2 M3 M4 M5 M6 M7 M8 M9 M10 M11 M12 $150.00 $200.00

As above with "Q."

27C $20 (10) M1,Q M2,Q M3,Q M4,Q M5,Q M6,Q M7,Q M8,Q M9,Q M10,Q M11,Q M12,Q $150.00 $200.00

"Approved" is on third line without "Q."

27D $20 (10) M1 M2 M3 M4 M5 M6 M7 M8 M9 M10 M11 M12 $150.00 $200.00

As above with "Q."

27E $20 (10) M1,Q M2,Q M3,Q M4,Q M5,Q M6,Q M7,Q M8,Q M9,Q M10,Q M11,Q M12,Q $150.00 $200.00

Civil Service

"Approved" is on second line, without "Q."

28	$20 (9)	C1 C2 C3 C4 C5 C6 C7 C8 C9 C10 C11	$150.00	$200.00

As above with "Q."

28A	$20 (8)	C1,Q C2,Q C3,Q C4,Q C5,Q C6,Q C7,Q C8,Q C9,Q C10,Q C11,Q	$125.00	$175.00

"Approved" is hyphenated, without "Q."

28B	$20 (10)	C1 C2 C3 C4 C5 C6 C7 C8 C9 C10 C11	$150.00	$250.00

As above with "Q."

28C	$20 (10)	C1,Q C2,Q C3,Q C4,Q C5,Q C6,Q C7,Q C8,Q C9,Q C10,Q C11,Q	$150.00	$250.00

"Approved" is on third line without "Q."

28D	$20 (10)	C1 C2 C3 C4 C5 C6 C7 C8 C9 C10 C11	$150.00	$250.00

As above with "Q."

28E	$20 (10)	C1,Q C2,Q C3,Q C4,Q C5,Q C6,Q C7,Q C8,Q C9,Q C10,Q C11,Q	$150.00	$250.00

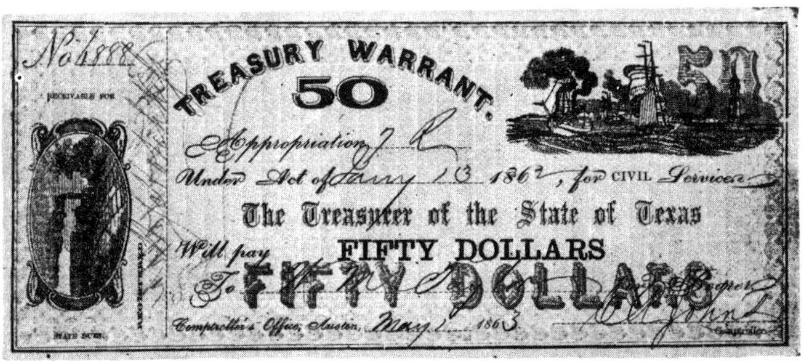

Train in oval at left, ships passing lighthouse at right. Yellow network over entire note, "50" and "FIFTY DOLLARS" in green.

Military Service

29	$50 (9)	M1 M2 M3 M4 M5 M6 M7 M8 M9 M10 M11	$150.00	$275.00

Civil Service

30	$50 (9)	C1 C2 C3 C4 C5 C6 C7 C8 C9 C10 C11	$150.00	$275.00

Fancy green back.

Military Service

31 $50 (6) M1 M2 M3 M4 M5 M6 M7 M8 M9 M10 M11 M12 $60.00 $85.00

Civil Service

32 $50 (6) C1 C2 C3 C4 C5 C6 C7 C8 C9 C10 C11 $60.00 $85.00

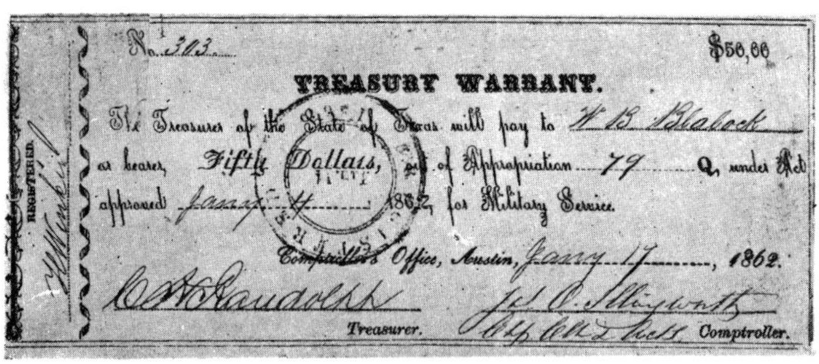

Typeset.

Military Service

33 $50 (11) M1 M2 M3 M4 M5 M6 M7 M8 M9 M10 M11 M12 extremely rare

Civil Service

34 $50 (11) C1 C2 C3 C4 C5 C6 C7 C8 C9 C10 C11 extremely rare

NOTE: it is conceivable, although unlikely, that the "$50" typeset note exists in the same varieties as the $5, $10, and/or $20 denominations.

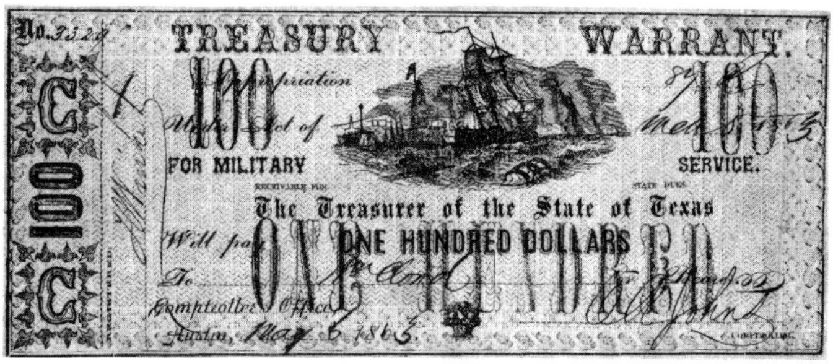

Ships passing a lighthouse. Red network covers the face of the note.
"100s" and "ONE HUNDRED" in dark red.

Military Service

35 $100 (9) M1 M2 M3 M4 M5 M6 M7 M8 M9 M10 M11 M12 $150.00 $250.00

Civil Service

36 $100 (9) C1 C2 C3 C4 C5 C6 C7 C8 C9 C10 C11 $150.00 $275.00

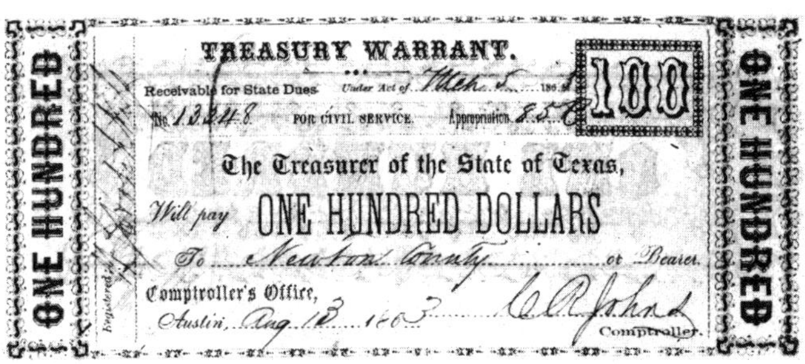

Fancy green back.

Military Service

37 $100 (6) M1 M2 M3 M4 M5 M6 M7 M8 M9 M10 M11 M12 $75.00 $110.00

Civil Service

38 $50 (6) C1 C2 C3 C4 C5 C6 C7 C8 C9 C10 C11 $75.00 $115.00

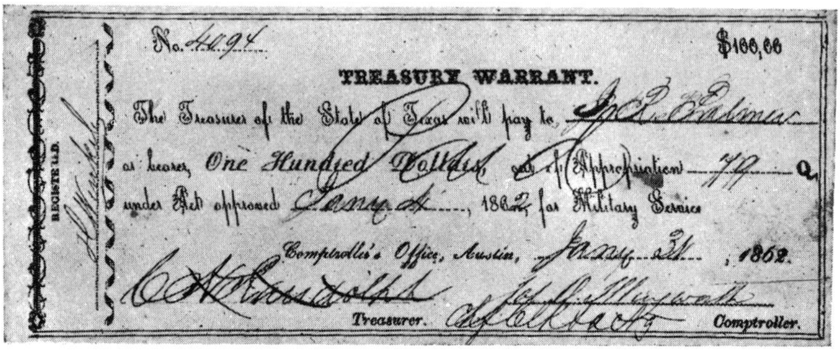

Typeset.

Military Service

39 $100 (11) M1 M2 M3 M4 M5 M6 M7 M8 M9 M10 M11 M12 very rare

Civil Service

40 $100 (11) C1 C2 C3 C4 C5 C6 C7 C8 C9 C10 C11 extremely rare

NOTE: it is conceivable, although unlikely, that the "$50" typeset note exists in the same varieties as the $5, $10, and/or $20 denominations.

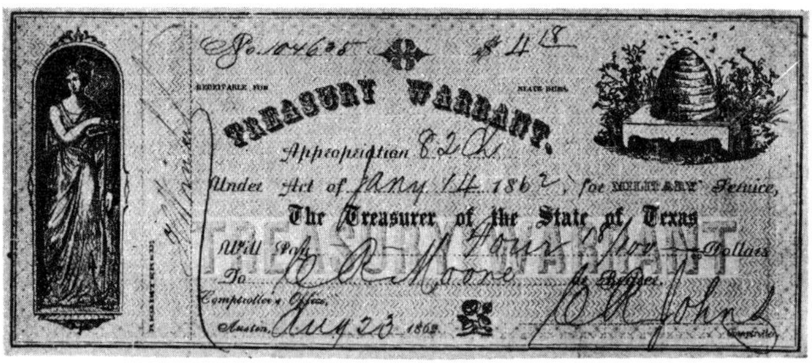

Liberty at left, beehive right; black with blue network that covers entire note.

Military Service

41 written denomination (6) M1 M2 M3 M4 M5 M6 M7 M8 M9 M10 M11 M12 $45.00 $125.00

Civil Service

42 written denomination (6) C1 C2 C3 C4 C5 C6 C7 C8 C9 C10 C11 $45.00 $125.00

Ceres seated at center, Indian maiden left, green and black.

Military Service

43 written denomination (6) M1 M2 M3 M4 M5 M6 M7 M8 M9 M10 M11 M12 — $50.00 $100.00

Civil Service

44 written denomination (6) C1 C2 C3 C4 C5 C6 C7 C8 C9 C10 C11 — $50.00 $100.00

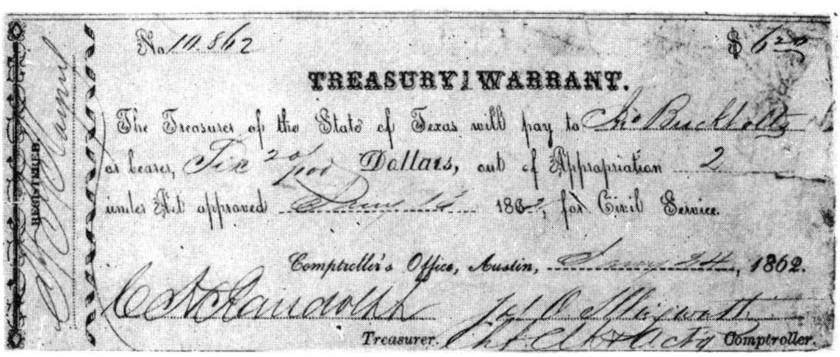

Typeset.

Military Service

45 written denomination (9) M1 M2 M3 M4 M5 M6 M7 M8 M9 M10 M11 M12 — $100.00 $250.00

Civil Service

46 written denomination (9) C1 C2 C3 C4 C5 C6 C7 C8 C9 C10 C11 — $100.00 $250.00

Written dates ("18" printed).

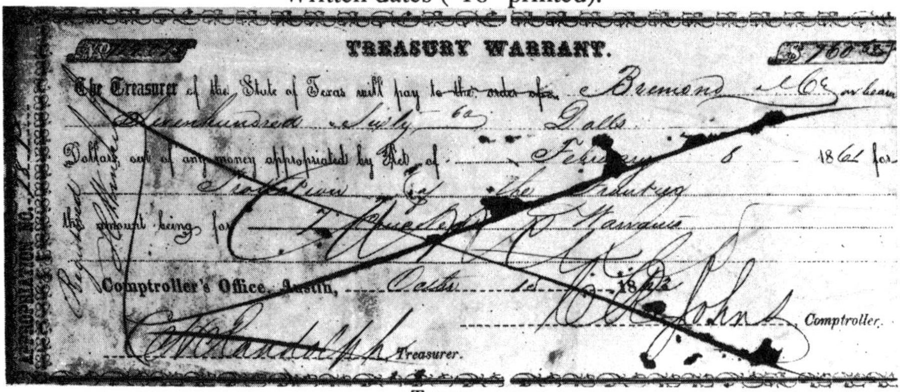

TREASURY WARRANT.

The Treasurer of the State of Texas will pay to the order of Bremond & Co. or bearer
Dollars, out of any money appropriated by Act of February 8 1861 for
the amount being for
Comptroller's Office, Austin, 18
Treasurer. Comptroller.

Typeset.

Military Service

47 written denomination (10) $90.00 $110.00

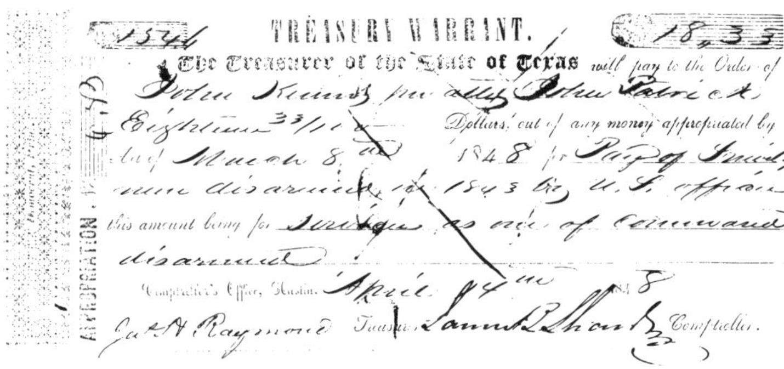

TREASURY WARRANT.

The Treasurer of the State of Texas will pay to the Order of
Dollars, out of any money appropriated by
1848 for
this amount being for
Comptroller's Office, Austin, 1848
Treasurer Comptroller.

49 written denomination (8) $80.00 $100.00

TREASURY WARRANT.

The Treasurer of the State of Texas will pay to the order of
Dollars out of any money appropriated by act of
for
the amount being for
Comptroller's Office, Austin,
Treasurer Comptroller.

PAID

55 written denomination (9) $80.00 $90.00

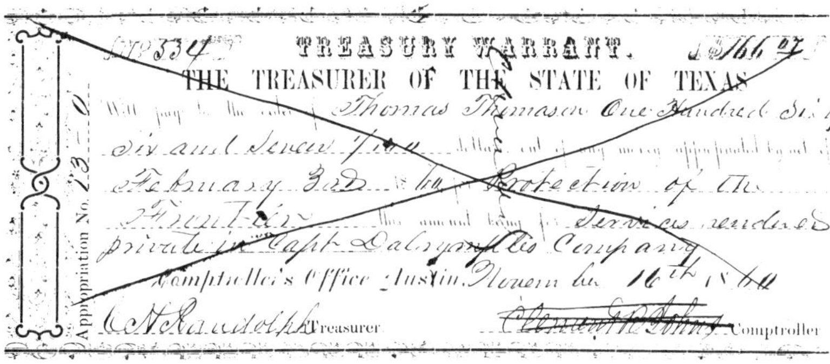

58 written denominations (8) $75.00 $85.00

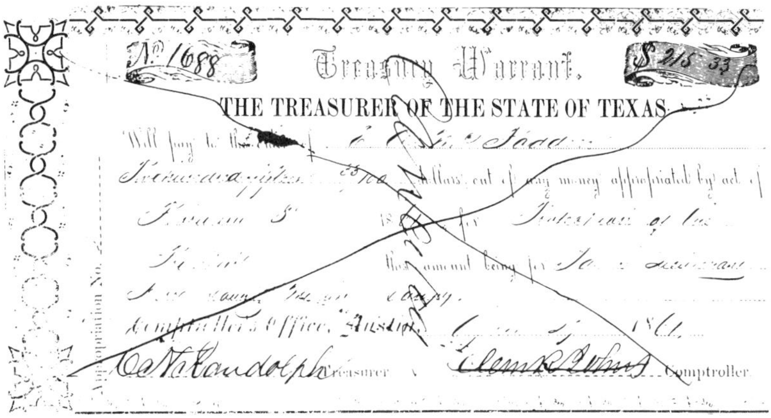

61 written denomination (9) $90.00 $110.00

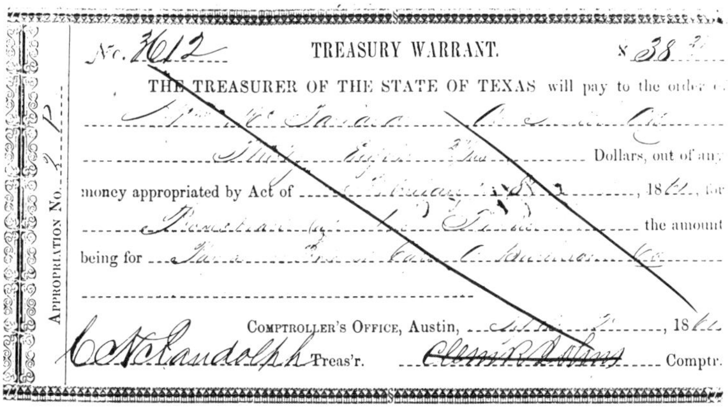

64 written denomination (7) $50.00 $80.00

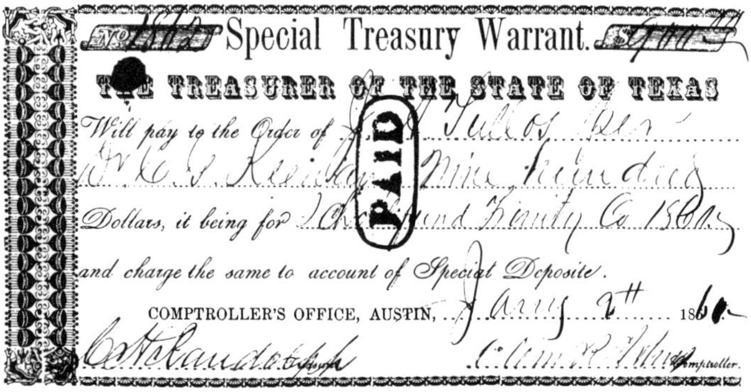
Special Treasury Warrant.
THE TREASURER OF THE STATE OF TEXAS
Will pay to the Order of
Dollars, it being for
and charge the same to account of Special Deposite.
COMPTROLLER'S OFFICE, AUSTIN, 186
Comptroller.

68 written denomination (9) $50.00 $100.00

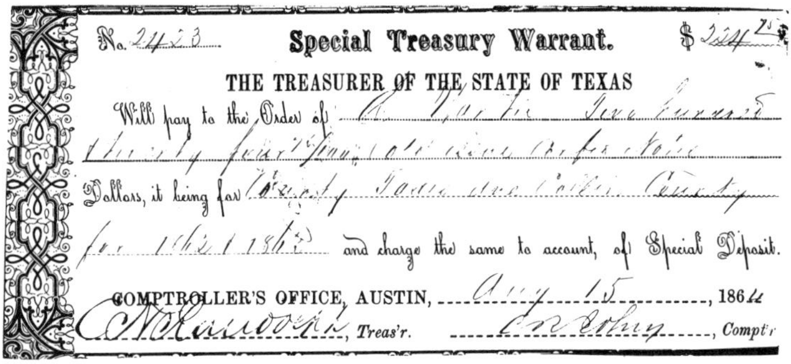
No. 2423 Special Treasury Warrant.
THE TREASURER OF THE STATE OF TEXAS
Will pay to the Order of
Dollars, it being for
and charge the same to account of Special Deposit.
COMPTROLLER'S OFFICE, AUSTIN, Aug 15, 1864
Treas'r. Compt'r

72 written denomination (9) $80.00 $100.00

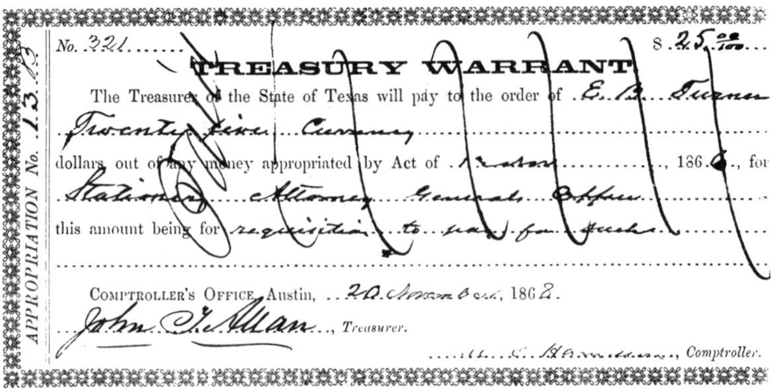
No. 321 $ 25.00/100
TREASURY WARRANT
The Treasurer of the State of Texas will pay to the order of
dollars, out of any money appropriated by Act of , 186 , for
this amount being for
COMPTROLLER'S OFFICE, Austin, 20 November, 1862.
John T. Allan, Treasurer.
Comptroller.
APPROPRIATION No. 13

80 written denomination (9) $90.00 $110.00

THE STATE OF VIRGINIA

$1,000,000 authorized by Act of March 14th, 1861.
$2,000,000 authorized by Act of April 30th 1861.
$2,000,000 authorized by Act of June 28, 1861.

"Hoyer & Ludwig. Richmond, Va."

Written dates of 1861

Three women left, Washington right. Red overprint.

1861-A $500 (11) A extremely rare

"Baldwin, Bald & Cousland. New York"

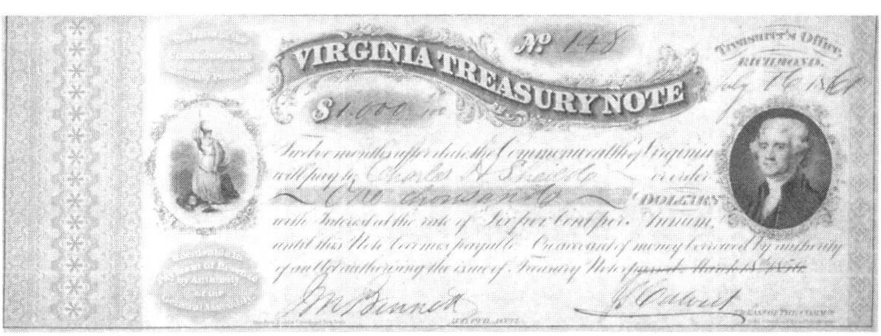

State seal left, Jefferson right. Orange-yellow overprint.

1861-B Written denominations (11) extremely rare

(only $1,000 denomination has been confirmed)

Bust of George Washington, red overprint.

1 $100 (10) A $3000.00 $4000.00

Ceres and Commerce with an urn, gladiatorial scene left, John Tyler right. Red overprint.

2 $50 (10) A B $2000.00 $2500.00

Bust of Washington center, Minerva left, green overprint.

3 $20 (6) A B C D $60.00 $130.00

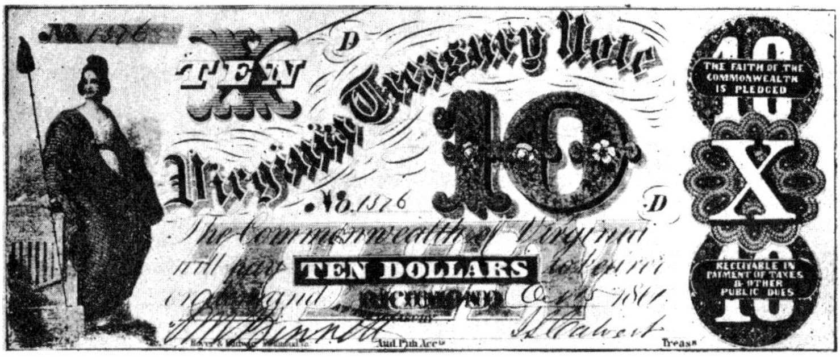

Liberty standing at left.

4 $10 (8) A B C D $65.00 $125.00

Ceres seated in large "V." Girl at left.

5 $5 (8) A B C D $65.00 $125.00

$4,000,000 Authorized by Act of Dec. 30th, 1861.
$1,300,000 Authorized by Act of Mar. 31st, 1862.

Engraved by "Keatinge & Ball. Richmond, Va."

Dated "Oct. 15th, 1862."

Governor Letcher center, Washington left, orange overprint.

6 $100 (7) A B C D $30.00 $85.00

Same as number 6 with red overprint.

6A $100 (9) A B C D $60.00 $150.00

Governor James M. Mason left, Ceres seated between Commerce and Navigation right, orange overprint.

7 $50 (7) A B C D $22.00 $50.00

Same as number 7 with red overprint.

7A $50 (9) A B C D $60.00 $150.00

8 $10 (5) A B C D $25.00 $40.00

Paper watermarked "Ten."

9 $10 (6) A B C D $25.00 $40.00

Paper watermarked "Five."

10 $10 (8) A B C D $40.00 $75.00

Paper watermarked "W.T.C.C. & Co."

11 $10 (7) A B C D $35.00 $65.00

Paper watermarked "J. Green & Sons 1862."

12 $10 (10) A D $150.00 $275.00

Dated "March 13th, 1862."

Bust of public account auditor Jonathan M. Bennett. Gladiatorial scene right, green overprint.

Plain paper.

13 $5 (3) A B C D $20.00 $30.00

Paper watermarked "Hodgkinson & Co. Wookey Hole Mill."

14 $5 (7) A D $75.00 $150.00

Paper watermarked "C S A" in block letters

15 $5 (7) A B C D $25.00 $50.00

Paper watermarked "J. Whatman."

15A $5 (8) A B C D $60.00 $125.00

Engraved by "Hoyer & Ludwig. Richmond, VA."

Ceres seated, bust of Governor John Letcher left. Red overprint.

Dated "May 15th, 1862."

16	$1 (5)	A B	$15.00	$30.00

Dated "July 21st, 1862."

17	$1 (2)	A B C D	$10.00	$20.00

Dated "Oct. 21st, 1862."

18	$1 (3)	A B C D	$10.00	$20.00

Act of March 28, 1879

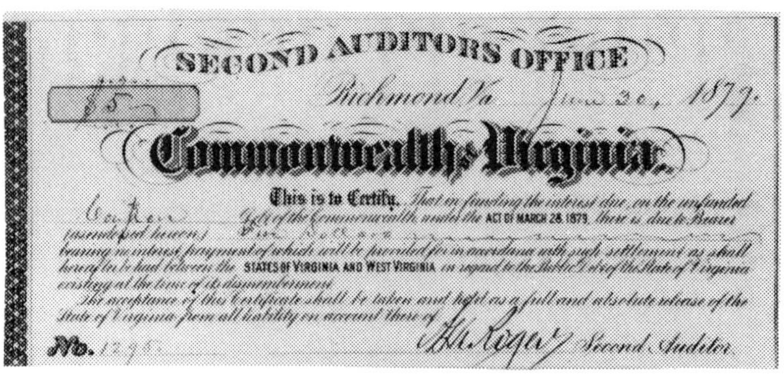

SECOND AUDITORS OFFICE

Richmond Va June 30, 1879.

Commonwealth of Virginia.

This is to Certify. That in funding the interest due on the unfunded Debt of the Commonwealth under the ACT OF MARCH 28 1879, there is due to Bearer ... bearing no interest payment of which will be provided for in accordance with such settlement as shall hereafter be had between the STATES OF VIRGINIA AND WEST VIRGINIA in regard to the Public Debt of the State of Virginia existing at the time of its dismemberment. The acceptance of this Certificate shall be taken and held as a full and absolute release of the State of Virginia from all liability on account thereof.

No. Second Auditor

Printed in orange on white paper.

1879A	written denominations (10)	$1200	$1500

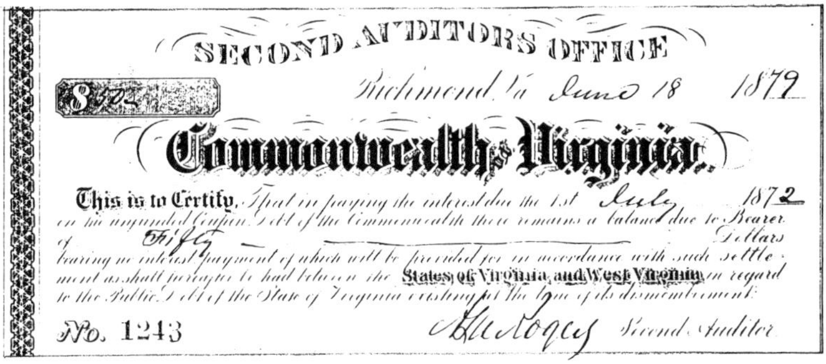

Similar, but green ink.

1879D written denominations (11) extremely rare

A Selected Bibliography on Confederate and Southern State Currency

Affleck, Charles, J. *The Obsolete Paper Money of Virginia, Volume II: Obsolete Bank Notes 1804-1865* (Virginia Numismatic Association: Hampton, VA) 1969.

Afflick, Charles, J. and Douglas, Ben M. *Confederate Bonds and Certificates* (Washington, D.C.) 1960.

Ball, Douglas B. *Confederate War Finance* Ph.D. Thesis (University of London, London School of Economics and Political Science) 1974.

Ball, Douglas B. "Confederate Financial Expedients in the Trans-Mississippi Department," in *The American Numismatic Association Anthology* (American Numismatic Association: Colorado Springs, CO) 1991.

Ball, Douglas, B. *Financial Failure and Confederate Defeat* 1992.

Bradbeer, William West *Confederate and Southern State Currency* (Reprint published by Aubrey Bebee: Omaha, NE) 1956.

Caldwell, Stephen A. *A Banking History of Louisiana* (Criswell Publications: Ft. McCoy, Fl) 1977.

Cassidy, Daniel G. *The Illustrated History of Florida Paper Money* (Jacksonville, FL) 1980.

Chase, Philip H. *Confederate Treasury Notes: The Paper Money of the Confederate States of America, 1861-1865* (Philadelphia, PA) 1947.

Criswell, Grover C. *Confederate and Southern State Currency (Criswell's and Criswell's Publications: Citra, FL) 1961.*

Criswell, Grover C. *Confederate and Southern State Currency Second Revised Edition* (Criswell's and Criswell's Publications: Citra, FL) 1976.

Criswell, Grover C. *Confederate and Southern States Bonds* (Criswell's and Criswell's Publications: Citra, FL) 1961.

Criswell, Grover C. *Confederate and Southern States Bonds Second Edition* (Criswell's and Criswell's Publications: Citra, FL) 1980.

Feller, Steve "The Ups and Downs of Civil War Currency," *The Numismatist 97* (4) 1984 pp. 697-704.

Freeman, H.L. *Florida Obsolete Notes and Scrip* (Society of Paper Money Collectors) 1967. This book is a part of the Wismer book project.

Garland, Paul E. *The History of Early Tennessee Banks and Their Issues* (Kingwood,TN) 1983.

Haseltine, John W. *Descriptive Catalogue of Confederate Notes and bonds* (Philadelphia, PA) 1876.

Haxby, James A. *Standard Catalog of United States Obsolete Bank Notes 1782-1866 Volumes 1 through 4* (Krause Publications: Iola, WI) 1988.

Hughes, Brent. Brent has written a marvelous series of articles on Confederate finances. They appear in *Paper Money* and *The Bank Note Reporter*.

Leggett, L. Candler, *Mississippi Obsolete Notes and Scrip* (Society of Paper Money Collectors) 1975. This book is a part of the Wismer book project.

Lerner, Eugene M. "The Monetary and Fiscal Programs of the Confederate Government," *The Journal of Political Economy* Vol. XLII, 1954, pp. 506-522.

Lerner, Eugene M. "Money, Prices and Wages in the Confederacy," *The Journal of Political Economy* Vol. XLIII, 1955, pp. 20-40.

Medlar, Robert, *Texas Obsolete Notes and Scrip* (Society of Paper Money Collectors) 1968. This book is a part of the Wismer book project.

Pennell, J. Roy, *Obsolete Bank Notes of North Carolina* (Anderson,SC) 1965.

Pick, Albert *Standard Catalog of World Paper Money (Volume 2 General Issues)* (Krause Publications: Iola, WI) 1990.

Roakes, Sam, Jr. "Financial Woes of the Confederacy," *Paper Money* Vol. 16 (3) 1977, pp. 158-163.

Rosene, Walter, Jr. *Alabama Obsolete Notes and Scrip* (Society of Paper Money Collectors) 1984. This book is a part of the Wismer book project.

Rothert, Matt, Jr. *Arkansas Obsolete Notes and Scrip* (Society of Paper Money Collectors) 1985. This book is a part of the Wismer book project.

Sebring, Thomas H. "Confederate Patterns: Sad Mementos of an Impossible Dream," *The Numismatist* 97 (4) 1984 pp. 688-695.

Sheheen, Austin, *South Carolina Obsolete Notes* 1960.

Slabaugh, Arlie R. *Confederate States Paper Money, Seventh Revised Edition* (Krause Publications: Iola, WI) 1991.

Thian, Raphael P. *Confederate Note Album for a Complete Collection* (Washington, D.C.) 1876.

Thian, Raphael P. *Register of the Confederate Debt* (Reprint by Quarterman Publications: Boston) 1972.

Todd, Richard Cecil *Confederate Finance* (The University of Georgia Press: Athens, GA) 1954.

Wismer, D.C. "Descriptive List of Obsolete Paper Money," *The Numismatist. This was a series of articles which appeared from 1922 to 1936.*

------ *America's Currency 1789-1866*, Coinage of the Americas Conference at the American Numismatic Society, New York; October 31 - November 2, 1985, (The American Numismatic Society: New York) 1985. This volume includes articles about Confederate and southern currency by Douglas B. Ball, Grover C. Criswell, Carl W. A. Carlson and Raymond H. Williamson.